The Ashley Cooper Plan

The Ashley Cooper Plan

The Founding of Carolina and the Origins of
Southern Political Culture

THOMAS D. WILSON

The University of North Carolina Press   Chapel Hill

This book was published with the assistance of the
Fred W. Morrison Fund of the
University of North Carolina Press.

Cover illustration: "A New Description of Carolina by Order of the Lords Proprietors,"
1672 map of the province from the early proprietary period. Courtesy of the North
Carolina Collection, Wilson Library, the University of North Carolina at Chapel Hill.

Library of Congress Cataloging-in-Publication Data
Wilson, Thomas D., Jr., author.
The Ashley Cooper Plan : the founding of
Carolina and the origins of Southern political
culture / Thomas D. Wilson, Jr.
pages cm
Includes bibliographical references and index.
ISBN 978-1-4696-2628-4 (pbk : alk. paper) —
ISBN 978-1-4696-2629-1 (ebook)
1. Political culture—Southern States—History. 2. City planning—
Southern States—History. 3. South Carolina—History—Colonial period, ca.
1600–1775. 4. North Carolina—History—Colonial period, ca. 1600–1775.
5. Southern States—Politics and government—To 1775. 6. Southern States—
Social conditions. 7. Shaftesbury, Anthony Ashley Cooper, Earl of,
1621–1683. 8. Cities and towns—Southern States. I. Title.
F272.w76 2016
306.20975—dc23
2015028006

Contents

Figures and Tables

Preface

Residents of South Carolina and visitors to the Lowcountry are familiar with the Ashley and Cooper rivers. The two rivers define the narrow peninsula occupied by the historic city of Charleston. They were named after a single person: Anthony Ashley Cooper, the 1st Earl of Shaftesbury, founder of the Province of Carolina.

Ashley Cooper and seven other noblemen established the Province of Carolina in 1670, chronologically midway between the foundings of Virginia and Georgia, the first and last of the original thirteen colonies. The province, which encompassed present-day North Carolina and South Carolina, created a social and economic framework in America that scholars in various disciplines have identified as a defining influence on national character.

Yet American history mostly neglects Ashley Cooper while celebrating other visionary founders such as Roger Williams, William Penn, and James Oglethorpe. The purpose of this book is to shine more light on the idealism underlying Ashley Cooper's "darling," as he called the colony, and then to follow the chain of events he set in motion to the present time. In doing so, it will be shown that he was influential in formatting one of America's three principal political cultures. Further, it will be argued that the connection of contemporary political culture to the past is not a weak one, as Ashley Cooper's *perspectives and ideology remain with us today.*

Ultimately, another purpose arises from the historical investigation, which is to offer inquisitive audiences practical new insight into the genesis of present-day political divides. In acquiring this new understanding, citizens and policy makers can become better advocates for progress in areas that currently seem to defy agreement. Readers who put this information to use may even be able to penetrate the veils of rhetoric separating them from their ideological critics, thereby attaining mutual understanding, if not agreement, in areas of critical concern.

The origins of today's political divisions is a vast subject area, but one that can be better understood in part by following a specific thread of history from Ashley Cooper's plan for Carolina to the formation of a unique regional political culture that eventually grew beyond its borders to acquire national prominence and influence. As this is also a broad subject area, attention is placed on the interactions between political culture and urban policy, specifically as it influences city planning and similar rationalistic professions. This path through history leads directly to a finding that America's urban-rural (or more precisely, urban-exurban) divide, enlarged by archaic political rhetoric, undermines critical thinking about serious contemporary problems.

Three European worldviews took root in colonial America—religious communitarianism in New England, commercial pragmatism in the Mid-Atlantic region, and "Gothic" class-structured republicanism in the South. Each of these was challenged during the eighteenth century by the new ideals of the Enlightenment. The extent to which those new ideals were accepted or rejected in America modified the three early worldviews and gave birth to three distinct political cultures— *egalitarian*, *pragmatic*, and *fraternalistic*—which survived the colonial period and grew with the nation. Scholars have assigned various other names to these cultures, but there is basic agreement over their genesis and character. Although there have been many realignments in American politics, the three political cultures—and the worldviews from which they are derived—are as strong in the twenty-first century as they were in the eighteenth century.

The three worldviews influence American character in ways that go beyond political culture. Religious denominations are often affiliated with a worldview and an associated political culture, as can be found with Southern Baptist Gothic republicanism and Unitarian humanism. Geographic patterns are also associated with the three traditions: Gothic republicanism is strongest in the South and in the nation's exurbs, Enlightenment values are associated with the East Coast and the West Coast and urban areas, and wide swaths in between tend to be more pragmatic in beliefs. The geographic pattern of political cultures has produced an acute, unresolved, urban-rural animus, which is exploited by special interests to divide America. Professions, or occupations, are sometimes aligned with a tradition. An example taken up in Chapter 5 is that of the urban and environmental policy and planning professions, which are associated with the rationalism and humanism of the Enlightenment. Such professions have been described as the "creative class" by the urban theorist Richard Florida. They may be more specifically described as *creative, progressive, scientific, and problem-solving* (or *creative-progressive* for short) professions to emphasize their inherent optimism about the power of reason to drive human advancement.[1]

The idea of the city investigated herein, beginning with Ashley Cooper's utopian colony, is an idea of civilization. From loosely connected, tribal agglomerations to economically and politically centralized societies, cities represent the character of cultures and the ways in which they envision themselves. American cities from colonial times have repeatedly reimagined and reinvented themselves in response to a changing world. But cities do so within the bounds of their inherited worldviews and political cultures. Understanding the evolution and potential of the American city requires understanding that context. The three colonial worldviews spread westward as the nation grew. Their visions for America have converged and diverged in cycles since colonial times, but always retaining their distinctive characteristics. The arc of those cycles is an evolutionary process that occasionally bends toward the precept that all men are created equal, but never without wrenching struggles.

Historical designs like the Ashley Cooper Plan are often viewed as artifacts rather than as models with continuing relevance to contemporary planning. Like an old painting on the wall, such old plans are revered for providing a glimpse into the past but seldom studied by people shaping the future of the city. An often acknowledged human weakness is a lack of a sense of the interconnectedness of past, present, and future. All events, however, have an enduring effect, and some have a powerful influence that continues over many generations. The Ashley Cooper Plan is one with continuing influence. It appeared to wither and die, but in fact it can be seen to have bridged seventeenth-century English republicanism with a new American republicanism. The bridge, however, was built with an additional component, the unshakable legacy of slavery.

Enlightenment ideals and values are repeatedly referenced in the following chapters, requiring definition for clarity. Subsequent usages of the word refer to the British Enlightenment, beginning in England with publication of Newton's *Principia Mathematica* and Locke's *Two Treatises* in the late 1680s and concluding with the American and French revolutions. The period was characterized by 1) adoption of inductive reasoning and systematic experimental methods in science and other fields; 2) rejection of natural hierarchy and unquestioning obedience to higher authority within the hierarchy; 3) assertion of human equality in the state of nature and acceptance of inequality only through social compact; and 4) belief in the capacity for incremental advancement through education and reassessment.

The focus on the city in this investigation also requires a note on terminology. The term "city planning" is used throughout in the broadest sense as shorthand for urban and regional planning, community planning, land-use planning, transportation planning, urban design, environmental design, landscape architecture, and urban and environmental policy making. City planning is frequently mentioned together with similar creative and problem-solving professions, specifically including environmental science (for example, climate science, ecology, and resource management); social science (for example, anthropology, economics, geography, and sociology); and social advocacy (for example, environmental justice, social justice, and legal services to the poor).

The word "city" is often used in the broad sense of civilization, as in "city upon a hill." American city planning was born with Ashley Cooper's plan for Carolina, but it did not remain the province of his republicanism. The American vision of the city was greatly influenced by the Enlightenment, an influence that has grown over time. Modern tension between Gothic republican and Enlightenment traditions places city planning, along with other creative-progressive professions, in an uncomfortably politicized position, a central problem addressed in this book.

The word "urban" is preferred over "city" by designers and is found throughout the lexicon: urban designers, New Urbanism, environmental urbanism, landscape urbanism, and so on. The word "city" is also out of vogue with planners, who more often describe their profession as urban and regional planning. Nevertheless, the word "city" is used throughout this book in order to expand its scope, thereby placing philosophical aspects of social organization at the heart of the discussion. To the philosopher or the historian of intellectual ideas, the city is more than design, infrastructure, environmental quality, or social justice; it is the essence of civilization and the ultimate subject of all discourse.

A note on names will be helpful to the reader. Anthony Ashley Cooper (1621–83) became the Earl of Shaftesbury in 1672, after the founding of Carolina, before which time his proper title was Lord Ashley. He is generally known in the historical record as Shaftesbury, or the 1st Earl of Shaftesbury. A distinction of generation is sometimes necessary, since Anthony Ashley Cooper, the 3rd Earl of Shaftesbury (1671–1713), is also often called Shaftesbury. A brilliant philosopher of the Enlightenment, the 3rd Earl was tutored by John Locke, the chief planner for Carolina. Anthony Ashley Cooper, 4th Earl of Shaftesbury (1711–71), was a leader among the Trustees who established the colony of Georgia; and Anthony Ashley Cooper, the 7th Earl of Shaftesbury (1801–85), was a noted reformer and philanthropist. The family name Ashley Cooper is not hyphenated here to be consistent with early texts, but it is currently most often written as Ashley-Cooper.

The 12th Earl of Shaftesbury, Nicholas Edmund Anthony Ashley-Cooper, presently resides at the Ashley Cooper estate in Dorset, England.

THE CONTENT OF this book covers more than three centuries and contains perspectives from a wide range of disciplines. The help of many people was essential. First, I would like to thank Joseph Parsons at the University of North Carolina Press for seeing potential in the project and arranging for three very astute readers to assess the early manuscripts. Alison Shay at the press facilitated the illustration plan. Jay Mazzocchi at the press had the critical role of editorial director for producing the book. Copy editing by Dorothea Anderson immeasurably improved the quality of the book. The entire team was consummately professional, and it was a pleasure to creatively engage with them.

Weaving perspectives from various disciplines throughout the book required critical review by several people. For that, I am most grateful to Dr. Philip Abbott, Dr. John Brooke, Dr. Kenneth C. Martis, and Dr. Angie Maxwell for in-depth reviews from the perspectives of American colonial history, southern history, political science, and cultural and political geography. I am also grateful to professors David Armitage, Harvard University; James Farr, Northwestern University; and John Milton, King's College, London, for addressing specific questions about "instructions" for settling Carolina prepared by John Locke for the Lord Proprietors.

I am particularly grateful for the assistance of Teri Norris, a technical artist experienced in working with urban planners, who prepared several of the illustrations and offered valuable insights as the work progressed.

Several institutions provided essential services. The Beaufort County Library located nearly all the books and hard-to-find materials necessary for writing the book. Grace Morris Cordial, Beaufort district collection manager, was supportive throughout, as was Stacey Inman, reference manager. The staff of the library at the University of South Carolina Beaufort were consistently helpful, as were those at the South Carolina State Archives. Special thanks is also due to Mike Berry with the South Caroliniana Library of the University of South Carolina and Mary Linnemann with the Hargrett Rare Book & Manuscript Library, University of Georgia.

Several friends and colleagues provided support when it was needed. Dr. Barry N. Haack and Dr. Imre E. Quastler were a constant source of moral support. Patrick O. Shay, AIA, was always a source of encouragement. Ian Hill, historic preservationist with the Beaufort County Planning Department, was also most helpful. I must express my appreciation for the South African planners who interned with me at Florida International

University and expanded my understanding of social equity issues. I am especially grateful to those who have stayed in touch over the years: Mlamleli Belot, Ashraf Adam, and Dr. Cecil Madell of Cape Technikon.

Nicholas Edmund Anthony Ashley-Cooper, 12th Earl of Shaftesbury, provided background formation. Mr. Richard Samways, the Shaftesbury archivist, was always prompt and informative in responding to my questions. I owe the North Carolina preservationist William Stroud my gratitude for facilitating the initial contact with Lord Shaftesbury.

The support of family can never be overestimated in a project as demanding as writing a book. Special thanks are due to my wife, Susan Townsend, and my aunt, Mary Wilson Heald.

Prologue

America: A Blank Slate for English Utopianism

Anthony Ashley Cooper was one of several English visionaries to see America as a blank slate for launching a utopian colony. Ashley Cooper led a group of prominent noblemen that founded the Province of Carolina as a planned colony governed by a model constitution. The design for Carolina formalized historically rooted social ideals and uniquely English principles of government into 120 articles, producing one of the most detailed constitutions ever written. Founded in 1670, Carolina was designed from inception to achieve balanced government, societal harmony, sustainable prosperity, impartial justice, and religious tolerance.

Orderly growth of planned cities and counties was an essential part of the design. The Ashley Cooper Plan for colonial settlement was guided by three principles: *consistency* with the colony's constitution; *concurrence* of development with infrastructure and administrative capacity; and *compactness* to promote efficient commerce and ensure defensibility. These principles were emphasized repeatedly in guidance documents sent to the colonists.[1]

Several English colonies preceded Carolina. Jamestown was the first substantial venture, established in 1607 for the purpose of extracting gold and other precious commodities from America, as the Spanish had been doing for a century. The colonies that immediately followed Jamestown, by contrast, were driven by religious idealism rather than the quest for wealth. Puritans, Baptists, Catholics, and others envisioned new colonies that would flourish with religious freedom. The compacts and constitutions adopted by those early colonies articulated ideals of "liberty of conscience," which matured into the first principles embraced later by the

Founders of the United States. None of those colonial founding documents, however, was as comprehensive in its underlying philosophy or in its detail as the constitution for Carolina.

Ashley Cooper, later the 1st Earl of Shaftesbury, planned Carolina as an idealized reinvention of traditional English society—which he knew as Gothic society—where order was maintained, prosperity attained, and liberty ensured through a balance of landowning interests and class interdependence. The plan established a social hierarchy sometimes characterized as neofeudalistic. It anticipated the necessity of toiling classes at its base, even slavery, but it did not contemplate full dependence on an enslaved labor force and the emergence of a slave society. The notorious dependence on chattel slavery in Carolina arose later at the instigation of Caribbean plantation owners, who were among the earliest settlers. Under Ashley Cooper's constitution, he and his seven associates and their descendants would form a permanent class of Carolina nobility, sharing power with an elected parliament. Under their guiding hand, modulated by the carefully crafted constitution, a traditional and virtuous English society would be reborn in the New World.[2]

Two other American colonies were subsequently founded with similarly ambitious plans, integrating strategies for social, economic, and physical development. In 1681, William Penn founded Pennsylvania, a colony that would provide religious freedom for Quakers, ensure religious tolerance toward others, adopt a secular constitution, and develop in accordance with a master plan. In 1733, James Oglethorpe produced a sequel to Ashley Cooper's Carolina when he founded Georgia, updating the earlier design with emerging ideals of the Enlightenment that envisioned a flatter, more equitable class structure. All three planned colonies were established on the premise that a detailed city and regional plan was essential to their social and economic aspirations.[3]

The design of Carolina—the *Ashley Cooper Plan*—is more than a mere historical artifact. The plan laid down a template for a political culture that would adapt and evolve. By the end of eighteenth century, a descendant of the original political culture had spread across the South. In the twentieth century, principally as a result of Great Depression white migrations out of the region, this uniquely American political culture dispersed northward and then westward throughout much of America. The character of cities, the role of city planning, and the contours of urban and environmental policy in much of America remain influenced by the social and political structure planted in Carolina by Ashley Cooper and his associates.[4]

The role of Carolina's first city planner, Ashley Cooper's protégé, John Locke, is also of continuing significance. Locke is considered by many to be an intellectual founder of American ideals, or first principles, and as such his still-relevant political theories can be understood in original context through the design of the Carolina Colony. Locke remained interested in the Carolina experiment and the American colonies after his mentor's death in 1682. His hand in the design of Carolina was closely tied to his pen as he began writing his most influential work, the *Two Treatises of Government*. The monumental work, years in the making, was finally published in 1689, a date that marks the beginning of the Enlightenment.[5]

The City upon a Hill

The model colony, the "city upon a hill," was a widely shared ideal among English visionaries of the seventeenth century. The phrase, derived from the Sermon on the Mount, was made famous by the Puritan leader John Winthrop in a sermon to fellow colonists en route to America. The vision Winthrop shared with his flock was that of a virtuous, exemplary society held together by a "bond of love" and faith in God. He believed the new Puritan society would become a model, offering hope for Christian salvation to the world as an alternative to the intolerance, persecution, and war that had tormented the British Isles and Europe throughout history.[6]

The power of Winthrop's phrase in capturing the ideal of a righteous and harmonious society has kept it alive, making it part of the sense of American destiny. The phrase was notably delivered in speeches about national purpose by presidents John Kennedy and Ronald Reagan, both of whom interpreted Winthrop's founding ideal as that of a model nation transcending "race or creed or even party affiliation," a nation "teeming with people of all kinds living in harmony and peace." Most of the original thirteen colonies that formed the United States were founded with an inspired vision and a sense of becoming a city upon a hill, or a model society.[7]

In reality, the Puritans' vision of a model society in America was neither socially utopian nor politically progressive. In the words of the historian David Hall, their "moral and social imperative was to enact the reign of Christ." Toward that singular end, they lived a pious, simple, dutiful, and community-oriented life governed by narrow interpretations of scripture. Yet, free of England's constraints, Puritan New England advanced so rapidly that it indeed set the stage for a new kind of political culture. Political scientists now trace a major strain of American political culture to the

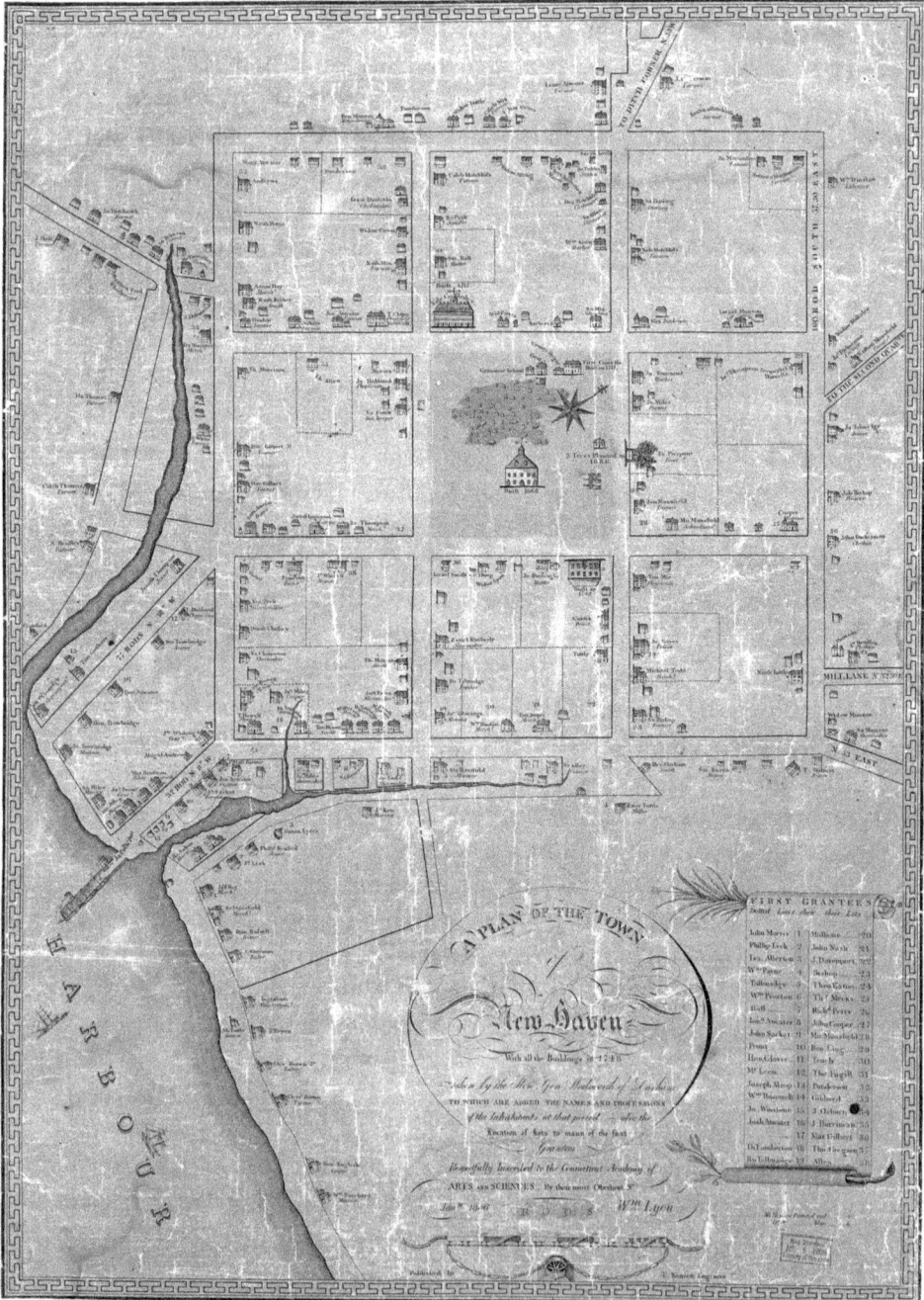

A PLAN OF THE TOWN

New Haven

With all the Buildings in 1748

Taken by the Hon. Gen. Wadsworth of Durham

TO WHICH ARE ADDED THE NAMES AND POSSESSIONS
of the Inhabitants, at that period — also the
Erection of Keys to many of the facts
Gardens

Respectfully Inscribed to the Connecticut Academy of
ARTS and SCIENCES, By their most Obedient S.

Feb. 6 1806   Wm. Lyon

HARBOUR

Puritans and to the broader category of Congregationalists, who settled New England with a similar ethic of hard work, piety, and community.[8]

The Puritan city upon a hill was, of course, a metaphorical city of spiritual virtue rather than a physical city of houses, streets, commercial buildings, and civic facilities. The Puritan life of farming, fellowship, and worship required little physical design. Initial settlements were compact to promote personal interaction, worship, and civic involvement, and they were efficient in terms of rights-of-way and lot patterns. Inevitably, however, as the towns of New England grew, they required more attention to design and were laid out in accordance with the civic, or "communitarian," values of the culture. A famous example is the plan for New Haven, Connecticut (Figure 1), which elegantly tied the physical city to the spiritual community.[9]

Down the coast from New England, other colonies would follow with various configurations of secular utopianism, religious idealism, and commercial pragmatism. Some would be inspired by England's unique constitutional tradition and the philosophers that built political theories upon it. The concept of a model civil society was first implanted in the English mind by Thomas More, the statesman, philosopher, and author who published *Utopia* (the first use of the term) in 1516. In his controversial novel, he imagined a society in which property was communally owned, agrarian labor was highly valued, and freedom of religion was a fundamental right. Two other utopian works were published in the next century as England began colonizing America. Francis Bacon, known for conceiving the modern scientific method, published *New Atlantis* in 1627. The novel envisioned a scientifically oriented society in which women had the right to vote, slavery was prohibited, and church and state were separated. The political theorist James Harrington had the most direct influence on colonial plans, including the Ashley Cooper Plan. Harrington published *The Commonwealth of Oceana* in 1656, in which he laid out a model constitution for a commonwealth founded on balanced government achieved through landownership equality among social classes. The idea that a more perfect society could actually be constructed in America,

(*opposite*) Figure 1. Historic Plan of New Haven. The 1638 "nine square plan" (shown in this 1748 plan update) was the second town plan in Anglo-America. It linked the physical city to the spiritual city, as had the design of St. Mary's, Maryland, in the previous decade. Like other plans that combine human-scale proportionality and civic space, the layout has survived the centuries and defines the core of modern New Haven. Illustration from the Library of Congress, Geography and Map Division.

far from the corrupting influences of the Old World, was a potent influence on the English visionaries who established the American colonies.

The Mid-Atlantic colonies developed with a mix of utopian, religious, and secular orientations. Originally settled by Dutch fur traders, who called the region New Netherlands, they acquired the motherland's tradition of pragmatic religious and ethnic tolerance. When England acquired New Netherlands in 1664, it created the colonies of New York, New Jersey, and Delaware. The region largely retained the commercial and pragmatic attitudes of the Dutch colonists, following the transfer of authority. Moreover, the desire of English settlers to avoid the destructive intensity of religious divisions at home reinforced a political culture that valued personal liberty and religious freedom. The physical city of the region was a practical city, efficient for commerce, civil administration, and defense, rather than the spiritual city of New England or the cultural city of other utopians. A vision of a greater society than the one left behind was an acquired sense, one that gained momentum as England challenged the emerging spirit of liberty in colonial America.[10]

If the American colonists needed a reminder of the painful experience of religious intolerance, they had Maryland to serve as an early example. The Province of Maryland was founded in 1632 as a haven for English Catholics as well as a commercial venture. The new colony was founded by Lord Baltimore, who envisioned a more tolerant society. The Maryland Toleration Act of 1649 briefly legalized freedom of worship for Catholics and other Trinitarian Christians, while providing the death penalty for others. The prescription for tolerance among certain Christians lacked permanence, as the colony more often mirrored the religious strife that consumed England through much of the seventeenth century. Anglicans, Puritans, and even Quakers rebelled against Catholic authority. In 1689, Puritans seized control, and Catholics lost their freedoms until they were restored after the American Revolution.

Maryland's unsuccessful grasp for religious tolerance ultimately added temperance to the American quest for liberty. As the Founders took on the task of writing a constitution, they confronted a "mosaic of religious denominations," and it became their task to prevent the ever-simmering potential for religious strife from consuming the new nation from within. Their eventual prescription for the malady was the First Amendment of the Bill of Rights guaranteeing freedom of speech and religion.[11]

The first capital of Maryland, St. Mary's City, is preserved today as testament to the visionary purpose of the colony. The town was laid out to reflect the colony's philosophy of tolerance (limited though it was), which in part required separation of church and state. The mayor's residence in St. Mary's was placed at the center of the town, while civic functions were placed at one end and church functions at the other. St. Mary's City remained the seat of colonial Maryland government until 1708.[12]

In 1660, after decades of religious strife in England and her colonies, the Puritan dictatorship of Oliver Cromwell, known as the Commonwealth of England, Scotland, and Ireland, was brought to an end. The Parliament of England restored the monarchy and returned the House of Stuart to the throne. Religious idealism that drove the founding of early American colonies established before the Commonwealth period was replaced by a broader spectrum of idealism underlying the establishment of subsequent colonies. The first such colony to be chartered following the Restoration was the Province of Carolina.

The Ashley Cooper Plan, through its desire to remake traditional English society, succeeded in planting a fourth political culture in America that briefly stood in contrast to theocratic-yet-civic New England, the pragmatic Mid-Atlantic region, and the more socially stratified plantations of the Potomac watershed. Carolina emerged in isolation, buffered from northern influences by wilderness and by Virginia, where early wealth seekers had given up the search for gold in favor of gentry agriculture. The Carolina and Virginia political cultures would eventually converge as a larger southern regional culture took form; first, however, Carolina would shed the more idealistic principles of the Ashley Cooper Plan while retaining much of the plan's class structure. The modern characteristics and geographic distribution of American political cultures born during the colonial period are taken up later, following a journey through Carolina developmental history.[13]

Ashley Cooper envisioned a new kind of society in Carolina, one quite different from other colonies. In contrast to Virginia, it would be carefully balanced in design to avoid an accumulation of power by one class of society. In contrast to New England, it would have a secular government capable of ensuring Protestant religious tolerance. The cities and hinterlands of the Ashley Cooper Plan were to adopt the ancient principle of *reciprocity* of duties and benefits among social classes, a hierarchy of need fulfillment in perpetual balance for the common good. However, in time, as slavery unintentionally became the primary source of labor in Carolina, the ancient idea of reciprocity quickly faded away; the wise nobility and the ethic of noblesse oblige were replaced by absolute authority of one *race* over another and the strong hand of one *class* over many. Ashley Cooper's balanced society was re-envisioned as a caste system that would sustain a plantation economy designed to enrich the few who sat atop the social pyramid. Intraclass adversarialism then overturned reciprocity.[14]

Ashley Cooper's political ideology and John Locke's political philosophy remained alive in America, even as their founding principles became warped beyond recognition in the social mores and settlement patterns that came to characterize the South. This irony of history will be dissected later in terms of historical geography, political culture, and the planning of American cities.

Model Colonies and City Planning in America

Anthony Ashley Cooper was the first of three founders of American colonies to envision a model society, a city upon a hill, and at the same time to design its villages, towns, and cities in concert with those ideals. With Locke's assistance, he designed Carolina with a constitution that addressed social structure, political institutions, and physical design with equal importance. Then they drilled deeper into those three areas by issuing detailed "instructions," essentially implementing regulations, to ensure that colonists would keep the elaborate system intact. The physical design template issued with the instructions called for balanced, sustainable growth consistent with the colony's constitutional principles. Only Pennsylvania and Georgia were conceived and designed with such care in linking political philosophy with physical design.

William Penn followed Ashley Cooper in 1681 with a plan for Pennsylvania based on principles of liberty that were similarly supported by, and integrated with, a design strategy for settlement. The constitution for the new colony was formalized the following year. Penn also appears to have been influenced by James Harrington's ideal agrarian commonwealth, which placed limits on land allocation, though not to the same extent as Ashley Cooper, who codified the agrarian law described in *Oceana* to achieve balanced government. Penn, a Quaker convert, had experienced religious persecution firsthand. He envisioned a colony where all people, regardless of religion, could worship freely and live together. Slavery was prohibited, and Penn's vision of social harmony extended to indigenous people as well; his treaty of friendship with the Lenape Indians was, Voltaire wrote, "the only treaty between Indians and Christians that was never sworn to and that was never broken."[15]

Pennsylvania was a planned colony in every sense. Settlement began only after a strategic and healthful site was selected on the navigable Delaware River and a capital city was laid out in a simple grid of large town lots for the colony's gentry. The colony's yeoman farmers were allocated 50-acre town lots and 450-acre farms in the surrounding rural townships. The settlement pattern was rural but sufficiently compact to ensure access to markets, schools, and churches—a more dispersed pattern, it was thought, to prevent the formation of civil society.

Penn's vision for a "green country town" integrated with the countryside was meant to make the capital, Philadelphia, more like the rural towns of England than the nation's crowded, morally corrupt, and polluted cities. Homes were surrounded by gardens and orchards to prevent overcrowding. A central area was reserved for a market, statehouse, and other buildings of civic importance. The original 1681 concept for the capital was replaced the following year with a more practical plan drawn up by surveyor Thomas Holme, who added more density as well as a central square and four outlying squares, giving Philadelphia more of the look of a city than Penn first envisioned and preparing it to become a colonial metropolis.[16]

The third visionary cited above, James Oglethorpe, founded Georgia in 1733 on principles similar to those adopted for Carolina. Georgia was the only American colony established during the Enlightenment, and the last of the thirteen colonies that would become the United States. The Oglethorpe Plan updated the agrarian principles underlying the Ashley Cooper Plan by nearly eliminating class structure and prohibiting slavery. Oglethorpe's vision of a sustainable yeoman society, based on a concept of "agrarian equality," was supported by an elaborate physical design intended once again to create a model society. An idealized depiction from promotional materials is shown in Figure 2. Oglethorpe, like Ashley Cooper, was influenced by James Harrington and Harrington's muse, Niccolo Machiavelli. Oglethorpe's references to Machiavelli suggest that he adopted the concept of *translatio virtutis* in conceiving Georgia—the idea that virtuous societies spring up in new lands as corrupting influences consume older nations.[17]

All three utopian plans, or models, were implemented to transcend the injustice and corruption of the homeland, thereby implanting higher ideals in the fabric of the American colonies at their inception. The concentration of idealistic beginnings in colonial America stood in sharp contrast to global European colonization, which was driven primarily by the desire for wealth and power.

The idea of planning cities in concert with forming a more perfect society, the city upon a hill, soon sprang up in other American colonies that had not been founded with utopian designs. The earliest effort at city

Figure 2. Idealized Depiction of Georgia. Designed sixty years
after Charles Town, Savannah was the first colonial city to be laid out in
accordance with Enlightenment principles, as reflected in this depiction of order
and harmony in the social and physical environment. The unique urban design at the
core of the plan has withstood the test of time and continues to serve the vibrant
urban environment of modern Savannah. Illustration provided by the
Hargrett Rare Book & Manuscript Library, University of Georgia.

planning took the form of regulations for siting towns. Colonists were consistently instructed by their English administrators to establish towns on high ground situated on navigable rivers and remote from unhealthy marshes; defenses and public facilities such as storehouses and market squares were to be constructed before private development took place. Specifications for street layouts were intended to address environmental conditions such as prevailing winds, a practice that dated to the revered Roman city planner, Vitruvius, whose work was brought to light and emulated during the Italian Renaissance.

Experience gained from building towns in the early seventeenth century led to more detailed laws and regulations that specified the layout of streets, reservation of civic space, and allocation of land for private lots. Such laws and regulations, originally set forth in colonial charters, compacts, purpose statements, and constitutions, were eventually adopted after 1776 in varying forms by the states and the federal government, beginning an American tradition of city planning. Those early laws and regulations were intertwined with the nation's founding principles and consistent with the intent of those principles.[18]

Before planned colonies emerged, beginning with Carolina in 1670, English colonies were established without a detailed framework for growth. Trade and defense dictated growth patterns in Virginia, while social organization around religion dictated the form of towns in New England. Eventually, however, organic growth in London and other Old World cities demonstrated beyond any doubt that unregulated growth led to dysfunctional congestion, aesthetic degradation, economic inefficiencies, fire hazards, crime and social anarchy, the spread of disease, and other health concerns such as air and water pollution. London's Great Plague of 1665–66 and the Great Fire of 1666, discussed further in Chapter 3, established a pivotal moment in English history after which city planning acquired greater importance.

The surge of creative ideas for rebuilding London after the Great Fire was made possible by the new intellectual freedoms that followed the Commonwealth. The founding of the Royal Society in 1660 established a community of scientists and attracted interest from nonscientists in the infinite possibilities of unleashed human reason. Many of those who were active in the Royal Society were keenly interested in cities. Robert Hooke, curator of experiments at the Royal Society, submitted a plan and surveyed parts of the city for rebuilding. Christopher Wren, a scientist, mathematician, and architect, designed many of London's most famous buildings. The most ambitious plans were put forward by John Evelyn, a writer, horticulturalist, and landscape designer, and Richard Newcourt, who had published a detailed map of London eight years before the fire. Both sought to completely redesign central London. The urban design concepts that emerged in the rebuilding of London were consonant with the new age of science and reason, an age that would soon blossom into the British Enlightenment.

The value of planning became evident not only to visionary founders like Ashley Cooper, but to subsequent administrators of the colonies. City planning became part of the legacy of the colonies as they transformed themselves into the United States.

Francis Nicholson (1655–1728) was the earliest colonial administrator active in city planning who was also a long-term resident of the colonies. He served as governor of Maryland, Virginia, and South Carolina and conceived the design of Annapolis and Williamsburg. Nicholson was influenced by the inspired designs for the rebuilding of London following the Great Fire and brought those ideas back to America, where he applied them. His plan for Annapolis, the new capital of Maryland, as pointed out by the planning historian John Reps, "introduced a new concept of civic design to colonial America." Nicholson's new concept included a legal framework for separating noxious activities that "annoy" or "disquiet" their neighbors, a precursor of the modern concept of zoning.[19]

The colonies founded before the pivotal 1660s subsequently adopted the new planning concepts. In addition to the design of Annapolis, the new planning ethic can be seen in Nicholson's plan of Williamsburg, the new capital of Virginia. Creativity entered British America's bloodstream, and towns and cities were designed accordingly. Some were carried to completion according to design (for example, New Haven, Connecticut, and Charlestown, Maryland); others remained on paper, surviving only as evidence of greater interest in city planning (for example, Radnor, South Carolina, and Eden, Virginia).

The Ashley Cooper Plan was the original Grand Model, as it was called at the time, adopted by the government of Charles II and his successors as a framework for development in the colonies. It synthesized proposals for rebuilding London after the Great Fire and applied them in colonial context. Going forward, towns and regions would be planned systematically in advance of settlement using a square-mile grid; standards would be adopted for streets, allowing ample width and efficient connectivity through a grid layout; town and country lots would be standardized; and sites would be set aside for civic and commercial uses.[20]

In following Ashley Cooper's (and Locke's) specifications, the capital of Carolina, Charles Town (now Charleston), became English America's first *comprehensively planned* city in the modern sense of that term. Implementation, however, was compromised by inexperience and pragmatism, as well as the competing objectives of the Caribbean slave-holders settling in the colony. Although the Ashley Cooper Plan was never fully implemented, it succeeded in settling a frontier colony, forming a rigidly hierarchical society, and designing towns partly in accordance with its original principles. The legacy of the plan, as will be seen over the course of subsequent chapters, spawned descendant plans that shaped growth for generations, and it remains present in America today.

The City of the American Enlightenment

At the signing of the Declaration of Independence in 1776, town planning was an accepted practice prescribed by law in several colonies, a practice retained as they became states. Numerous American cities had matured under the guidance of inspired plans, including Charles Town (1672) Philadelphia (1682), Albany (1695), Williamsburg (1699),

Annapolis (1718), New York (redesigned in 1731 by the British), Savannah (1733), New Haven (1748/1638), and Alexandria (1749). Town planning acts of the time addressed the siting of new towns, the form of towns, and sometimes details of the layout of streets and lots. Colonial Virginia's "Act for Building a Town" of 1662 became the basis for town planning laws later adopted by the states of Virginia and Maryland. Similar laws existed in other states, many of them influenced by the physical design elements of the Ashley Cooper Plan.[21]

Where a law did not exist, plans were often implemented to orchestrate growth. In South Carolina during the early 1730s, Governor Robert Johnson implemented a plan for establishing towns on the western frontier of the colony. The objectives of creating these planned towns were to create a protective buffer against attack by Indians or Spanish and to increase opportunities for European settlement to counter the threat from an ever-growing enslaved majority. Eleven townships were identified at strategic intervals, 60 miles inland on principal rivers. Not all were built or survived when they were, but several became prominent towns.[22]

City planning was reinforced as an early American value by a concept shared by many if not most of the Founders: the idea that "nature's God" created a universe that operated under mathematically harmonious laws. In the new paradigm of the Enlightenment, the old idea of God as a whimsical, emotional, often angry father figure was rejected as accumulated myth perpetuated by "priestcraft" (a favored term of deists). The new idea of God was that of a rational Supreme Being whose true nature was rediscovered in part through Isaac Newton's demonstration of order and precision in all Creation. Planning beautiful and orderly cities was consistent with this view of God, and among most of the Founders that view was a given.

Freemasonry adopted the Newtonian worldview and nearly became a tolerant and scientific Christian denomination. John Desaguliers, a leader of the growing Freemasonry movement of the 1720s, was a member of the Royal Society and author of "The Newtonian System of the World, the Best Model of Government: An Allegorical Poem." Freemasons referred to God as "The Great Architect of the Universe," and they saw their society as originating with the sacred design of Solomon's Temple. As a society of builders of ancient cities, city planning was in the genetic code of Freemasons. Many of the Founders were Freemasons, including George Washington, John Hancock, and Benjamin Franklin.

Newtonian order and harmony entered the mainstream of Enlightenment discourse through other channels as well. One of those was formed by Ashley Cooper's famous grandson, the 3rd Earl of Shaftesbury, who wove the Newtonian worldview into the emerging philosophy of his teacher, John Locke. His moral and humanistic philosophy was published in one of the most influential works of the time, *Characteristicks of Men, Manners, Opinions, Times* (1711). Shaftesbury's work was taken up and expanded by Francis Hutcheson, who brought together David Hume, Adam Smith, and others who created a nucleus for the Scottish Enlightenment. It is impossible to overestimate the profound influence of the many channels of Enlightenment philosophy on the Founding Fathers.

Newtonian order and harmony and the new humanism of the era were synthesized by the Founders in the form of the design of the new nation's first planned city, its capital, Washington. The capital city stands as testimony to the fact that in the era of the Founding Fathers the concept of planning cities was woven into the fabric of the nation's Enlightenment-based ideals. Sited at the heart of the nation, the capital rose up as a comprehensively planned city, supervised in its design and development by George Washington and Thomas Jefferson.

The French engineer and designer Pierre L'Enfant, a Freemason and a friend of Alexander Hamilton who had served in the Continental Army, was commissioned to lay out the city. Jefferson supplied L'Enfant with plans of Amsterdam, Milan, Paris, and other great cities. The plan observed natural topography while laying out a city of the people. According to the National Park Service, "As the capital of a new nation, its position and appearance had to surpass the social, economic and cultural balance of a mere city: it was intended as the model for American city planning and a symbol of governmental power to be seen by other nations." The L'Enfant Plan of 1791 for Washington remains one of the world's most renowned city plans, a literal city upon a hill.[23]

While the United States was founded with an ethic for planned cities, it should be pointed out that Washington was built on land donated by Maryland that had long since been vacated by Native Americans and that many other planned cities in the colonies and first thirteen states were carved out of wilderness. Planning cities on such a blank slate did not interfere with private property rights. Modern city planning, by contrast, must necessarily balance public benefits with well-established patterns of private landownership. The simple fact pointed out here is that land planning for a range of purposes—infrastructure, aesthetics, health, economic development, social organization, and defense—was an early value consistent with the nation's founding principles. It is not argued that civic planning was or is a higher value than private property rights, but rather that both are highly valued American cultural traditions. Striking a balance between those values, embedded as they are in first principles, is a subject taken up later.

There were alternatives to planned cities, and they were largely rejected at the founding of the nation. Administrative cities, for example, could have been founded without any effort to shape the hinterlands beyond. Garrison towns might have been sited for strategic value, certainly with an expectation of growth around them, but again without any concern for the economic hinterlands of the colony or state. Organic cities might have been expected to arise naturally as central places in agricultural regions, around trading posts, or at transportation hubs. Yet most of the colonies and the first thirteen states perceived value in planning the location, distribution, and design of towns.

Standardized *regional* planning much like that adopted for Carolina, Pennsylvania, and Georgia was adopted by the United States almost immediately after the Revolution. The young nation's attraction to Newtonian order and harmony in land-use planning is seen with the Land Ordinance of 1785, which established a hierarchical, rectangular survey grid to replace the localized, irregular British system of metes and bounds. The new system created a framework of townships and square-mile sections for the development of cities and their economic hinterlands. The ordinance reflected the value placed on public education by reserving section 16 in each township for public schools.

Although the nation was founded with an ethic of city planning infused into its national priorities, that ethic suffered erosion in the nineteenth century until health and sanitation concerns renewed interest in planning (and brought about zoning) at the approach of the twentieth century. Today, the city planning ethic varies regionally and among political cultures. In the South, city planning had ambitious origins and enduring effects with the Ashley Cooper Plan and the Oglethorpe Plan. For nearly two centuries after the founding of the United States, the South continued to embrace an urban vision that matched its predominant rural character, building cities with strong centers composed of vibrant commercial districts, neoclassical buildings, elegant public places, and efficient grids. Beginning with the civil rights movement, however, city planning became increasingly identified with heavy-handed government. As southerners headed for the suburbs, their historical antigovernment bias, rooted in preserving slavery, was extended to the traditional city. The legacy of resistance from the time of Ashley Cooper to the present is explored further in Chapter 5.[24]

Southern political culture, well established by the American Revolution, inherited the social hierarchy of the Ashley Cooper Plan without its original goal of class reciprocity. It inherited a sense of ordered space and ethic of rational planning to the extent it served the needs of the white middle class and the domineering oligarchy (or the "aristocracy," as it viewed itself). In recent times, as the South has become the center of gravity for modern conservatism, resistance to class-neutral city planning has spread out of the region to other areas of the nation. Efforts to orchestrate growth consonant with rational planning models, for example, are challenged today by those who see such plans as violating individual liberty and private property rights, a principle conservatives associate with Lockean natural rights. The role of government in framing priorities for development is thus increasingly rejected as a new form of "tyranny," especially as strict-constructionist private property advocates align themselves with social conservatives, who fear that government is a force in undermining their values. Additionally, in the present climate of political divisiveness, xenophobic fears of a United Nations threat to national sovereignty through Agenda 21 coupled with predictions that Islamic law could be adopted in the United States have added new recruits into the mix of opposition to city planning. Such an assertion seems farfetched until one sees firsthand the extent to which such fears are cropping up at the state and local levels (see Chapter 5 for an assessment).[25]

Two points central to this book refute contemporary claims that planning has acquired a new, Far Left agenda that is alien to American traditions. The first is that American cities have been comprehensively planned from the earliest times, often with a vision consonant with principles underlying the founding of the nation. The second is that city planning and associated urban policy take form within the context of political culture, and that there are, by most reckonings, three distinct political cultures in the United States with planning traditions that date back to the nation's founding. These points will be reinforced throughout the chapters that follow.

The American Idea of the City

Most people today think of themselves as living in a city. Yet the newness of cities in human history is stunning. For over 95 percent of approximately 200,000 years of human existence, we have lived without cities, roaming the earth in nomadic bands and subsisting as hunter-gatherers. Permanent settlement began only about 10,000 years ago with the advent of agriculture, and cities arose only about 6,000 to 7,000 years ago with the capability of producing food surpluses and conducting trade (Uruk in Mesopotamia being the best-known example, if not the first city). The success of early permanent settlement was reinforced through the Neolithic Age, during which humans learned to fashion tools for farming as well as hunting purposes.[26]

From the end of antiquity and the rise of Classical Greece 2,600 years ago, cities have been considered the engines of civilization, driving economic, scientific, and cultural advancement. They are places of creative energy and new ideas that can also magnify the most sinister of human ambitions. But in their primal form, cities were governed like clans, with rigid hierarchies of members segregated in their roles by physical strength, dominant personalities, specialized knowledge, age, and gender. The primal hierarchy was famously altered in the Greek city-states when reason and compassion emerged as new forces capable of shaping society. However, even Athenian democracy retained most of the primal hierarchy as its basic superstructure, and even Aristotle, the father of political science, saw the city in terms of a hierarchical social pyramid.

It was not until the Age of Enlightenment took form in the late seventeenth century that alternatives to the primal hierarchy, a rigid social pyramid, could be envisioned. The Greek Stoics, early Christians, and many others throughout history have envisioned a more equitable society, but until the Enlightenment the idea of equality was a spiritual vision, not one that would constitute a first principle at the foundation of a government.

From the time of Aristotle (384 B.C.–322 B.C.) to that of Ashley Cooper, democracy was considered mob rule, an impractical, unworkable form of government. In 1675, Ashley Cooper, by then risen to the title of Earl of Shaftesbury, asserted in Parliament that the nation's finely tuned balance of governmental powers prevented it "from tumbling into a democratic republic." The concept of a functioning democratic republic had no traction anywhere up to that time. Yet within Ashley Cooper's new vision of a constitutional republic, articulated in the Grand Model, were ideas of reciprocity and social justice that amounted to a final step in advancing an ancient system toward recognition of democracy as a viable principle of government. Locke, who outlived Ashley Cooper by twenty years, was the agent who carried the prospect of democracy forward into the Enlightenment. His assertion in the *Second Treatise* that everyone has a right to defend personal "life, health, Liberty, or possessions" is the source of the right of everyone to "life, liberty, and the pursuit of happiness," a first principle of American democracy, found in the Declaration of Independence.[27]

Locke is a controversial figure because of the apparent contradiction between his writing on equality and his role in planning and establishing the rigid class system in Carolina. He is indisputably a primary source for the American ideals of democracy and fundamental human equality. Those revolutionary ideals assert that all people are fundamentally equal, and from that premise the nation has progressively expanded the idea of liberty over the arc of its history. Thus slavery was ended; former slaves gained the right to vote; the franchise to vote was extended beyond property owners; women gained the right to vote; and poll taxes and literacy tests aimed at restricting voting were abolished. Advocates at the forefront of extending liberty and human rights to all people are increasingly called "progressives" rather than "liberals" to emphasize the advancements made possible under the nation's first principles. Many professions are also progressive in the sense that their practices require giving equal weight to all parties affected by their work. City planners belong to one of the professions that embraces equality and democracy as a core value, while also endorsing America's strong protection of private property rights. Such a commitment to Enlightenment values sometimes results in criticism from those who are concerned that equality and democracy are only viable within the framework of a republic that preserves a traditional social or class pyramid. The sharpening intensity of this conflict will be taken up in more detail in chapter 5.

The democracy movement launched in the Enlightenment has consistently flattened the traditional social pyramid that shaped society and politics from Aristotle to Ashley Cooper. It replaced top-down authoritarianism with bottom-up empowerment grounded in Locke's premise that power is derived from the people through a social contract. At the same time, the mythology of cities and civilizations has been challenged as never before in history, creating an anarchy of hierarchy. The neoconservative historian Leo Strauss, in *The City and Man* and elsewhere, has diagnosed this trend as carrying with it the seeds of the destruction of Western civilization. To Strauss, if a society is to be democratic, it must also retain a shadow hierarchy of thought-leaders who advance a set of ideals by winning the tacit support of the people. That support is won by cultivating a mythology of greatness and destiny, a seduction that one might call an opiate for the masses if the phrase were not already taken. The neoconservative position is that political philosophers from Aristotle to Ashley Cooper were right, that pure democracy is mob rule. Empowerment of the people, a central value of progressive political philosophy, is misguided and will destroy the great civilization inherited from Classical Greece. Planners, with their emphasis on public participation, are sometimes seen as complicit in the erosion of tradition and authority.[28]

The city upon a hill is therefore a very different construct for progressives and conservatives in America today, and increasingly so as the latter has become tied to southern political culture and its historical suspicion of government intervention and outside influences. The future of the city—the nucleus of civilization—is at stake, and both sides realize it. City planning is finding itself at ground zero in battle after battle in that war of ideas.

The progressive's core values of equality and democracy run counter to the natural state of humanity, the hierarchical social pyramid described by Aristotle and prevalent across the world until the Enlightenment. The new idea of the Age of Enlightenment was that through the gift of reason, man can improve upon the primitive, natural hierarchy built on power, intrigue, and leverage. A world can be designed where the ideals of equality, justice, and opportunity are adopted as core values and continuously extended to more and more people. As the deists of the Enlightenment asserted, man can and should exercise reason to emulate the beauty and harmony of God's design. Such an effort requires not only designing a new ship of state to replace the ancient model, but then trimming the ship's sails to set a modern course. Enlightened city planning, urban policy, and resource management are essential to maintaining a course that preserves equality and social justice and at times widens its embrace.

The conservative's core values are individual liberty and republicanism. Those values are consistent with the natural state of humanity, the given order of the world until the Enlightenment offered an alternative. Neoconservatives assert that such a hierarchy reflects the accumulated wisdom of Western Civilization dating to Classical Greece. Libertarians claim that individual liberty will naturally result in the best forms of social order. Religious conservatives believe that God has created a hierarchy, the Great Chain of Being, the natural order of things in the spiritual and physical realms (see Figure 6 in Chapter 1). To these ideological conservatives, pure equality and democracy are delusions, impossible to attain. There must always be visionaries and leaders, myth and faith, and masses to be guided in the discovery of life's meaning. The ship of state is not new but ancient, its best course set by a destiny shaped in belief in cultural superiority. Private interests are best left unhindered to build the city; planning and public policy to promote equality and social justice rob the "makers" of society of liberty essential to human advancement.

Ironically, the names of the American Democratic and Republican parties originally ran counter to conservative and progressive core values. The Democratic Party, dating organizationally to Andrew Jackson and philosophically to Jefferson, supported the rigid social hierarchy of the Solid South. The Republican Party, founded by abolitionists and having Abraham Lincoln as its first president, was the party that redesigned the ship of state as prescribed by Enlightenment humanism. A century later, the Civil Rights Act of 1964 led to a mass defection of southern Democrats to the Republican Party, encouraged by a Southern Strategy crafted by President Nixon and perfected under President Reagan. The polarity of the two parties reversed and their core values became more appropriately aligned with their names: Democrats championed equality and broad democracy and Republicans championed a more hierarchical ship of state consistent with the classical tradition of republicanism.

Today's great challenge faced by city planners, urban designers, urban policy makers, environmental scientists, social equity advocates, and many others operating in the sphere of Enlightenment values is to accommodate a new form of conservatism that rejects the pragmatic center for a strongly ideological worldview that is skeptical of democracy. The political divide has sharpened as ideological conservatives place increasing emphasis on local and state politics, retooling the Southern Strategy to embrace the rise of the Tea Party. The new conservative view is no longer played out primarily on the national stage and in the realm of international geopolitics. It has become intensely local, with frequent interventions by libertarian and Tea Party activists opposed to city planning and design initiatives. Such initiatives, in their view, empower "takers" and undermine "makers," turning the traditional social pyramid upside down.

The new Southern Strategy is now a national strategy with a synergistic relationship among elected officials, private concerns, and grassroots organizations (principally Tea Party groups). It blames "big government" and often the United Nations for upending the traditional values of society. Previously benign planning proposals have become politically charged. Land-use plans, zoning ordinances, and sustainable development practices are now attacked as relocation schemes aiming to concentrate people in United Nations–prescribed "habitat zones." Development standards such as building heights and housing densities are perceived as a confiscation of private property rights.

Planners and local elected officials are no longer simply trying to balance the rights and aspirations of the community with those of individuals. They are now enmeshed in new rhetoric about the nation's history, its first principles, and forces out to destroy its traditions. To counter the war of words against planning, planners and other public officials need to have a better grasp of history and the ability to argue the merits of their actions in historical terms. By doing so, they can reassure policy makers that their decisions are consistent with American traditions and values.

Anthony Ashley Cooper began a planning tradition in America in 1770, and John Locke authored the first comprehensive set of city planning "instructions"—in essence regulations that prescribed where urban growth should occur, where areas should remain rural, and how development should be spatially organized in terms of private lots, civic space, and public rights-of-way. The Ashley Cooper Plan became part of an American tradition of city planning present at the founding of the United States. The American system of jurisprudence has upheld that tradition, always finding balance between civic and private interests. The ideological attack on contemporary planning is taken up further in the Epilogue, where language dating to the Founders and their muses—including Ashley Cooper and Locke—is shown to be consistent with the theories and practices of contemporary planning.

First Principles and the Future of the City

The values associated with city planning and other creative and problem-solving professions are those of the Enlightenment: inductive reasoning, harmonious design, equality, and democracy. Those values date to the founding of the United States and the early spread of humanistic ideals, and they are consonant with the values of the Founders and the sentiments found in the Declaration of Independence and the Constitution. Yet virtually nothing is said by such practitioners about the foundation of their values. By contrast, conservative critics of professions like city planning claim with confidence to be grounded in the nation's first principles and founding documents. The result is two separate forms of discourse and no real communication. Since the Right is not going to change its rhetoric, as it would be "relativism" to do so, the other side of the conversation will have to acquire a historical dialectic to convey its ideas to its opponents effectively.

The planning profession has adopted a formal code of ethics, with a "primary obligation to serve the public interest," to recognize the "long range consequences" and "interrelatedness of decisions," and to "seek social justice." Urban designers employ a charrette (design workshop) process based on the same core values of participatory democracy. Transportation planners prioritize projects with statutory guidance from citizen advisory committees. Until recently, Enlightenment values were shared by most scholars, elected officials, and public figures, and they were accepted by the general public. The rise of a new form of conservatism, one associated with neoconservatism and libertarianism rather than pragmatism, has gained momentum. Its values are more traditional or classical than Enlightenment-oriented. The new conservatism is, by design, as active at the state and local level as it is nationally, a fact of life that professions like city planners can no longer ignore.[29]

Attacks on city planning are often based on perceived violations of America's first principles. Such presumed violations are articulated by a host of policy institutes ("think tanks") sitting near the top of the conservative organizational pyramid. Unlike progressive policy institutes, which primarily deliver their findings to policy makers, conservative think tanks also hone their work products for popular consumption, as with the Heartland Institute's billboard campaign comparing climate scientists to mass murderers and the John Birch Society's steady supply of anti-sustainable development literature to local Tea Party groups.

Conservative think-tank messages are often a mixture of technical information and historical first principles, messages that often imply profane treatment of the most sacred text, the Constitution. This approach arouses justifiable indignation. The idealistic language and scholarly assessments of American constitutional history generated by conservative think tanks provides cover for deeper disturbances. Lying underneath the indignation over violating first principles and "trampling on" the Constitution is a deeper sense of indignation fueled by the rhetoric of the Far Right. One such festering concern is the quest for fairness in a complex world; another is the desire to band with similar people in an increasingly diverse society. In banding together, the aggrieved feel they are doing something about undeserving people who appear to be bilking hardworking Americans through their enablers, the liberals, and big government.

The honorable defense of first principles and the Constitution conceals such deeper feelings, which, if spoken, might sound classist, racist, or xenophobic. The Enlightenment legacy of rational problem solving and social justice at the core of planning ethics is perceived as liberal facilitation of the demands of people with alien cultural values or as lacking a work ethic. Planning actions are sometimes perceived as part of a government "redistribution" of wealth from the deserving to the undeserving, from the makers to the takers. Arguing against Enlightenment values head-on is unproductive, but attacking practitioners of those values from first principles cleanses political discourse and places the attackers on high ground.

The tactic suggested by most observers for assuaging the concerns of indignant conservatives is to engage in respectful, constructive dialogue. This is a valid but superficial prescription, but ultimately stronger medicine will be required. Professions newly caught up in political crossfire must also learn to address the substantive issues driving conservatives and their aggrieved followers. Moreover, they must learn to present factual counterarguments to elected and appointed officials in succinct and memetic (catchy) arguments. An essential part of winning arguments in public debate is reducing them to the nubs that people can remember. No matter how long and elegant an argument might be, it will fail to equip decision makers with a rationale for supporting it if it fails to deliver succinct, reproducible ideas.

Professions like city planning therefore should be prepared to advocate for their positions on two levels, objective and subjective. On the objective level, they should understand historical first principles and their embodiment in the Constitution. They should also understand the relationship between first principles and the history of American city planning, a history that dates to the Ashley Cooper Plan, with threads traceable farther back to the Puritans. On the subjective or emotional level, city planners and those concerned with urban futures must be prepared to address an implicit fear in a conservative population that their plans and policies yield a zero-sum result. That is, any improvement in the condition of one group (the perceived unworthy takers) will diminish the equity held by another group (the self-identified worthy makers). There is a sense that hardworking Americans, believed to make up 53 percent of the public, is under siege by the 47 percent who have become dependent on government and want "free stuff" (a meme introduced by presidential candidate Mitt Romney and used by conservatives during 2012 election campaigns).[30]

While the first level, particularly the history of city planning, is the present subject, the second area is inseparable from it in public discussion and is therefore taken up in a more general fashion. The inclination of city planners is to ignore subtext and vaguely stated public concerns; but they do so at their peril when underlying issues continue to define opposition to planning initiatives. City planners should learn to refute the idea that society is bifurcated into makers and takers. Methods for exposing the fallacy of vast dependency are proposed in the "language of democracy" taken up in the Epilogue. The means to deliver a factual refutation of the fallacy is readily available in such documents as comprehensive plans and in the ever-increasing power of graphic illustration to compress an abundance of data into understandable bites.

So what are the first principles upon which the nation was founded? The Founders supplied part of the answer in their writings. They cited earlier writings of specific people as inspirational to their vision of democracy and republican government. Their models came from the English political philosophers James Harrington, John Locke, and Lord Bolingbroke; from Scottish Enlightenment thinkers, including Francis Hutcheson, David Hume, and Adam Smith; and from the giants of the French Enlightenment, Voltaire, Montesquieu, and Rousseau.

Locke's concept of social contract and the natural right to "life, liberty, and estate" are well-known precursors to the Declaration of Independence. Several others, however, were developing similar concepts during the Enlightenment. Hutcheson, a disciple of Anthony Ashley Cooper, the 3rd Earl of Shaftesbury (the subject Ashley Cooper's grandson), wrote a series of essays on the ideas of invisible union, inalienable rights, and posterity's liberty and happiness. Voltaire and Montesquieu both resided in London for a time during the 1720s, where they interacted with Bolingbroke and his circle of writers and intellectuals, which included Alexander Pope and Jonathan Swift. They all diagnosed corrupt leadership as the source of social ills across Europe.

Bolingbroke drew from Harrington (who in turn drew from Machiavelli) in developing the idea of a "patriot king" who would restore the nation to its first principles. The idea of clearing away the old regime with its accumulated corruption developed into a powerful notion on both sides of the Atlantic. In part, the Founders saw themselves as clearing away corruption and restoring England's ancient principles of liberty in America; in part they were creating entirely new principles of equality and democracy.

While the new ideas of the "long eighteenth century" (beginning with the Glorious Revolution in 1689), the Age of Enlightenment as it would be known, inspired the Founders, earlier settlers and their mentors were also influential. In addition to John Winthrop and the city upon a hill, Roger Williams was significant to the Founders in at least two ways. He was the first to advocate the modern idea of separation of church and state. It was Williams who wrote of a "wall of separation" between the church and the secular world, words later invoked by Jefferson to describe his position on separation of church and state. Williams also espoused the idea of a home as a castle, a place of ultimate liberty, secure from the prying eyes of government and religious institutions. Before coming to America, Williams was an associate of the famous English jurist Sir Edward Coke, who first articulated this thesis, now known as the Castle Doctrine, as a principle of law. Separation of church and state and the Castle Doctrine are the first of first principles, although there is variation of interpretation.

Ashley Cooper, with Locke, established a pivot point from that earlier time to the Enlightenment. The Grand Model for Carolina replicated the traditional English social pyramid, a feudal hierarchy by today's standards; but it also advanced new ideas, including tolerance of religious diversity (which did not go as far as Locke preferred) and trial by a jury of peers, in addition to modern city planning concepts. The creation of a plan for the colony became an elaborate thought experiment in political philosophy and first principles. Ashley Cooper immediately went on to modernize republicanism (after its failure under Cromwell), and Locke went on to become not only one of the most influential philosophers of the Enlightenment, but of all history. Locke departed from Ashley Cooper's republicanism into liberalism (considered foundational to modern conservatism).

The first principles on which the United States was founded vary according to the eye of the beholder. The prime example is freedom of worship and its corollary, separation of church and state. It is the first principle most visible today to the city planner. A wave of state and federal laws sponsored by conservatives in the 1980s ostensibly aimed at protecting religious freedom by exempting houses of worship from most zoning standards. The unstated impetus behind these new laws was the recruitment of evangelicals and conservative churches into the base of the Republican Party. The new laws became political statements asserting the rights of churches over other sectors of society. After 2001 and the rise of Islamophobia, a new wave of religious legislation has aimed to restrict freedom of religion for non-Christians, especially Muslims.

Most first principles incorporated into the Declaration of Independence and the U.S. Constitution came from the early aspirations of colonists, from ancient principles of English law, and from emerging Enlightenment values. The list shown below summarizes those first principles that can be identified in the codes of the thirteen colonies and the nation's founding documents. What should be readily apparent in the list is that most of the first principles are philosophical concepts subject to interpretation.

Yet they are sufficiently clear in purpose when they reach their ultimate arbiter, the Supreme Court, to preserve the republican ideal of liberty and to expand the Enlightenment ideal of equality.

SELECTED FIRST PRINCIPLES OF THE FOUNDERS
Freedom of Conscience, Speech, Religion
> Freedom of religious practice
> Tolerance of religions and cultures (for example, Native Americans)
> Castle Doctrine (home as castle secure from intrusion)

Balanced Government
> Separation of powers (executive, legislative, judicial)
> Social contract (power derived from the people)
> People's militia (a standing army is a threat to the people)
> People's government (citizen representative, short sessions)
> Agrarianism (diffusion of power across the land)
> Separation of church and state (wall of separation)
> Secret ballot

Natural Rights and Equality
> Natural rights of life, liberty, property/pursuit of happiness
> All people created equal

When those first principles are viewed through modern political lenses, they sometimes take on strange forms. As John Adams foresaw, "The history of our revolution will be one continued lye [lie] from one end to the other." The journey taken herein back through a strand of incipient first principles planted in America by Ashley Cooper and Locke attempts to set aside such biases and review the events and ideas of the time. In doing so, it discovers that extreme political ideologies of today often bear little resemblance to first principles, even as political cultures maintain their historically subideological temperaments. This finding is of particular importance to those who plan the growth of cities and regions, build local economies, promote social equity, and protect environmental resources.[31]

Ashley Cooper revived republicanism from the devastation of the English Civil War, drawing concepts of balanced government from Harrington's *Oceana* and combining them with more traditional principles. Classical liberalism, also known as Lockean liberalism, is Locke's reformulation of republicanism. Locke outlived Ashley Cooper by two decades, a period that was his most productive as a philosopher. His work is understood to be foundational to modern conservatism and libertarianism, a legacy that can be seen in the mission statements of think tanks with those orientations. The John Locke Foundation, based in North Carolina, is one such example. The foundation's Shaftesbury Society (that is, Anthony Ashley Cooper, 1st Earl of Shaftesbury, Society) sponsors speakers who discuss conservative and libertarian policies. The foundation is "committed to individual liberty and limited, constitutional government," and it "seeks a better balance between the public sector and private institutions of family, faith, community, and enterprise."[32]

It has been argued that the political philosophy and grand models of colonial founders had little relevance to the core value of liberty held by the populace. Libertarian historian Murray Rothbard, an associate of Ayn Rand, has thus argued that libertarianism was fundamental to the American spirit. He finds that this was demonstrated over and over by the people, who, enabled through republican government, rejected the heavy hand of British autocrats. The conservative and libertarian Ludwig von Mises Institute, based in Auburn, Alabama, which claims a faculty of more than 350 members, promotes Rothbard's account of American history.[33]

In Ashley Cooper's Carolina, and later in Oglethorpe's Georgia, according to Rothbard's libertarian thesis, the founders' model colony, fraught with paternalistic ideals, was replaced by libertarian principles that emerged from the people. In both cases, the colonists themselves claimed their freedom and threw off the yoke of oppression. Never mind, apparently, that what followed in Carolina was a caste system that supplied a generous amount of liberty to only a precious few, the elite white minority that ruled over an enslaved majority.

In Pennsylvania, to cite another Rothbard example, William Penn's heavy hand as a sort of feudal lord was ignored by an anarchist colonial assembly. Yet an essential function of republican government is to prevent mob rule, which requires statesmanship, leadership, and compromise among factions. In its purest form, libertarianism and laissez-faire government permits forces of repression sitting atop the social pyramid to act with impunity in trampling on the rights of those with less power and influence. One person's model libertarian garden of liberty is potentially another person's hell on earth, certainly where religious freedom and minority rights are concerned.[34]

Rothbard's characterization of Oglethorpe's Georgia reveals a pattern of detail in documentation to support libertarian preconceptions. Mixed in with considerable factual detail, he asserts that Georgia was slave-free for pragmatic reasons that had nothing to do with principle. To support that conclusion, he erroneously contends that Oglethorpe owned slaves on a South Carolina plantation and invested in the slave trade. Rothbard was correct in stating that Georgia had pragmatic reasons for banning slavery, but he was incorrect in asserting that an antislavery principle was not among them. Rothbard was also incorrect in asserting that Oglethorpe owned slaves, a notion based on a fallacious rumor circulated by slave merchants who sought to discredit him. Nor did Oglethorpe invest in the slave trade, except while serving very briefly as a director with the Royal African Company before establishing Georgia. Oglethorpe, as a matter of record, was deeply opposed to slavery and can reasonably be called the first abolitionist. While a vocal minority of white Georgians, known as the Malcontents, were eager to adopt the Carolina caste system, their efforts did not constitute a libertarian uprising. Rothbard's counterfactual claim paints Oglethorpe as a misguided humanist who imposed unreasonable rules on the colony, a claim used to support his view that libertarian principles emerged from the people as a natural response to oppressive regulation.[35]

Rothbard's portrayal of Oglethorpe as elitist and the "ambitious Ashley Cooper" as a purveyor of "feudal rule" immune to "market processes" is an effort to force historical facts into a preconceived theoretical framework. Both men had humanistic goals for their colonies, which may be at the heart of Rothbard's libertarian disdain for them. Ashley Cooper sought to instill the ancient principle of reciprocity of duties and benefits among classes within society, and Oglethorpe sought to flatten the class pyramid by preserving opportunities for yeoman farmers. Both goals are entirely consistent with modern democratic principles, and both efforts were undermined by the seductive profitability of slavery.[36]

It was the alteration of the Ashley Cooper Plan by libertarian slave owners that created a neofeudal state in Carolina, overran Georgia with the same feudalistic state, and advanced westward across the South. The political culture that arose from libertarian philosophy allowed the primitive social pyramid, with little or no liberty available to those in the rigidly controlled lower tiers, to become the status quo. It reinforced a brutal system of slavery that persisted until the nation's other two political cultures, with egalitarian traditions, intervened.

The irony of the libertarian prescription is that it would have society revert to a native state in which a more rigid class pyramid would inevitably emerge. As Samuel Johnson asked, "How is it that we hear the loudest *yelps* for liberty among the drivers of negroes?" The first principle of liberty for all, however, requires a compact to limit free exercise of impulses that do harm others. Democracy requires idealism, constitutionalism, and vigilance to prevent degradation of its availability to all people in all classes. The idea of democracy was known to Aristotle, but it was an unworkable ideal until the Enlightenment. Although the Ashley Cooper Plan was rigidly hierarchical, class reciprocity substituted for what it lacked in democracy. It was the first step in America toward a democratic republic, a step that Locke helped to eventually complete. Penn and Oglethorpe followed Ashley Cooper with refinements in the progression toward democracy until it was put into constitutional form by Jefferson. The libertarian South, however, retained for a minority the liberty to rule and enslave the majority.[37]

John Winthrop envisioned a metaphorical city upon a hill, a place of virtue that others in the world would look up to and emulate. Three competing visions of the American city emerged during the colonial and founding periods, not the singular libertarian impulse portrayed by Rothbard. One saw the city as the inevitable center of civilization, a place of learning and creativity and the spread of ideas and innovation. Another saw the city as the network of towns and villages where civic and religious values thrive. The third saw the large, unregulated, relentlessly growing city as an engine of corruption. Ashley Cooper, Penn, Oglethorpe, and Jefferson envisioned the third, preferring an agrarian state. Within each there were elements of traditional authority and hierarchy and elements of Enlightenment idealism. The former soon dominated the South, and a long train of abuses was set in motion in the southern colonies—slavery, Jim Crow laws, resistance to civil rights laws, and now New Jim Crow laws—and along with it, a legacy of deep hostility toward the city as a dynamic force for human advancement.

There is no reason, other than primitive tribalism, that the three visions should not interact to produce a greater vision, particularly if the idealism and first principles of Ashley Cooper and Oglethorpe are understood and gain new appreciation. The advancement of civilization has always been about the city and the synthesis of ideas it makes possible. The creative engine of the Mid-Atlantic metropolis, the civic humanism of the New England town, and the connection with nature of the southern landscape all have a place in the larger idea of the city upon a hill. But civility and synthesis are not on today's menu, and the daily specials go to those with the sharpest elbows.

The next three chapters dissect the Ashley Cooper Plan in terms of its first principles, design strategies, and implementation. The remaining chapters trace the effects of the plan from colonial times to the present day, showing that the plan provided the initial framework for southern political culture and set up the tension that now exists between advocates of humanistic urban policy and those who demand a more libertarian growth model. It is essentially the same tension that existed in the eighteenth century between advocates of Enlightenment ideals and advocates of pre-Enlightenment hierarchical society.

CHAPTER ONE

Carolina

The First Planned Colony

In the seventeenth century, following the peaceful and prosperous reign of Queen Elizabeth I, England descended into a long period of religious strife and civil war. During the same period, amid rising domestic chaos, the nation began forming an empire and sending tens of thousands of colonists to the shores of America. The first colonists were in search of fortune, but they were soon followed by a much larger wave of colonists who were in search of "freedom of conscience"—the freedom to practice one's faith and live the life it prescribed. It was not until 1670, and the founding of the Province of Carolina—more than sixty years after the founding of Jamestown—that England adopted a comprehensive approach to colonization designed to promote the multiple goals of economic development, orderly growth, social stability, impartial justice, and religious tolerance.

America was not only a blank slate for utopian visionaries; it was ultimately a laboratory of innovation for carrying out those visions. The eventual arrival of Enlightenment concepts of equality, natural rights, and the social contract heightened the expectations of colonists and broadened their idea of liberty. A wide range of new laws were enacted in the colonies consistent with those expectations. A more level society without nobility and structural privilege emerged, standing in sharp contrast to the durable class pyramid of the mother country. While the new ideals of the Enlightenment embraced in America were largely England's intellectual property, the motherland failed to recognize them and instead produced the "long train of abuses" that drove Americans to sever their cultural and political bonds.

Anthony Ashley Cooper, in founding the Province of Carolina, contributed a formative paradigm to American society, one that preceded the Enlightenment but that would become permanently engaged with those newer ideals. The new paradigm was a plan for a commonwealth modeled on an idealized concept of English manorial society, an ancient form of feudalism known to Ashley Cooper as Gothic society. The utopian plan, which envisioned a traditional class pyramid, was soon adapted to support a new kind of social hierarchy, an increasingly rigid system of oligarchic masters ruling an enslaved majority. The society that emerged was a hybrid with features of Ashley Cooper's utopian plan and the English Caribbean plantation system. The hybrid society became entrenched in Carolina by the end of the seventeenth century. Ashley Cooper's Grand Model, as he called his utopian plan, modified to support a slave society, would survive to become a cultural hearth of southern political culture in the United States.

Ashley Cooper and seven other noblemen were granted a charter from Charles II in 1663 to establish Carolina. Subsequently, Ashley Cooper, with the consent of his associates, developed the "Grand Model of government" (one of the specific uses of the term "Grand Model"), which was formalized in March 1669 as the Fundamental Constitutions of Carolina (the word "constitutions" was equivalent to "constitutional articles," thus plural). He did so with the assistance of his protégé, John Locke, yet to become the famous political and empiricist philosopher.

The Grand Model conceived by Ashley Cooper with Locke's assistance was much more than a framework for colonial government. It was a prescription for building a new society modeled on British ideals of liberty, property, and class. It was also a plan for settlement of a region that was almost untouched by Europeans. The Fundamental Constitutions prescribed exactly how land would be subdivided, and it laid out the principles by which towns would be established. Subsequent "instructions" from the two men (and perhaps one or two other proprietors), derived from the principles laid out in the Fundamental Constitutions, provided the first settlers with additional detail on the siting and design of towns and allocation of land. It would be the first comprehensive effort at city and regional planning in British America.

The Fundamental Constitutions formally remained in effect until 1729, long after the deaths of Ashley Cooper and the other seven founding proprietors. While the Fundamental Constitutions were periodically amended to accommodate real-world exigencies, they were never fully implemented. In practice, the actual government of Carolina retained elements of the original design but set its own course. The footprint left by the Carolina experiment created a permanent impression on the American cultural landscape. The legacy of Ashley Cooper's Grand Model in its altered form can be found in the designs of towns and the settlement patterns of the region; it is present in the stratification of southern society; and its elements are traceable from the plan's origin to present-day American political culture.

The evolving relationships among physical settlement patterns, class structure, and political culture obscure the enduring impact of Ashley Cooper's formative model. However, one can trace the threads that connect past to present, beginning with seventeenth-century political theory and its projection to American shores. Modern conservatives are particularly interested in doing so, frequently arguing their positions on the basis of "first principles," such as those outlined in the Prologue, and often tracing the lineage of their beliefs to Ashley Cooper, Locke, and later English and Scottish philosophers of classical liberalism such as Adam Smith.

Shaping City and Society in the New World

The Ashley Cooper Plan was conceived and implemented during a period of colonial expansion between the Age of Discovery and the Age of Enlightenment. During the former age, a span of time from the Renaissance to the early seventeenth century, European nations enriched themselves through global trade and created global empires. During the latter age, which began in the late seventeenth century, science and humanism became dominant themes and the modern ideas of equality and democracy were born. Whereas the Age of Discovery occurred at a time when rigid social hierarchy drove European advancement, the Enlightenment emphasized both social interdependence and individual worth. The Enlightenment also brought about a revolution in which reason and science led to the creation of modern financial institutions, systematic government accounting practices, and the Industrial Revolution.

A rational and systematic approach to colonial settlement and city planning in European colonies emerged in the later seventeenth century— the predawn of the Enlightenment—as England, France, Spain, and the Netherlands secured their hold on much of the world. The languages, cultures, and conventions (for example, time and calendars) of these three nations became international standards. Their settlement practices, derived in part from Roman practices, became a universal template.

As European powers competed, they also created planning frameworks that uniquely responded to intense international geopolitics and mercantile economic theory. The Netherlands was almost exclusively trade oriented during the seventeenth century, and its cities were points of contact to conduct business with indigenous people, with little form beyond the practical grid and defensive perimeters. France was similarly trade oriented and produced few major cities that reflected the attention to design promoted by Louis XIV, with Quebec and New Orleans being notable exceptions. Spain was far more ambitious and conquest oriented, making indigenous people minions of the empire. To meet the needs of such a vast empire, Spain adopted the Laws of the Indies over the course of more than a century, consolidating them into a single body of law in 1680. The Laws specified how colonies were to develop economically and socially and how they were to be governed. City planning specifications were highly detailed and designed to meet regional development needs as well as to strengthen geopolitical influence.[1]

England lacked Spain's grand design for international dominance; but its early emphasis on populating the American colonies with farmers secured its hold on territory, and the relatively close proximity of those colonies to the homeland ensured the timeliness of communications and supplies. Royal charters issued for each new colony gradually became more specific over the course of the seventeenth century, providing increasing detail for economic, government, and military planning. Ashley Cooper's Grand Model consolidated earlier practices into an entirely new framework similar to the Spanish Laws of the Indies. The consolidation and standardization of colonial practices completed England's transition to the status of a world power equal to Spain. In 1707, England and Scotland united, becoming the Kingdom of Great Britain, after which the term English Empire would apply.

Today, throughout the world, cities retain the character of their European designers. Cities of Spanish origin are typically organized around a central square where civic and commercial life is concentrated; churches and government buildings that were designed to exhibit the power of the empire and to endure for centuries remain, often as the most prominent structures; new streets are laid out to continue the original grid that defined blocks of commercial and home lots fronting the street and providing interior yards; major transportation routes leading into cities became boulevards defining important neighborhoods and commercial corridors. Those cities today are often vibrant and visually stunning.

The cities of former English colonies often have a central square or waterfront promenade around which civic and commercial buildings were originally composed, but typically with less architectural prominence and durability than in their Spanish counterparts. The street grid is tiered, composed of major transportation routes, prominent streets, and narrower streets. Lots were designed so that buildings could be set back from the street and surrounded by yards. The agrarian orientation of English gentry and nobility made their cities greener, less dense, and less vibrant. The impact of the Great Plague and the Great Fire of 1666 reinforced the impulse to build less concentrated cities. The English colonial city reflected the design parameters of Ashley Cooper and John Locke more than any other colonial planners.

The physical and social imprint left by the English on America during this time established a political culture in the Province of Carolina, aspects of which endure to the present in the southern United States in the form of large-footprint land-use patterns, neoagrarianism, and opposition to urban interests. This ethic has been reinforced over three separate eras: antebellum slavery, the New South (with the undertow of Jim Crow), and the post–civil rights era. The last, most recent, era advanced progress toward equality as framed by the Founding Fathers while reinventing new institutions of repression known as the New Jim Crow. Thus, in spite of the structural changes brought on during these distinct periods, the basic social order associated with the Ashley Cooper Plan remains as a consistent thread.[2]

The Ashley Cooper Plan represented a strain of political philosophy with accompanying forms of settlement that arrived on America's shores in the late seventeenth century and stood in sharp contrast to concepts of settlement that arrived in the early eighteenth century. The former was built on a quest for liberty; the latter, arriving during the Age of Enlightenment, brought the concept of equality to America's shores. Those two strains would also manifest themselves in two distinct spatial patterns. One would support a slave-based economy and agrarian society. The other would support a more compact urban society and eventually an industrial economy.

Anthony Ashley Cooper, 1st Earl of Shaftesbury

Anthony Ashley Cooper was one of the most powerful men in England during the turbulent Commonwealth, Protectorate, and Restoration periods of the seventeenth century. He first emerged as a leader on the national stage following the English Civil War and the execution of Charles I. He then served in the world's first modern republican government, the Commonwealth of England, led by Oliver Cromwell. When Cromwell became too powerful, he shifted allegiance from the Commonwealth back to the monarchy and became an architect of the Restoration. For his service in restoring Charles II to the throne in 1660, he was made Baron Ashley of Wimborne St. Giles in 1661 and the Earl of Shaftesbury in 1672. He climbed the ladder of political power, reaching the highest positions of government, but the rapid climb was accompanied by hard falls: he was investigated, arrested, and twice imprisoned in the Tower of London. He was a risk taker who navigated the unstable and dangerous political terrain of seventeenth-century England with intense intellectual energy, despite chronic physical disability.

In 1675, Ashley Cooper turned against the monarchy a second time. Charles II was headed down the same path toward absolutism taken by his father. Changing sides again was a potentially fatal choice, but Ashley Cooper was driven by a political philosophy of balanced government, known then as "Gothic polity" or "Gothic balance," according to which no branch would accumulate excessive power. He chose to act upon that philosophy rather than remain loyal to the king he had helped put back on the throne. His philosophy of Gothic balance endured to have a profound effect not only in England but also in America, where he planted the seed of Gothic balance in Carolina, and where his protégé, John Locke, became the intellectual fountainhead of modern democracy.[3]

Ashley Cooper's political derring-do and shifting allegiances precipitated criticism of his character by some of his contemporaries. He was portrayed as vain, untrustworthy, crafty, and Machiavellian and as an unprincipled "changeling." On the other hand, even his critics readily admitted that he was intelligent, learned, eloquent, witty, charming, and gallant. He was offended by his critics' attacks and went about writing an autobiography to set the record straight. Only fragments remain, but in this surviving passage he made his goal clear: "Whoever considers the number and the power of the adversaries I have met with and how studiously they have, under the authority of both Church and State, dispersed the most villainous slanders of me, will think it necessary that I . . . write my own memoirs, that it may appear to the world on what ground or motives they came to be my enemies."[4]

After his death in 1683, those who worked for him and knew him best rose to his defense, though to little lasting effect. Benjamin Wyche, an employee of the household, composed a rebuttal: "A Vindication of the

Character and Actions of the Right Honorable Anthony Late Earl of Shaftesbury." John Locke began a memoir, but it too was never completed. Locke also composed an epitaph in Latin, translated as follows: "In courtesy, sharpness of understanding, persuasiveness, judgment, courage, perseverance, faithfulness, you will scarcely find an equal anywhere, and nowhere a superior. Of Civil and Religious Liberty, a vigorous and unwearied defender. While liberty stands, neither devouring Time nor yet more devouring Envy shall obliterate the memory and praise of a life spent in public service."[5]

Locke's epitaph was considerably expanded by Ashley Cooper's great-grandson, the 4th Earl of Shaftesbury, for a monument erected at the family estate in Wimborne St. Giles. The 4th Earl also commissioned Benjamin Martyn, secretary to the Georgia Trustees, to write a biography that would offer an accurate portrayal, from the family perspective, of the patriarch's life. The project was delayed, but the biography was eventually published a century later, in 1836. A second redemptive biography was published by William Dougal Christie in 1871.[6]

Despite such efforts at redeeming Ashley Cooper's reputation, historians perpetuated negative characterizations up to the mid-twentieth century, when a biography published by K. H. D. Haley in 1968, titled simply *The First Earl of Shaftesbury*, proved to be a "watershed" in Shaftesbury historiography. Haley showed Ashley Cooper and his Whig Party as having greater ideological depth than previously thought, and he emphasized the historical context of intertwined religion and politics. His work led to a new generation of scholarship in which Ashley Cooper's actions have been reexamined and elevated to higher ground.[7]

Modern reexamination of Ashley Cooper's life reveals a man who was consistent in his political philosophy and who only changed loyalties when the government drifted too far toward absolutism (tyranny of the monarch) on the one hand or toward democracy (tyranny of the majority) on the other. His actions in and outside government from the 1640s through the early 1680s illustrate that he acted with consistency of principle. Rather than achieving personal gain from his bolder actions, as some contended, he put himself at risk, as when he switched allegiance from Royalists to Parliament in 1644, leaving his estates, the source of his wealth, "behind enemy lines."[8]

Ashley Cooper's political career took off after the Civil War of the 1640s. On May 19, 1649, less than four months after Charles I was beheaded, Parliament enacted a law declaring England to be a Commonwealth. The next action by the new Cromwell government was to draft a constitution.

The "Instrument of Government," adopted in 1653, became one of the world's first written constitutions. It is unclear whether Ashley Cooper played a role in drafting such a radically new document, but he served on its implementing committee.[9]

Ashley Cooper also served on the Hale Commission, established in January 1652 to examine the nation's laws and legal procedures. Led by the politically neutral legal scholar Matthew Hale, the commission recommended adoption of numerous progressive reforms. Although none were enacted into law during the Commonwealth period, several survived on paper to become law at a later time. These two prominent appointments marked Ashley Cooper's entry onto the national stage.

The experience in establishing a new foundation for England's government would provide Ashley Cooper with a wealth of experience and knowledge from which to conceive the "Grand Model" for Carolina in the late 1660s. The Carolina design was greatly influenced by the publication of James Harrington's utopian *The Commonwealth of Oceana* in 1656, discussed later in the chapter, where Gothic balance is explored in more depth. The decade of the 1650s was one of serious reflection about government, and many of the ideas that emerged from that reflection found their way forward into the Enlightenment and the creation of modern democracies.

The second Parliament of the Commonwealth, elected in 1653, became known as Barebone's Parliament, named after Praise-God Barebone, a member of the Fifth Monarchist sect that believed in the imminent Second Coming of the Messiah in the year 1666. The "saints" of the new Parliament set about preparing England for the biblical end-time. Barebone's Parliament would not survive to carry out its mission. Cromwell restructured the Commonwealth government into a Protectorate, over which he and military governors increasingly ruled with near-dictatorial authority. By the mid-1650s, Ashley Cooper was distancing himself from Cromwell, and by the end of the decade he was an enemy of the Protectorate, a clear threat to Gothic balance.

In the late 1650s, he joined with others in Parliament in planning a return to constitutional monarchy. One of those who facilitated the return of the king was Edward Hyde, 1st Earl of Clarendon. Another was George Monck, 1st Duke of Albemarle, Cromwell's governor of Scotland. Monck marched south to London and negotiated a peaceful change of government. Clarendon was made chief minister of the new government. Charles rewarded Clarendon and Monck in part by naming them proprietors of the Province of Carolina, along with Ashley Cooper and five others who supported his return to the throne.

The Restoration returned the House of Stuart to power in England, Scotland, and Ireland without decisively resolving the questions of divine right, authority of the Church of England, and freedom of conscience. One might compare this to the later founding of the United States without resolving the question of slavery: the seeds of civil war were planted. England in the 1660s, however, was prosperous and relatively calm for the time being.

Ashley Cooper's power and influence grew rapidly during the decade following the Restoration. He was made chancellor of the exchequer in the Clarendon government and served on the committees that set a new course for the nation's trade policy, including colonial planning and development. Trade policy was set with the Navigation Act of 1660; vital trading entities (for example, the East India Company) were reorganized or created; strategic territories (for example, New York, Tangier, Bombay) were captured or acquired; and the new colony of Carolina was chartered and designed with standards that would apply to future colonies.

The Second Anglo-Dutch War over trade dominance brought on military setbacks for which Chief Minister Clarendon was blamed, along with his handling of the Plague and Great Fire of London. He was dismissed in 1667 and replaced by five members of the Privy Council, including Ashley Cooper, who was then at the peak of his influence. The group, which served from 1668 to 1674, became known as the Cabal Ministry, after the acronym formed by their names (Clifford, Arlington, Buckingham, Ashley-Cooper, and Lauderdale). The relatively calm years of the Cabal Ministry afforded Ashley Cooper and Locke time to plan and implement the Province of Carolina.[10]

Ashley Cooper's rise continued into the early 1670s. In 1672, he became a member of the Privy Council's Committee on Trade and Foreign Plantations. He then developed a war strategy to contend with the growing dominance of the Dutch in world trade. He famously argued before Parliament that "delenda est Carthago" (Carthage must be destroyed), echoing Cato in calling for war, against the Dutch in this instance. Unknown to most, however, in 1670 Charles had signed the so-called Secret Treaty of Dover with the French in which he promised to become a Catholic. In 1673, the Catholic threat became clear when James, Duke of York, married a Catholic. Charles headed off opposition by dismissing Ashley Cooper and others who questioned an emerging Catholic monarchy. Parliament reacted with the Test Act, creating a religious test for public employment that precluded Catholics. Previously unresolved questions between Parliament and the Stuart monarchy began to strain the relationship.[11]

By 1675, Ashley Cooper (now the Earl of Shaftesbury) saw Charles II as gravitating toward absolute monarchy, as his grandfather and father, James I and Charles I, had done before him. He was also concerned that Charles's Catholic brother and potential successor, James, Duke of York, would give Catholicism new prominence. Ashley Cooper saw Catholicism intertwined with absolute monarchy across Europe, and he believed that a Catholic king invoking the principle of divine right would bring tyranny to England.[12]

Ashley Cooper collaborated with Locke on *A Letter from a Person of Quality to His Friend in the Country*, a tract written in 1675 as an appeal to country lords to once again defend England's liberty and Protestantism. The letter, which authorities believe was written with Locke (although disguised to reveal neither), reflected their shared political beliefs. In essence, they believed that the king and the bishops and their Tory allies were shifting the nation back toward rule by divine right, the thesis upon which absolutism rested. Ashley Cooper took this message directly to the House of Lords in the same year, warning the nobility that its role in maintaining balance of powers and preventing tyranny was about to be undermined.[13]

As Ashley Cooper warned of looming tyranny, he also worried that new elections had not been called since 1661. He began demanding frequent parliaments, fundamental to the ancient English system of Gothic balance. "Frequent new parliaments," he proclaimed, were "the people's right." In 1676, Charles sent word to Ashley Cooper to leave London, but he refused and continued to organize opposition to king and court. In 1677, he challenged Parliament's right to sit without new elections, leading to a charge of contempt, for which he and three supporters were sent to the Tower.[14]

In 1678, after a year of imprisonment, Ashley Cooper apologized, and Charles ordered him released. He was made lord president of the Privy Council in 1679, but he was not co-opted by the appointment. Undeterred in his mission, he escalated the drama over Catholic succession by introducing the Exclusion Bill, designed to prevent James, Duke of York, from succeeding to the throne. A political crisis ensued that lasted for three years. The crisis recast the Whig political faction, with Ashley Cooper among its founders, into an opposition party to the more royalist Tories. As tensions mounted, he became increasingly estranged from Charles and his supporters.[15]

As the Exclusion Bill was being considered, a plot was uncovered in which Catholics abetted by foreign elements were accused of planning to assassinate the king, overthrow the government, and massacre English

Protestants. The Popish Plot, as it came to be called, was in large part a contrived event, as many witnesses were exposed as unreliable. Nevertheless, it heightened religious tensions at a time that was useful to Ashley Cooper in thwarting a Stuart shift to Catholic absolutism.

Ashley Cooper saw the Tories becoming stronger and feared they would arrest and try him again. Nevertheless, in March 1679, he delivered a speech to Parliament warning of threats to the nation's system of balanced government driven by Catholic plotting by those close to the king. Charles attempted to appease Ashley Cooper by appointing him lord president of the Privy Council; however, the move failed to rein in the criticism. He proceeded to argue that James, Duke of York, as a Catholic should be prevented by law from succeeding Charles. When the Duke, who had been exiled to Europe, relocated to Scotland in October 1679, Ashley Cooper called a meeting of the Privy Council to discuss the matter. Charles finally had had enough and removed him from the council.

Ashley Cooper, still undaunted, continued through Parliament to press against succession by the Duke of York. The Tory government reacted by arresting him on suspicion of high treason in 1681, and he was again sent to the Tower of London. The government's case was weak, however, and he was soon acquitted. When Charles became gravely ill in May 1682, Ashley Cooper attempted unsuccessfully to orchestrate a rebellion and force succession to the Protestant Duke of Monmouth, Charles's illegitimate son. Facing the prospect of another prosecution, Ashley Cooper fled the country in November 1682 and settled in Amsterdam. Having become ill as he fled, he quickly prepared a will and died a few days later, on January 21, 1683.

The plotting initiated by Ashley Cooper continued after his death with the Rye House Plot, an attempt to ambush and assassinate Charles and James as they traveled outside of London with only a light guard. The plot was uncovered in June 1683, and most of those involved were executed. Locke, who may have been involved, went into exile. The next attempted coup d'état occurred in 1685 when the Duke of Monmouth led an armed revolt against James II, who had succeeded to the throne earlier that year. The revolt became known as the Monmouth Rebellion. It was quickly put down, and the duke was executed. James, the Catholic monarch of officially Protestant England, was finally deposed in 1688 by forces of Parliament and allied forces from the Dutch Republic. The event, which soon became known as the Glorious Revolution, installed Dutch head of state William of Orange and his wife, Mary (James's Protestant sister), as jointly ruling monarchs. Ashley Cooper's aim of preventing a European-style Catholic monarchy with absolutist leanings was finally secured, sixteen years after his death.

Ashley Cooper's political philosophy formed in a world where constitutional traditions were associated with Protestantism and absolutism was intertwined with Catholicism and papal supremacy. However, he was skeptical of religious influence in government regardless of denomination (see Chapter 2 for more on his views on religion). Religion of any kind was a threat to Gothic balance if it became too powerful. Under England's ancient traditions, the country lords had a duty to serve the interests of the people and the nation. It was their responsibility under Gothic balance to prevent accumulation of power through religious justification of absolutism or the use of standing armies to enforce it. He thus argued in favor of frequent parliaments dominated by the members of the landowning nobility, who would not become professional politicians of the city. It was these men who would raise armies from their own militias, as in ancient times, when necessary for national defense.

While Ashley Cooper was indisputably a traditional aristocrat who believed in a rigid social hierarchy, his view of slavery is open to interpretation. His grandfather was a member of the Virginia Company, with a view of "aristocratic imperialism" tempered by "visions of republicanism." Ashley Cooper himself co-owned a 205-acre Barbados plantation with twenty-one servants and fifteen slaves from 1646 to 1654; but that was before Barbados became England's first slave society. Until a tipping point was reached in the 1660s, chattel slavery was antithetical to English traditions. Queen Elizabeth I, in 1563, upon hearing of the first English shipment of slaves from Africa to the Caribbean, expressed deep concern: "If any Africans were carried away without his free consent it would be detestable and call down the vengeance of Heaven upon the undertaking."[16]

Ashley Cooper was probably not worried about incurring the wrath of God by permitting slavery in Carolina. He believed that slaves were part of the natural hierarchy of an agrarian society, but he probably did not envision his colony in the New World evolving from a society with slaves (which he clearly foresaw) to a slave society. This conclusion is supported by analysis of his correspondence, which shows no interest in the sort of planning that would be necessary for the widespread implementation of slavery. While the Barbados Concessions of the Articles of Agreement of 1664 and the Fundamental Constitutions of 1669 both reference slavery, subsequent instructions to the colonists authored by Ashley Cooper and Locke omit all such detailed references to it while retaining otherwise similar wording.[17]

An understanding of the process by which his plan for Carolina led to the formation of a slave society addresses two fundamental questions about American political culture. First, to what extent did slavery in Carolina shape the evolution of the American South to a slave society? Second, in what way was the secretive and enigmatic John Locke ultimately influenced by his mentor when he asserted that all men are created equal?

LIKE MANY COUNTRY lords, Ashley Cooper owned a rural estate and rented a house in London, the former being the source of income and the latter being the base of power. Both residences were of sufficient size to house a large staff, including executive assistants, who handled business and professional affairs. Ashley Cooper's Dorset estate in Wimborne St. Giles has remained in the family for ten generations. He began construction on St. Giles House in 1650, taking inspiration for its design from the famous architect Inigo Jones. The estate has remained under family ownership to the present.[18]

Two of Ashley Cooper's descendants acquired fame as great as that of the patriarch himself. Anthony Ashley Cooper, the 3rd Earl of Shaftesbury (1671-1713), published numerous influential philosophical essays that synthesized the Enlightenment precepts of his teacher, John Locke, with those of Isaac Newton. Published as *Characteristicks of Men, Manners, Opinions, and Times*, the collected essays was one of the most widely read books of the eighteenth century.

The second famous descendant was the 7th Earl of Shaftesbury (1801-85), one of the great English philanthropists of the Victorian era. His work led to limits on child labor and many other social reforms. He was memorialized by the fountain, the Angel of Christian Charity, at the end of Shaftesbury Avenue in Piccadilly Circus.[19]

Anthony Ashley Cooper, the 4th Earl of Shaftesbury (1711-71), although not one of the more famous descendants, was notable for his role as a trustee of the utopian Georgia Colony. It was the 4th Earl who retained Benjamin Martyn, a published playwright and secretary to the Georgia Trustees, to write a biography of his great-grandfather.

Nicholas Edmund Anthony Ashley Cooper, the 12th Earl of Shaftesbury (b. 1979), is the present occupant of the St. Giles estate. The 12th Earl and his wife, Dinah Streifeneder, Countess of Shaftesbury, a veterinary surgeon, have adopted the 7th Earl's commitment to philanthropy as a model in their own lives. Their interests include conservation and support for children with disabilities. The 12th Earl has also had notable success in the music business and the art world.[20]

John Locke, Carolina's Chief Planner

John Locke (1632–1704) is recognized as one of the great philosophers whose ideas were foundational to the Enlightenment. Much of his work was accomplished while serving Anthony Ashley Cooper. The two met during the summer of 1666 when Ashley Cooper visited Oxford to see his son, then a student, and to receive medical treatment. Locke was filling in for the physician he ordinarily would have seen. At the time, Locke was studying medicine and natural philosophy, having earlier received bachelor's and master's degrees from the university. He became Ashley Cooper's personal physician and moved to his London residence, Exeter House, where he lived for eight years. Beyond treating Ashley Cooper's liver ailment, it is not clear what role he had in the household until he became officially employed with the Carolina proprietors.[21]

Locke is known today as an architect of Enlightenment idealism, the father of classical liberalism, and the first of the British empiricist philosophers. He articulated concepts that became fundamental principles of modern democracies: religious tolerance, separation of church and state, balance of powers, and the idea that legitimate government derives its power from a compact with the people who agree to be governed. The American Declaration of Independence contains his words "long train of abuses" as a justification for ending the people's compact, or contract, with their government. Thomas Jefferson adapted Lockean language for the Declaration in crafting the famous phrase "life, liberty, and the pursuit of happiness." Jefferson identified Locke along with Francis Bacon and Isaac Newton as "the three greatest men that have ever lived, without any exception."[22]

Between 1667 and 1669, Locke likely worked closely with Ashley Cooper in developing the plan for establishing the Province of Carolina, including its famous Fundamental Constitutions. Once the colony was founded in 1670, he drafted many of the implementing regulations for its settlement, including standards for the design of towns and plans for regional development. Locke's role during that period, while still in his thirties, was officially one of a secretary and technical adviser rather than that of a framer of the vision for the colony. Unofficially, however, given the high regard in which he was held by Ashley Cooper, it is likely that he asserted some personal influence in framing the plan for Carolina. Yet he was a protégé of Ashley Cooper at this point in his career, not the strategist behind the politician. As the historian of philosophy J. R. Milton has written, "By the time Locke joined his household, Shaftesbury was a politician of immense and remarkably varied experience, who no more needed a political adviser than Mozart needed a musical adviser."[23]

Locke lived in France from 1675 to 1679 but resumed working on the Carolina project upon his return to England. He left the country again in 1683, shortly after Ashley Cooper's death in exile, fearing he might be implicated in the Rye House Plot, the attempt to assassinate Charles II and his brother and heir to the throne, James, Duke of York. He remained in exile in the Dutch Republic during the subsequent reign of James II, until the king was deposed in 1688 by the Glorious Revolution. The revolution ushered in the enlightened age for which Locke had long prepared himself.

Locke began writing the famous *Two Treatises of Government* while employed by Ashley Cooper and completed the work in exile, crafting it in part as a justification for the new monarchy of William and Mary. The work earned him the respect of the future king and queen, and Locke returned to England with Mary in 1688 during the revolution. His influence as an administrator, policy maker, and philosopher rose during the reign of William and Mary, and it continued to rise under William after Mary's death in 1694.

During William's thirteen-year reign, the government of England (Britain was not yet a formal entity) was greatly professionalized. Banking and trading institutions were modernized, government debt was financed through the markets rather than by wealthy individuals, and men of the caliber of Locke and Isaac Newton (who oversaw the mint) were brought into government. Locke acquired more authority in the government and wielded influence on colonial policy at a broader level. While he retained an interest in Carolina during this period, he no longer had a direct role in aligning settlement practices in the province with the principles set forth in the Fundamental Constitutions.

The experience assisting Ashley Cooper with the design for Carolina and working with him in the sphere of national politics increased Locke's interest in political philosophy and influenced his two monumental works, *Two Treatises of Government* and *An Essay Concerning Human Understanding*. Both works, initially published anonymously, would be widely read during the course of the eighteenth century, influencing the intellectual climate that sustained the Enlightenment and precipitated the American and French revolutions.

Locke begins the first treatise with the statement that "slavery is so vile and miserable an estate of man, and so directly opposite to the generous temper and courage of our nation; that it is hardly to be conceived, that an Englishman, much less a gentleman, should plead for it." Locke's critics point to what they see as striking contradictions in his work. On one hand he was a great advocate for the principles of liberty; on the other hand, he had a role in designing a class hierarchy for Carolina notable for its structural servitude and enslavement. He also was an investor in the slave-trading Royal African Company, secretary to the Council of Trade and Plantations, and a member of the Board of Trade. In those various capacities, his critics maintain, he contributed to forging a colonial system that enriched a few and enslaved many.[24]

The Fundamental Constitutions of Carolina established a Gothic, oligarchic frame of government that empowered a class of plantation elite with near-absolute power over a class of enslaved laborers. Opposition to slavery and hereditary power in Locke's later writings has been interpreted by his most severe critics as hypocrisy or at best a restricted view of those people entitled to basic human rights. Other authorities, however, believe that Locke evolved from one position to another and perhaps learned a difficult lesson from his early involvement in the creation of the Province of Carolina. The latter position is consistent with Locke's disposition as portrayed by his biographers, who have shown him to be receptive to a wide range of ideas in his early years rather than one who fixed on a particular worldview at the beginning of his career as a social and political philosopher. It may even be the case that Locke subtly influenced the removal of references to slavery found in the instructions to colonists, beginning in July 1669.[25]

One difficulty in absolving Locke of condoning slavery using the argument that he simply evolved is that he finished writing *Two Treatises* while engaged with Peter Colleton, son of John Colleton, in amending the Fundamental Constitutions for a third time in 1682. Colleton was both a Carolina proprietor and a Barbados plantation owner. If Locke believed in the proposition that all men are created equal in a state of nature and slavery is vile, then his continued work on behalf of the Lords Proprietors could be considered the height of hypocrisy, especially in view of the fact that it was he who added and later retained the words "power and" in the original 1669 version that stated, "Every Freeman of Carolina shall have absolute power and Authority over his Negro slaves of what opinion or Religion soever." Had Locke published *Two Treatises* at the same time he was revising the Fundamental Constitutions, the accusation of hypocrisy would seem to have merit, but it was published later, making an assessment difficult.[26]

Locke's secretiveness regarding his deeper convictions may have been largely a matter of self-preservation. He was, perhaps, engaged in esoteric communication, a form of communication attributed to philosophers by the late political scientist Leo Strauss. When Locke was engaged in the Carolina project, one's personal well-being depended on staying within certain boundaries in discussing class, religion, or politics. Ashley Cooper, who led a life of intrigue pushing those boundaries, taught him caution in words, if not in deeds. Others who were less cautious suffered the consequences. Algernon Sidney, another republican political philosopher whose *Discourses Concerning Government* was widely read by the American Founders, was executed for his dissenting opinions and actions. When he was implicated with Ashley Cooper in the Rye House Plot, he was tried and beheaded. On the scaffold at his execution in 1683 he stated, "We live in an age that makes truth pass for treason." It was a climate that made Locke extremely cautious in his public statements, yet revolutionary in anonymity.[27]

The historian Holly Brewer has recently brought to light evidence supporting an understanding of Locke as one who was associated with an oligarchic colonial design yet one framed within an incipient egalitarian and humanistic conception of government. Brewer found notes taken by Locke that support an effort to end slavery in Virginia; and she has argued that Locke became empowered as a result of the Glorious Revolution of 1689 to carry out his liberal political philosophy in a more enlightened era. The revolution, a major turning point in English history, ended a line of Stuart monarchs—James I, Charles I, Charles II, and James II—who leaned toward absolute monarchy and a rigidly hierarchical society. William and Mary were Stuarts of a different sort, steeped in Holland's liberal culture. It was under William, after Mary's death in 1694, that Locke rose to a position of authority with the Board of Trade that enabled him to influence national policy. Once in that position, and without further need to conceal his political philosophy, Locke, Brewer believes, sought to plant a new paradigm of liberty in America.[28]

Locke's rendering of the Fundamental Constitutions was therefore likely a reflection of Ashley Cooper's traditional view of social hierarchy, one that was more liberal and idealistic than that of the Stuarts but that fell within the limits of pre-Enlightenment doctrine. Locke was no doubt inspired by Ashley Cooper's commitment to republican principles, and the constitutions were his first exercise in structuring those principles for real-world application. The initial process of drafting the constitutions was a difficult learning experience and a transitional period from which he conceived entirely new ideas concerning republican government, democracy, and slavery.

Locke's experience with Carolina was and still is of importance on multiple levels. He and Ashley Cooper designed a society within the limits imposed by an ancient social pyramid, one that in principle achieved Gothic political balance and equitably allocated duties and benefits among classes. The balance of duties and benefits within a society, class reciprocity, was perhaps the highest pinnacle of social equality conceived before the Enlightenment and stood in sharp contrast with the nineteenth-century rhetoric of paternalism. As their project strained under the tension between utopianism and oligarchic plantation elitism with increasing reliance on slavery, it bequeathed two paths forward in America: one that reverted to traditional hierarchical society and another that became modern democracy.[29]

Seventeenth-Century Political Culture

The roots of American political idealism can be traced back through Locke and Ashley Cooper to James Harrington. Harrington was born into a wealthy English family and educated at Trinity College, Oxford. After touring Europe (a common rite of passage for the upper classes), he was introduced to Charles I, who liked him and appointed him to a position within his household. When Charles was arrested during the Civil War, Harrington was also briefly imprisoned. He was among the few with the king at his execution in January 1649.

Although Harrington admired the king, he was no supporter of the monarchy. Soon after Charles was executed, he began writing *The Commonwealth of Oceana*, which portrayed a utopian government resembling the new Commonwealth of England under Cromwell. With the refinements detailed in *Oceana*, England could come to represent an ideal form of government. The resemblance to the government was insufficient; when the manuscript for *Oceana* went to the printer, it was seized by Cromwell's government before it could be published. Harrington successfully appealed for its release through Cromwell's daughter, and it came out in print in 1656.

After the Restoration of the monarchy under Charles II, Harrington was arrested as a traitor and sent to the Tower of London. Harrington had always been open about his political theories and apparently never engaged in seditious activity. When questioned, "Why did he, as a private man, meddle with politics? What had a private man to do with politics?" he answered,

> There is not any public person, nor any magistrate, that has written on politics worth a button. All they that have been excellent in this way, have been private men, as private . . . as myself. There is Plato, there is

Aristotle, there is Livy, there is Machiavel. . . . I can sum up Aristotle's Politics in a very few words: he says, there is the Barbarous Monarchy—such a one where the people have 110 votes in making the laws; he says there is the Heroic Monarchy—such a one where the people have their votes in making the laws; and then, he says, there is Democracy, and affirms that a man cannot be said to have liberty but in a democracy only.[30]

Pressed on whether he believed that, he replied,

I say Aristotle says so. I have not said as much. And under what prince was it? Was it not Alexander, the greatest prince then in the world? I beseech you, my lord, did Alexander hang up Aristotle? Did he molest him? Livy, for a commonwealth, is one of the fullest authors; did not he write under Augustus Caesar? Did Caesar hang up Livy? Did he molest him? Machiavel, what a commonwealthman was he! But he wrote under the Medici when they were princes in Florence: did they hang up Machiavel, or did they molest him? I have done no otherwise than as the greatest politicians: the King will do no otherwise than as the greatest princes.[31]

Nevertheless, he was held in miserable conditions, untried and refused the right of habeas corpus. He was moved twice to other prisons, and his health declined severely. When he was finally released, he was mentally and physically nearly destroyed. He married an old family friend and struggled to continue writing but produced little more. He died in 1677 and was buried by the grave of Sir Walter Raleigh.

During his later life, Harrington was a political hot potato. He had no significant following, and no political faction would claim him. To the present time, he remains an obscure figure, in part due to his difficult writing style and frequent references to Classical Antiquity. Yet the force of his ideas, however inaccessible, crept into the political and intellectual circles of England. Ashley Cooper was the first to adopt his theories and put them before the public, although partially disguised and without mentioning him by name.

The historian J. G. A. Pocock traces Harrington's influence on Ashley Cooper (who was now the Earl of Shaftesbury) to a speech he delivered to the House of Lords, October 20, 1675, in which he opens by saying "our all is at stake."

My Lords, 'tis not only your interest, but the interest of the nation, that you maintain your rights; for let the House of Commons, and gentry of

England, think what they please, there is no prince that ever governed without nobility or an army. If you will not have one, you must have t'other, or the monarchy cannot long support, or keep itself from tumbling into a democraticall republique. Your Lordships and the people have the same cause, and the same enemies. My Lords, would you be in favour with the King? 'Tis a very ill way to it, to put your selves out of a future capacity, to be considerable in his service.[32]

Pocock characterizes the speech as beginning with "straight Harringtonian doctrine," which posits that the king's minions must be organized in either a feudal structure or within and about his household. In either case, tension will exist between the military class and the king so as to make it an unstable form of government. The role of the nobility is to maintain balance and prevent such instability.[33]

Opposition to a standing army as a source of tyranny at that point became a central tenet of the political movement associated with Ashley Cooper, first known as the "country party" and later conceived in America as republicanism. The word "country" meant "nation," but it was also a movement based on the nation's rural traditions. The country party agenda stood in contrast to that of the "court party," which from Ashley Cooper's time to the mid-eighteenth century increasingly represented urban interests—commerce, finance, and the executive branch of government. The rural-urban political dichotomy attained its greatest intensity during Robert Walpole's tenure as leader of the Whig government, from 1721 to 1742. Walpole's executive authority as first minister was such that he is considered Britain's first prime minister.

Ashley Cooper argued that "the only ancient and true strength of the nation" resides not with the army but with the militia. Composed of the people and controlled by a broad base of nobility, the militia is essential to liberty. The abuses of a standing army controlled by the king were of concern not only in England, but also in America, where the British army trampled on liberty in the colonies. This fundamental concern survived to modern times, finding expression in the famous warning by President Dwight Eisenhower about the power of the "military-industrial complex."[34]

The navy, by contrast, represented no threat to liberty. It could not be deployed by a tyrant to suppress domestic freedom. Instead, it defended the nation from invasion, policed colonial shores, and protected the commercial fleet. In doing so, it paid for itself, unlike a standing army, which could drain the treasury. The patriotic British song "Rule, Britannia!" encapsulates this view of the navy as the main line of defense in preserving the nation's freedom and independence with the lines, "Rule, Britannia! rule the waves: / Britons never will be slaves."[35]

In Pocock's assessment, "The standing army was a bogey intended for country gentlemen, part of a hydra-headed monster called Court Influence or Ministerial Corruption, whose other heads were Placement [patronage], Pensions, National Debt, Excise, and High Taxation." Those on the other side of the political divide constituted the "court party," and they were opposed to the calcified "Gothic" model of government based on a balance of power among the monarch, nobility, and common people assured by England's "Ancient Constitution"—the body of historic laws such as the Magna Carta.

Returning to Harrington as the progenitor of republicanism, *Oceana* set forth a detailed analysis of forms of government throughout history, concluding that a commonwealth, "a government of laws and not of men," was the ideal model. He proposed two fundamental constraints on political power in a commonwealth essential to balanced government: limits on the ownership of land and on access to political office. "The fundamental laws of Oceana, or the centre of this commonwealth," he wrote, "are the agrarian and the ballot." In the case of land, Harrington proposed an "equal agrarian," an equal distribution of land among classes such that no class of society would acquire a dominant share. In the case of political office, he proposed franchising as large an electorate as possible, with voting through secret ballot, term limits to political office, and rotation of office among social classes. In his words,

> An equal commonwealth is such a one as is equal both in the balance or foundation, and in the superstructure; that is to say, in her agrarian law and in her rotation.
>
> An equal agrarian is a perpetual law, establishing and preserving the balance of dominion by such a distribution, that no one man or number of men, within the compass of the few or aristocracy, can come to overpower the whole people by their possessions in lands.[36]

Harrington drew extensively from history to support his conclusions. He cited Aristotle as warning that "immoderate wealth, as where one man or the few have greater possessions than the equality or the frame of the commonwealth will bear; is an occasion of sedition, which ends for the greater part in monarchy." Further, he said he agreed with Machiavelli "that a nobility or gentry, overbalancing a popular government, is the utter bane and destruction of it."

Harrington was among the first to formulate the idea of natural law, an idea now associated most closely with Locke. "There is a common right, law of nature, or interest of the whole, which is more excellent, and so acknowledged to be by the agents themselves, than the right or interest of the parts only." He maintained that "law of nature" was best accomplished when the people of the commonwealth were oriented to the land. Citing a mythical figure from English history, a device he employed throughout *Oceana*, he warned of the ill effects of imbalanced land ownership on the people: "Take heed how their nobility and gentlemen multiply too fast, for that makes the common subject grow to be a peasant and base swain driven out of heart, and in effect but a gentleman's laborer."[37]

He returned to Aristotle for support in maintaining that commonwealths built on "the country way of life" are stronger. Commonwealths built on "city life," like Athens, are less stable. The "urban tribes" of Rome, as well, were less strong than the "rustics." A people employed on the land "in making farms and houses of husbandry of a standard" in a sustainable commonwealth should be "maintained with such a proportion of land to them as may breed a subject to live in convenient plenty, and no servile condition, and to keep the plough in the hands of the owners, and not mere hirelings."[38]

The Ashley Cooper Plan for the Province of Carolina was heavily influenced by Harrington in structuring just such a balance in the design of its towns and counties. The historian Thomas Leng has noted that the Fundamental Constitutions allowed settlers to operate outside "Anglocentric social order," thereby implementing Harrington's concepts without distorting influences. Ashley Cooper envisioned a self-sufficient colony achieving Gothic balance by allocating each proprietor land in each county, but with more land allocated to colonists. The landowning gentry and nobility would constitute an aristocracy that would govern society. The design would overcome many of the problems that arose in Virginia, where self-serving merchants acquired excessive power. In Ashley Cooper's view, merchants were essential but not well suited to lead the country. Aristocrats at the top of the social pyramid were the nation's natural leaders, responsible to the people, and most qualified to perceive the greater good.[39]

Sixty-three years later, the Oglethorpe Plan for Georgia reprised the Carolina Grand Model with even stronger requirements to maintain Harrington's Gothic agrarian balance. Oglethorpe continued to advocate rural virtue throughout his long life, which encompassed most of the Enlightenment. He contacted Oliver Goldsmith after reading *The*

Deserted Village, published in 1770. The poem laments the loss of an idyllic Auburn village, the "loveliest village of the plain" (a name later given to Auburn, Alabama). The two men became close friends and took the conversation to Samuel Johnson's influential literary circle.[40]

Oglethorpe and Goldsmith argued that the village, like much of rural Britain, lost its character and sustaining agrarian economy to the disinvestment and greed of the new class of urban gentry—men who favored trade and cared little for people of the land.

> A time there was, ere England's griefs began,
> When every rood of ground maintain'd its man;
> For him light labour spread her wholesome store,
> Just gave what life requir'd, but gave no more:
> His best companions, innocence and health;
> And his best riches, ignorance of wealth.[41]

Trade and city commerce had yielded wealth and luxury at the expense of village life. Farms became playgrounds for the rich as the poor deserted their villages for the city.

The debate over rural virtue never ended and remains part of the political landscape of modern times. One the one hand, some perceive a continuum of rural virtue and urban decay. On the other hand, many observers perceive a continuum of rural stagnation and urban innovation. Jefferson weighed in on the side of Harrington, Ashley Cooper, Oglethorpe, and Goldsmith, comparing the "mobs of great cities" to sores and asserting that "it is the manners and spirit of a people which preserve a republic in vigor." That sentiment was expressed as the Industrial Revolution began to accentuate the contrast between urban and rural life. The Garden Cities movement attempted to blend the virtues of both, but real success in doing so is seen only now on a large scale as developers begin building towns with all the amenities and accessibility of cities in rural environments.[42]

Harrington's contribution to seventeenth-century thought was limited, and his concepts would not be fully explored until the early 1700s. More broadly, his arguments in favor of a commonwealth added to the sense that English republicanism was a work in progress, one in need of refinement after the failure of the disastrous Cromwellian experiment in republican government. The idea of rural virtue articulated by the country party originated with Harrington and was refined by Ashley Cooper, Locke, Oglethorpe, Jefferson, and others associated with republicanism. Today in the United States, echoes of this strain of republican political theory are intensifying as the major political parties align themselves with urban and rural populations. Cities spawned corruption, greed, excess, sloth, and addiction to luxury.[43]

Theories of republican government stood in contrast to the absolutist tendencies of the House of Stuart during the seventeenth century. James I (reign 1603–25), successor to Queen Elizabeth I, advanced the idea of the divine right of kings and a social order that was largely maintained through inheritance. The monarchist beliefs of the Stuarts resonated throughout the century, but they were met with the counterpoint of the republicans. That backdrop provided the milieu in which Ashley Cooper and Locke conceived the plan for colonial settlement that they called the Grand Model. The plan, with considerable modification but enduring fundamentals, became a growth guide for the Province of Carolina, eventually becoming the model for the growth of other colonies in the region. Class reciprocity would disappear from the plan, and the plan's spatial structure, designed to perpetuate "Gothic" governance, would be recalibrated for a plantation system that increasingly relied on the enslavement of Africans and the displacement of Native Americans. The virtues of the "Gothic" model and its republican derivative failed to find full expression in Carolina. The Ashley Cooper Plan mutated into a new form of tyranny that fit neatly into the Atlantic Triangle Trade system.

Establishment of the Province of Carolina

The Province of Carolina, Latin for Charles, was named in honor of Charles I by his son, Charles II. The Lords Proprietors, allies of Charles II at the Restoration, implemented the plan for the colony in 1670. They and their heirs ultimately governed, with waning authority, until 1729. The boundaries and initial principles of governance were laid out in the charter of 1663. The charter granted title to lands south along the present-day Georgia coast and north to the Virginia Colony, the band of latitude ranging from 31 degrees north to 36 degrees north, depicted in Figure 3. The charter was revised in 1665, widening the band to extend from 29 degrees north (thus including the Spanish settlement at St. Augustine, Florida) to 36 degrees 30 minutes north (a span shown in Figure 3). The charter granted the colony all land westward to the Pacific Ocean.

The colony was permanently settled in 1670 when colonists from Bermuda and Barbados joined an expedition from England in relocating to Carolina. Charles Town was established at a location selected by Ashley Cooper on the estuary of the subsequently named Ashley and Cooper rivers, where he envisioned a "great port towne." The colonial capital

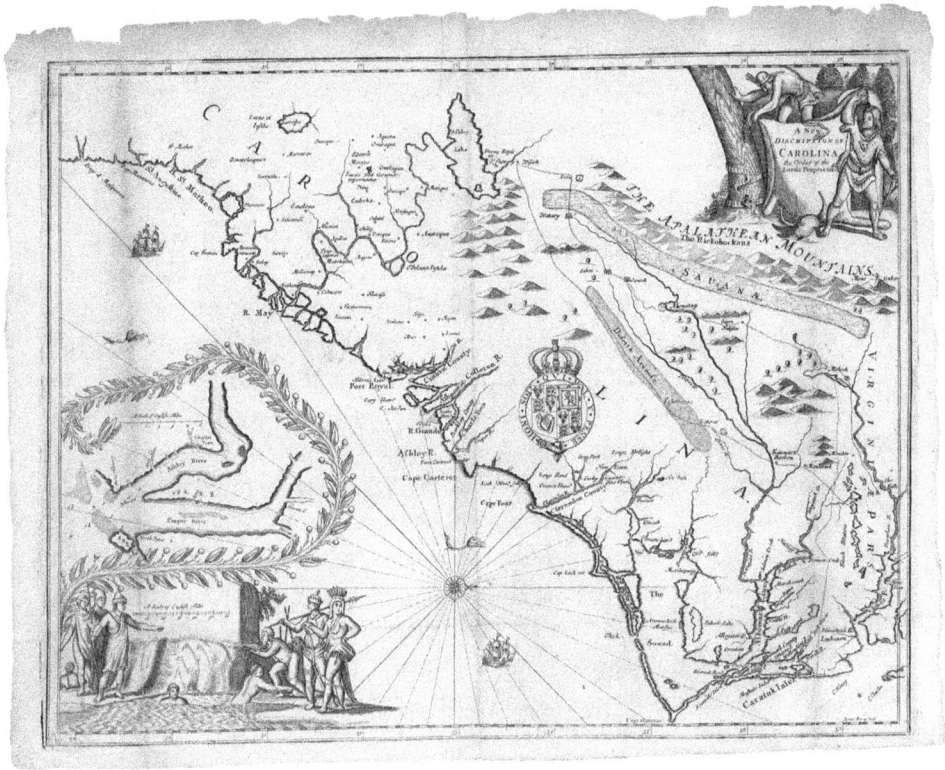

Figure 3. A New Description of Carolina by Order of the
Lords Proprietors. This 1672 map of the province from the early proprietary
period is oriented as if looking at it from England. The inset shows the hub of colonial
activity at the confluence of the Ashley and Cooper rivers. Illustration provided
by the Wilson Library of the University of North Carolina.

was situated near latitude 33 north, midway between the northern and
southern borders of the colony. Charles Town soon became the major port
city that Ashley Cooper envisioned, and it remained Britain's only major
settlement south of Virginia until Savannah, founded in 1733, matured
into an active port city in the mid-1700s. Charles Town remained Britain's
principal city south of the Chesapeake Bay through the colonial period,
and it retained that status for decades following the American Revolution.

The northern part of Carolina Province was placed under a deputy governor in 1691 and became the separate colony of North Carolina in 1712.
The original proprietors, however, retained control over both colonies
until 1719, when colonists rebelled against their authority. The crown responded by appointing a royal governor and initiating a process of buying

out the proprietors. The transition was completed in 1729 when the royal colonies of North Carolina and South Carolina were formally established.

From 1666 to 1682, Ashley Cooper was the most active of the Lords Proprietors in planning, promoting, and settling the colony. The proprietors possessed the highest authority in the colony, although a colonial government was established, consisting of a governor and council, half of whom were appointed by the proprietors, and a popularly elected but weak assembly. They were culturally immersed in the concept of noblesse oblige and class reciprocity, believing that their position of authority conferred upon them a deep responsibility to the people. The idea of a more democratic republic simply was not imaginable to them.

Of the eight proprietors, none ever saw their colony. Only one, Sir William Berkeley, came to America, where he served as governor of Virginia from 1641 to 1652 and 1660 to 1677. Some were more active than others, however, in settling the colony. Peter Colleton notably arranged for relatives and other settlers from Barbados, with many of their slaves, to begin rice cultivation in Carolina; his family maintained plantations in the Carolina Lowcountry after his death. The names of all the Lords Proprietors are found throughout the Carolinas in towns, counties, and rivers, as seen already occurring in Figure 3. Short biographies of each can be found in the Appendix.

Each of the proprietors was designated an owner of vast tracts of land within the colony. Colonial practices at the time amounted to government-supported investments, according to which the king granted land and military protection in expectation of promoting lucrative commerce and geopolitically trumping other European powers in foreign lands. The purposes of colonization under the Stuarts were primarily mercantile growth and geopolitical strength. Ashley Cooper and the Lords Proprietors refined and formalized this model so that it provided specific practices in settling colonies.[44]

Ashley Cooper and Locke included a set of articles in the constitutions whereby each proprietor would have a system of governance for his individual holdings that would mesh with the overall system for the colony. The constitutions also contained a detailed framework for the Ashley Cooper Plan, including a Grand Model for cities that influenced colonial development more broadly. The details of his plan and its underlying philosophy are the subject of Chapter 2.

The Fundamental Constitutions were drafted for the proprietors by Locke under the direction of Ashley Cooper. There were multiple reasons for drafting the guiding document. According to Ashley Cooper, the principal purpose was to provide a "compass" to "steer" the new colony. However, the Fundamental Constitutions contained assurances that made them a recruiting device as well as a governmental model. Provisions for citizenship, religious tolerance, and land grants of various sizes were designed to appeal to a range of potential settlers.[45]

The emphasis on balanced landownership as a foundation for representation in government was of central importance, a design likely inspired by Harrington's utopian model set forth in *Oceana*. It is this system that has led many historians to assail the Fundamental Constitutions as a feudal system of land tenure backward even for its time, and a great mistake of Locke's otherwise brilliant career. The codification of "absolute power" by freemen over slaves is particularly repellent from the modern perspective. Critics, however, miss the essential features of the Grand Model that were visionary and humanistic. Representative government, religious freedom, limitations on the power of the aristocracy, a secret ballot, and reciprocity were core principles of the plan that later became axioms of the Enlightenment.[46]

The Fundamental Constitutions were never ratified by the freemen who formed the colonial government. Nevertheless, many of the most appealing features of the document took effect as laws and regulations for the colony. The character of the colony was thus shaped by the Fundamental Constitutions, even though they were neither formally adopted nor thoroughly implemented.[47]

The Ashley Cooper Plan and English Manorial Tradition

The Grand Model may be described as an idealized form of manorial or neofeudal society. "Feudalism," however, is an imprecise term sometimes defined narrowly to describe a society found in Europe during the Middle Ages in which the lords of large manors (estates) regulated the affairs of their agrarian tenants and the residents of adjoining villages. In England, feudalism evolved with unique features, influenced in part by the country's Ancient Constitution. The term in use during Ashley Cooper's time to describe this uniquely English form of feudalism was "Gothic society." The elite at the apex of the class pyramid in Gothic society constituted a stratum of nobility that advised the government, paid taxes to support it, and supplied soldiers to the king for the defense of the nation.

Gothic society was disappearing from England in the sixteenth century with the rise of the yeoman and gentry classes and as standing armies and militias replaced conscripted forces under knights and higher nobles. But to Harrington and Ashley Cooper, the role of the nobility in Gothic society and the reciprocity of benefits the ancient system provided to all strata within the class hierarchy remained as essential ingredients of balanced government and a stable, productive society.

Gothic society may be defined as a rigidly hierarchical society led by a king who rules with the support and by the consent of a property-owning aristocratic class, who in turn rule over lower classes of people within their dominions. Gothic society encompasses "manorialism," in which the lord of the manor owns a large estate, manages common pasture, and leases or allots land to freemen or tenant farmers with specific obligations such as cash or crop share rent. Figure 4 illustrates a typical manorial plan with a manor house, church, village, and pond clustered together and surrounded by farms, common pasture, and natural areas.

England's social hierarchy changed rapidly during the sixteenth and seventeenth centuries. It retained elements of the earlier Gothic manorial system, but it bore little resemblance to the European feudalism of the Middle Ages. The period of change immediately preceding Ashley Cooper's rise to power was one in which the highest ranks of the social pyramid lost influence. The nobility in particular suffered a decline of wealth and landholdings relative to the gentry: the nobility wielded less military might; the new practice of granting titles for cash rather than merit devalued rank; attitudes changed toward the tenantry, as renters not workers created an adversarial relationship; it came to be out of touch through increasingly extravagant living in the city and long absences from the countryside; it lost influence to an increasingly educated untitled elite of administrators; and its authority was challenged by the rise of individualism and new religious attitudes that promoted freedom of conscience over hierarchy and obedience.[48]

The structure of English society is a matter of record. From the time of the Domesday Book, a census and land inventory produced for William the Conqueror following his invasion of England in 1066, national censuses provided population counts by social class. Although terms were poorly defined and applied inconsistently, the hierarchy can be discerned as follows:[49]

Nobility. An aristocratic, largely agrarian hierarchy consisting of
  dukes, marquesses, earls, viscounts, and barons; knights were
  traditionally a lower order of warrior nobility.
Gentry. A class of wealthy landowners who owned manors and
  controlled tenants and laborers much like the nobility; a new class
  of urban gentry began to arise in the seventeenth century that
  rivaled the influence of the rural gentry.

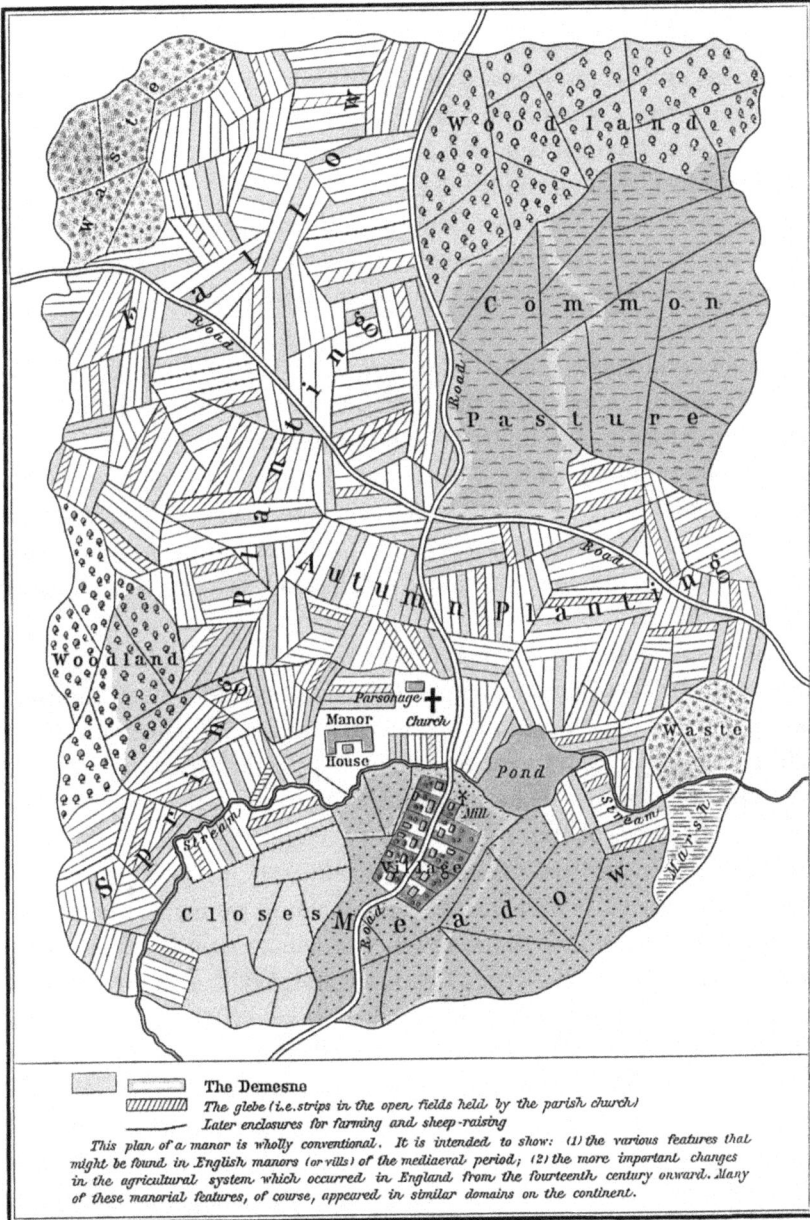

Figure 4. Traditional English Manorial Plan. Traditional English
society from the Middle Ages to the sixteenth century was organized around
the manor. The Ashley Cooper Plan for Carolina drew from this ancient system,
formalizing many of its features in the Fundamental Constitutions.
Illustration from William Shepherd, *Historical Atlas*.

Yeomen. A term that encompassed many occupations of people who made up a middle class but was most often applied to free, landowning farmers.

Freemen and Tenant Farmers. Freemen of the manor or freeholders were tenant farmers, not often distinguishable from yeoman farmers. Husbandmen were a category more difficult to define that straddled freemen and laborers.

Laboring Classes. The lower tier of society consisted of serfs, villains, wage laborers, and indentured servants; slaves were disappearing as an enumerated class by the seventeenth century.

Changes within the English class pyramid over the sixteenth and seventeenth centuries benefited the yeoman farmer perhaps more than any other class. Greater availability of land through sale by the crown as well as reclamation increased the wealth and expanded the numbers of yeomen farmers. Changing interclass relationships produced greater social mobility, allowing lower classes to rise to higher ranks. Isaac Newton notably rose from the yeoman class to knighthood, as had William Harvey and John Milton.[50]

There was less geographic mobility in England than social mobility. The shires and parishes (similar to the later counties and towns in America) were populated for generations by the same families of all classes. Those falling on hard times were taken care of, but vagrants from other towns were apprehended by the local constable, whipped, and set on the road toward their towns of origin.[51]

The English upper and middle classes saw rural society as a product of many centuries of evolution, bringing gradual improvements that created an exceptional nation. They revered their Ancient Constitution, the body of documents such as the Magna Carta that codified liberty and prevented tyranny. Ashley Cooper and Locke had no reason to alter the fundamental structure of British society in planning the Province of Carolina. Rather, they used it as a model to restore and apply traditional society in the New World. Toward that end, and in order to ensure the commercial success of the colony, the Fundamental Constitutions sharpened the lines defining the traditional class pyramid and clarified the spatial organization associated with that hierarchy.

Ashley Cooper and Locke were classically educated men, and there was nothing in their knowledge of history that suggested there was any model superior to this system that might be applied to America. Throughout human history, societies had been organized into pyramidal hierarchies, and they believed that none of the others had enjoyed the protection of liberties that existed in England.

Ancient Egypt, the longest surviving civilization known to Ashley Cooper and Locke, thrived for three millennia with a pyramidal social structure. Classical antiquity, the period of Greco-Roman civilization in the Mediterranean world, even with the conception of democracy and the communal influence of Christianity, thrived under a rigid pyramid-shaped hierarchy. Plato envisioned such a structure attaining its greatest success while led by philosopher-kings, who would pilot the ship of state with attention "to the seasons, the heavens, the stars, the winds, and everything proper to the craft if he is really to rule a ship."[52]

Aristotle, perhaps the most influential philosopher in history, wrote that "the first governments were kingships, probably for the reason that of old, when cities were small, men of eminent virtue were few." After monarchy, two other principal forms of government emerged, oligarchy and constitutional government. Each form of government was pyramidal in its pure form. Each could be corrupted: monarchy into tyranny, oligarchy into self-interest of the wealthy class, constitutional government into democracy, or rule by many. The last, which would have flattened the class pyramid, he viewed as unworkable mob rule. Thus, to Aristotle and to so many philosophers to follow, a stable, thriving society was a pyramidal society. To the extent that democracy could thrive, it would by necessity have to be restricted to the upper strata of society.[53]

Aristotle placed *magistrates and officers* at the top of the class pyramid, for "the state cannot exist without rulers." The *wealthy class*, or those "who minister to the state with their property," were next in the order. Those engaged in *justice, deliberation, and politics*, who were essential to the state, formed the next social class. *Soldiers*, the "warrior class," needed "if the country is not to be the slave to every invader," were next. Going down the pyramid, other classes were *traders*, who are engaged in commerce; *craftsmen*, who contribute to luxury and "grace of life"; and *farmers*, "the food-producing class." At the bottom were *serfs*, *laborers*, and *slaves*. Aristotle's social pyramid varied with the type of government, but it always took the form of a pyramid, as illustrated in Figure 5.[54]

Aristotle posed a fundamental question that Locke sought to answer and that is central to modern politics. Are good laws primarily good for the higher classes, or are they good in an immediate and direct way for the many? He believed that an overall good could be achieved, recommending rule the by middle class as the most stable form of constitutional government. His prescription for a degree of social mobility did not apply

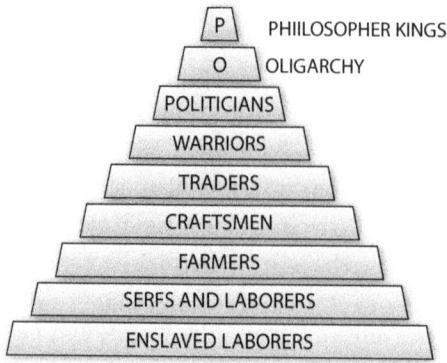

Figure 5. Aristotle's Class Pyramid. The concept of a class pyramid found in Aristotle's *Politics* influenced the concept of class structure until the eighteenth century, when the Enlightenment ushered in a new paradigm. Illustration by Teri Norris.

to the lower classes. Those classes were deemed incapable of practicing the kind of virtue necessary for wise leadership.[55]

The idea of democracy arose in ancient Athens a century before Plato's generation. It conferred the right to vote and to hold government office on male citizens, but restricted citizenship primarily to those born to citizens. Most of those in the toiling classes were not citizens, so that only a small minority of those who lived in Athens participated in its governance. The idea of freedom and democracy for all was inconceivable to the ancient mind and would not emerge as a serious theory of governance until the Enlightenment.

Christianity in its earliest and purest form promoted democratic behavior, but it did not propose democracy. Believing the Second Coming was imminent, Christians had no reason to challenge the class pyramid of Mediterranean society. While Paul said that all should take bread and wine together in the Eucharist and blamed the wealthy for bringing social segregation to the ritual, he refrained from a broader challenge to established order: humans are "subject to the governing authorities. For there is no authority except from God, and those that exist have been instituted by God." The emergence of an organized and increasingly hierarchical church strengthened the class pyramids within its domain. As the church became a vast bureaucracy, coexisting in parallel with political bureaucracies, the idea of a level society and basic democracy surfaced in only a few places, such as Savonarola's Florence of the late fifteenth century.[56]

The concept of a Great Chain of Being, or *scala naturae*, emerged to reinforce pyramidal class structure on earth and place it within the greater pyramidal structure of God's universe. Human beings were seen as occupying the stratum between heaven and spiritual existence, on the one hand, and the purely physical world on the other. Figure 6 illustrates the

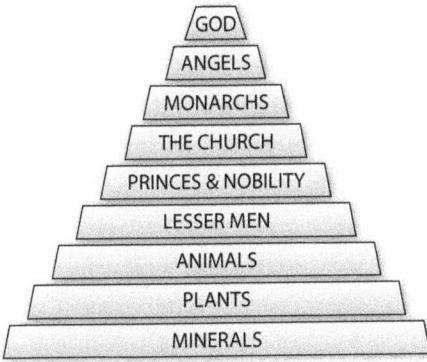

Figure 6. The Great Chain of Being. Social and theological hierarchies were mutually reinforcing concepts until challenged by the Enlightenment. The Great Chain of Being became a justification for southern slave society. Illustration by Teri Norris.

essence of the concept, which for pre-Enlightenment theologians could be much more detailed.

The powerful effect of the concept of the Great Chain of Being was felt not only in theology but in the early scientific paradigms of anthropology, sociology, and biology. It reinforced a rigid worldview and suppressed a more dynamic view. Its grip was loosened in the Enlightenment when science and deism became less inclined to accept a priori principles as ultimate truth. It was during the middle Enlightenment that hierarchical society and the institution of slavery were effectively challenged in public debate by James Oglethorpe, as he fought to create a more level society in the colony of Georgia. Two of Oglethorpe's associates late in his life, Granville Sharp and Hannah More, were among those who carried the antislavery message forward by creating the antislavery movement. Their efforts introduced a profound disruption in the fundamental assumptions underlying the Great Chain of Being.[57]

It was not until the Enlightenment that democracy was popularly considered a viable and natural form of government. In *Two Treatises of Government*, Locke reasoned that liberty was an entitlement derived from natural rights, a parallel construct to the natural laws described by Isaac Newton in *Principia Mathematica*, published in 1687. Locke's influence extended through the Enlightenment to later influences such as Francis Hutcheson and the other philosophers of the Scottish Enlightenment. Hutcheson's concepts of "invisible union," "inalienable rights," and "posterity's liberty and happiness" merged with Locke's philosophy of social contract and the natural right to "life, liberty, and estate" to find expression in the American Declaration of Independence. The Enlightenment concluded with the American and French revolutions, which introduced the new idea that "all men are created equal."[58]

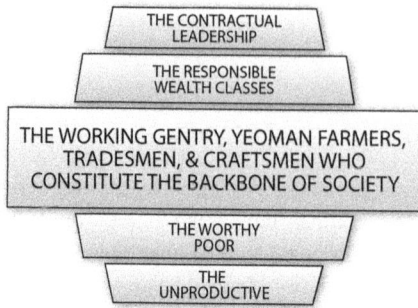

Figure 7. The New Society of the Enlightenment. The Enlightenment flattened the social pyramid by introducing the idea that all people are born equal in the state of nature. The new idea of fundamental equality was open ended, eventually allowing women, oppressed minorities, and others to claim equal rights. Illustration by Teri Norris.

The Enlightenment shattered the idea, held throughout history, that virtually any society, regardless of its culture or government, was structured as a class pyramid. A large middle class of farmers, tradesmen, craftsmen, and even laborers constituted "the people," whom government was presumed to serve through a fundamental contract. James Oglethorpe founded the colony of Georgia in 1733 on that basis, while prohibiting slavery and guaranteeing indentured servants the right to yeoman farms at the end of their service. Thomas Jefferson, like Oglethorpe, envisioned a better society composed of a backbone of yeoman farmers. Modern democracies and the concept of social equity emerged from the Enlightenment, and these political ideals are widely held today as superior ones.[59]

The Province of Carolina, however, was envisioned and established before Locke's *Two Treatises* took final form at the dawn of the Glorious Revolution in 1689. The Fundamental Constitutions transferred the pyramidal structure of a Gothic society to America and, in doing so, planted a classical theme in American politics that played counterpoint to the Enlightenment theme of a more level society, depicted in Figure 7.

The Effect of the Ashley Cooper Plan

Although the Fundamental Constitutions were not adopted and the Grand Model was never fully implemented, the plan was sufficiently formative to shape the economic, social, and spatial character of Carolina and neighboring provinces. Colonists who settled those areas during the colonial era were funneled through Charleston, where they experienced its pyramidal socioeconomic hierarchy before fanning out through the southern region. There they replicated the model's hierarchy, most particularly the large-scale, slave-based plantation system.

Table 1. Timeline of the Founding of Carolina in Historical Context

1688	James II deposed in the Glorious Revolution
1683	Ashley Cooper died in exile in Holland; Rye House Plot uncovered
1682	Ashley Cooper went into exile in Holland
1678	Ashley Cooper released from the Tower
1677	Ashley Cooper sent to the Tower for contempt
1672	Ashley Cooper made 1st Earl of Shaftesbury
1670	Founding of the Province of Carolina (detailed timeline in Chapter 2)
1669	The Fundamental Constitutions of Carolina adopted by the proprietors
1666	The Great Fire of London; Locke becomes Ashley Cooper's physician
1665	The Great Plague of London
1663	Province of Carolina authorized by royal charter
1660	The Restoration: reign of Charles II begins
1656	James Harrington's Oceana published
1653	The Protectorate replaced the Commonwealth
1649	Charles I executed; Commonwealth of England established
1642	English Civil War began
1640	Ashley Cooper elected to Parliament
1632	John Locke born
1621	Anthony Ashley Cooper born
1620	Plymouth Colony founded by the Pilgrims
1607	Jamestown founded by the Virginia Company

Wealth and power resided in South Carolina through the colonial era and for some time afterward. Its economy thrived on the Atlantic Triangle Trade heavily oriented to the enslavement of Africans. Charleston held a prominent position in this triangular trade system, in which commodities produced largely in the Caribbean and the southern colonies were shipped to the northern colonies and Britain, which in turn exchanged manufactured goods in Africa for slaves, which were sent to the New World. The thriving city benefited from its position on the trade route, which followed the Gulf Stream from the Caribbean and along the southeastern coast, without having to invest heavily in infrastructure.

The lucrative trade enjoyed by South Carolina created entrenched land-use patterns associated with slavery and a white caste system. As early as the 1660s, Carolina settlers reported that the colony could not exist without slavery. By the 1670s, slaves formed as much as a third of the Carolina population. In the 1700s, the importation of slaves accelerated in Carolina while it decreased in Virginia, the other main importer. Throughout the eighteenth century, nearly all of South Carolina's productive parishes had a majority black population, while the opposite was the case in Virginia. At the same time, the nonslaveholding white population of tradesmen, small farmers, and others also increased.[60]

The land-use pattern established by the Ashley Cooper Plan during the initial settlement of Carolina was never completely wiped away to create a blank slate for a new kind of society. Its manorial or Gothic structure remained in place, and it was merely adapted to transfer more authority to new occupants of the upper tier of the social pyramid, reinforcing a white caste system. Thus, the form of Ashley Cooper's plan remained in place while its philosophical content was gutted. The ideal of reciprocity of advantage among social classes failed to materialize. The concepts of natural rights, the social contract, and human equality eventually emerged from— perhaps in part because of—the wreckage of the Grand Model in Carolina.

CHAPTER TWO

The Carolina Grand Model

During the Age of Discovery, explorers from England, France, and Spain charted the Atlantic Coast of North America and brought back promising reports on its potential for exploitation and colonization. Sir Walter Raleigh (1554–1618) explored the Mid-Atlantic region and ventured as far south as Florida. He envisioned a large colony, to be named Virginia for Elizabeth, the Virgin Queen, encompassing much of the area that would become Carolina. Virginia was successfully colonized in 1607 with the founding of Jamestown, but a charter granted by Charles I in 1629 for a colony to the south was never acted upon. Another attempt to colonize territory to the south would not be made until 1663, when Charles II granted a charter for the Province of Carolina, named for his father, Charles, Carolus in Latin, who had issued the earlier charter.

Apparently the proprietors were not among those who believed that the numerology of year 1666 portended the end-time, even as the Great Plague consumed England in 1665 and the Great Fire burned much of London the following year. Ashley Cooper and his associates were busy designing a utopian Carolina during that perilous time, though not God's paradise as envisioned by Barebone and the Fifth Monarchists. Instead of presaging the Second Coming, the two catastrophes stimulated imaginative plans for rebuilding London, plans that in turn inspired Ashley Cooper to pursue a physical design for the towns and hinterlands of Carolina to match his political design for the colony.

Contemplating city planning and political philosophy at the same time, as Ashley Cooper did, made a lot of sense, given the recent succession of events: religious strife, civil war, regicide, experimental government gone awry, the return of monarchy, plague and fire, all occurring in a twenty-five-year period. Cities were growing in size while growing apart politically from rural Gothic society. Ashley Cooper believed that cities in the new colonies should grow in a more orderly fashion, for political stability as well as for public health and safety. Earlier migrations to Virginia produced class disharmony, while migrations to New England by religious sects such as the Puritans produced orderly development patterns reflecting social uniformity. Future colonies would need to be more stable and resilient than Virginia and more diverse than New England, given the rapid growth of empire that lay ahead.

The term "Grand Modell of government," or simply Grand Model, was used by Ashley Cooper to describe the political system conceived for Carolina, coupled with its physical design, or settlement pattern. It was a framework for class structure, colonial administration, governance, land allocation, and city planning that embodied the lessons learned from a quarter century of strife.

Once put to paper, the framework became the Fundamental Constitutions of Carolina. Ashley Cooper and Locke also applied the term "Grand Model" to the design of the colony's towns, counties, and hinterlands. The second usage is found in detailed "instructions" sent to colonial administrators. A subset of these was described as "agrarian laws." The second usage was not entirely separate from the first, as the design of towns, as well as other specifics regarding the settlement of Carolina, was intended to flow from the principles set forth in the Fundamental Constitutions. Thus the term "Grand Model" is used here to represent both the constitutions (articles) and the instructions, including (especially) the "agrarian laws."

In addition to the constitutions and instructions, the proprietors also issued numerous regulations that were called "temporary laws." They understood that a small population struggling to establish itself on the American frontier could not possibly form itself overnight into the complex social system they envisioned. Pragmatic steps consistent with constitutional principles would be required to build a foundation for a future model society.

The idealistic vision fashioned by Ashley Cooper with Locke's assistance was one of a regimented, hierarchical, prosperous, stable, and sustainable society. The turmoil created by the English Civil War was caused by commonwealthmen, early republicans, who embraced experimental governance to the point of bringing about democratic (the word was a pejorative before the Enlightenment) chaos to replace an absolutist monarchy. The design for Carolina formalized England's Ancient Constitution, with its system of Gothic balance to prevent such a disastrous unraveling in the future. Ashley Cooper believed that England's Gothic class structure was one in which an enlightened nobility preserved balanced government, while the monarch ruled within the bounds of traditional authority and "the people" willingly performed their roles in society, knowing that they benefited from the security and wealth created by the ruling class.

Ashley Cooper's early school of republicanism was not the more socially level version that appeared in the Enlightenment. His "country party" republicanism contained at its heart an ideology of distinct social and geographic classes. The nation's landowning nobility provided the guiding wisdom and the economic strength to lead the country. Along with the landowning classes under them, the gentry and upper yeomanry, they were spread across the land and represented every sort of interest. They represented the farmers, tradesmen, and laborers in a mutually supportive relationship—a system of reciprocity with advantages for all classes. It was the nobility that had the ultimate responsibility to maintain the Ancient Constitution and protect the nation's vital interests by keeping king and court focused on their core executive duties. Thus, to Ashley Cooper, the House of Lords was the most important policymaking body of government: "The king, governing and administering justice by his House of Lords, and advising with both his Houses of Parliament in all important matters, is the Government I own, I was born under, and am obliged to."[1]

Early republican political philosophy with its Gothic social hierarchy was an essential piece of the framework implanted in the Province of Carolina and eventually infused into the regional political culture. Ashley Cooper and Locke formalized the Gothic-republican system with a detailed settlement plan for Carolina, an integrated design that is herein eponymously named the Ashley Cooper Plan. The plan was progressive for the time in its approach to religious tolerance for Protestant sects, in creating a system of justice that would minimize corruption, and in establishing a well-defined role for government in facilitating and regulating commerce. It was conservative and traditional by constitutionally legislating a class structure with a permanent upper class of nobility and a permanent underclass of serfs and slaves (though it did not contemplate slavery on the scale that would emerge).

Ashley Cooper and Locke, having experienced the turmoil of the English Civil War followed by an experimental Commonwealth, lived the nightmare of unbalanced government described in Aristotle's *Politics*. The constitutions for the Carolina Province would restore the principles of the Ancient Constitution with a precision and formality that would prevent such a slide into chaos by empowering wise and educated nobility to rule the land while guaranteeing the rights of the people.[2]

The Fundamental Constitutions of Carolina

The Fundamental Constitutions drafted by Locke under Ashley Cooper's direction were adopted by the proprietors on March 1, 1669, as the framework for governing the province. The full document was composed of 120 "constitutions," as Locke preferred to call them (meaning "articles"), which detailed in 8,086 words a comprehensive and integrated model for government, class structure, and landownership. By comparison, the U.S. Constitution contained 4,555 words in the original, unamended text. The comprehensiveness of the document went further than Harrington did in *Oceana* in detailing an ideal system of government, one capable of maintaining a stability that would prevent future civil wars and social chaos.[3]

The Fundamental Constitutions created a palatinate, an area ruled by a nobleman, the palatine, who was granted special autonomy to control a frontier territory. The precedent for the palatine model had been created six centuries earlier by William the Conqueror, who established the county palatine of Durham on the unstable Scottish frontier. The name "palatine" was derived from the Latin *palatium*, meaning "palace." The Carolina palatine was to be the eldest of the Lords Proprietors, a permanent aristocratic leadership class that sat at the apex of authority in the class pyramid. The Fundamental Constitutions explicitly stated in its preamble that it was the Lords Proprietors' intent to avoid "erecting a numerous democracy," as much a threat to Gothic balance as a tyrant-king.

The next several sections examine the various facets of class, property, government, religion, agrarian economics, and infrastructure planning encompassed by the Fundamental Constitutions. The proprietors recognized that these formal structures would not be erected immediately on a distant frontier, and thus, as noted earlier, they issued the "instructions" and "temporary laws" for immediate, practical guidance to the first colonists.[4]

Class Structure, Land Ownership, and Settlement Planning

Articles one through twenty-seven established the eight Lords Proprietors as Carolina's hereditary nobility and asserted that they alone permanently held the highest positions of authority in the province. Under the leadership of the palatine, the other seven proprietors would exclusively hold the "seven great offices" of the palatinate: "admirals, chamberlains, chancellors, constables, chief justices, high stewards, and treasurers." Subsequent articles set forth the rights and privileges of this hereditary ruling class.

The heirs of the proprietors would succeed them to those offices, and if there were no heirs, a member of the nobility would be raised to office by the other proprietors. Proprietors absent from the province were empowered to appoint a resident deputy to fulfill the duties of office.

Two tiers of hereditary nobility were created below the proprietors, the highest of which was the *landgrave*, a term borrowed from German feudal tradition. Each county in the province would have one and only one landgrave. The next tier of nobility was the *cacique*, a term for leader or chieftain used by Native Americans. Each county in the province would have two caciques. These two ranks of nobility were used throughout the proprietary period and continued to be used through the colonial period by those who claimed inherited nobility (see Chapter 4 for a discussion of the perpetuation of the oligarchy, or "aristocracy," in the South).[5]

The proprietors anticipated that there would be other large landowners in the province, and for that reason they created a tier in the class pyramid for *lords of manors*. This landowning class corresponded to the lower level of nobility in Britain, such as the powerful landowning knights and gentry who controlled large estates with sizable populations of farmers, tradesmen, and laborers settled on or near their lands.

The province was to be divided into counties of 750 square miles, an area typical of southern counties in the United States today. Each county would consist of eight signiories, eight baronies, and four precincts; the precincts in turn would be divided into six colonies. Each signiory, barony, and colony was to consist of 12,000 acres. The eight signiories were the domains of the eight proprietors. The eight baronies were divided so that the one landgrave in each county owned four baronies and the two caciques each owned two baronies, such that they were "hereditarily and unalterably annexed to and settled upon the said dignity."

Based on the parameters described above, the total amount of land owned by the nobility in any single county was limited to 192,000 acres, or 300 square miles, which constituted two-fifths of the total area. The historian Thomas Leng has observed that the allocation of three-fifths of the land to freemen was intended to create a large class of farmers, thereby establishing agrarian balance and avoiding an imbalance that had developed in Virginia, where the landowning aristocracy was at cross-purposes with a powerful merchant class. As stated in the constitutions, the land was to be allocated "amongst the people; so that in setting out and planting the lands, the balance of the government may be preserved."[6]

The "people" were the lords of manors and the lower-ranking freemen of the province who had the right to own property, vote, and hold local offices, subject to minimum landownership requirements. The lesser freemen constituted what might be described as the middle class of the province, but they did not possess the broad-ranging upward mobility associated with a modern middle class. They were primarily the gentry and yeoman farmers, but also (in lesser proportion) the merchants and tradesmen of the colony.

Below the middle-class freemen lay the toiling classes, who had virtually no civil rights. The *leetmen*, known in other feudal contexts as vassals, serfs, or villeins, were peasant laborers who owed fealty to masters among the higher classes. They were expected to voluntarily enter into their class status, presumably attracted by the reciprocal benefits of physical and economic security, then register in a place of permanent residence. Once registered, however, leetmen were within the sphere of control of their master and not allowed to travel from their place of registration without his permission; nor could they vote or hold elective office. If they were married, their masters were required to allocate a ten-acre kitchen garden to the couple, for which they would pay a share of the produce as rent.

Below the leetmen were the *slaves*, a class who could not own land and had no civil rights, except to practice their religion. They were chattel property of the landowning classes who could be bought or sold as a commodity. The enslavement of people at this point in history was legal in England, and it was an accepted practice virtually everywhere. In Christian Europe, it was reinforced by the theological precept of the Great Chain of Being (see Figure 6 in Chapter 1). Mass enslavement that later came to characterize Carolina and eventually the entire region was not envisioned under the Fundamental Constitutions as originally drafted. The colony thus began as a *society with slaves* (common throughout history), and later became a *slave society* (comparatively uncommon in history).[7]

The proprietors retained the right to dispose of their land until 1700, after which time it would descend to their male heirs or, if none, to female heirs or other general heirs or to the other proprietors (who would choose a new proprietor). The number of eight proprietors was to be maintained as a constant, with surviving proprietors choosing landgraves to succeed those who were deceased. After 1700, new proprietors would take up "the name and arms of that proprietor whom he succeeds; which from thenceforth shall be the name and arms of his family and their posterity." A landgrave or cacique could become a proprietor and acquire a signiory, and then his former title and land would "devolve into the hands of the lords proprietors."

Twelve counties were to be initially established, encompassing a total area of 9,000 square miles, essentially the entire coastal plain of present-day South Carolina. Each proprietor was to choose one land-grave for eight of the counties, with the remaining four selected by the palatine's court, which was made up of the proprietors themselves. The twenty-four caciques would be selected in the same manner, so that the entire nobility was created by the proprietors. Once the first twelve counties were established, a second group of twelve would be created in the same manner, "according to the proportions in these fundamental constitutions" (that is, articles). Subsequent sections of the Fundamental Constitutions preserve the class pyramid created by the proprietors and the landholdings associated with that hierarchy, as illustrated in Table 2.

The nobility was vested with broad authority over those on their land: "In every signiory, barony, and manor, the respective lord shall have power, in his own name, to hold court-leet there, for trying of all causes, both civil and criminal; but where it shall concern any person being no inhabitant, vassal, or leetman of the said signiory, barony, or manor, he, upon paying down of forty shillings to the lords proprietors' use, shall have an appeal from the signiory or barony court to the county court, and from the manor court to the precinct court." This provision is the first use in the document of the term "manor," which is defined as a land grant of 3,000 to 12,000 contiguous acres in a single colony from the palatine's court.

The Fundamental Constitutions placed further limitations on the ability of lords of signiories, baronies, and manors to subdivide, sell, or otherwise alienate their land. The ownership system was designed to keep the class hierarchy and original land grants intact through successive generations and under all conceivable conditions.

The lords of every signiory, barony, or manor retained administrative authority over their leetmen and leetwomen, who did not "have liberty to go off from the land of their particular lord and live anywhere else, without license obtained from their said lord, under hand and seal." Further, "All the children of leet-men shall be leet-men, and so to all generations." However, it appears that the abdication of liberty was meant to be initially voluntary: "Whoever shall voluntarily enter himself a leet-man in the registry of the county court, shall be a leet-man." A married leet-man and leet-woman was to be granted ten acres, but they were compelled to pay their lord up to "one-eighth part of all the yearly produce" generated from their land.

Table 2. Land Allocation and Agrarian Balance by County

Tract Type by Class	Tracts per County	Tract Acreage	Total Tract Acreage	Percentage for Agrarian Balance
Signiory	8	12,000	96,000	20
Barony	8	12,000	96,000	20
Colony	24	12,000	288,000	60
County Total	40	—	480,000	100

The Grand Council and Supreme Courts of Government

A "court" was an administrative unit of government in the sense of a "department" today. A court included the judicial functions associated with the modern use of the term. Eight supreme courts were to be formed, the first of which was to be "called the palatine's court, consisting of the palatine and the other seven proprietors." An elaborate formula was prescribed for the other seven courts whereby they were controlled by the nobility.

The parliament was to be constituted by elections from the nobility. The palatine's court had the power to call parliaments, to hold elections, to designate port towns, to maintain the public treasury except for funds granted by parliament for a specific public use, and to exercise other powers granted by the king. The palatine had the authority of general of the army, or he could assume the position of chief justice in any proprietors' court.

The *chief justice's court* tried all civil and criminal appeals from lower courts. The *councilor's court* had custody of the great seal under which the palatine's court issued commissions and grants. It also had various other duties, including state matters such as treaties with Indian nations. The *constable's court*, headed by the proprietors and supplemented by twelve assistants called lieutenant-generals, had authority to order and determine "all military affairs by land, and all land forces, arms, ammunition, artillery, garrisons, forts, &c., and whatever belongs unto war." In time of war, the constable was to become the general of the army and those under him were to appoint lower officers. The *admiral's court*, headed by one of the proprietors, had responsibility for inspection of ports and navigable tidal rivers, for public shipping and storage of goods, and for all maritime affairs. *The treasurer's court* would consist of a proprietor and his six under-treasurers to manage public revenue and treasury. The *high steward's court* would consist of a proprietor and six comptrollers to manage "foreign and domestic trade, manufactures, public buildings, workhouses, highways, passages by water above the flood of the tide, drains, sewers, and banks against inundation, bridges, posts, carriers, fairs, markets, corruption or infection of the common air or water, and all things in order to the public commerce and health."

The high steward's court was also responsible for land surveys, the site selection of towns, and town planning. It was illegal for anyone to establish a town without the court's approval. The court also had power to approve public buildings, highway and bridge construction, drainage projects, and improvement of navigable waterways. A form of eminent domain was enacted that included compensation to property owners.

The *chamberlain's court*, consisting of a proprietor and six vice-chamberlains, had responsibility for "the care of all ceremonies, precedency, heraldry, reception of public messengers, pedigrees, the registry of all births, burials, and marriages, legitimation, and all cases concerning matrimony, or arising from it; and shall also have power to regulate all fashions, habits, badges, games, and sports."

A *grand council*, consisting of the palatine and seven proprietors and the forty-two councilors of the several proprietors' courts, was given the authority to settle controversies arising from the various courts. The grand council was the final authority on appeals. It also had the exclusive responsibility to prepare the agenda of matters going before parliament and to "dispose of all the money given by the parliament [for] any particular public use."

The eldest of the Lords Proprietors residing in Carolina would serve as the palatine's deputy, holding all of his powers. If no proprietor resided in the colony, procedures were set out for selecting someone else for the position from their heirs, the landgraves, or the caciques.

Courts of Justice

Ashley Cooper's service on the Hale Commission in 1652 provided valuable experience for designing a legal system from the ground up. The commission's task of evaluating the nation's laws and legal procedures was thwarted by systemic inertia and special interests. With Carolina, he had a blank slate to apply all that he had learned since the Hale Commission.

Below the chief justice's court, which tried appeals, were the local courts, where legal actions were initiated. Local courts were to be formed in every county, consisting of the sheriff and four justices, one for every precinct. The sheriff was required to reside in the county and own at least 500 acres. A court was also to be established in every precinct, consisting of a steward and four justices residing in the precinct and owning at least 300 acres. They were to serve as judges in all criminal cases except treason, murder, and any other capital offenses, with the exception of cases involving the nobility. Appeals would rise to the county court. No case could be tried twice in any one court, and all civil or criminal cases would be tried by a jury of peers. Capital cases would be tried by a commission of the grand council meeting at least twice a year. The panel "shall come as itinerant judges to the several counties."[8]

Jurors in the precinct courts were required to own at least 50 acres of freehold. In the county courts, the minimum was 300 acres of freehold. In the proprietors' courts, the minimum was 500 acres of freehold. Juries were to consist of twelve men; verdicts were to be issued at the "consent of the majority." Legal representation for a fee was declared "vile" and prohibited with few exceptions. Lawyers who "plead for money or reward" were prohibited.

Parliament

The Carolina parliament would consist of the proprietors or their deputies, landgraves, caciques, and one freeholder out of every precinct, in the number shown in Table 3. Every member would have one vote. A member of parliament was required to have at least 500 acres of freehold within the precinct from which he was elected. Voters were required to own at least fifty acres of freehold within the precinct of their residence. Parliament would assemble on the first Monday of November every other year. The Fundamental Constitutions would be read at the opening of every parliament, and all present were required to assent to it.

Elections to the biennial parliament by freeholders were to take place on the first Tuesday in September for the parliament seated the next November. All acts of parliament required ratification in open parliament by the palatine or his deputy and three more of the Lords Proprietors or their deputies.

As the province was expected to grow in units of twelve counties, the parliament would also grow, with freeholders maintaining a majority and proprietors having an increasingly small share of the votes. However, parliament had little authority, and major decisions rested with the grand council.

Provisions were made to avoid a "multiplicity" of laws and regulations, with the potential to "have great inconveniencies, and serve only to obscure and perplex [, and thus] all manner of comments and expositions on any part of these fundamental constitutions, or on any part of the common or statute laws of Carolina, are absolutely prohibited."

Table 3. Composition of Parliament for Twelve Counties

Class	Members	Qualifications
Proprietors	8	Hereditary right
Landgraves	12	Hereditary right
Caciques	24	Hereditary right
Freeholders	48	Freehold of 500 acres

Administration of Precincts and Colonies

A registry of "deeds, leases, judgments, mortgages, and other conveyances" would be maintained in every precinct, and the position of register filled from among the freeholders owning at least 300 acres. A registry of births, marriages, and deaths would be maintained in every signiory, barony, and colony. The person holding the position of "register" of a colony was required to own at least 50 acres in the colony. Births, marriages, and deaths of the proprietors, landgraves, and caciques were to be recorded in the chamberlain's court.

Every colony would have a constable, elected annually by the freeholders. The constable was required to own at least 300 acres in the colony. Assistants to the constable were also to be elected annually by the freeholders.

Incorporated towns were to be governed by a mayor, twelve aldermen, and a common council of twenty-four. The common council was to be elected by the householders of the town; the aldermen would be chosen from common council; and the mayor would be selected from the aldermen by the palatine's court.

The success of the colony was deemed dependent on designated port towns, and it was made unlawful to unlade cargo at any other location. The first port town on every river would be situated in a colony, and it would be a maintained as a permanent settlement.

Practice of Religion

At the time of the English Civil War, religion and government were almost inextricably intertwined. Following the Restoration, the close relationship was cautiously questioned, which set the stage for it being addressed head-on during the Enlightenment. Ashley Cooper and Locke were among the first to take substantive steps toward legalizing the concepts of freedom of conscience and the disentangling of church and state.

Although religion was woven into government and through society at large, England had a tradition of anticlericalism and the questioning of religious institutions. The clergy were seen by many as self-serving and readily causing war and suffering over their narrow interpretations of scripture and dogma. Ashley Cooper articulated these concerns and probably set an example for Locke to follow in *A Letter Concerning Toleration*.[9]

Two quotes by Ashley Cooper found among Locke's works exemplify their shared view of religion:

> The clergy . . . have truckt away the Rights and Liberties of the People in this, and in all other countries wherever they have had the opportunity, that they might be owned by the Prince to be Iure Divino, and maintain'd in that Pretention by that absolute power and force, they have contributed so much to put into his hands; and that Priest and Prince may, like Castor and Pollux, be worshipped together as Divine in the same temple by Us poor Lay-subjects; and that sense and reason, Laws, Properties, Rights, and Liberties, shall be understood as the Oracles of those Deities shall interpret, or give signification to them, and ne'r be made use of in the world to oppose the absolute and free Will of either of them.[10]

In other words, the intimate and collusive relationship between religion and government, "priest and prince," is a perfect formula for tyranny. Here he is quoted again by Locke on this subject:

> I observed the leaders of the great parties of religion, both laity and clergy, ready and forward to deliver up the rights and liberties of the people, and to introduce an absolute dominion; so that tyranny might be established in the hands of those that favoured their way, and with whom they might have hopes to divide the present spoil, having no eye to posterity, or thought of future things.[11]

While Ashley Cooper questioned religion broadly, his greatest concern was over Catholicism, or, more precisely, "Popery," a term that distinguished denominational political culture from religious belief. As seen in Chapter 1, he saw the Catholic nations, with their culture of divine right and absolute power, as an existential threat to England's long-standing principles of civil liberty and constitutional government.

In drafting the Fundamental Constitutions, Locke seemed willing to press the right of freedom of conscience farther than others, arguing for a broad application of religious tolerance. The Lords Proprietors, however, ultimately adopted a narrower provision: "No man shall be permitted to be a freeman of Carolina, or to have any estate or habitation within it, that doth not acknowledge a God, and that God is publicly and solemnly to be worshipped." Specifically, they provided that the Church of England, as "the only true and orthodox [church] and the national religion of all the King's dominions," would be the sole religion supported by the parliament of Carolina, which would pay for the construction of churches and the salaries of its ministers.

After this formal acknowledgment of the established Church, they recognized that a diverse society represents a "compact with all men" and that a violation of that compact would constitute a "great offence to Almighty God, and great scandal to the true religion which we profess." Furthermore, "Jews, heathens, and other dissenters from the purity of Christian religion may not be scared and kept at a distance from it, but, by having an opportunity of acquainting themselves with the truth and reasonableness of its doctrines, and the peaceableness and inoffensiveness of its professors, may, by good usage and persuasion, and all those convincing methods of gentleness and meekness, suitable to the rules and design of the gospel, be won ever to embrace and unfeignedly receive the truth." In view of these principles, "any seven or more persons agreeing in any religion, shall constitute a church or profession, to which they shall give some name, to distinguish it from others."

Privacy of religion, however, was not one of the principles to which the proprietors subscribed. Members of a church were required to enter their names and the date of their declaration in a registry maintained in the precinct of their residence. All persons age eighteen and older were required to be a member of a church or profession of faith, in order to have "any benefit or protection of the law."

Followers of all recognized religions were required to subscribe to three basic rules:

1. "That there is a God."
2. "That God is publicly to be worshipped."
3. "That it is lawful and the duty of every man, being thereunto called by those that govern, to bear witness to truth; and that every church or profession shall, in their terms of communion, set down the external way whereby they witness a truth as in the presence of God, whether it be by laying hands on or kissing the bible, as in the Church of England, or by holding up the hand, or any other sensible way."

Assemblies of people not embracing these rules would be considered "riots" and punishable as such.

Religious persecution, hate speech, and all forms of intolerance were forbidden, as was any statement in any "religious assembly [that spoke] irreverently or seditiously of the government or governors, or of state matters."

Native Americans were acknowledged to be an important concern to the colony. While they were "utterly strangers to Christianity," the proprietors conceded that their "idolatry, ignorance, or mistake gives us no right to expel or use them ill." Similarly, people from other nations who settled in Carolina would "unavoidably be of different opinions concerning matters of religion, the liberty whereof they will expect to have allowed them, and it will not be reasonable for us, on this account, to keep them out, that civil peace may be maintained amidst diversity of opinions."

Chattel Slavery

The issue of slavery was first addressed in the context of religion in article 107 of the Fundamental Constitutions:

> Since charity obliges us to wish well to the souls of all men, and religion ought to alter nothing in any man's civil estate or right, it shall be lawful for slaves, as well as others, to enter themselves, and be of what church or profession any of them shall think best, and, therefore, be as fully members as any freeman. But yet no slave shall hereby be exempted from that civil dominion his master hath over him, but be in all things in the same state and condition he was in before.

Slavery in the British Isles existed for centuries, before and after Roman occupation, but it involved only small numbers of people. Chattel slavery was rendered obsolete with Gothic feudalism, according to which the villein, or serf, supplied labor for the lord of a manor. Neither Ashley Cooper nor Locke sought to eliminate slavery from Carolina, imagining that a frontier society would require various forms of labor, including slaves taken as prisoners of war or in the emerging African slave trade. The constitutions specified that liberty for enslaved people and their descendants would not be attainable, even through religion: "Every freeman of Carolina shall have absolute power and authority over his negro slaves, of what opinion or religion soever."

This is where Locke's commitment to liberty and equality has been questioned by his critics. Part of the complication of understanding Locke is that he began his career as a philosopher in an age that did not question traditional class hierarchy but instead sought balance and reciprocity within the traditional social hierarchy. He ended his career as a philosopher at the dawn of the Enlightenment, when he contributed to the emergence of an entirely new ideal of equality and social mobility. His personal evolution from twilight to dawn in the new age remains unclear. What is clear is that he sought social justice for all classes, first through balance and reciprocity among classes and later through a less classist vision of society.

The fact that the Fundamental Constitutions say little about slavery, while going into great detail about every other aspect of society, suggests that the documents were not envisioned as a cornerstone of the colony. That is, as surmised earlier, a *society with slaves* was expected, but a *slave society* was not envisioned. The Ashley Cooper Plan was far more concerned with Harrington's vision of *Oceana* and the establishment of an ideal English province than with slavery. While the practice of mass enslavement on Caribbean plantations was well known to Ashley Cooper, the other proprietors, and Locke, their early focus on labor supply centered on peasant families and indentured servants.

Slavery of course emerged as the primary source of labor in Carolina, and fifty years after the founding of the colony, a majority of its people were enslaved Africans. The Ashley Cooper Plan did not cause that result, but it was adapted by Caribbean settlers to sustain it. The institution of slavery they created and perpetuated for two centuries is described in Chapter 4.

Property and Taxation

No person was permitted to "hold or claim any land in Carolina by purchase or gift, or otherwise, from the natives, or any other" person or group. Land must be obtained "from and under the lords proprietors, upon pain of forfeiture of all his estate, movable or immovable, and perpetual banishment."

Beginning in the year 1690, landowners were required to "pay yearly unto the lords proprietors, for each acre of land, English measure, as much fine silver as is at this present time in one English penny, or the value thereof, to be as a chief rent and acknowledgment to the lords proprietors, their heirs and successors, forever." The palatine's court had the lawful responsibility to obtain a "new survey of any man's land, not to oust him of any part of his possession, but that by such a survey the just number of acres he possesseth may be known, and the rent thereon due may be paid by him."

Other forms of valuable property found or obtained in the form of "wrecks, mines, minerals, quarries of gems, and precious stones, with pearl-fishing, whale-fishing, and one-half of all ambergris, by whomsoever found, shall wholly belong to the Lords Proprietors."

Revenues and profits received collectively by the Lords Proprietors would be divided into ten parts, with the palatine receiving three parts and each proprietor one. In the event the palatine's deputy was governing the colony, he would receive one share and the nonresident palatine would receive two shares.

Militia Duty

Freemen and all other inhabitants of Carolina above the age of seventeen and under the age of sixty were required to "bear arms and serve as soldiers, whenever the grand council shall find it necessary." The maintenance of a well-regulated militia was a tradition in England with a long history. The formation of armies of the people, under the control of the nobility, prevented the king from maintaining a standing army that might empower him to rule as a tyrant. Ashley Cooper was an opponent of a standing army in England, and he sought to prevent the formation of one in Carolina as a potentially destabilizing force.

An essential aspect of a regimented society was its ability to organize for defense. In threatening times, the nobility would rise to lead an army of the people, built from the militias of the manors and villages across the land; soldiers were not professionals who might threaten society from within.

In Carolina, as in other English colonies, the idea of a regulated militia became engrained in society. The right to bear arms to support a militia later became the basis for the Second Amendment of the Bill of Rights. Largely forgotten now, however, is the purpose of maintaining a militia as an alternative to a standing army.

Adoption and Effect of the Fundamental Constitutions

The proprietors believed that the Fundamental Constitutions were essential to the success of the colony, and that all citizens of the colony should be aware of their content. Toward that end, they required that a copy of the document must be kept by the register in every precinct. Every resident of the precinct above the age of seventeen having any estate or other possession in Carolina or expecting the protection or benefit of its laws was required to submit the following oath of allegiance before a precinct register:

> I, NAME, do promise to bear faith and true allegiance to our sovereign lord King Charles II, his heirs and successors; and will be true and faithful to the palatine and Lords Proprietors of Carolina, their heirs and successors; and with my utmost power will defend them, and maintain the government according to this establishment in these fundamental constitutions.

All persons admitted to any office in Carolina were also required to swear the oath of allegiance to the Fundamental Constitutions. A nonresident swearing to the oath of allegiance before any precinct register was to be recorded as a naturalized citizen.

The final paragraph of the constitutions reads as follows: "These fundamental constitutions, in number a hundred and twenty, and every part thereof, shall be and remain the sacred and unalterable form and rule of government of Carolina forever. Witness our hands and seals, the first day of March, sixteen hundred and sixty-nine."

Assessment of the Grand Model

Locke and Ashley Cooper attempted to establish a society regulated by a body of clear, unambiguous, and just laws. Many of the provisions in the Fundamental Constitutions were progressive for the time: freedom of religion; a multitiered government of elected freeholders; a justice system of regularly elected freeholders rather than one of professional lawyers and judges who were thought to be corruptible; trial by a jury of peers; and a system of government designed to efficiently build and maintain infrastructure and increase the wealth of all of its freeholders.

The ideals of class reciprocity and balanced government were perhaps the pinnacle of social justice until the Enlightenment replaced those ideals with the entirely new concepts of democracy, equality, and social mobility. The grip of a rigid class pyramid was, for the first time in human history, about to be replaced by a more dynamic structure. The ancient pyramid, however, would remain entrenched in Carolina and an essential part of southern political culture. The Fundamental Constitutions established the proprietors at the top of the class pyramid as a permanent ruling class and the leetmen and slaves at the bottom of the class pyramid as a permanent underclass. In between, there was only modest room for social mobility as the colony's lower nobility made up of landgraves and caciques were a constitutionally protected class. The gentry and the lower tier of freeholders enjoyed the only prospect of mobility, much as the yeomen of England were able to rise into the gentry class.

The rigidity of the society envisioned by the Fundamental Constitutions was intended to promote order, safety, liberty, and prosperity. The social disruption, slaughter of war, and loss of lands by the nobility during the English Civil War would be forever avoided by the rational system established by the Fundamental Constitutions. However, the effect of the framing document in the eyes of settlers who would soon begin populating the province was to diminish liberty, opportunity, and the potential for widespread prosperity. In modern democratic republics, the amount of control exercised by the proprietors would be perceived as a totalitarian nightmare on the order of Orwell's *1984*.

Initial Implementation of the Grand Model

When the plan to settle Carolina was implemented in 1668, the proprietors recognized that planting people on the frontier was a messy business and that their Grand Model would require modifications to meet the exigencies of initial settlement. Communications were slow, compounding their ability to resolve problems; settlement patterns were uneven and lacked the critical mass to put administrative structures in place; and people arriving on the frontier were pragmatic out of necessity, and in most cases by character, and thus unlikely candidates to endorse the utopian constructs set forth in the constitutions. Additionally, and most importantly, America was not quite the blank slate envisioned in England; it was populated by indigenous nations that had adapted to environmental conditions entirely unknown to Europeans. Among the nations well established in the region were the Creek, who traded along the Savannah River, the Cherokee in the mountains to the west, and the Algonquian in Albemarle Sound.

Earlier European attempts at settlement south of Virginia had proved futile, sometimes due to a hostile reception by indigenous people and other times due to challenging environmental conditions. The Spanish were the first to claim the region and to establish trading relations with indigenous peoples. It was the French, however, who established the first European settlement. Jean Ribaut, a Huguenot naval officer, was sent to explore the territory north of Spanish America for prospects of French colonization. His expedition of 1562 established the town of Charlesfort in Port Royal Sound, on present-day Parris Island (a Marine Corps training installation that allows public access to the historic site). The outpost was abandoned before it could be resupplied from France, but it has the distinction of being the first town in what would become English-speaking North America, predating St. Augustine by thirteen years. The Spanish subsequently occupied the site from 1566 to 1587, renaming it Santa Elena; they continued to claim the territory, and threaten Carolina, until James Oglethorpe definitively secured it for Britain in the 1740s.

Europeans only began settling the region that would become Carolina in large numbers in the 1650s, when Virginia farmers expanded south into the vast estuary that would later be named Albemarle Sound (after Carolina proprietor George Monck, 1st Duke of Albemarle, who had been instrumental in restoring the monarchy). Shortly before the Charter of 1663 was granted to the proprietors, a group of New Englanders established a settlement farther south in present-day North Carolina, along the Cape Fear River. Once the settlers found themselves under the authority of the proprietors, they petitioned to have the same rights of democratic self-government they had enjoyed up to that time. The undemocratic Fundamental Constitutions had not yet been conceived by the proprietors, but they instinctively rejected the request. Soon after, a group from Barbados was allowed to establish another settlement in the area, and Sir John Yeamans was appointed governor. Some of the original settlers returned to New England, but the proprietors directed Yeamans to encourage them to return with an offer of limited self-rule. Some accepted the offer, and by 1664 the proprietors recognized three counties—Albemarle, Clarendon, and Craven.

These counties, all situated near the Cape Fear River, never matured into formal jurisdictions. A single settlement named Charles Town grew to a population of 800 by 1666. However, it was never fully embraced by the proprietors, and, lacking their support, it wanted for provisions that would sustain it. After a hurricane in 1667, the town was abandoned.

The proprietors developed a preference for a more southern settlement with natural harbors and less vulnerability to storms. John Yeamans's son, William, was sent to establish a new, principal settlement farther south at Port Royal Sound, long known to European explorers as a safe natural harbor with considerable high ground along its perimeter.

The first mission to the province was undertaken in 1669, following adoption of the Fundamental Constitutions. The proprietors each contributed £500 to supply ninety-two colonists and crew members and outfit three ships, the *Carolina*, the *Port Royal*, and the *Albemarle*. The small fleet sailed in August, stopping in Ireland to take on more settlers, then proceeding to Barbados, where it would acquire even more. En route to Barbados, the *Albemarle* was lost in a storm. At Barbados, the expedition was joined by John Yeamans, who leased a replacement ship. Finally sailing directly for Carolina, the fleet encountered another storm that sank the *Port Royal* and blew the remaining ships all the way to Virginia.

The last phase of the mission was led by William Sayle after Yeamans decided to return to Barbados. Sayle was an elderly adventurer who had lived in the Bahamas for more than twenty years and claimed proprietary rights to a portion of that territory. A Puritan, he had arrived in the Bahamas with a plan to establish a colony with religious freedom. It was to be an egalitarian society with equal allocations of land and a representative parliament. As such, he was not an ideal match for the proprietors and their plan for feudal class structure. Other settlers, however, proved to be a much better match. They came from Barbados, the easternmost island in the Caribbean region. Barbados had a well-established class structure tied to a slave-based plantation system. Their leader, John Yeamans, had settled in Barbados in 1650, where he became owner of a large plantation and a public official. His first expedition to Carolina in 1665 produced a small settlement in present-day North Carolina. His second was conducted in concert with Sayle's expedition.[12]

Yeamans was to be the first governor, but he transferred that position to Sayle and returned to Barbados. Sayle died in 1671, and deputy governor Joseph West, with the support of the colonists, became governor. West's formal appointment by the proprietors was issued in July 1669. Yeamans returned and was appointed governor by the proprietors, who had ultimate authority in the matter. Yeamans was granted land from the proprietors, and he brought slaves from Barbados to work the plantation. He also controlled trade to the colony, for which he reaped excessive profits. His greed caused the proprietors to replace him in 1674 and reinstate West to the governorship.

Sayle scouted the coast, observed the terrain, and identified navigable rivers and sounds. Seeing natives, however, he did not go ashore. Upon return to England, he was appointed to be first governor of the province in July 1669. The proprietors issued instructions to the colonists so that it would be clear how they intended to implement their Grand Model with so modest a beginning:

> In regard to the number of people which will at first be set down at Port Royal, will be so small, together with want of landgraves and caciques, that it will not be possible to put out grand model of government in practice at first, and that notwithstanding we may come as nigh as the aforementioned model as is practicable.
>
> 1. As soon as you arrive at Port Royal you are to summon all the freemen that are in the colony, and require them to elect five persons who being joined to the five deputed by the proprietors are to be your council. . . .
>
> 2. You are to cause all the persons so chosen to swear allegiance to . . . the king . . . the proprietors . . . and the form of government. . . .
>
> 3–4. You and your council are to . . . build a fort . . . which is to be your first town. . . .
>
> 5. If you place your first town . . . on the maine [mainland], then shall the six next adjoining squares of 12,000 acres be all colonies, so that the people may at first plant together in convenient numbers.
>
> 6. You are not to suffer anyone to take up lands within two miles and a half of any Indian town. . . .

7. You are by and with the concent of your council, to establish such courts . . . as you present think fit . . . till our grand model of government can come to be put in execution.

8. You are to summon the freeholders . . . to select twenty persons, which together with our deputies for the present are to be your parliament. . . .

9–11. You are to take notice that we do grant unto all free persons above the age of sixteen years that do come to Port Royal . . . 150 acres of land [with additional acreage for each servant and those who have completed their terms of service, on a declining scale through 1672].

12. You are to cause the land to be laid out in squares containing each 12,000 acres [for signories, baronies, and colonies].

13. You are to order your people to plant in towns, and one town at least in each colony so ordering and laying out the towns as you and your council shall think most convenient and profitable for the people yet to inhabit them. You are not to suffer the inhabitants of any of the colonies to have a greater proportion of front of their land to the river than a fifth part of his depth.

14. Any person having brought servants, to plant [shall obtain a warrant from the surveyor general on which shall be recorded an oath of allegiance, the form of which is described].

15. We having sent a stock of victuals, clothes and tools for the supply of those people, who through poverty have not been able to supply themselves . . . are to order the storekeeper how much of each sort shall be delivered weekly . . . and how much . . . shall be delivered to any of the Indian caciques to purchase their friendship and alliance.[13]

The proprietors continued to issue instructions as needed to settle Carolina before it was sufficiently populated to fill offices and form a parliament.

Sayle returned in 1670 with colonists from England, Ireland, and the islands, arriving first at Port Royal Sound near the future site of Beaufort. There he was intimidated by the indigenous people and sailed northward at their suggestion to a more hospitable site. The alternate site was 70 miles up the coast at the confluence of two large rivers. Those rivers would be named the Ashley and the Cooper in honor of Anthony Ashley Cooper. Sayle encamped on the west bank of the Ashley. The site proved unsuitable as a permanent town, and a better site was found the following year on the peninsula separating the rivers.

Colonists from various places soon began arriving in Carolina's first town, named Charles Town for Charles II. In order to keep the new colony on its intended course, the proprietors issued additional instructions to the governor and council of Ashley River in May 1671. First, they were directed to hold an election of the freeholders to choose twenty representatives, who with the proprietors' deputies would form the parliament, which was authorized to enact laws consistent with the constitutions. Parliament was also directed to select five of its members to join with the proprietors' deputies and five of the eldest members of the nobility to form the grand council. The instructions named John Locke, John Yeamans, and James Carteret as landgraves entitled to future baronies in the county.[14]

Instructions for establishing county boundaries, surveying property lines, laying out towns, and situating the capital city were included with the instructions. Settlement was to proceed in an orderly and compact manner to promote efficient allocation of resources, effective administration, and viability of commerce. The detailed settlement plan is taken up in Chapter 3.

Additional instructions issued at this time advised the colonists to "avoid taking up great tracts of land sooner than they can be planted." The proprietors were concerned about achieving efficiencies in land-use patterns to support commerce and provide for effective defense. Thus, initially, each proprietor would be allocated three signories, and each landgrave and cacique would be allocated one barony. When seventy-two colonies were settled, a member of the hereditary nobility would then have the right "to take up the proportion of land due to his dignity." To further promote efficient land use, baronies were required within seven years to support at least thirty settlers, and manors were to support at least fifteen.[15]

The proprietors envisioned the practice of "English husbandry"—a model of growth based on family farms coexisting with large estate farms, a variety of crops and domesticated animals forming the foundation of the economy, and an upwardly mobile labor force freed of obligation following short-term indentures. However, pressed by the Barbadians, greed and the desire for quick profits trumped the proprietors' vision of a more balanced and sustainable economy. Instead of traditional husbandry, the Barbadians vigorously pursued a large-scale monoculture similar to sugar in the West Indies. In the 1680s, they found the ideal crop in rice.[16]

None of the founding proprietors ever ventured to Carolina to assume the role of palatine, establish the nobility, and form the government envisioned by the Grand Model. The leaders who emerged were men who owned vast tracts of land and merchants who could link them to the Atlantic Triangle Trade. Tapping into that trade (initially with rice, later with cotton) had the potential to create great wealth and enormous estates, but they were estates of a new and rapidly rising gentry class, not those of an enlightened nobility imagining itself to be creating a just, stable, prosperous, and sustainable society. The gentry class of Carolina grew in parallel with its partners in England, a new class of gentry that emerged out of state-sponsored commerce with a compass oriented to self-interest.

The Influence of Barbados

Many of the colonists arriving in Carolina came from Barbados, where English sugar plantations had reached the limits of growth on the island. The Barbadians brought their experience as plantation operators and merchants to Carolina at a formative stage. Barbadian John Yeamans emerged as a good fit with the proprietors' Gothic social model, having formed such a society himself, though without any idealistic intent.

Barbados is located where the Caribbean Sea meets the North Atlantic Ocean and where strong southeast trade winds could drive seventeenth-century ships coming from Africa at a fast 180 miles a day. Its geography enabled it to become England's lucrative entry point in the Atlantic Triangle Trade. The island was small at 166 square miles, but its economy grew spectacularly in the mid-1600s after planters adopted Brazilian methods for producing sugar and modified them with ever-present Dutch commercial ingenuity. Barbados became the richest and most populous English colony in the mid-seventeenth century.[17]

At the time of the founding of Charles Town, Barbados was entering a period of decline from hurricanes, overpopulation, crop failures, large plantations crushing the viability of smaller ones, and instability arising from a slave population that exceeded that of free residents. Thousands sought to leave, and many of those looked to Carolina for new opportunities. Barbadians arriving in Carolina soon began reshaping the Grand Model to the Barbadian experience: an economic model of large-scale monoculture and the social model formed in England's first slave society. Approximately half of those arriving in Carolina in the decade after Charles Town was founded were from Barbados or elsewhere in the Caribbean.[18]

Barbados had a diverse population that created a unique economy and society on the island. There were Portuguese who were experienced in operating plantations with slave labor, Dutch traders who were the most sophisticated businessmen of the age, and Virginia merchants, French planters, sailors, government bureaucrats, pirates, priests, and seekers of fortune and adventure. English plantation owners were among the most influential Barbadians to migrate to Carolina, but there was a wide range of others as well. A parish priest described them as "a perfect medley or hotch potch, made up of bankrupt pirates, decayed libertines, sectaries and enthusiasts of all sorts who have transported themselves hither and are the most factious and seditious people in the whole world." It was not a group that would readily submit to the authority of the proprietors or their deputies in the colony.[19]

At the time of the founding of Carolina, the slave population in Barbados was already greater than that of the free population, and by 1700 enslaved people constituted over 70 percent of the population. Over the course of sixteenth-century development on the island, it evolved from a frontier society with slaves to a highly regimented slave society. The concept of chattel slavery was unfamiliar to the English until it emerged on Barbados.[20]

The slaveholders of Barbados learned to control the majority black population through a system of harsh laws and racial differentiation. The impetus for tightened oversight and regulation followed an island-wide revolt in 1675 for which over 100 plotters were arrested, tortured, and executed. The 1688 Act for Governing Negroes formalized the system of control. Its preamble read,

> Whereas the Plantation and Estates of this Island cannot be fully managed . . . without the labour and service of great number of Negroes and other slaves and inasmuch as [they] . . . are of a barbarous, wild and savage nature, and such as renders them wholly unqualified to be governed by the Laws, Customs and Practices of our Nation: It [is] therefore becoming absolutely necessary, that such other Constitutions, Laws, and Orders, should being this Island framed and enacted for the good regulating or ordering of them, as may both restrain the disorders, rapines and inhumanities to which they are naturally prone and inclined.[21]

Legalized oppression brought on a cycle of resistance, rebellion, and even more oppression; and thus another island-wide revolt in 1692 resulted in more than 200 arrests and over 90 executions.

The adoption of such laws and regulations created and intensified racial differentiation. When Barbados was a *society with slaves*, Africans were seen as individuals; but as the island became a slave society it looked upon Africans as savages and it rationalized its harsh treatment of slaves as necessary to civilize and Christianize them. Slaves were forced to wear coarse linen clothing, were discouraged from speaking their native languages, and were instructed to cease practicing their religions. When they disobeyed or broke the law, they could be flogged, beaten, or branded or have their ears cropped or their nostrils slit; in severe cases, they could have appendages amputated and be forced to eat the severed parts; they could be covered with honey and put on an ant hill; they could have gunpowder ignited in orifices; and they could be burned alive. Whatever kind of treatment was necessary to maintain order in the slave society became accepted practice. Slaveholders held absolute power, while slaves had no rights and no dignity. As Carolina transformed into a slave society in the 1690s, it drew heavily from the Barbadian model.[22]

Monoculture was another facet of the Barbadian model with transference to Carolina, other English colonies in America, and eventually the southern United States. Sugar monoculture inspired rice monoculture in the Lowcountry, tobacco monoculture in Virginia, and eventually King Cotton across the Deep South. The "radical simplification" of the landscape, as the historian Walter Johnson described it in *River of Dark Dreams*, perpetuated greed and vulnerability in systems unable to withstand shocks from environmental or market forces. The emphasis on a single lucrative crop was so intense that none of those economies were able to produce much of their own food, relying heavily on imports rather than wasting money to produce crops for local consumption.[23]

Sir John Colleton, one of the proprietors, was also a Barbadian landowner. He died in 1666 before the founding of Charles Town, but his eldest son, Peter, inherited his proprietorship and promoted the Barbadian model in Carolina, subtly competing with the Grand Model. Sons Thomas and James were landgraves. The historian Richard S. Dunn wrote: "Planters like the Colletons and Middletons [a common name in the Lowcountry today] enjoyed privileges in Barbados more tangible than the aristocratic trappings dreamed up by Shaftesbury and Locke in the Fundamental Constitutions of Carolina." They were motivated to perpetuate that status in Carolina. Ashley Cooper and the other proprietors, however, were unaware that the Barbadian model was about to wield greater influence on the colony than their own unique design.[24]

Eventually, Charles Town (renamed Charleston in 1783) would come to resemble Bridgetown, the principal town of Barbados. As Richard Dunn wrote, "Charleston's brittle, gay, and showy society, compounded of old world elegance and frontier boisterousness, echoed the Barbadian atmosphere of a century before. So it was the Barbadians [who] helped to create in North America a slave-based plantation society closer in temper to the islands they fled from than to any other mainland English settlement." In the nineteenth century, Charleston would become wealthier and more sophisticated. It acquired the power and wherewithal to assume an important role in articulating an idealized portrayal of southern slave society. As the North intensified its attacks on slavery, Charleston stood on the front lines in defending southern political culture and the "peculiar institution" of slavery. The South, Charlestonians maintained, had reached a point in the advancement of civilization where virtuous men were free to become wise and thoughtful leaders. They were the nobility of Ashley Cooper's Gothic society.

Amendments to the Grand Model

In November 1691, the proprietors issued new laws in the form of forty-three articles that expanded on the Fundamental Constitutions and superseded previous temporary laws and instructions. It was a house-cleaning measure in part, but also a strong reaffirmation of proprietary authority over the growing and evolving province. The new laws covered the creation of two new counties and the granting of land in those counties; provision of ferry service; land allocation for renters who could not afford to purchase land; and the lease of proprietary land for hunting, fishing, and other limited uses.

The new laws confirmed that the proprietors alone would hold the palatine's court and the other seven great offices named in the Fundamental Constitutions. The rights of the hereditary nobility were reaffirmed. Furthermore, the palatine had sole authority to name a governor, a position not mentioned in the Fundamental Constitutions (except as the palatine's deputy), and the other heads of each great office. Subsequent instructions similarly affirm the various branches of government down to the county level.[25]

The new laws named the four counties settled to that date as Albemarle, Colleton, Berkeley, and Craven. They specified county boundaries, including inland limits to 35 miles in a straight line. The significance of the limit was to create a precise boundary from which to form new colonies as the province grew. It would also restrict settlers from invasive activities in the Indian nations. The plan to orient new counties to rivers remained in place, and rules for creating counties were restated and expanded.[26]

New regulations for settlement, twenty-two in number, were also issued in February 1692. The earlier, detailed plans drawn up by Locke remained largely intact; however, the new regulations made minor adjustments and provided specific guidance for settlement of the new counties of Craven and Colleton. The new plans are taken up in greater detail in the next chapter.[27]

Carolina in the New Century

The proprietary government maintained authority in Carolina for over fifty years until it was overthrown by colonists in 1719. Three generations of Lords Proprietors held the position of palatine and the "seven great offices" reserved for the nobility at the apex of the colony's class pyramid.

By the beginning of the eighteenth century, the original eight proprietors had all died. The new generation of proprietors for the most part continued policies set by the earlier generation. John Locke outlived the original proprietors and went on to serve as an official with the Board of Trade until his death in 1704. Serving under King William, who reigned from 1689 until 1702, Locke enjoyed greater latitude to advance his political philosophy than he had under the proprietors. His involvement with the proprietors during this time, if any, was peripheral, although he remained close to the Ashley Cooper family. The second and third earls of Shaftesbury were proprietors in Locke's late life.

At the turn of the century, the European population of Carolina was just over 3,000 and the slave population was about 2,400. At this time, the population of Native Americans in the Carolina coastal plain was greater than that of colonists and slaves combined. Quite by design, the proprietors had created the frame of a province that would mature to have the substance of a neofeudal society.

A visitor to Carolina writing to the Board of Trade saw a different future, sending it this description of the province in 1699: "There are but few settled inhabitants in this province, the lords have taken up vast tracts of land for their own use, as in Colleton County and other places, where the land is most commodious for settlement, which prevents peopling the place, and makes them less capable to preserve themselves."[28] The visitor, a pragmatic businessman, was probably unaware of, and certainly unconcerned with, the vision for a model society still being implemented by the proprietors. Instead, he saw a strategically situated colony with enormous trade potential. After elaborating on the colony's trade potential, he focused on the strategic value of the capital:

Charles Town bay is the safest port for all vessels coming thro' the gulf of Florida in distress, bound from the West Indies to the northern plantations; if they miss this place they may perish at sea for want of relief, and having beat upon the coast of New England, New York, or Virginia by a northwest wind in the winter, be forced to go to Barbados if they miss this bay, where no wind will damage them and all things to be had necessary to refit them.[29]

The writer was correct in his assessment of Carolina's potential if populated with gentry farmers and merchants rather than land-acquiring nobility. The pattern created by the proprietors, however, would remain substantially in place, and the gentry would merely displace the nobility as owners of vast tracts of land and lords of commerce. In doing so, civic virtue would no longer be an accompaniment to the acquisition or maintenance of wealth.

The proprietors had no reservations about establishing a society built upon the labor of slaves and serfs. Arguably, no objection to slavery and serfdom had ever been articulated to that point in human history. Man's natural state of being was hierarchical, as far as they were concerned, and some concept of the Great Chain of Being was a fundamental assumption. An articulation of human rights that envisioned an alternative to the class pyramid would await the impending Age of Enlightenment. What the proprietors and their resident philosopher, John Locke, believed when they adopted the Fundamental Constitutions was that wisdom and compassion created a decent life for people in all strata of society.[30]

The proprietors continued to govern Carolina in the eighteenth century, although their authority was slipping and they faced frequent petitions from colonists unhappy with their regime. In 1704, the Carolina parliament passed an exclusion act limiting the rights of dissenters and making the Church of England the state church. The proprietors approved the act over the objections of Ashley Cooper's grandson, Maurice Ashley. Dissenters in the province sent representatives to England to call attention to the injustice. The prolific writer Daniel Defoe (best known today as the author of *Robinson Crusoe*) was retained to write a tract opposing the action.[31]

Defoe presented the tract, entitled "Party-Tyranny," to parliament in 1705. His presentation covered the origin and history of the colony, arguing that its original principles were never properly implemented: "I am certain of this, they handed the infant government into the world without leading-strings, and turned it loose before it could stand alone; by which means, like young Romulus, it has got a wolf to its nurse, and is like to be bred up a monster."[32]

The original proprietors were negligent in implementing their creation, Defoe maintained, but the present proprietors cared only about personal gain and in pursuing self-interest and had deprived colonists of their fundamental rights as Englishmen. They are, he wrote,

> like a landlord to his tenants, they have their eyes upon the rent; their concern, if any, is not of affection, but of interest; they are step fathers and strangers to the government, and they have shown it; for their ears have been stopped, and shut to the complaints of their oppressed people; they govern them as sub-tyrants, and connive at their tyrannies because they are not furnished with the affection of love to the people they govern.[33]

The proprietors and officials in Carolina eventually got the message and amended the legislation governing church and state relations.

Another injustice facing the proprietors was Indian relations. Carolina Indian traders "were a particularly odious lot," in the words of one historian, who "habitually swindled and debauched the Indians with whom they traded." They offered credit to the Indians, thereby inducing them to run up debt they could never pay off. The trade was supported by government officials, making it difficult for the proprietors to monitor and regulate. Others, including William Bull, who would have a major role in the later royal government, saw the trade as unethical and dangerous, and to the extent they could, the proprietors adopted more progressive policies toward Indians. Bull had more of an appreciation of the Fundamental Constitutions, as his father had earlier served as deputy to the 3rd Earl of Shaftesbury.[34]

As the political philosophy of the original proprietors faded into history, oversight by their heirs became increasingly lax. While there were many settlers attracted by a guarantee of religious freedom and a fair and wise government, many other settlers were adventurers and opportunists who had no interest in the higher rationale behind the constitutions and regulations of the proprietors. Slavery became a particularly sensitive matter. In the words of historians George Rogers and James Taylor, "Greed overcame the moral scruples that some settlers surely had about owning slaves."

African slaves, first brought from Barbados and later directly from Africa, were found to withstand the summer heat and tropical diseases better than Native Americans. When rice cultivation was perfected and became a profitable export in the 1690s, many more slaves were needed. The slave trade accelerated, and by 1708 the number of enslaved people exceeded the number of free people in the province. The black population of South Carolina would increase to double that of whites in the following decades and remain larger for 200 years, until the 1920s, requiring increasingly repressive laws to prevent rebellion.[35]

The Barbadians were the first to bring African slaves to Carolina, and they emerged as the first organized group to oppose proprietor regulations. Many of them settled on Goose Creek, a tributary of the Cooper River. These Goose Creek men, as they were known, became wealthy from the slave trade and other dubious ventures, including trading with pirates. The less oversight by the proprietors, the better, as far as they were concerned, and to justify their opposition to regulations, they promoted an image of themselves as defenders of provincial liberty.[36]

Another divisive issue arose with increased settlement in the north, which had little connection with the more settled south in and around Charles Town. In 1710, the proprietors divided the province into North Carolina and South Carolina, each with its own governor. Such concessions to local authority prolonged their government, but its demise was inevitable.

Colonists became organized and toughened, with new leaders emerging from the challenges of life on the nation's frontier, many of them Goose Creek men. In 1702, Governor James Moore led an attack on their adversaries at St. Augustine, burning the town by the castle. In 1704, Moore led another expedition into Florida, attacking Native Americans allied with the Spanish. In 1706, new leaders Governor Nathaniel Johnson and Colonel William Rhett repulsed an attack on Charles Town by Spanish and French forces. In 1711, Colonel John Barnwell led an attack on the Tuscarora people in North Carolina, after which he became known as Tuscarora Jack. Colonel Moore, the former governor, led another attack on the Tuscarora, decisively defeating them in 1713. The Yemassee War of 1715 became a mortal challenge to the province when several native nations rose against the province and killed more than 100 colonists at Port Royal; reinforcements from North Carolina and bringing slaves into the battle were required to defeat the insurrection.[37]

The threat posed by pirates was also repulsed, although some colonists, including Goose Creek men, preferred to keep them around as trading partners. Pirates, including Edward Thatch (also spelled Teach), or Blackbeard, and Stede Bonnet, operated with impunity along the coast until 1718, when Blackbeard was captured and killed by the Royal Navy and Bonnet was captured by Rhett and executed.[38]

Table 4. Timeline of the Founding of Carolina

1660	The Restoration; Charles II restored to the monarchy
1661	Ashley Cooper becomes Chancellor of the Exchequer
1662	Charles II issues the Declaration of Indulgence for religious tolerance, a measure supported by Ashley Cooper
1663	Charles II grants charter for the Province of Carolina
1665	Carolina charter amended to expand the colony; the Great Plague strikes London
1666	September—The Great Plague ends and the Great Fire destroys much of London; October—Ashley Cooper and Locke meet at Oxford
1667	Ashley Cooper becomes the second A in the CABAL ministry
1669	March 1—adoption of the Fundamental Constitutions; July 26—William Sayle appointed first governor; Joseph West appointed commander in chief of the fleet to Barbados; August—first expedition to Carolina by the proprietors
1670	Charles Town founded on the Ashley River
1672	Charles II issues the Royal Declaration of Indulgence expanding religious tolerance, a measure supported by Ashley Cooper; Ashley Cooper made the Earl of Shaftesbury and becomes Lord Chancellor of England
1691	New laws passed amending the Fundamental Constitutions
1692	Craven and Colleton counties created and new planning regulations issued for settlement

During this period of instability and war, the proprietors were of little help to the province. As Defoe had said years before, they simply had "their eyes upon the rent." The proprietors' secretary during the last decade of their administration, Richard Shelton, effectively ran the colony as the proprietors became less engaged. Shelton had little authority over those in the province and concentrated on the business interests of the proprietors rather than political philosophy or governance.[39]

In 1719, whites in the colony were sufficiently organized, confident, and battle tested to successfully rebel against the proprietors. In December of that year, they reorganized the assembly and became self-governing (see Table 4). The following year, with the black population twice that of whites, the new assembly authorized watchmen to detain blacks on sight, a measure that would become standard practice. In 1740, the colony erected a legal framework for regulating the lives of slaves that would remain in effect until the Civil War.[40]

Influence of the Grand Model on Later Settlement

By 1700, three decades after going into effect, the Fundamental Constitutions and instructions were largely abandoned. The new generation of proprietors was not interested in creating a model colony, and the colonists were certainly not interested in political philosophy. The parties on both sides of the Atlantic were focused on practical matters, not on a society that would endure for centuries. The utopian vision of the original proprietors reflected in article 79 of the constitutions, requiring refreshment of original principles through the expiration of laws that had been on the books for a century, had become an anachronism of the seventeenth century. The Age of Enlightenment was about to usher in an age of humanism in which neither Gothic society nor slave society had a place.

While the utopian Gothic-republican society planned and put in motion under the constitutions was, not surprising in retrospect, never fully implemented, it was also never entirely dissolved. It left an imprint that settlers in the province sought to change to their advantage rather than to radically alter. As a consequence, the society envisioned by the proprietors was merely replaced by a new class pyramid with wealthy slaveholders and merchants occupying the pinnacle. The permanent underclass of slaves grew larger, and the lower class of white servants and laborers remained disenfranchised. It was a social structure linked to an increasingly prosperous plantation economy, which would evolve into a distinct political culture, one that would become a model for the southeastern region. Ashley Cooper's Gothic utopia thus survived to become one of the competing traditions in American society. Other traditions, influenced by the Enlightenment, would take America down a more progressive path leading to urbanization, industrialization, and education and upward mobility for the masses.

CHAPTER THREE

The Grand Model and
Frontier Reality

Anthony Ashley Cooper, or Shaftesbury, as he is better known to history, lived to see the implementation of his plan for the Province of Carolina. However, estranged from the king and distracted by politics, he was increasingly kept from being as deeply involved in the project as he might have preferred. By 1682, twelve years after the founding of Carolina, his political situation had become so precarious that he fled to Holland, where he died in exile. A few months later, when the Rye House Plot was discovered, John Locke also went into exile. The political distraction and eventual departure from England prevented Ashley Cooper and Locke from supervising the course of events in Carolina at a critical time. Locke's fortunes improved dramatically in 1688 when he returned to England with William and Mary during the Glorious Revolution, and his subsequent influence on the colony was present but subtle.

Most of the productive work crafting the implementing regulations for the settlement of Carolina occurred during the early 1670s and again in the early 1680s. The first period corresponded with the initiation of settlement and the peak of Ashley Cooper's influence in government. It was during this first period that most of the town and regional planning standards were issued. Afterward, Locke spent a few years in France, but he returned to England and resumed his involvement with the Lords Proprietors in 1679. It was during this second period that the site of the provincial capital, Charles Town, was selected and additional design standards were issued for the towns of Carolina. The plan for regional development was reiterated to settlers at this time and once again framed within the original principles of the Fundamental Constitutions.

The argument made earlier that Ashley Cooper and Locke were applying the political theories of James Harrington, author of *The Commonwealth of Oceana*, is supported not only by the agrarian framework found in the Fundamental Constitutions, but also through instructions issued in 1671 and in a set of more detailed "agrarian laws" issued by the Lords Proprietors in 1672. The laws specified how, where, and to whom land would be allocated and how it would be settled. The resulting distribution of land among social classes was carefully designed to achieve a durable class structure and support balanced government.[1]

The first set of detailed instructions for the layout of towns is found in a letter dated May 1, 1671, and sent to the governor and council of Ashley River. The instructions contained a "model," or plan, that required streets to be oriented to the cardinal points of the compass in a grid. The second set of instructions containing the agrarian laws, reinforcing the first, was sent to the governor and council once they had settled upon the new site, at the peninsula formed by the mouths of the Ashley and Cooper rivers. Dated June 21, 1672, the new instructions were predicated on "a right and equal distribution of land" taken up in an "orderly" manner. Charles Town as well as other towns established in the colony were "to be laid out into large, straight, and regular streets, and sufficient room left for a wharf if it be upon a navigable river." Only one port town was permitted on any navigable river, and it was to be the primary settlement for that region. The plan envisioned that each county in the province would be associated with a navigable river, and its principal settlement would be a port town on that river. (Details of the town planning instructions and agrarian laws are taken up in the "Urban Design" section of this chapter.)

Influences on the Grand Model

The Great Plague of 1665–66 and the Great Fire of London in 1666, as noted earlier, strongly influenced development of the Grand Model. The former created an awareness of the need for health considerations in siting and designing towns. The latter led to intensive discussions of urban design in rebuilding London in a safer, more economically vibrant, manner and with greater attention to aesthetics. Those discussions coincided with the period when Ashley Cooper was contemplating the design of towns in Carolina, soon thereafter to be joined in the effort by Locke.

Charles II encouraged designers to submit proposals for a master plan for rebuilding London, and many were received. Several notable designers submitted ambitious and creative plans, including Robert Hooke, curator of experiments at the Royal Society; Christopher Wren, scientist, mathematician, and architect; John Evelyn, writer, horticulturalist, and landscape designer; and Richard Newcourt, cartographer. Their designs ranged from Evelyn's baroque plan with grand avenues to euclidean plans with a regular grid and public squares. Charles, however, found that the urgency of rebuilding and restoring the economy would have to take precedence over the more elaborate plans, no matter how inspired.

Christopher Wren's plan was the most practical, and he was commissioned as the designer for rebuilding London. City authorities attempted to inventory land and structures and develop a plan of compensation for redesigning the city, but massive alterations in the fabric of the city proved logistically, politically, and legally impractical even under Wren's design. Those who remained in the city were in survival mode, and those who had left were anxious to return, and their labor was needed. Without an inventory and compensation plan, none of the grand squares and avenues could be built. The existing street network was left in place, and the rebuilding effort concentrated on improvements to environmental health and fire safety. Wood structures were prohibited, obstructions to traffic and ones that blocked access to the river were removed, and, where feasible, streets were widened. Wren concentrated on designing and rebuilding the city's churches, including the famous St. Paul's Cathedral, seat of the bishop of London.

Ashley Cooper and Locke met at Oxford in October 1666, just a month after the fire. As a minister of Charles's court, Ashley Cooper would have been fully informed of plans to rebuild, and he probably shared such information with Locke. Rebuilding plans were submitted at the time Locke became an aide and confidant to Ashley Cooper, thus making it likely they reviewed the various plans for rebuilding the city as they became available. Such a review would have occurred almost simultaneously with planning for Carolina.

Health and safety concerns arising from the catastrophes included the need to allow for circulation of fresh air and to create firebreaks. Designers responded by providing more green space and wider streets. Building on higher ground to avoid unhealthful marshes was also given more attention. Plague and fire spread from close contact, therefore deconcentration was a primary concern. This concern was perpetuated in colonial charters and is reflected even today in America, where state and local planning and zoning laws often contain vestigial language about the unhealthful effects of "over-crowding" in high density "slums."

Wide streets, a continuous street network, and focal points for interaction were deemed essential for commerce and civic order as well as a healthful environment. The plan submitted by Richard Newcourt (1610–79), although not implemented, appears to have left an impression on those who reviewed it. It might well have become the preferred plan, but it was set aside because the urgency of restoring London required more expedient measures. As seen in Figure 8, the plan created a high degree of connectivity and civic space. Its order and harmony reflected the new science of the Royal Society, presaging the Newtonian theme of order and harmony central to the British Enlightenment (lyrically presented in the writings of Ashley Cooper's grandson, the 3rd Earl).

The connection between the Newcourt plan and the design of towns in Carolina is circumstantial but compelling. The resemblance has led authorities on town planning to cite it as a likely source for later designs. John Reps, an authority on the history of town planning, has also seen its influence in the famous plans for Philadelphia (1683) and Savannah (1733).[2]

It is unlikely that Locke knew much about ancient town planning or Renaissance proposals for the ideal city, but some of that knowledge probably found its way to him through designers such as Wren, Evelyn, and Newcourt. Design concepts from classical antiquity, such as Roman city planning, would not be fully appreciated in England until the Enlightenment. In drafting planning guidelines for Carolina, Locke may have drawn ideas about urban design from the more famous classical figures. Aristotle in *Politics* identifies Hippodamus (498–408 B.C.) as having "invented the art of planning cities." The regular street grids found in Piraeus and Militus were designed by the Greek planner. Vitruvius (c. 75–25 B.C.), the transformative Greco-Roman architect and town planner, was probably unknown to Ashley Cooper and Locke, but they would have been familiar with urban grids laid out by the Roman army. The Roman army *castra*, or encampments, were designed with two main arteries, the *cardus maximus* and the *decamanus maximus*, which met at a central civic feature. The design included a street grid that paralleled those principal streets.[3]

Locke's reading of Aristotle's *Politics* (and perhaps Ashley Cooper's as well) would have readily led him from the discussion of land distribution to town planning. Aristotle examined the proposition that "the equalization of property is one of the things that tend to prevent the citizens from quarreling" and then immediately took up the discussion of Hippodamus and city planning. Locke and Ashley Cooper would have understood this discussion as foundational to their application of Harrington's political philosophy.[4]

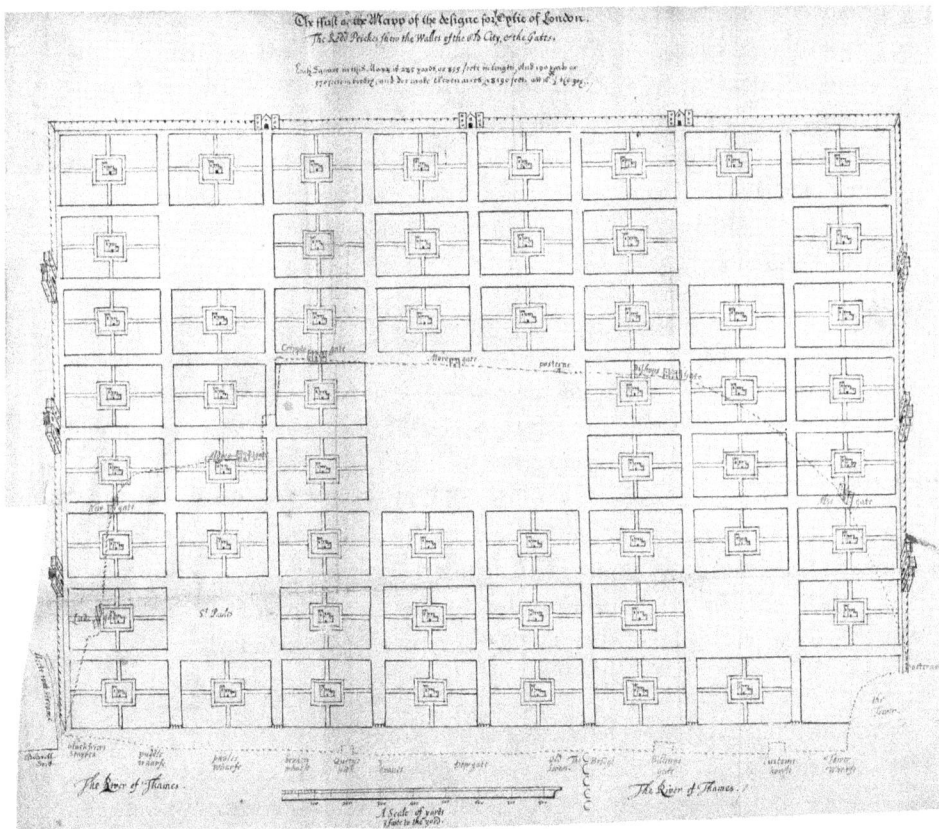

Figure 8. Newcourt Plan of London. This plan by Richard Newcourt
was one of several designs proposed for rebuilding London after the Great Fire
of 1666. A faint dashed line shows the location of the city's ancient wall.
Courtesy of London Metropolitan Archives, City of London.

Whatever the sources, Ashley Cooper and Locke came up with a plan for
Carolina towns that was classically geometric. Yet it was also subdivided much
like the Newcourt plan to create rectangular neighborhood units within the
town grid. Their objectives establishing a network of planned towns were to
strengthen defenses, facilitate commerce, and promote civic responsibility
within the social hierarchy defined in the Fundamental Constitutions.

Planning Principles for Towns and Regions

The instructions and agrarian laws issued by the Lords Proprietors in 1671
and 1672 gave precise direction to the colonists on the Ashley River on how

to lay out the towns and counties of the province. The Lords Proprietors made it very clear that the instructions were a logical extension of the Fundamental Constitutions and were to be treated as such. Towns throughout the province were to be situated on rivers. Initially, since the first counties were to be located on the coast, the first towns were to be settled near the mouths of the rivers, where those first counties were established.

The influence of Harrington's agrarian political philosophy can be seen in the preamble to the laws:[5]

> Since the whole foundation of the settlement is founded upon a right and equal distribution of land, and the orderly taking of it up is of great moment to the welfare of the province. And though the regulation of this need not be perpetual, yet since all the concernment thereof will not cease as soon as the government comes to be administered according to the form established in the Fundamental Constitutions, that the distribution and allotment of land may be with all fairness and equality, and that the conveniency of all degrees may be as much as is possible in their due proportion provided for, we, the Lords Proprietors of Carolina have agreed upon these following temporary agrarian laws.

Harrington's *Oceana*, written twenty-five years earlier, was a model for republican government based on balanced land allocation, and it repeated the prescription of agrarian equality over and over, as in this passage: "Where there is equality of estates, there must be equality of power, and where there is equality of power, there can be no monarchy." Before the emergence of a powerful urban gentry, created by mercantile trade and accelerated by the Industrial Revolution, land was the primary source of wealth and power. The plan for Carolina was the implementation of *Oceana*, with a great deal of new thinking by Ashley Cooper and Locke.[6]

Before digging deeper into Locke's urban design, it should be noted that Harrington's philosophy continued to be a direct influence on republican political philosophy beyond the seventeenth century. Philosophy preceded design, as it should (but often does not). The Gothic interpretation of Harrington by Ashley Cooper and Locke retained features of England's historical manors and towns in the design of Carolina. Harrington's agrarian commonwealth remained central to later planners, notably James Oglethorpe, Gothic republicanism gave way to Enlightenment ideals, and designs changed accordingly. Oglethorpe's 1733 design for Georgia towns envisioned a much flatter social pyramid than the one constructed for Carolina. Oglethorpe's reinterpretation was reflective of, and a step in the progression of, political thought that led to the American and

French revolutions, the formation of modern democratic republics, and new ideas about cities and how they relate to their hinterlands.[7]

Ashley Cooper and Locke, however ancestral they were at this point to modern republican principles, remained immersed in the Gothic paradigm, a political model that resembled feudalism more than democracy. The people at the top of the class pyramid were an enlightened class of nobility that would maintain order in society, practice noblesse oblige, respect the principle of class reciprocity, and generate wealth and progress in the nation. Today they might consider themselves the "1 percent" or the "job creators." As such, it was not strange that the nobility would assume responsibility for establishing the form of government, the settlement patterns, and the social standing of the colonists.

The Regional Development Plan

Before any settlement could take place, the surveyor was to identify a navigable river as an axis of orientation for a county. That principal axis was to be placed within a north-south, east-west grid, to the extent possible, beginning at the mouth of the river. The 12,000-acre grid units, or "squares," were to be laid out such that the first two on the right-hand side entering the river were baronies, followed by three colonies that "belong to the people." The next two were to be signiories belonging to Lords Proprietors, and the next three were to be colonies. After that, the two-three-two-three pattern continued, until a county of forty squares was completed.[8]

On the left-hand side of the river, the pattern began with three colonies, followed by two signiories, three colonies again, and two baronies. The pattern intentionally placed colonies opposite signiories and baronies along the river, giving the nobility oversight of the people and access to their services.[9]

The ten squares on either side of the river near its mouth constituted a nucleus for the further development of the county. The additional thirty squares would be allocated adjacent to those already in place to maintain a compact and orderly settlement process. Where the topography made it impossible to precisely align the squares, the surveyor, at the direction of the grand council, was to allocate the land as close as possible to the principles set forth in the Fundamental Constitutions, instructions, and temporary laws of the Lords Proprietors. The pattern, for example, should continue to be allocated in a one-one-three ratio, or one-fifth of the land to signiories, one-fifth to baronies, and three-fifths to colonies "for the people."[10]

In keeping with the intent to maintain a compact, efficient growth pattern, criteria were set out to ensure that each square was properly settled before new squares were allocated. Thus, "no proprietor shall choose a second signiory till he hath an hundred inhabitants upon his own particular signiory," and the same applied to the landgraves and caciques. Thus a member of the nobility acquiring a fourth square would need to have settled three previous squares in a compact manner with at least 100 people settled on each one to work the land.[11]

Ashley Cooper and Locke envisioned the initial settlement of twelve contiguous counties in what might be called, in modern terms, a regional development plan. Each county would contain an allocation of signiories, baronies, and colonies in the prescribed one-one-three ratio. Following the same principle of compact growth applied within counties, new counties would be formed "as closely and compactly together" as possible. Land speculation, which might hinder orderly growth, was prohibited by requiring the landgraves, caciques, and lords of manors to substantially settle on their land within seven years with a minimum of thirty inhabitants.[12]

Since the province would be settled in groups of twelve counties at a time, twelve landgraves only would be created, beginning with each phase of settlement in the ratio of one landgrave per county set out in the Fundamental Constitutions. Similarly, there would be twenty-four caciques created for each group of twelve counties, or two per county. The remaining baronies would be allocated to freeholders, some of whom would be lords of manors or the gentry of the province (as distinct from the hereditary nobility). Since each proprietor would own a signiory in each county, each group of twelve counties would result in ninety-six signiories. And since each county would contain twenty-four colonies, a settled block of twelve counties would contain 288 colonies. With the total number of squares fixed at forty per county and 480 for the region, and given the minimum population of 100 persons per square (the number required in a square before the next could be allocated), the total population for a twelve-county region would be at least 48,000.

When it became time for a new region to be settled in the interior of the province, without access to navigable rivers, "the forty squares constituting a county, shall be as closely and compactly together as may be, and be marked an appropriated eight of them for signiories, eight of them for baronies, and the remaining twenty-four for colonies by the direction of the grand council." Locke's repetition made it clear that the pattern was to hold throughout the province, even where topography varied considerably from that of the initial settled regions.[13]

Ashley Cooper and Locke envisioned the grid for the province overlaying existing Native American settlements. Thus any "square of 12,000 acres wherein any Indian town stands, and the square next to it are to be left untaken up and unplanted on for the use of the Indians." Furthermore, "No Indian upon any occasion or pretense whatsoever shall be made a slave, or without his own consent carried out of Carolina."[14]

The Lords Proprietors were self-taxed to finance the settlement of new counties, and once settled, the other hereditary nobility and the freeholders were to be taxed to maintain the government and finance the infrastructure of the province. Fines were levied upon those members of the hereditary nobility who took possession of their 12,000-acre square but failed to populate and improve it. The threat of a fine would prevent gaps from appearing in the settlement that would reduce the spatial efficiency of the overall development pattern.[15]

Revenue for the Lords Proprietors was determined by article 115 of the Fundamental Constitutions, which would not take effect until they were satisfied that their initial investment was satisfactorily reimbursed. The article provided that "revenues and profits belonging to the Lords Proprietors," accrued from rents as well as business profits, would "be divided into ten parts, whereof the palatine shall have three, and each proprietor one." In other words, they were free during this time to extract what the market would bear and the people would tolerate to get their investment back.[16]

The governor and council might find during their implementation that the agrarian laws governing the settlement required modification. Locke made it clear that they could recommend such changes, but the Lords Proprietors reserved the right to approve any such amendments. In actual practice, however, provincial administrators laid out and granted land according to the dictates of topography rather than those of the Grand Model.[17]

The first signiory in the colony was granted to Ashley Cooper in 1675. It was located on the south side of the Ashley River near Charles Town. The plat of the tract compiled by attorney and historian Henry A. M. Smith in the early twentieth century shows irregular boundaries rather than the prescribed squares. Smith's 1906 reconstruction was based on a 1716 survey, with the addition of interior subdivisions to 1780. The Colleton tracts, by contrast, were surveyed as squares. Later subdivisions into working plantations are intact today as private preserves and exclusive communities.

The Ashley Cooper tract passed to Shaftesbury's son, the 2nd Earl, and then the 3rd Earl, and then his brother, Maurice Ashley, remaining in the family until 1717. Afterward it was subdivided into tracts ranging from 300 to 3,000 acres and later subdivided further for towns and smaller farms while retaining large tracts for plantations. Ashley Cooper obtained written title for the land from the Native Americans claiming rights to it, thus acting in a manner consistent with the Lords Proprietors' stated desire to maintain honorable relations with indigenous people, even though the family held title to the land from the king of England. The land was purchased in exchange for "a valuable parcel of cloth, beads and other goods and manufactures."[18]

The site of the Ashley Cooper signiory on the upper Ashley River, known as St. Giles Kussoe, is currently being excavated by an archaeological team assembled by the Historic Charleston Foundation. Archaeologists and historians previously discovered the foundation of one of the oldest brick structures in the region. The original settlement is described by the archaeological team as "a fortified plantation and Native American trading outpost, actively used for just a decade, 1675–1685." The team has recovered and analyzed more than 5,000 artifacts since 2011.[19]

A latter day "Domesday Book" of proprietary land grants and later subdivisions and assemblies of land was prepared by Henry Smith in the early twentieth century, and in 1988 it was republished as a three-volume set by the South Carolina Historical Society. The first volume richly documents the history of sixteen signiories and baronies, showing original boundaries and subsequent alterations of fourteen. One of the earliest 12,000-acre tracts was granted to Lord Proprietor Sir John Colleton, who died before receiving his grant; two tracts were later allocated to his sons. The Colletons were Barbadians, the constituent group of early settlers who would wield the most influence in shaping politics, class structure, and land use. The signiories ware further subdivided, but Smith's maps show that the remaining tracts were sufficiently large to support the system of slavery to which they had become accustomed in Barbados.[20]

John Colleton's eldest son, Peter, was granted a signiory, which became known as Fairlawn Barony, in 1678; it was situated on the west side of the western branch of the Cooper River. The boundaries shown by Smith, which are closer to the prescribed square, are based on a map from 1789 and other "old maps and deeds." The northern boundary is shown as 369 chains, or 24,354 feet, which if squared would equate to 13,616 acres. With the intruding river bend, a total area of 12,000 acres appears accurate.[21]

The Fairlawn tract remained in the family, members of which were the only descendants of the original Lords Proprietors to live in the province. Large portions of the Colleton tract were conveyed to Thomas Broughton in 1708 and 1712, becoming Mulberry Plantation, which remained in the Broughton family for nearly two centuries. At least two other notable plantations, Epsom and Exeter plantations, were also subdivided from the tract.[22]

Peter Colleton's brothers, James and Thomas, were also granted 12,000-acre tracts and made landgraves. Thomas Colleton's tract, named Cypress

Barony, was shown on an early survey as measuring 358 chains, which would equate to 12,816 acres if the tract was square. The barony was given an early exception to be divided into thirds. Later subdivisions created working rice plantations. Large tracts remain in private ownership today, including the well-known and picturesque Mulberry Plantation. Thomas's son, Peter (after his uncle), inherited the estate in 1692 and sold it to Barbadians in 1707. According to Smith, the property came with "one dwelling house, one kitchen, one barn and one dairy and milk-house . . . , six negro men one negro boy about 17 years of age five negro women two suckling young children one negro girl eight hundred head of cattle great & small two teams of oxen two carts one plough and harrow and five new saddles."[23]

James Colleton's tract, named Wadboo Barony, was located on the upper Cooper River. Whereas Thomas and son Peter did not settle in the province, James took possession of his property and became active in Carolina politics. Wadboo Barony became a productive cotton plantation and is now an exclusive gated community.[24]

The allocation of 12,000-acre tracts throughout the Lowcountry by the Lords Proprietors established a land-use pattern that supported a rigid social hierarchy. Those original tracts were frequently subdivided into large tracts for family members, political allies, and other members of the powerful gentry, thus perpetuating an agrarian economy that depended increasingly on slave labor. The Goose Creek men at the center of this agrarian economy were the slave merchants and plantation elite of Barbados. These "ruthless rogues" permeated the social and spatial patterns established by the Lords Proprietors, seizing political power as they did so. As Locke observed at the time, "The Barbadians endeavor to rule all." They succeeded not only in acquiring power during the proprietary period, but in shaping the political future of South Carolina. Their "cultural stamp" (reflected in Figure 9a-b) left a lasting impression, one that overwhelmed Georgia's resistance to slavery in the mid-1700s and later fanned out across the South.[25]

Those who embraced slavery and other conditions set by the Goose Creek men, including supremacy of the Anglican Church, prospered in Carolina. Puritans, Quakers, and other nonconformists who settled in the colony were among those who left it over the issues of slavery and religious intolerance. Some, of course, altered their standards to remain and prosper in the region. Revolutionary War hero Nathanael Greene, a Quaker, "became not only a slave owner, but a slave purchaser, a characteristic which gave no little umbrage to his quondam [former] friends the Quakers," according to Greene's biographer, William Johnson.[26]

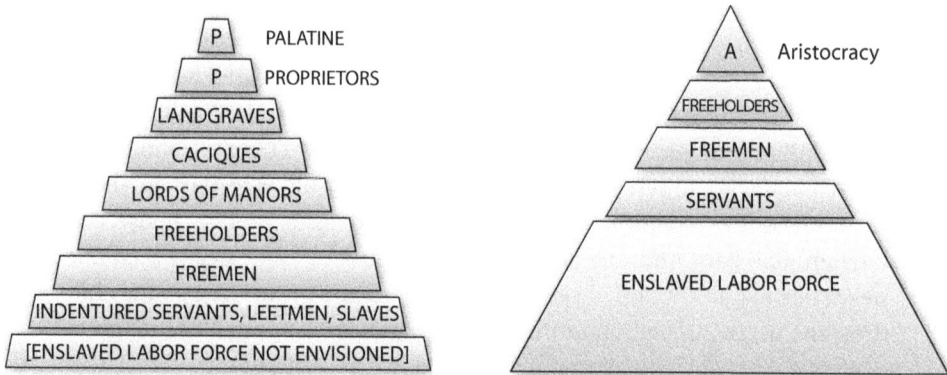

Figure 9. The Planned and Emergent Class Pyramids.
(a) The Carolina Grand Model. The model's Gothic class structure was
essentially Aristotelian. Each class was expected to have reciprocal benefits
from the order and security provided by the system. Slavery was not initially
envisioned as the primary source of labor but became so after West Indian plantation
owners settled in the colony. Illustration by Teri Norris. (b) The Carolina Caste
System. The plantation elite, a self-styled aristocracy, replaced the proprietors at
the top of the pyramid. They retained the titles of landgrave and cacique long
after the Lords Proprietors relinquished their claim to the colony. The idea
of a master race made up of the upper tiers evolved to secure total
control of the black labor force. Illustration by Teri Norris.

Urban Design

Locke's plan for towns anticipated that people would live in planned areas
situated strategically throughout the province. Thus, informal settlements
that could mushroom into unplanned towns were not permitted. Towns
were "to be laid out into large, straight and regular streets, and sufficient
room left for a wharf if it be upon a navigable river." There would be only
one town on any navigable river for the first thirty years of settlement. At
least one town would be reserved for the freeholders in each colony, where
the population density would be greatest. Like all other towns, those in
the colonies would have street grids that were "straight, broad and regular," and the task of laying them out would be performed by the surveyor
of the province. Aside from those constraints, the freeholders of a colony
were authorized to choose the location of any other towns.[27]

To promote interest in Carolina and accelerate settlement, the Lords
Proprietors offered to make a freeholder a landgrave if he brought 600 settlers to the colony within a year. If he brought over 900, he would have the
right to nominate a cacique, and if he brought 1,200, he would have the right

to nominate two caciques. All freeholders were required to bring supplies for a year. Therefore those bringing others with them had the burden of ensuring that a large store of supplies was transported to Carolina with their people.[28]

The location of the capital city for Carolina was to be determined by the Lords Proprietors during the early stages of settlement. A special precinct would be identified for the capital, and a special plan would be adopted for the surrounding area, where eight signiories would be laid out adjacent to the town, one for each of the Lords Proprietors.[29]

The surveyor was ordered to map the county into the grid of 12,000-acre squares for land allocation as set forth in the Fundamental Constitutions. The grid was to be oriented to the cardinal compass points (north, south, east, and west). During the process of laying out lots, the deputies and the surveyor were advised to "reserve convenient high ways from the colony town to the plantations . . . beyond it, and from one colony town to another."[30]

Locke listed twenty articles with the Lords Proprietors' instructions of May 1, 1671, and he attached a plan or "model" for the capital and future towns. The streets were to be formed in a uniform linear grid, and encroachment into street rights-of-way was specifically prohibited. Principal streets were to be 80 feet in width, with a "back street" or alley of 40 feet. Secondary streets were to be 60 feet, with back streets of 30 feet. The street grid would form "squares" (blocks) of 600 feet on each side.[31]

Residents were to build "their houses fronting to those streets so laid out and take so many foot as in the front of their building toward the street in breadth, and so far backward toward the next street behind, in length as shall be convenient for outlet, belonging to the said house, that so when hereafter the town shall come to be built with good houses, the streets also may be large, convenient and regular." In towns built on existing or potentially navigable rivers, "nobody shall build a house within eighty feet of the low water mark, but it shall constantly be left for a wharf for the public use of the town." The Lords Proprietors encouraged them, however, to locate "as far up in the country as may be to avoid the ill air of the lowlands near the sea, which may endanger their health at their first coming."[32]

Locke's plan provided for a generous common of 200 acres. He specified that it would be used initially, as the town grew, to plant kitchen gardens. Once produce was available from outlying farms, the common would be used for raising cattle. After twenty-one years, the use of the common would be determined by the residents, which might be continued use as pasture or "exercise of the people, enlargement, or any other conveniences of the said town as occasion shall require."

Table 5. Grand Model Planning and Development Specifications

POLICY FRAMEWORK

A. Consistency. Development should be consistent with the Fundamental Constitutions.
B. Concurrence. Development should be phased for effective administration and infrastructure.
C. Compactness. Development should be compact to promote business efficiency and public safety.

PROVINCIAL STRUCTURE

A. Primary planning and development units.
B. Counties of 750,000-square-mile area.
C. Tracts ("squares"); forty per county.
D. Capital city: to be sited on a navigable river within a colony.
E. Towns: sited within colonies; location of home lots for colonists.
F. Land grants: initial grants of 150 acres per free person, plus additional 100 acres per servant.
G. Infrastructure: waterfront preserved for access and wharfing; farm-to-town roads to be provided by proprietary government.

REGIONAL PLAN

A. Location of counties: Situated on the right and left sides of navigable rivers as viewed from sea.
B. Types of tracts: colony (C), signiory (S), barony (B)
C. Size of tracts: 12,000 acres
D. Number of tracts per county: C = 24; S = 8; B = 8
E. Siting Pattern for Tracts, from river bank inland:
    a. left river bank: C-C-C-S-S-C-C-C-B-B
    b. right river bank: B-B-C-C-C-S-S-C-C-C
F. Agrarian balance: C, hereditary nobility, 96,000 acres; B, raised nobility, 96,000 acres; C, "the people," 288,000 acres.

URBAN DESIGN

A. Location of towns. To be sited on navigable rivers where there is healthful upland.
B. Grid layout. Square blocks with "large, straight, and regular streets."
C. Block size. 600 feet per side.
D. Street specifications. Primary: 80 feet, back lanes 40 feet; Secondary: 60 feet, back lanes 30 feet.
E. Lot size. 75 feet by 280 feet; 60 feet by 285 feet. Proprietors: 5-acre town lots.
F. House size. Minimum: 16 feet by 30 feet, 2 stories.
G. River access and buffer. Riverfront lots limited to 1:5 ratio, frontage to depth; 80 foot public access and infrastructure buffer.

Notes: Policy framework terminology draws from Dr. John M. DeGrove's growth-management model adopted by the state of Florida in the 1970s and 1980s. Most of the detail in the table was derived from Ashley Cooper et al., "Instructions," July 27, 1669; Ashley Cooper et al., "Carolina Instructions," May 1, 1671; and Ashley Cooper et al., "Agrarian Laws," June 21, 1672. A number of other documents reemphasize consistency, concurrence, and compactness.

The surveyor was instructed to create a "home lot" for each freeholder in a town and an "out lot" in a place of his choosing outside the planned area of the town. The total allocation of land should not exceed 5 percent of the freeholders' "whole right." Thus, if he held an agrarian land grant of 100 acres, his home lot and out lot combined could not exceed 5 acres.[33]

Frontage on rivers was allocated judiciously to preserve access for all. Frontage was thus limited to one-fiftieth of a freeholder's lot length. The restriction was also applied to rivers that were "capable of being made navigable." These various planning development principles and standards sent to the colonists by Locke are summarized in Table 5.[34]

Instructions from the Lords Proprietors issued for recruitment of people from Ireland provide a glimpse as to how they imagined the settlement of the province progressing. The instruction dated August 31, 1672, stated that for a period of one year, freemen from Ireland would be allocated 100 acres of freehold in one of the colonies. They would be allocated an additional 100 acres for each male servant over the age of sixteen, and 70 acres for each male servant under age sixteen or each female servant. Once a servant fulfilled the term of service, he would be entitled to an allocation of seventy acres, thus becoming freeholders of the province. Once again, the plan for a compact and efficient development pattern is evident in the instructions. For "better settlement," freeholders were required to locate within towns "and not build their houses straglingly from one another, such solitary buildings be uncapable of that benefit of trade, the comfort of society and mutual assistance, which men dwelling together in towns are capable of giving one another."[35]

Instructions dated May 1674 provided to Andrew Percivall, apparently a newly created landgrave, referred to 50-acre land allocations for settlers under his leadership. The 50-acre total consisted of "five acres for a house and garden lot, ten acres in the common cow pasture, and thirty-five in a piece beyond the common." When they were able to cultivate it, they were also entitled to a 300-acre farm lot.[36]

By 1680, the Lords Proprietors had determined that the site for the principal port town would be located near the confluence of the Ashley and Cooper rivers. The town would be named Charles Town, and it would henceforth be the sole place for the loading and unloading of cargo. The governor and council were instructed that the Lords Proprietors were to have 5-acre lots allocated in the new town. They were reminded to "still take care of the regularity and straightness of the streets," as previously directed. Furthermore, to expedite development of the town, each allocation of a house lot was to come "with a proviso, that the foundation of his house shall be laid in less than one year, and a house erected before the [passage] of two years."[37]

A person having already built a house and desiring to build one or more additional houses would be allocated land for that purpose, provided any houses built were at least 30 feet long, 16 feet wide, and two stories in height ("besides garrets"). However, any such additional houses were to be built within twelve months of taking possession of the lot.[38]

By the 1680s, the province had settlers arriving in sufficient numbers to warrant the creation of new counties, and more instructions were issued by the Lords Proprietors. Ashley Cooper, however, went into exile in Holland in 1682 and died in January 1683. Locke's involvement was also curtailed at this time, although it appears he later reengaged himself with the Lords Proprietors and may have done additional work for them. In any case, he retained an interest in the province.

Carolina continued forward under the Fundamental Constitutions, even though the original prime mover and his architect were no longer directing its affairs. However, as new tracts of land were surveyed farther inland and in less habitable coastal areas, the euclidean geometry of the Grand Model began to come up against the complexity of the topography. In particular, the irregularity of river tributaries made it necessary to issue complex instructions for land allocation. In November 1682, instructions from the Lords Proprietors illustrate their commitment to the Fundamental Constitutions and Locke's Grand Model for development, with detailed rules for applying those principles to constrained terrain. Procedures for the allocation of tracts between tributaries forming narrow necks of upland, for example, were spelled out in great detail. Particular attention was given to fair and efficient access to frontage on navigable rivers. The 12,000-acre squares were limited to 346 chains (at 66 feet to a chain) of frontage. Smaller lots had proportionately less frontage. The limitation prevented landowners from having more length of frontage than depth, thereby assuring equal access, a principle from the original agrarian policy framework.[39]

The same set of instructions from the Lords Proprietors continued the policy of compact development, limiting the geographic range for the formation and allocation of new tracts of land. No land grants were permitted beyond 30 miles south of the Stono River, 50 miles north of the Ashley and Cooper rivers (which join at the coast), or 60 miles inland.

Such instructions concentrated on the southern settlements (the future South Carolina), as that was where the natural harbors were found and growth was concentrated.[40]

Later Instructions on Town Planning and Design

The second generation of Lords Proprietors, including the 2nd Earl of Shaftesbury, continued issuing instructions to Carolina officials on town planning into the 1690s. Locke remained close to the Shaftesbury family and interested in the colony, and he probably influenced the instructions and may have even actually written some of them. Although not an employee of the family at that time, he was close to the 2nd and 3rd Earls.

In November 1691, detailed instructions were sent to the governor that covered a range of subjects, including towns. At this point, the province had grown to four counties, ranging from Albemarle County in the north to Colleton County in the south, a span that covered most of present-day coastal North Carolina and South Carolina. More counties were anticipated, some of which would be established inland under very different conditions. It was therefore urgent to reassert the tenets of the Fundamental Constitutions and subsequent instructions on settlement of the colony.

The 1691 instructions stated that the inland boundaries of counties would be measured from the principal river "in a straight line from the sea" for 35 miles. New counties inland from those boundaries were also to be oriented to the principal river where possible. Boundaries were also to be as closely oriented to north-south and east-west axes as possible.[41]

In February 1692, "Rules and Instructions for Granting of Land" were issued for the province. All navigable rivers in a county were to have a town, and a site of 500 acres was to be set aside for its development. The site for the town was to "be as far up as the biggest ship that can come over the bar of the said river can safely and conveniently sail." The site was to have sufficient elevation for storage of "wholesome" fresh water in underground cisterns. The site should also "be (if possible) far from marshes, swamps, or standing water."

The initial plan to create a grid of 12,000-acre square units remained in place. The grid square within which the town was to be located was to be designated a colony, or a place to settle "the people." So also were "the next two squares on the same side of the river adjoining to it," and the squares behind those.

The next set of detailed instructions from the Lords Proprietors, covering diverse matters, was issued on May 20, 1692. These instructions clarified who would succeed as palatine, among other administrative matters. In doing so, they reaffirmed the tenets of the Fundamental Constitutions and the feudal system they maintained. Other measures for expedient local administration were also covered. Growth of the province also required that they confirm county boundaries. From north to south, Albemarle County ran from Virginia to the Albemarle River; Craven County boundaries were specified in terms of vectors that placed it between Albemarle and Berkeley counties; Colleton County was situated between the Stono River and the Combahee River, extending 35 miles on a straight line inland. Procedures for establishing other counties were also reviewed.[42]

On June 18, 1702, the Lords Proprietors issued instructions to Nathaniel Johnson, governor of North and South Carolina, that the Fundamental Constitutions, temporary laws, and instructions governing the province were to be inspected and amended by him with the grand council and assembly. A new framework of laws replacing the former laws would in due course be reviewed and approved by the Lords Proprietors. Blank deputations for landgraves and caciques were to be canceled. It was further ordered that the new authorities "are to take great care that the Indians be not abused and that all means be used to civilize them and that you endeavor your utmost to create a firm friendship with them and to bring them over to your part for your better protection and defense against the enemy the neighboring French and Spaniards against whom you are to protect our said province and we assure you of our utmost assistance for your security."[43]

The Fundamental Constitutions were effectively withdrawn as the law of the land. The ancient system of reciprocal duties and benefits within the social hierarchy was replaced by a tyrannical system of chattel slavery.

The Emergence of Charles Town as a Gentry Capital

Charles Town was founded in 1670 and initially situated on the south bank of the Ashley River. The Lords Proprietors and the grand council recognized this as a temporary site and within a year identified an alternate site for the town on Oyster Point at the confluence of the Ashley and Cooper rivers. Although a layout for the town was drawn up in 1672 by the surveyor general, John Culpepper, following the specifications supplied by Locke, the first town lots were not allocated until 1679. The relocation of the town was completed in 1680. Locke's original sketch plan for the city was lost or destroyed, but early maps by Culpepper and others contain elements of the original design.[44]

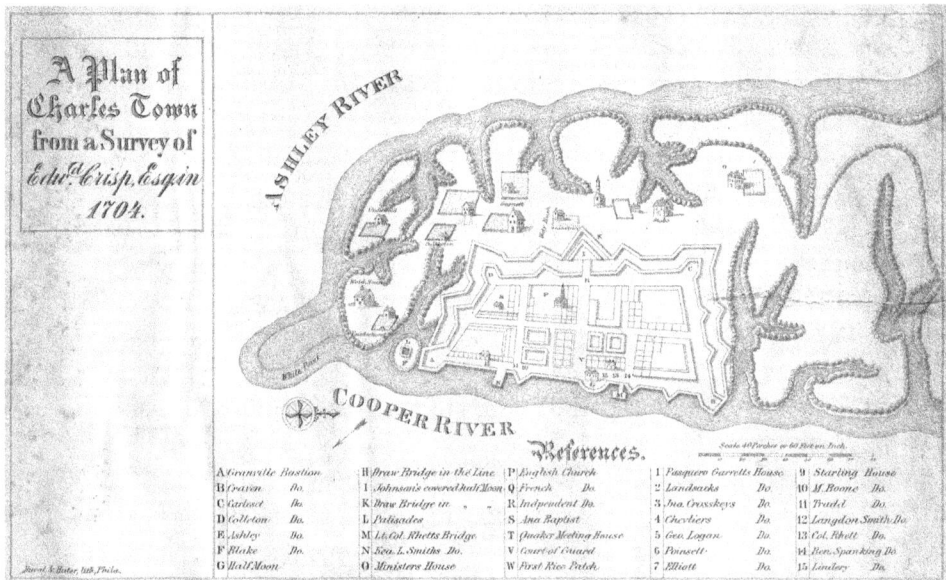

A Plan of
Charles Town
from a Survey of
Edw.ᵈ Crisp, Esq.in
1704.

ASHLEY RIVER

COOPER RIVER

References.

A	*Granville Bastion*	H	*Draw Bridge in the Line*	P	*English Church*	1 *Pasquero Garretts House*	9 *Starling House*

Figure 10. Crisp Map of Charles Town, 1704. In the early 1700s, the
city was continuing to grow roughly in accordance with Locke's model, but the
plan was abandoned soon after. Charles Town was only 90 miles from the newer
planned city of Savannah, but, in sharp contrast to the latter, its increasing
irregularity of urban form reflected a pre-Enlightenment political culture.
From the South Caroliniana Library, Kohn-Henning Collection.

Locke's "Grand Model" for the town continues to be referenced today
in describing the oldest section of Charleston's historic district, although
Locke used the simpler term "model" in his letters. However, a new survey
and plan was completed by William Bull and John Herbert in 1723 (a
decade later, Bull would assist James Oglethorpe in laying out the famous
plan for Savannah). Charles Town was resurveyed in 1746, and a new plan
was adopted by law. The plan shown in Figure 10 is probably that of Bull
and Herbert, which was largely based on Culpepper's layout.[45]

The regularity of the Grand Model can be discerned, though barely, in
the general layout of the modern city of Charleston. As with most matters,
colonists ignored the details when they could get away with it and altered
the plan over time. The street grid put in place lacked the hierarchy specified
by Locke, and internal development within the grid became organic and irregular rather than following the prescribed lot pattern. Future generations
continued to alter the plan in accommodating growth to the confined space
of a narrow peninsula. Charleston's history in this respect stands in sharp

contrast to Savannah, 90 miles to the south, where the original plan was closely followed for 120 years and today remains substantially intact.

Charleston fulfilled the expectations of the Lords Proprietors and the destiny of geography by becoming the capital of Carolina, a hub of southern culture, and the principal seaport in the southeast. It has retained many features of that early status to the present day.

A principal difference between Charles Town as envisioned by the Lords Proprietors and Charleston as it emerged as a major city in the eighteenth century is one of class structure and leadership. The Lords Proprietors installed a class of hereditary nobility (landgraves and caciques) that they believed would adopt their philosophy and uphold their authority. Below the nobility were the classical strata of gentry and yeoman farmers and laboring classes necessary to build a model society, one that reflected the traditions and first principles of the English nation.

The Lords Proprietors succeeded in creating a class pyramid nearly identical to the one they envisioned, with one essential difference. The proprietors themselves, the wise nobles who would instill virtue in the new land, were replaced by an enlarged gentry, or "political aristocracy," in the phrase of the historian Eugene Sirmans, of plantation owners and merchants. The new gentry, some of whom were experienced businessmen from Bristol and London specializing in overseas trade, would be guided entirely by self-interest rather than political philosophy, except inasmuch as it justified their actions. Some began buying baronies and other large tracts, and in so doing benefited from the slave trade as well as the use of slaves on their plantations.[46]

Beaufort and George Town

The geographic prime directive in Carolina's founding documents was to form a county around every navigable river and establish a town near the mouth of that river. After Charles Town, Beaufort was the next settlement to fulfill that directive. Georgetown would do the same to the north, but after the proprietary period. By 1735, both had grown sufficiently large to compete with Charles Town for trade. Charles Town, however, would remain the seat of power and eventually become an embodiment of southern culture.[47]

On December 20, 1710, the proprietors determined that a seaport town would be established on Port Royal Island, the largest island in Port Royal Sound. The town of Beaufort was subsequently founded and chartered on January 17, 1711. The name of the town was to be Beaufort Town. The town appears to have been laid out with streets and regular lots by 1716. An Act of 1740 required property owners to erect a house on their lot within three years at a size of at least 15 feet by 30 feet with a brick chimney. A single square was laid out at the intersection of Carteret and Craven streets and marked for a castle (later called a citadel), with four adjoining lots designated for civic uses.

Beaufort became the principal town at the southern reaches of the colony, but it was later eclipsed by the founding of Savannah, 40 miles to the south, in 1733. The early layout of the town remained in place as it grew, imbuing it with both functionality and aesthetic appeal. Beaufort has preserved its historic character up to the present time, becoming a highly regarded tourism and retirement destination. It is the county seat of Beaufort County.

Earlier settlements on Port Royal Sound during the proprietary period failed to take root, having been routed by Spaniards and Indians. Scots Covenanters were the first in the proprietary period to settle in the area, establishing Stewart Town 5 miles from Beaufort. The town was burned by the Spanish in 1686, and some of the Scots returned to Scotland and others went elsewhere in Carolina. In 1732, Fort Frederick was built near the former site of Stuart Town to guard Carolina's southern frontier. James Oglethorpe deposited the first colonists to settle Georgia in the barracks at the fort while he scouted the Savannah River, 40 miles south, for the future site of the town of Savannah.

The Town of Port Royal was established in 1874 near the site of Stuart's Town, founded two centuries earlier. The town claims to date even farther back, to 1562, when Jean Ribaut established Charlesfort on Parris Island, which is within the town's incorporated area (see Chapter 2). Other barrier islands on Port Royal Sound became noteworthy for the enslaved African people who evolved into the Gullah culture. St. Helena Island is considered one of the prominent examples of enduring Gullah culture; Hilton Head Island, now a major resort town, once had a large Gullah settlement; and Daufuskie Island's Gullah people were the subject of Pat Conroy's novel *The Water Is Wide*.

Georgetown was founded in 1729, the first town to be established after the proprietary period. It is located about 70 miles northward of Charleston on Winyah Bay at the confluence of the Great Pee Dee River and the Waccamaw and Sampit rivers. The Georgetown area was initially settled as early as 1705 on land granted to John Perrie, an Irishman who became wealthy in Antigua. Perrie and members of his family also obtained grants and sent an experienced merchant and twenty-five slaves to begin settling the land. By 1729, Georgetown was settled by numerous families who had acquired the Perrie estates, prompting Governor Robert Johnson to initiate establishment of the town.[48]

The plan for the town took the form of a 4-by-8-block grid layout prepared by Elisha Screven, one of the principal landowners. The town maintained the grid layout as it grew, and much of it is preserved today. The town is listed on the National Register of Historic Places. A steel mill built adjacent to the historic district produced a stark contrast between a pristine historic streetscape and waterfront and a smoky, soot-covered neighboring section of town.

As with Port Royal, Georgetown claims to be the site of what could be the earliest European settlement within the present boundaries of the United States. In 1526, a Spanish expedition established a small colony on Waccamaw Neck named San Miguel de Gualdape. The site, however, was occupied for only about three months.

Smaller towns established after Beaufort and Georgetown adopted the Grand Model, even though it was no longer in force, rather than simply forming in a spontaneous and organic fashion.

The Early Towns of the Royal Colony

In 1730, Governor Robert Johnson implemented a plan to create nine new towns on the colonial frontier. The scheme would create a band of white settlements to protect the core of the colony from the Spanish and French, as well as from hostile Native Americans. It would also increase the proportion of white settlers in the colony at a time when slaves outnumbered white settlers by two-to-one, while creating an outer ring to contain escaping slaves and quell slave rebellions.

In the assessment of Henry Smith, these new towns, as well as others founded at this time, "embodied the urban vision of the Lords Proprietors" coupled with that of Governor Johnson. The location and orientation of towns, their street grids and lot patterns, the allocation of parcels for civic uses, and other design elements were planned in advance of settlement. Although many of the towns never grew as planned, their layouts offer insight into the emerging culture and its ideas about urban design.

French James Town was located about 50 miles northwest of Charles Town on the Santee River. The name was acquired from the Huguenot settlers who arrived in the area in the 1680s. As seen in Smith's reconstruction of a 1716 plat, the riverfront was reserved for public uses and a common. A line of small lots, probably for a mix of uses, formed the first tier of lots, with increasingly larger lots farther from the river.[49]

Childsbury was founded on the western branch of the Cooper River, 25 miles north of Charleston, on land granted to James Child in 1698. It was laid out in 1714 or earlier. Child's will provided public land for a college or university. The town was abandoned by 1736. The symmetry in the plan is remarkable and may have been inspired by plans proposed for the rebuilding of London after the Great Fire of 1666.

The town of Edmundsbury was located on the west bank of the Ashepoo River on the main road from Charleston to the south. It was laid out in 1740 and ceased to exist after 1757, becoming one of several planned towns that became extinct as urban functions became more centralized in Charleston and other cities. The plan provided for a 16.5-acre common and church land on a civic square on the principal street from the river.

The planned town of Radnor was not settled as designed, but it is worthy of mention because of its location and design. The town was strategically sited at the Combahee River ferry crossing, but it developed with only a few houses. William Bull obtained half of a barony (a large land grant from the Lords Proprietors) in September 1732. Bull and his son Stephen further subdivided the land into Sheldon and Newbury plantations, respectively. The town of Radnor was laid out on an adjacent tract on the Combahee River at the ferry crossing in 1734. The town had a 70-acre common "for the use and benefit of the inhabitants," as well as a square (inspired in design by his friend Oglethorpe) for the market and separate lots for a chapel and a free school. The town disappeared from maps after 1757.[50]

The town of Purrysburg was established on the Savannah River in 1732 by Swiss Protestants led by Jean Pierre Purry. The town was a thriving settlement for two decades, after which its residents began dispersing and integrating into the general population.

The Carolina town plans of the early royal colonial period reveal a remarkable consistency with the Grand Model: sited on a strategic river location; designation of waterfront for public use; gridiron street pattern; substantial street width; standard lot sizes; and designated public space to accommodate civic uses such as markets, schools, and churches. The design would be replicated over subsequent generations, altered slightly by the streetcar era of the late nineteenth century, and then far more substantially by the automobile era of the twentieth century. Historic towns across the South are an extension of this legacy.

Political Culture after the Proprietary Period

At this point, the reader should be able to discern features of the Ashley Cooper Plan that survived the proprietary period. First, there was the class pyramid of Gothic England planted in Carolina so firmly that titles of nobility remained in use for over a century. An accompanying sense of aristocratic privilege survived even longer. Second, there was the agrarian ethic that centered power with the landed nobility and gentry and diminished that of the urban gentry class. Third, there was Locke's urban and regional plan, parts of which were taken to create a network of smaller towns aimed at serving the plantation as economic engine. The city was a function of the country in Carolina and across the South, even as the Industrial Revolution permanently reversed that relationship in the North. Slaveholders through the late colonial period built or more often rented houses in Charles Town that resembled their plantation houses, firming up the home-away-from-home relationship.[51]

A political culture built on plantation slave dependency was well established by the end of the proprietary period. The elaborate class pyramid fashioned by Ashley Cooper and Locke, based on a system of agrarian equality and class reciprocity, had been transformed into a three-tiered pyramid of slave masters, freemen, and a majority underclass of enslaved laborers. The system was reinforced by the lucrative Atlantic Triangle Trade that enriched its participants in the North American and Caribbean colonies, England, and Africa. The greatest concentration of wealth among the fewest active participants in the Atlantic trade network was in South Carolina. Charleston became one of the wealthiest cities in the world, and its residents cultivated a relationship with the nobility of England to acquire the aristocratic dignities they saw as befitting their wealth.

South Carolina was managed by the Lords Proprietors from its founding in 1670 to 1720, when a royal governor was appointed by George I. While the first generation of proprietors was actively involved in designing the colony and implementing their plan, their successors were less engaged. Later proprietors who inherited or purchased an interest in Carolina were neither idealists nor good stewards of their province. In 1704, the colonial parliament passed an exclusion act limiting the rights of dissenters and making the Church of England the official state religion. The proprietors approved it, with objections from Maurice Ashley, Ashley Cooper's grandson. The dissenters in the colony sent representatives to England to protest. It was at this point that Daniel Defoe was retained to write the tract entitled "Party-Tyranny" opposing the action (see Chapter 2).

In 1729, the government of George I bought out the last proprietor holding an interest in the province and completed the conversion of North and South Carolina into royal colonies. By that time, a political culture was well established in the more settled coastal region of South

Carolina (the Lowcountry), where the Goose Creek men dominated politics. Made up in large part of Barbadians and other West Indians familiar with a slave-based economy, an even more rigid social hierarchy than that planned by the original Lords Proprietors had been built.[52]

Life on the frontier in the colony's early years had a leveling influence on its society. Nobility, gentry, freemen, indentured servants, and enslaved laborers—all the strata of society—pulled together to survive in an alien world. As they did so, they shared some aspects of common humanity that later entirely disappeared. Cruelty of one to another existed, of course, and relations were unthinkably harsh by present standards; but the historical record reveals that early Carolina society was cohesive and relatively tolerant, certainly less brutally racist than it would become in the early eighteenth century.[53]

As Carolina developed close ties to Barbados and became more of a "colony of a colony" (a phrase that exaggerates the relationship), it tended to follow the island's path toward a rigid hierarchy. Initially, Barbados planters saw indentured servants as their primary source of labor, as did the proprietors. Indenture contracts, however, varied widely, adding uncertainty to the labor supply. In Barbados, most were five to seven years in duration and then were reduced to three to five years to attract more interest. Some Irish were taken as slaves in an effort to establish a permanent labor force, but Africans were eventually available in larger numbers. When Africans were found to be accustomed to a hot, humid climate and less troublesome than the Irish, they became the preferred source of labor. Africans cost a third of what Irish servants cost to maintain, and they proved to be better workers. Once Africans made up a large base in the social pyramid, the Irish acquired greater social status and rose to an intermediate tier in the hierarchy.[54]

The social pyramid rigidified from the bottom up as classes within its layers acquired status and authority in relation to those underneath them. A plot against slave masters in Barbados in 1688 that precipitated a rigid slave code (see Chapter 2) alarmed Carolinians, and in 1690 the first of many laws regulating slaves was adopted. In the minds of whites, blacks from then on were a distinct race, better off serving as slaves and being Christianized than living as "savages" in Africa.

Rice cultivation became the first major export crop for the colony. It was labor-intensive work, and it increased demand for African slaves. Experimentation with rice production on Wadboo Plantation by James Colleton proved successful, and techniques for growing the crop in tidal basins were perfected by 1683. Production increased dramatically in the

1690s. Africans in coastal West Africa (in an area west of Elmina known as the grain or rice coast) were experienced at growing rice, and their expertise became a great asset to the plantation owners.[55]

In 1708, the number of enslaved people in South Carolina exceeded that of the free population. The slave population at that time was made up primarily of Africans but with a considerable number of Native Americans. By 1730, the black slave population was double that of the white population, and by 1760, enslaved people constituted more than 90 percent of the population in many parts of the Lowcountry. It would not be for another 200 years (as enumerated in the 1930 census) that the white population in South Carolina exceeded the black population.[56]

A spiral of racial tyranny set in as the plantation elite sought more wealth from their plantations. The enslaved population increased, and the burdens of labor became more grueling. Laws were adopted and continually revised to control the lives of slaves and suppress any possibility of rebellion. The movements and activities of blacks were strictly regulated, militias were formed to rigidly and swiftly enforce the laws, and punishments were contrived to be as severe as the mind could imagine. The enslaved population, pressed to the limit of endurance, developed subtle means of resistance that could be applied on a continuous basis. When an opportunity arose, some plotted rebellion and escape to Indian or Spanish territory. With each attempt to secure freedom, the laws and punishments became more severe.

A mythology developed within the white population that enslaved Africans were contented people who occupied their proper place in the Great Chain of Being. The records of the period, readily accessible through modern library and archive technology, clear the fog of history and prove the opposite. Charles Wesley and his brother John Wesley, the founder of Methodism, were among those who documented the horrors of slavery in South Carolina. The brothers had been recruited by James Oglethorpe in 1734 to serve in the slave-free colony of Georgia. Charles Wesley wrote the following description of one slave owner's practices:

> Colonel Lynch cut off the legs of a poor Negro, and he kills several of them every year by his barbarities. Mr. Hill, a dancing-master in Charleston, whipped a female slave so long that she fell down at his feet, in appearance dead; but when, by the help of a physician, she was so far recovered as to show some signs of life, he repeated the whipping with equal rigour, and concluded the punishment by dropping scalding wax upon her flesh: her only crime was overfilling a tea-cup! These horrid

cruelties are the less to be wondered at, because the law itself, in effect, countenances and allows them to kill their slaves by the ridiculous penalty appointed for it. The penalty is about seven pounds, one-half of which is usually remitted if the criminal inform against himself.[57]

Alexander Garden, the Carolina doctor after whom the gardenia was named, wrote in 1755 that slaves working in rice cultivation were driven beyond their limits: "Labor and the loss of many of their lives testified the fatigue they underwent, in satiating the inexpressible avarice of their masters." The "barbarity" and cruelty of slave masters and overseers, he wrote, caused slaves to have a miserable life and often to die from exhaustion and exposure.[58]

Slaves were forced to punish or execute other slaves, and in 1740 the practice was legalized in part as a terror tactic for subjugation. Before a slave was hung by another slave, other slaves were gathered to witness the execution. Executions were made as dramatic as possible, sometimes by piking the heads of the executed.[59]

New ministers were often mortified by the treatment of enslaved people, if not the institution of slavery itself, but found themselves socially ostracized and professionally isolated if they objected. They adapted to the institution of slavery by adopting the position that earthly obedience was the only ticket to heaven. Ministers observed all the horrors but shared them with few. One wrote in 1709 that "a poor slavewoman was barbarously burnt alive near my door without any positive proof of the crime she was accused of." He recorded many instances of cruelty to slaves, which increased as masters feared rebellion. Some created extreme forms of torture, such as a "hellish machine" the size of a coffin in which the victim was kept for days, unable to move or eat. Objections by ministers were ineffective, and they learned to withhold them to maintain their social standing. Some ministers took slaves themselves, and they learned to avoid the subject of cruelty to slaves in sermons so as not to offend parishioners.[60]

In time, the church as an institution accommodated slavery as an institution, finding justifications for it in scripture as well as in the human invention of the Great Chain of Being. Ministers learned to support the idea that the white race, and even an aristocratic race within the white race, were superior beings destined to rule. They joined the southern, slave-holding elite and their minions and abandoned their church counterparts in the Middle Atlantic and New England regions, creating the Southern Baptist and Southern Methodist churches.

The more repressive whites became, the more outwardly docile and inwardly rebellious enslaved people became. Occasional "explosions of rage" against the system "were almost always suicidal." Behavior described by whites as "uppity" or "saucy" was a passive form of resistance that normally enabled an enslaved person to avoid punishment. However, even such behavior became reason for punishment by the late 1730s. The cruelty was noted across the river in Georgia, where a colonist wrote in 1738 that Georgia's system of yeoman farms was preferable to Carolina's "inhumane and abominable using of Negroes."[61]

Slaves were sometimes able to return the terror in the form of poisonings, an art learned from their knowledge of plants. A maid was burned alive for an attempted poisoning. Arson was another means of rebellion sometimes employed as repression increased. Organized resistance in the form of plots and rebellions were an inevitable result of extreme repression. The Stono Rebellion, which took place within 20 miles of Charles Town in 1739, was the most shocking. It became a turning point in South Carolina history.[62]

The rebellion began when an estimated 60 to 100 rebels seized horses, weapons, and food with the goal of reaching Florida, where the Spanish offered freedom to English slaves. The uprising was nearly crushed the first day by the militia, but fighting continued for a week before the rebellion was completely contained. By then, however, the rebels had come to within 30 miles of the Georgia border. Not all of the rebels were captured; one of the leaders remained at large for three years.[63]

The few freedoms available to the enslaved people of South Carolina (for example, having families, visiting friends, hunting and fishing) were always tenuous, but they nevertheless provided a modest sense of a better future. After the Stono Rebellion, the white elite could no longer tolerate even such meager freedoms. All rights were taken away legislatively, Christian instruction emphasized submissiveness and obedience, and the laws of the caste system were enforced more efficiently than ever before.[64]

As repression became more efficient and as southern white society grew more dependent on it to maintain its way of life, outside attacks on the system increased and the need to defend it also arose. The blatant absence of class reciprocity of benefits derived from the system was obscured with a new rhetoric of paternalism. In the nineteenth century, intellectual southerners were advancing the idea that racial paternalism was a high achievement of civilization.

Racial Myth and Reality

Race underlies much of the American experience, and South Carolina has been a force in shaping racial attitudes across the South and beyond. This section looks at the concept of race as it evolved from the founding of Carolina to the present day. It will be shown that South Carolina constructed a racial mythology consistent with its political culture and led other slaveholding states down that path as it increasingly diverged from reality. The origin of racial mythology is relevant at this point because it is part of the fabric of history in which Carolina's past is woven into America's present—a fabric within which American patterns of social hierarchy and spatial development have taken form. Chapter 4 will build on this discussion of the origin and evolution of racial mythology in exploring its effects.

Over the course of the seventeenth century, British colonies in the South and in the Caribbean developed economies dependent on large-scale plantation monoculture and enslaved labor. Initially, white settlers and black slaves worked with a degree of cooperation to create a new life in the wilderness. The English had no cultural experience with chattel slavery and therefore no legal framework within which to formalize it. Englishmen were proud of their nation's tradition of liberty, and thus it took time for them to condone and then rationalize slavery. African slaves were seen as physically different, but until the late seventeenth century there was no sense that Africans were innately suited for enslavement.[65]

With the establishment of successful monocultures—first sugar in Barbados and then rice in the Carolinas—a rigid social hierarchy emerged, with a self-described aristocratic planter class, now often described as the plantation elite, governing from the top. Lower tiers of whites acquired a sense of racial status and the potential for upward mobility in relation to slaves. Racial distinctions became increasingly well defined in cultural attitudes and under the law, in order to sustain white prosperity and privilege in the face of ever-harsher conditions imposed upon the black labor force.[66]

During the eighteenth century, the slave population became much larger than the white population in the Carolina Lowcountry and the Caribbean. Slaveholders came to consider slaves a "domestic enemy," even though they were deemed property essential to the economy. The *enemy within* became paired with the *enemy outside*—in the Lowcountry it was Native Americans, then Spanish, French, British, and Yankees. Such a terrifying worldview of perpetual, mortal threats within and without justified the institution of state tyranny in Carolina and its eventual replication across the South. The fear of internal and external enemies coordinating insurrection remains a familiar theme in American political culture, as subsequent chapters will bring to light.[67]

Harsh repressive measures instituted to prevent slave rebellion necessitated an evolution in white attitudes toward blacks. Thus blacks came to be considered a race of uncivilized savages who could only be saved through Christianity and then made to accept their plight as slaves and their place in God's Design, the Great Chain of Being. In the words of the historian Winthrop Jordan, who wrote the first comprehensive analysis of white attitudes toward blacks, enslavement and prejudice were "equally cause and effect . . . dynamically joining hands to hustle the Negro down the road to complete degradation."[68]

The dynamic "hustle" continued into the nineteenth century, with new and elaborate refinements to southern racism. Blacks were not only imagined to be barely removed from African savagery but also barely removed from any depravity that could be conceived to occur on that Dark Continent, including cannibalism. Slaveholders across the South, with intellectual leadership from South Carolina, convinced themselves that the system they had created, the "peculiar institution" of southern slavery, was in fact the highest pinnacle of civilization ever attained by man. It was a system piously rooted in Christianity that bequeathed enormous benefits to slaveholders, middle classes, and slaves alike. Southern whites came to believe that blacks as a race were happiest and most fulfilled in life when serving as slaves. The belief was articulated to the U.S. Senate by South Carolinian John C. Calhoun in 1837, in what has become known as the Positive Good Speech:[69]

> Never before has the black race of Central Africa, from the dawn of history to the present day, attained a condition so civilized and so improved, not only physically, but morally and intellectually. . . . I hold that in the present state of civilization, where two races of different origin, and distinguished by color, and other physical differences, as well as intellectual, are brought together, the relation now existing in the slaveholding States between the two, is, instead of an evil, a good—a positive good.[70]

The argument that Africans were primitive savages and cannibals, fortunate to be enslaved by Europeans, is one that took more than a century of practice to perfect. By the early twentieth century, at the height of the Jim Crow era, the language of mutual benefit was found in the popular prose of southern scholars such Frank Owsley and Donald Davidson, who confidently claimed that "half savage blacks" of America were barely removed from the "cannibals and barbarians" of Africa. This intractable dogma made "race . . . the defining essence of the South," in the judgment of southern historian Paul Conkin, who profiled Owsley, Davidson, and the other Southern Agrarians.[71]

The overtly degrading racism of Owsley and Davidson was not present in the work of all the Southern Agrarians, but their inability as a group to attain any self-awareness over the effects of slavery attests to their tacit acceptance of the myth of black savagery and white benevolence. In the collaborative work of the Southern Agrarians, *I'll Take My Stand* (a phrase taken from the song "Dixie"), the rural way of life in the South, a "culture of the soil," is romanticized as if it were essentially disconnected from centuries of slavery.[72]

The myth of race as a basis for class and of slavery as a positive good began in the rapid and intense development of sugar plantations on Barbados. The myth was refined and rationalized in the context of the hybrid class hierarchy of Carolina. A model of repressive slave laws and rhetorical justification for them emerged in South Carolina. The Carolina model went on to acquire additional layers of rhetorical justification across the antebellum South. The process did not stop with the Civil War but resumed with additional mythological support in the Jim Crow South. Leaders such as George Wallace spoke with certainty on the subject: "All those countries with niggers in 'em have stayed the same for a thousand years." Wallace, like most white southerners, believed blacks to be innately lazy and predisposed to criminal behavior unless under the thumb of white authority. The historian Dan T. Carter, writing about both periods, has shown that the southern obsession with race was as strong in the 1960s as it was in the 1860s.[73]

As the *mythology* passed from generation to generation, it became increasingly divorced from the *realities* of Africa, race, and slavery. Knowledge of Africa and Africans was attainable from many sources, but it would not have supported the essential myth upon which the "peculiar institution" was built and sustained. Knowledge, therefore, was ignored by the plantation elite even as its members claimed an advanced degree of wisdom and knowledge afforded them by their unique position as leaders of a perfected civilization.

A case in point illustrating how knowledge might have defeated myth is evident with James Oglethorpe, the founder of Georgia. Oglethorpe confronted advocates of slavery in neighboring Carolina when he established a yeoman-agrarian vision for Georgia Colony in 1733 and soon after made it explicitly slave free. The debate between the two sides was so intense that Oglethorpe developed a lifelong interest in the problem of slavery. The more he read about Africa and Africans, the more committed he became to abolition. In a letter written in 1776 to Granville Sharp, who later joined William Wilberforce and others in formalizing the abolition movement, Oglethorpe demonstrated a deep knowledge of African history and respect for African people. Such knowledge, which influenced Britain to abolish slavery, was entirely ignored by the South as it constructed and perpetuated self-serving racial mythology.[74]

Knowledge of Africa in England and America in the seventeenth and eighteenth centuries was limited to histories written by North African scholars such as Ibn Battuta and Leo Africanus, whose works had been available for centuries. Had such sources been consulted, a different understanding of Africa would have emerged to contradict southern mythology. West African history and ethnography is particularly revealing, in view of the fact that nearly half of the slaves bound for North America came from that region. In 1352, four and a half centuries before the English explored the region, Ibn Battuta described the black people of present-day Mali as quite the opposite of the savages, barbarians, and cannibals of southern mythology: "They are seldom unjust, and have a greater abhorrence of injustice than any people. Their sultan ['mansa'] shows no mercy to any one guilty of the least act of it. There is complete security in the country. Neither traveler nor inhabitant in it has anything to fear from robbers or men of violence."[75]

In 1513, Leo Africanus described Timbuktu in present-day Mali as an especially advanced city: "Here are many shops of craftsmen and merchants, especially those who weave linen and cotton cloth. . . . The region produces corn, cattle, milk and butter in great abundance. . . . The inhabitants are a people of gentle and cheerful disposition. . . . Here there are many doctors, judges, priests and other learned men, that are maintained at the king's cost."[76] It was not until the very end of the eighteenth century that the English-speaking world had an account of the interior of Africa by one of its own. The explorer Mungo Park traveled through the interior of West Africa, up the Senegal River, across the Sahel, and down the Niger River. Park's extensive travels led him to conclude that "whatever difference there is between the negro and European, in the conformation of the nose, and the colour of the skin, there is none in the genuine sympathies and characteristic feelings of our common nature." A drawing published in 1799 with Park's book, *Travels in the Interior Districts of Africa* (Figure 11), shows a very different picture of Africa than the mental images constructed by southern slaveholders.[77]

The illustration portrays a town with fenced family compounds in the foreground and a carefully laid out community in the background. People

Figure 11. "A View of Kamalia." This drawing of a West African town in
the 1790s shows highly organized urban form and complex economic activity. The
reality of African life stood in sharp contrast to its portrayal by southern slaveholders.
From Mungo Park, *Travels in the Interior Districts of Africa*.

are seen working cooperatively in various types of economic activity. They are
free and better off for it than their enslaved brethren. Nothing here or anywhere in Park's account supports the racial mythology developed to defend
slavery, a mythology that became a defining part of the American experience.

Park described Sego (Segou), the capital city of the Bambara Empire
on the Niger River, in rapturous terms: "The view of this extensive city;
the numerous canoes upon the river; the crowded population, and the
cultivated state of the surrounding country, formed altogether a prospect of civilization and magnificence, which I little expected to find in the
bosom of Africa."[78] Park's journey occurred at a time when the European
"scramble" to colonize and exploit Africa was only beginning to impact
its political geography. Many West African nations developed in a manner similar to England's Gothic traditions, in some cases with a greater
level of advancement due to nearly 3,000 years of trans-Saharan trade.
Complex sub-Saharan societies emerged around 300 A.D., as seen with
ancient Jenne on the Niger River. Iron smelting, crop cultivation, and pot-
tery making in West Africa date to at least 400 B.C. The Empire of Mali in

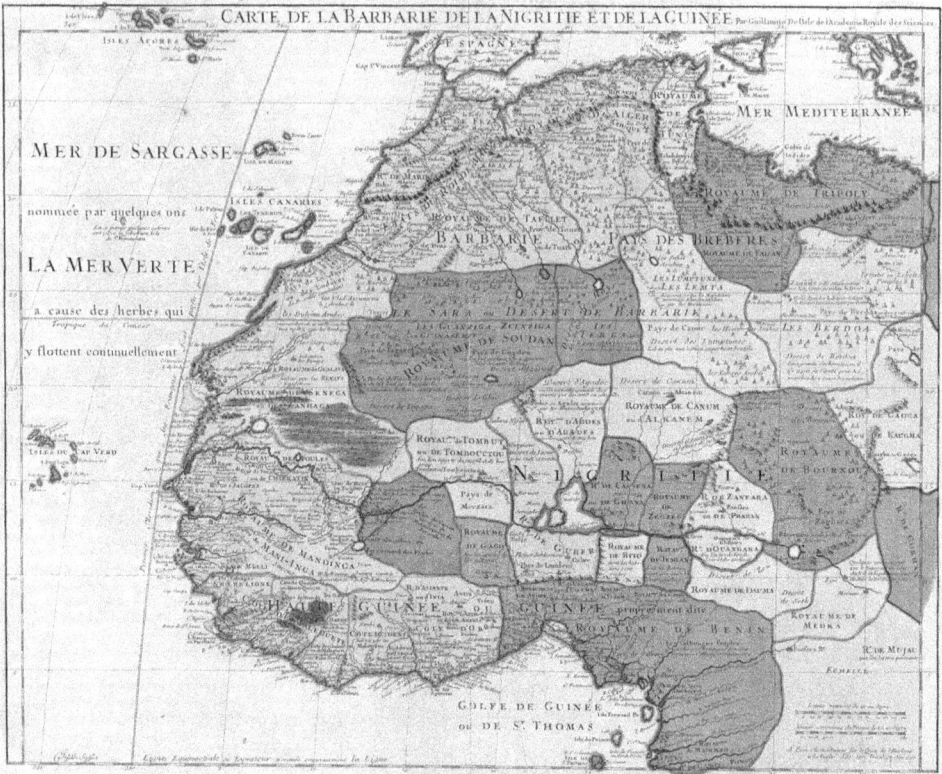

Figure 12. Map of West Africa, 1707. The precolonial nations of West Africa were formed over centuries of intraregional and trans-Saharan trade. The vast scale of the Atlantic slave trade destabilized the region and ushered in over two centuries of European colonial rule. Illustration from the Library of Congress, Geography and Map Division.

the fourteenth century extended across the Senegal, Gambia, and Niger rivers for over 1,000 miles; it maintained a standing army and a professional government supported by a tax on trade. In the eighteenth century, as the Atlantic slave trade reached its maturity, there were nearly thirty highly organized nations and city-states making up the political geography of West Africa (as seen in Figure 12). Much of the rest of sub-Saharan Africa was similarly organized.[79]

As West African trade with Europeans increased, trans-Saharan trade decreased, and nations based on ethnic traditions and centuries-long trade relationships withered. New colonial nations arose with no regard to historical patterns. The slave trade then became an essential part of the economic engine of the Atlantic Triangle Trade.

Rather than rescuing Africans from savagery, barbarism, and cannibalism and endowing them with the benefits of civilization, as southern mythology depicted history, slavery reduced men to a permanent, abused underclass while destroying the nations of Africa.

Conclusion

Historians have debated whether the "peculiar institution" of American slavery, with its self-serving "positive good" mythology, was driven primarily by social or by economic forces. Was it the invention of the plantation elite, who believed so strongly in the virtue of their culture that they forced the economy to bend to it? Or was it a result of the "invisible hand" of economic forces guiding individuals to make rational decisions accruing to their personal benefit and thereby shaping a new kind of slave society?

In looking at the interrelated development of Barbados and Carolina, one finds both forces at play. Barbados was the creation of commercial imperatives, and slavery could be predicted within the economic framework of classical liberalism. South Carolina, however, was created with a Gothic Grand Model, wherein the economy was a function of society rather than the other way around (see Table 6). The answer to the culture-versus-economy question, therefore, resides in the extent to which the Grand Model survived as an influence in Carolina and elsewhere, a question pursued further in Chapter 4.

The Ashley Cooper Plan—the Grand Model codified in the Fundamental Constitutions and various regulations—left a permanent imprint on Carolina. The Goose Creek men were driven by the Barbadian experience, but at the same time they adapted themselves to the Grand Model because it conferred upon them nobility and purpose. The emergent Carolina nobility, the colony's wealthy slaveholders, replaced higher purposes of the Grand Model (including reciprocity and noblesse oblige) with a self-serving mythology of aristocratic entitlement. Nevertheless, the *appearance* of traditional Gothic hierarchy and a stable agrarian society was an essential pretense of Carolina's hybrid political culture.

Although the Barbadians and their allies altered the vision of the Lords Proprietors and then overthrew that government, land allocation and class structure remained much the same long after the proprietary period. The nobility that Ashley Cooper believed would lead a virtuous model society was replaced by an agrarian elite and a merchant gentry class whose self-interest led Carolina into an age of prosperity built upon slavery.

Table 6. Timeline of the Settlement of Carolina and Georgia

1671	The first set of detailed instructions for the layout of towns was issued in a letter dated May 1, 1671
1672	A second set of instructions was issued on June 21, 1672, stating principles of "a right and equal distribution of land" taken up in an "orderly" manner
1675	The first signiory, located on the south side of the Ashley River near Charles Town, was granted to Ashley Cooper
1680	A plan for relocating Charles Town to Oyster Point was adopted by the Lords Proprietors.
1682	Instructions from the Lords Proprietors in November demonstrate their commitment to the Fundamental Constitutions and the Grand Model
1683	Anthony Ashley Cooper, 1st Earl of Shaftesbury, died in Holland
1691	Detailed instructions were sent to the governor in November that covered a range of subjects, including towns
1692	"Rules and Instructions for Granting of Land" were issued for the province
1702	The Lords Proprietors issued instructions to the governor that the Fundamental Constitutions, laws, and instructions governing the province were to be inspected and amended
1711	Town of Beaufort established
1712	Carolina divided into northern and southern provinces
1729	Town of Georgetown established; final buyout of the Lords Proprietors completed
1730	Governor Robert Johnson implemented a plan to create nine new towns on the colonial frontier
1733	Georgia founded
1739	Stono Rebellion
1743	Oglethorpe returned to England the final time
1752	Georgia Trustees return control of the colony to the crown; Carolina slaveholders lead a "parade" of slaves into the colony

Since many scholars either diminish the role of South Carolina in forming American political culture or attribute its role to being a conduit for the slave society created in Barbados, it will be useful at this point to isolate the spectrum of permanent influences on the colony exerted by the Ashley Cooper Plan, summarized below in five points.

1. South Carolina had a planned land-allocation system, whereas development was haphazard on Barbados. In the view of South Carolina historian Eugene Sirmans, "The land system proposed in the Constitutions had far-reaching effects. . . . No one can deny that the Constitutions, with its provisions for a local aristocracy and

incredibly large land grants, speeded the development of a landed gentry in South Carolina."[80]

2. South Carolina had a formal constitution, whereas Barbados had no such guiding instrument. South Carolina historians have described an emergent "political culture" that was ultimately "embedded in the Fundamental Constitutions," a founding code "generally felt to have influenced [the] character of the state as it developed."[81]

3. The Fundamental Constitutions established a social hierarchy modeled on the Gothic traditions of England, led by country lords rather than men of commerce.

4. The nobility created by the Fundamental Constitutions was perpetual and hereditary at the highest echelons. The sense of entitlement to social position and authority did not fade with the Fundamental Constitutions but continued for generations.

5. While there were superficial similarities between Charles Town and Bridgetown, the former became a far more influential urban center in part because of the planning that guided its development and relationship with plantations.

The Grand Model was adapted to protect those at the top of the class pyramid and suppress those at the bottom. Enslaved people were largely confined to plantations surrounded by marshes, rivers, and inhospitable wilderness, making escape nearly impossible. They were generally prohibited from entering towns without their masters, and the regularity of design made towns easily patrolled. Market squares and other civic spaces were adapted for use as armories, citadels, and guardhouses for the protection of white citizens living in the midst of an enslaved black majority.

A slave-based economy adorned with aristocratic pretentions would be perfected in South Carolina, thereby exerting a greater influence on the development of southern political culture than the region's two other slave societies, Virginia and Louisiana. The Carolina system would spread into Georgia after Oglethorpe's departure, then westward, becoming a model for the American South. Chapter 4 investigates how Carolina political culture became one of the core traditions contributing to the multifaceted character of the United States.

CHAPTER FOUR

The Grand Model and the
Genesis of Southern Political Culture

This chapter investigates the hypothesis that the United States is composed of three primary political cultures, one of which substantially originated in colonial times with the Ashley Cooper Plan. The assertion that attitudes and actions of the present time can be traced back to a point of origin ten generations earlier appears on its face to be a decidedly spurious notion rather than a serious hypothesis. Certainly, most *individuals* today looking back ten generations would be hard-pressed to find a single ancestor with a discernible influence on the present generation. On the other hand, Nicholas Ashley Cooper, the 12th Earl of Shaftesbury, can readily single out Anthony Ashley Cooper, the 1st Earl of Shaftesbury, from among 1,024 ancestors to that generation as the person who established his family culture. In a similar sense, the first Ashley Cooper arguably fathered a plan that conjoined with other definable influences to frame an American political culture.[1]

The search for a point of origin of a culture appears even less strange when one considers that many of the great traditions of civilization are traceable to a single person. Aside from the messianic origins of the world's two largest religions, which count half the world's population as adherents, some argue that Western Civilization owes its path of advancement to a single patriarch, Abraham. Certainly Ashley Cooper was neither a messiah nor a cultural patriarch, but he was an instrumental figure in the creation of an American political tradition. His idea of a republican society built upon Gothic traditions became the rootstock upon which Barbadian slave society was grafted. With Virginia slave society to the north and French and Spanish slaveholding territory to the west and south, Carolina slave society was able to propagate throughout the southeastern region until meeting and blending with its hierarchically compatible neighbors, thus creating an enormously powerful region with many shared political values.

Earlier chapters have shown that Ashley Cooper influenced American political culture in two ways. The first influence was direct and readily discernible: Carolina retained his agrarian plan for large-scale plantations owned by an elite class and modified it for a slave society. The colony abandoned the balancing elements of the plan—a strong yeoman class and the ethic of reciprocity—but it faithfully implemented the design for a powerful plantation elite that saw itself as an entitled aristocracy. In his breakthrough work, *The Mind of the South*, W. J. Cash maintained that few of the plantation elite remained in the South by the nineteenth century, and their numbers were diminishing; yet the model they bequeathed left the smaller backcountry planter with "his feet firmly planted on a road that logically led to aristocracy." To this, Cash added the following quote from the abolitionist Hinton R. Helper: "The white victims of slavery . . . believe whatever the slaveholders tell them; and thus are cajoled into the notion that they are the freest, happiest, and most intelligent people in the world." The mythology constructed by the plantation elite, the "current of unreality" as Cash called it, remained in place to be shared by all whites.[2]

The historian Bertram Wyatt-Brown, who led advancements in the field of psychohistory, confirmed Cash's intuitive understanding of the South as a society enmeshed in hierarchy and patriarchy where whites were "highly conscious of even the subtlest distinction in rank among themselves." Historians have also convincingly demonstrated that the region's plantation elite, though declining in number, maintained a firm grip on the levers of power. It will be shown subsequently that the mechanisms of control were often transmitted from South Carolina to new states as they joined the Union.[3]

The second influence stemming from the Ashley Cooper Plan was indirect and less readily discernible: as the Carolina plantation elite became increasingly dependent on an enslaved labor force, it developed a culture of resistance to outside authority, one that evolved into a defining characteristic of regional political culture. The direct effect was the formation of a distinct "Carolina way," as the early Georgians called it. As a direct influence of the Ashley Cooper Plan, a tenacious pre-Enlightenment, Gothic foothold was introduced into America. Virginia was inclined to adopt new Enlightenment values and to reconsider the long-term viability of the institution of slavery, but Carolina was irrevocably set on a more traditional historical path. The stratification of society widely questioned during the Enlightenment was instead embraced and reinforced in Carolina and its descendant culture. Ashley Cooper's personal reach for a utopian society, the pinnacle of his Gothic political philosophy, succeeded in one monumental way—in maturing John Locke's political philosophy to the point where it would ignite the Enlightenment—an enormous achievement but not the one Ashley Cooper could have expected.[4]

The indirect effect of a culture of resistance developed in waves. One might make a case that it was born in Ashley Cooper's resistance to successive regimes in England. In America, however, it began with the struggle to gain secure footing in a geopolitical no-man's-land claimed by Spain, coveted by France, and held by several Indian nations. An overlapping struggle soon emerged in which the colonists found themselves pitted against the Lords Proprietors over basic tenets of the Fundamental Constitutions. Resistance to proprietary authority persisted through a second generation of colonists over colonial management and religious freedom. After fifty years of resistance to proprietary authority, the colonists gained greater autonomy as a royal colony, then immediately mounted vigorous resistance to the authority of the Georgia Trustees over the neighboring colony's prohibition of slavery. Carolina ultimately succeeded in extending slavery into Georgia, only to begin a struggle against northern states to secure slavery in perpetuity through the Constitution. Upon winning the constitutional fight with northern states, a new fight began over protection of slave "property" and the establishment of future slave states. Resistance to northern abolitionist sentiment escalated into the Civil War. A culture of resistance remained palpable as the southern states reversed the effects of emancipation in the segregationist Jim Crow era. A century after slavery ended, the civil rights era struggle once again provoked southern resistance, reinforcing a sense of regional unity in the face of outside agitation. Continuous resistance to external forces evolved into a visceral hatred of the federal government and a well-honed rhetoric with which to defend its peculiar institutions.

The resistance to outside authority that began with a fight against Ashley Cooper's utopian constitution might be characterized as a cultural *reaction formation*, to borrow a phrase from Freudian psychoanalysis. Reaction formation is defined as "the tendency of a repressed wish or feeling to be expressed at a conscious level in a contrasting form." A classic example is that of repressed homosexuality that develops into hatred of homosexual behavior. In the case of Carolina, a deep-seated anxiety over slavery was turned into an exaggerated defense of its opposite, liberty.

W. J. Cash, who read Freud closely, argued that the region deeply resented its persecution and "in its secret heart always carried a powerful and uneasy sense of the essential rightness of the nineteenth century's position on slavery." In facing continuous external challenges to the way of life created by its self-styled aristocracy, Carolina and eventually the entire South reacted by developing a revulsion for external authority coupled with a strident moral defense of its socioeconomic system.[5]

The tension between an American political culture formed before the Enlightenment and another political culture formed as the Enlightenment flourished established a polarity in national character reflected by political parties. Conservative and progressive parties or their factions have at times balanced each other out, to the nation's benefit. At other times, one or the other has become more extreme to the detriment of the nation. One might also argue that too little tension between political parties is detrimental, as when weary politicians abandoned Reconstruction rather than reforming it, allowing nearly a century of Jim Crow repression to emerge and replace enslavement in their desire to avoid painful but necessary structural change.

The plantation elite that ruled South Carolina through the eighteenth century and into the nineteenth century up to the Civil War was composed largely of Charleston merchants and slaveholders. The historian Robert Weir described their rule as one of "pervasive conservatism that retarded change in many areas of life," a political culture attributable in large part to the compulsion to defend their quasi-aristocratic way of life and the system of slavery that made it possible and resist external pressure to change.[6]

Carolina political culture spread into Georgia in the 1740s, clandestinely at first, then openly, after the Georgia Trustees transferred the colony to the crown in 1752. At that point, the "Carolina way" became the Georgia way. James Oglethorpe's reprise of Harrington's agrarian equality coupled with Enlightenment values gave way to tyranny, as had Ashley Cooper's earlier utopian design. Slaveholders and slave traders had long sought an open market in Georgia, and once available, they moved in quickly.[7]

The interior regions claimed by the Carolina and Georgia colonies came fully under Carolina's influence after 1752. Native Americans, weakened by European diseases, could not stop the advance of the "Carolina way." The alliances built and the trust nurtured by Oglethorpe and the Georgia Trustees were replaced with a more competitive relationship in which the Carolinians sought dominance through regulatory schemes and military superiority. Many of the surviving Native Americans were removed and their lands were seized in a series of repressive actions that culminated in the Trail of Tears in 1830.

Without the ancient tradition of class reciprocity or the Enlightenment philosophy of human equality or strong resistance from Native American nations, the Carolina slave system advanced south into Georgia and then westward at a rapid pace to the Mississippi, where it met the established plantation culture of Louisiana. At the same time, the plantation culture of Virginia and the Potomac River valley advanced across the Appalachians, where it joined Carolina political culture in the region of Tennessee. After the Revolution, the states of Kentucky, Tennessee, Louisiana, Mississippi, and Alabama built a society based on Carolina, Louisiana, and Virginia plantation socioeconomics models and were admitted to the union in rapid succession between 1792 and 1819.

The plantation system was destroyed by the Civil War, but the pre-Enlightenment class pyramid remained psychologically if not economically intact. The agrarian elite who sat atop the pyramid knew from generations of experience that small farmers and other whites in the middle tier had to feel empowered, and their source of empowerment was in their superiority to the formerly enslaved class at the base of the pyramid. Generations of southern poverty followed the Civil War, but with racism built into the class pyramid, there would never be an alliance between aspiring whites and blacks to improve their economic position in the region.

As poverty-stricken whites and blacks migrated steadily out of the South in the last third of the nineteenth century, and then in a torrent between 1913 and the 1960s, the class pyramid and physical and social segregation accompanied them. Cities from the Northeast to the West Coast were racialized, southern-style, to some degree. The change outside the South was held in check, however, by the more pragmatic and democratic (less hierarchical) cultures dominant in other regions.

In 1964, Republican presidential candidate Barry Goldwater developed a southern strategy for attracting traditionally Democratic white voters based on "states' rights," a racially loaded term in the context of the Civil Rights Act passed that year. In the 1968 presidential campaign, Republican candidate Richard Nixon deployed a similar strategy, also using the shield of "states' rights." The term "Southern Strategy" was popularized by Republican strategist Kevin Philips in *The Emerging Republican Majority*, published following Nixon's victory. The strategy was continued in Nixon's 1972 campaign and subsequently adopted in Ronald Reagan's presidential campaigns. During this period, racial rhetoric became more subtle, as conservative positions on the economy and religion took center stage. The strategy successfully broadened the appeal to conservatives in all regions, resulting in resounding Reagan victories in 1980 and 1984, in which he carried forty-four and forty-nine states, respectively.

Republican success was most dramatic in the South. Goldwater won 55 percent of the southern vote in 1964, and Reagan won 72 percent in 1984. The Reagan second term landslide, however, was an outlier, given that African American voters were moving to the Democratic Party as fast as white southerners became Republicans. Republican presidential candidates continued to carry the region in total and electoral votes, but with lower percentages. In Senate elections, the Solid South remained true to its principles as those principles moved from one party to the other. All Deep South senators were Democrats in 1960, and all but one were Republicans in 2012. In the House of Representatives, southern Republicans held only 1 percent of seats in 1960, but since 2000 they have held over 60 percent. Democrats argue that gerrymandering and voter suppression engineered by increasingly Republican-controlled state governments is stretching the demographic ceiling beyond the proportion of white Republican voters in the South.[8]

The Party of Lincoln radically realigned itself by successfully deploying southern class pyramid psychology to reverse regional political polarity. Ironically, the strategy also realigned the political parties to more closely resemble the nation's regional political cultures. The pre-Enlightenment class pyramid of Ashley Cooper's time is found at the core of the modern Republican Party. The flattened social structure of the Enlightenment is found at the core of the Democratic Party. The parties have changed, but political divisions remain, all descendants of the southern, the Mid-Atlantic, and the New England political cultures formed in colonial times. Red, purple, and blue reflecting those divisions have now been popularized by the media as the three primary colors of American political culture.[9]

This brief account of the evolution of southern political culture is expanded later in the chapter with a spotlight cast on South Carolina's continuing influence in the region and in the broader culture. The investigation will reveal the historical roots of current political divisions and associated policies for growth and development—policies that affect the natural environment and shape the cities of tomorrow.

Before presenting additional historical detail, the following section will acquaint the reader with a range of theoretical frameworks that attempt to explain American political culture. The section is essential to understanding the findings and conclusions presented later.

Theories of American Political Culture

Theories of American political culture began with Alexis de Tocqueville, the French political historian who toured the United States extensively in the early 1830s. The tour resulted in publication of *Democracy in America*, which analyzed the regional character of the young nation. Of particular note, Tocqueville traced the essence of the American spirit of democracy to the Puritans, who he found exemplified the values of honest work, civic responsibility, and a more level society. Those admirable traits, he maintained, survived the course of time to become a permanent part of American character, outliving the tarnish of wars with Native Americans and other colonists, intolerance of dissenters, and infamous witch trials. Puritan ideals, Tocqueville believed, were the transformative principles that enabled the United States to eliminate royalty and nobility while lifting all classes of society to greater liberty, economic opportunity, and social mobility.

The political scientist Daniel J. Elazar identified three traditions of political culture in America, generally consistent with Tocqueville's characterizations. New England political culture of the Puritans evolved to become *moralistic political culture*. This component of American character emphasizes community and civic virtue over individualism. It promotes the idea of participatory democracy and the positive role of government in addressing common problems. The Mid-Atlantic region produced *individualistic political culture*, which views government as a utilitarian necessity and seeks to limit its intrusion into private activities. Private initiative is held to be of higher importance than the public sphere. The South produced *traditionalistic political culture*, which elevates social order and family structure to a prominent role. It embraces a hierarchical society as the natural order of things, consistent with Gothic society and the Great Chain of Being. Elected leaders are respected men who use the reins of government to secure and perpetuate the existing social order. Leaders are expected to preserve traditional values and maintain limited government; they are not expected to be reformers or innovators.[10]

Elazar wanted to avoid category names with political undertones and value associations. As a result of this cautiousness, his categories are not intuitively obvious. The more intuitive names *egalitarian* (or humanistic), *pragmatic*, and *fraternalistic* are offered here as alternatives, as presented in Table 7a. The term "egalitarian" reflects the observations of Tocqueville and others on the orientation of New Englanders to community and a relatively level society (see Table 7b). The term "pragmatic" describes the

Table 7a. Principal Regional Political Cultures

Elazar Categories	Region of Origin	Intuitive Name
moralistic	New England	egalitarian
individualistic	Mid-Atlantic	pragmatic
traditionalistic	South	fraternalistic

Table 7b. Principal Metropolitan Political Orientations

Metro Geography	Influence	Political Name
urban	Enlightenment	progressive
suburban	Dutch trade culture	moderate
exurban	Gothic society	conservative

orientation to trade, industry, commerce, and practical government prevalent in the Mid-Atlantic region. A fourth term, *progressivistic,* is applied to both moralistic and individualistic political cultures to reflect their greater openness to progress and support for creative, progressive, scientific, and problem-solving (*creative-progressive,* for short) professions. Finally, the term "fraternalistic" captures the hierarchical and paternalistic aspects of traditional southern culture, as well as the racial and cultural uniformity in the top layers of the social pyramid. The characterization of southern political culture as "paternalistic" is accurate to the Civil War, but since then it has become more fraternalistic, as political control by the agrarian elite has given way to unity—one might say "brotherhood"—in largely white, exurban subregions.[11]

The political scientist J. David Woodard has noted that urbanization, interregional migration, and economic growth have made the South less distinguishable from other regions. He notes with Elazar that civil communities are replacing traditional communities as a result of these forces. Woodard examined demographic variables, including income, education, and population diversity, and found three distinctive subgroups within the South. *National states* strongly resemble other states outside the region with advanced economies; they are Texas, Florida, Georgia, and Virginia. *Emergent states* are those that are approaching that status; they are North Carolina and Tennessee. Others he identifies as *traditional states,* which retain many historical characteristics; they are the Deep South states of South Carolina, Alabama, Arkansas, Louisiana, and Mississippi. Nevertheless, Woodard identifies six facets of southern identity that "have a commanding influence" on its political culture: physical geography and climate, agrarian economy, racial legacy, religious values, one-party politics, and political leadership. Woodard, an adviser to conservative politicians, leans toward the right in minimizing the extent to which the South retains and exports racism as a normative influence on political culture, while also being accurate in his appraisal of past racism.[12]

Woodard acknowledges the pioneering scholarship of the historian V. O. Key in identifying the elements of southern political culture. A central observation in Key's work is that the South alone produced a one-party system, one designed for the exclusive purpose of protecting white privilege. The racially focused system, however, was "ill-designed to meet the necessities of self-government" and chronically unable to solve a broader spectrum of problems. In *Southern Politics*, the first systematic study of southern political culture, Key wrote: "The South, unlike most of the rest of the democratic world, really has no political parties—at least as we have defined them. A single party, so the saying goes, dominates the South, but in reality the South has been Democratic only for external purposes, that is, presidential and congressional elections. The one-party system is purely an arrangement for national affairs."[13]

In 1949, when *Southern Politics* was published, Jim Crow was firmly in place and white authority was internally secure. Since the Civil Rights Act of 1964, the one-party system in the South has adapted to defend against the internal threat of newly empowered black voters. The uniformity of white southern political affiliation, first in national politics, now at all levels, has exacted a price—weakened government set up for defensive maneuvers rather than effective problem-solving. Weak government, of course, is held up as an unchallenged ideal within the South's one-party system. Unfettered private initiative, in that view, will lift the region from its chronic problems across a wide range of socioeconomic indicators, if only the tyranny of the federal government were removed.

The cultural geographer Donald Meinig concurred with Elazar's three primary political cultures in his acclaimed work, *The Shaping of America*. Meinig, however, is more specific about the influence of South Carolina: "This South Carolinian style of politics emerges so blatantly and becomes such a powerful force in the affairs of the Republic that we must acknowledge it as a distinct political culture, even though it does not appear in Elazar's comprehensive scheme but remains submerged in the broader 'traditionalistic' [category]." However, like many authorities on political culture, Meinig traces southern political culture back through Carolina to Barbados (see the conclusion to Chapter 3 for a summary of the counterargument to this position).[14]

The historian and journalist Colin Woodard developed an alternate typology in an analysis of the spatial patterns of American political culture. In *American Nations: A History of the Eleven Rival Regional Cultures of North America*, published in 2011, Woodard delineated regions that correspond closely with those of Elazar. Traditionalistic political culture in Elazar's typology corresponds to three of Woodard's regions—Deep South, Tidewater, and Greater Appalachia. Similarly, Elazar's moralistic and individualistic cultures closely match Woodard's Yankeedom and Midlands categories. Woodard delineates newer political cultures in the western United States, but he acknowledges the influence of the earlier cultures. Woodard's Deep South political culture was begun in Charleston and shaped by the Barbadians, apparently with none of Ashley Cooper's Gothic society surviving. Woodard's work built on the earlier work of the political strategist Kevin Phillips (*The Emerging Republican Majority*, 1969) and the cultural journalist Joel Garreau (*The Nine Nations of North America*, 1981).[15]

The historian David Hackett Fischer traced the origin of four American folkways to regional counterparts in England. Folkways include political culture, but they also encompass religion, settlement patterns, language, and many other facets of culture. The Puritans of East Anglia brought their folkways to Massachusetts in the migration that occurred between 1629 and 1641. People of the distressed south of England populated Virginia between 1642 and 1675, implanting their folkways in that region. The people of England's North Midlands brought their folkways and beliefs to the Mid-Atlantic region between 1675 and 1725. Finally, immigrants from England's north borderlands brought their folkways to the American backcountry over the course of the eighteenth century. These primary influences blended with other cultural and geographic influences to form America's unique mix of regional cultures. In Fischer's view, however, South Carolina became "a distinct culture region, but it never developed into a major cultural hearth."[16]

The conclusion that there are four regional folkways linking Britain with America is compelling, and on close examination enriches (rather than contradicting) the thesis that Carolina produced one of America's three primary political cultures. The Scots-Irish who populated much of America's backcountry began arriving in large numbers in the early 1700s, forming a fourth "great folk migration." More than a quarter million people migrated in the eighteenth century, the largest migration up to that time. They came from the north of Ireland and the border region of Scotland and England and brought with them a tradition of independence, libertarianism, and militant Christianity, as well as a legacy of "incessant violence [that] shaped the culture of the border region." Many arrived in Philadelphia and other cities, but quickly moved into the backcountry. They settled throughout the South, and by the end of the century many were living in the Carolinas. Andrew Jackson and John C. Calhoun were among the descendants of borderlands immigrants.[17]

Fischer describes the Scots-Irish as xenophobic, negrophobic, and anti-Semitic, but also hostile to the large plantation slaveholders and the state governments they controlled. The "strong mood of cultural conservatism" among them persisted from the seventeenth century to the present. They had an "intense concern for equality of esteem," individual autonomy, and "natural freedom," as they referred to their nearly ungoverned frontier way of life. They became known as "crackers," a term of disparagement brought from England. They subscribed to the principles of "minimal government, light taxes, and the right of armed resistance to authority" for infringement of liberty. Their "intolerance for contrary opinions" made their advocacy of those principles a ready source of conflict. An attraction to the backcountry was consistent with Daniel Boone's desire for "elbow room." It was an expression of natural freedom and a facet of libertarianism—frontier improvisation versus the orderliness of settlement in New England and cities on the Atlantic Coast.[18]

These were the same people of the backcountry described by W. J. Cash and Bertram Wyatt-Brown. As individuals, they fiercely defended the equality of their social status while perversely aiming to become more like the plantation elite they despised. The relationship between elite class and backcountry "crackers" became symbiotic over time, as the former established new state governments modeled after South Carolina across the Deep South and the latter populated those states. As Cash wrote, "The tradition of aristocracy met and married with the tradition of the backwoods." Together they forged a region that was proslavery, agrarian, and anti–federal government.[19]

Other theories of political culture are somewhat less geographically specific. The political scientist Louis Hartz laid out a compelling argument for a dominant political culture in *The Liberal Tradition in America*, published in 1955. Hartz argued that John Locke's influence on America was so profound that his political theory, known as classical liberalism, established a set of common beliefs for the nation (see Chapter 1 for a discussion of Locke's *Two Treatises of Government*). America "begins with Locke [and] stays with Locke," thereby shedding the European feudal tradition and never adopting a modern socialist tradition. The two essential

Lockean ideals that shaped America were equality and liberty. Political parties, however, may emphasize different sides of government's role in maintaining these ideals:

> There are two sides to the Lockean argument: a defense of the state that is implicit, and a limitation of the state that is explicit. The first is to be found in Locke's basic social norm, the concept of free individuals in a state of nature. This idea untangles men from the myriad associations of class, church, guild, and place, in terms of which feudal society defined their lives; and by doing to, it automatically gave to the state a much higher rank in relation to them than ever before. The state became the only association that might legitimately coerce them at all.

The South broke from its Lockean and Jeffersonian past (as Hartz framed it) around 1830 in a feudal reaction that brought the region into alignment with South Carolina's full frontal, "positive good," defense of slavery. It became "radicalized" by the 1850s through "its love of chivalry, its faith in force, its ethos of blood and soil." But the "Gothic dream" of the South disappeared remarkably fast, unable to compete with the dominant strain of liberalism underlying American political culture. Southern mythology, or "fantasy," as Hartz called it, was in his view ultimately unable to survive the influence of liberalism, even among southerners.[20]

New support for Hartz can be found in recent research by the cognitive linguist George Lakoff, as well as in fMRI brain-mapping by cognitive scientists and in the findings of anthropologists that humans evolved with dominant cooperative capacities. Lakoff maintains that America began with Enlightenment values, which emphasized a moral foundation for government based on protection and empowerment rather than traditional conservative "frames" of authority, discipline, and obedience. Since about the time Hartz published his work, according to Lakoff, conservatives have become adept at reframing freedom and liberty in particular as core conservative values, thereby redirecting political discourse away from traditional and genetically innate American progressive values of equality, cooperation, empathy, and connectedness. The implications of Lakoff's findings are explored further in the Epilogue.[21]

The political scientist Richard Ellis has argued that Locke is less of a consensus figure than a multifaceted philosopher with appeal to rival beliefs. Ellis identified five distinct political cultures, which generally correspond to the grid-group theory framework proposed by the anthropologist Mary Douglas. The three most prevalent are *individualism, egalitarianism,* and *hierarchy* (which generally correspond to Elazar's traditionalistic, individualistic, and moralistic categories, respectively). The other two are *fatalism* (originating from slave culture) and *hermitude* (Thoreau-like individualism). The first two, individualism and egalitarianism, are particularly enduring strains of American political culture, but not as immutable as Hartz's classical liberalism. Each claims the Lockean ideals of equality and liberty, but what they are claiming is only a piece of Locke, and one that is not necessarily consistent with the whole. Some political cultures see equality as *process*, while others see it for its *results*. Similarly, Americans agree with Locke that "justice gives every man a title to the product of his honest industry," but they differ on what "honest" means. While Ellis finds "welcome relief" in Elazar from the consensualist theories of Hartz and others, he argues for deeper analysis. The "fundamental weakness" of Elazar's categories, he maintains, is that it is derived from "regional variations" rather than multidimensional analysis.[22]

A new multidimensional approach to defining political culture was taken in *Our Patchwork Nation*, a collaboration by the journalist Dante Chinni and the political geographer James Gimpel. In the book, they analyzed county-level demographic data to look beyond the coarser red, blue, and purple state categories framed for public consumption by the news media, seeking more fine-grained patterns in American political culture. Chinni and Gimpel identified twelve cultural communities found throughout the United States, with varying degrees of geographic concentration. Their categories ranged from "boom town" and "monied burbs" with 118 million people between them, to "Mormon outposts" and "tractor country" with only 4 million people combined. The categories are teased out of statistical data, and they offer a more realistic portrayal of the geographically discontinuous cultural fabric of the nation than blanket state and regional categories. The extent to which the twelve cultures are franchised by primary cultures sustained by major political interests is unclear.[23]

In a similar collaboration between a journalist and a social scientist, Bill Bishop and Robert Cushing offered more quantitative evidence for the Chinni-Gimpel thesis. In *The Big Sort*, they showed that with 5 percent of the population moving from county to county each year, people are sorting themselves into communities rather than regional political cultures or red and blue states. Political culture is now often more visible at the city or county level. A well-known example is Los Angeles and Orange counties in California, where populations have been sorting themselves for decades into increasingly Democratic and Republican enclaves. In "landslide counties" where one party typically wins an election by a vote margin of 20 percent or more, patterns are becoming clear. Republican landslide counties have increasingly large populations of churchgoers, among other sorting factors, while Democratic landslide counties have increasingly large populations of immigrants. The sort is also found in high-tech and low-tech cities. Populations of the former increasingly exhibit more interest in cultures and places, more engagement in individualistic activities, and more optimism; the latter exhibit greater church attendance, more community projects and social activities, more support for traditional authority, and more family-oriented activity. Bishop and Cushing conclude that an increasingly cocooned population is diminishing America's sense of national consensus.[24]

For the present, it is safe to stay with Elazar's typology as regional characteristics remain strong (though perhaps not for many more decades). According to Elazar's assessment, moralistic political culture became well established in New England, the Upper Midwest and portions of the West. Individualistic political culture became characteristic of the Mid-Atlantic states west to Illinois, and beyond to much of the West. Traditionalistic political culture grew dominant in the South, where class hierarchy is fundamental to social organization, as revealed in the migration patterns shown in Figure 13. Figure 14 shows the generalized distribution of the three primary political cultures at full maturity in the twentieth century.

The three political cultures began reshaping America's urban geography during the mass migrations from the South in the early and mid-twentieth century. Metropolitan areas in all regions are often seen trending toward historic New England and Mid-Atlantic political traditions, whereas rural and exurban areas throughout the nation have trended toward southern, or fraternalistic, political culture. Still, the urban-suburban-exurban divisions are influenced as much by occupation, education, income, and other demographics as by regional political culture. Resistance to external threats, part of the essence of southern political culture, has not been central to the political culture of the rural North. However, the resistance orientation of traditionalistic southern political culture gradually diffused through metropolitan regions across the nation, first through migration, then as a political strategy (the Southern Strategy), and more recently through media technology advances and market segmentation (for example, Fox News versus MSNBC).

Table 7b suggests a different typology for political variation associated with metropolitan regions, which may be described as a political orientation rather than a political culture. Highly urbanized areas are strongly influenced by institutions of higher learning and research, social diversity, and the presence of a "creative class" (a term popularized by urban theorist Richard Florida).

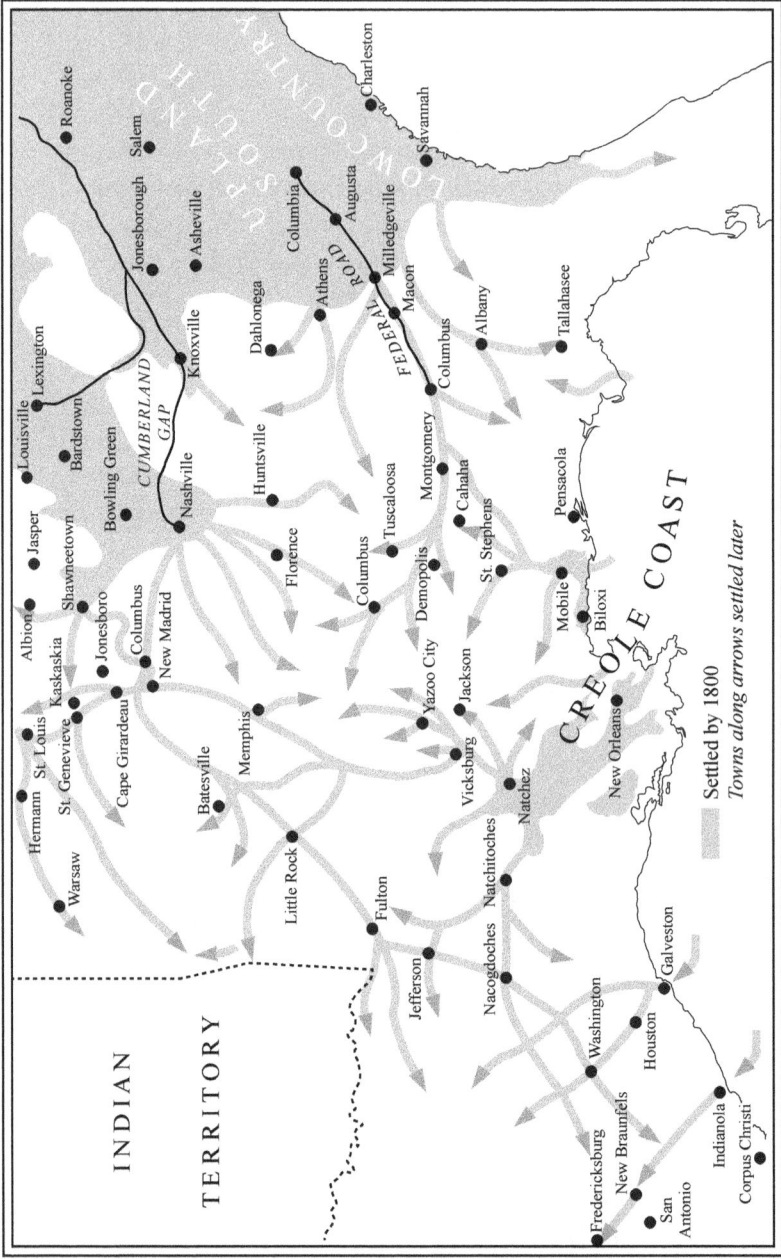

Figure 13. Migration Patterns and Diffusion of Political Culture. Carolina migrants can be seen settling the Deep South and meeting Virginia migrants in the Lower Mississippi region, where both cultures blended with Louisiana influences. From D. W. Meinig, *The Shaping of America*, courtesy Yale University Press.

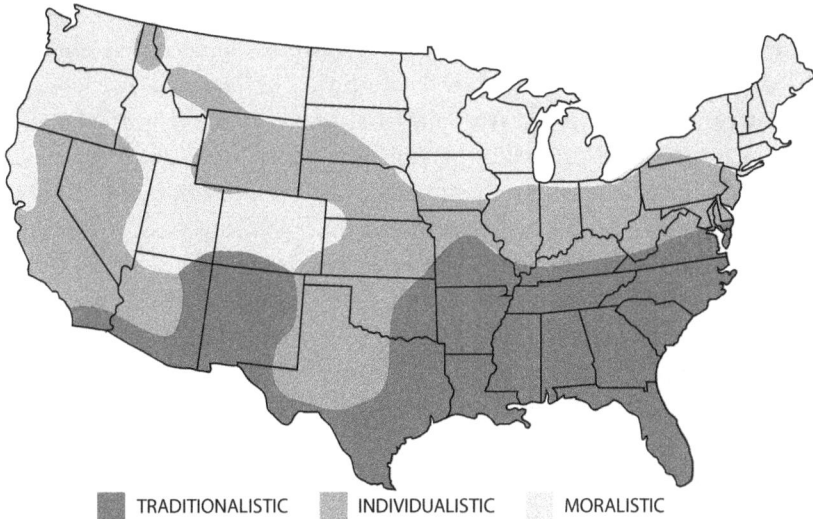

TRADITIONALISTIC   INDIVIDUALISTIC   MORALISTIC

Figure 14. Generalized Map of American Political Cultures. Elazar's three primary political cultures shown here are based on established regional character. In recent decades, the same political cultures have formed within metropolitan regions throughout the country. Illustration by Teri Norris (after Jordan-Bychkov and Domosh, *The Human Mosaic*, 9th ed., 187).

The urban orientation toward science and humanism falls within the tradition of the Enlightenment and may be described as a *progressivistic* political orientation, as suggested earlier. The progressivistic urban orientation is distinct from the generally *moderate* and pragmatic political orientation of the suburbs and the more *conservative* political orientation of the exurbs.

James Carville, a Democratic Party political adviser, captured the essence of geographic diffusion of political culture with his observation that "Pennsylvania is Philadelphia and Pittsburgh with Alabama in between." In the South, the Republican base resides in rural areas, small towns, exurbs, and white enclaves. However, many southern cities lean Democratic, including Charleston, the birthplace of traditionalistic political culture. The city has reelected Mayor Joseph Riley, a Democrat, since 1975.[25]

Recent research led by the social psychologist Peter J. Rentfrow supports both regional and urban-rural theories of political culture, while finding that psychological variables allow for a more fine-grained geographical analysis similar to that of Chinni and Gimpel. The research on American "psychological topography," based on multiple samples of over a million respondents, supports Elazar's regional theory of political culture while finding that migration frequency contributed to the formation of a distinct western political culture (exhibiting pragmatic traits of Elazar's individualistic Mid-Atlantic region). Rentfrow's quantitative analysis discovered three primary political cultures. The "relaxed and creative region" predominant in the West places a high value on open-mindedness, tolerance, individualism, and the pursuit of happiness. The "temperamental and uninhibited region" predominant in the "quintessential blue states" of the Northeast is largely made up of people who are passionate, competitive, and liberal. The "friendly and conventional region" predominant in the South and other red states is characterized by conservative social values, family, low levels of social tolerance, and maintenance of the status quo. The researchers found "overwhelming evidence for regional variation across the United States on a range of key political, economic, social, and health indicators."[26]

Research by the psychologists Jesse Harrington and Michelle Gelfand published in 2014 lends further support to Elazar's theory. The research identified nine variables associated with political culture and developed a composite index to rank all fifty states on a scale of "tightness" (many strongly enforced rules and little tolerance for deviance) and "looseness" (few strongly enforced rules and greater tolerance for deviance). The rank order of states on the scale produced a cluster of southern states exhibiting tightness, a cluster of northeastern and West Coast states exhibiting looseness, while midwestern and Mountain West states ranked in the middle. The clusters were nearly identical to Elazar's traditionalistic, moralistic, and individualistic regional political cultures. The researchers conclude that by understanding "why differences in tightness–looseness arise at the state level, we can better appreciate our intranational differences and, ultimately, manage our own diversity therein."[27]

Another study by psychologists synthesizing a large body of research examined psychological variables underlying political orientation, specifically conservatism. They evaluated eighty-eight studies involving 22,818 cases in twelve countries. The study found support for an overarching theory that "political attitudes and beliefs possess "a strong motivational basis" and that such motives "satisfy various psychological needs." Variables include fear and aggression, dogmatism and intolerance of ambiguity, uncertainty avoidance, need for cognitive closure, personal need for structure, terror management, group-based dominance, and system justification. Conservative ideology at its core is associated with "psychological management of uncertainty and fear." The outcome of these motives is primarily "resistance to change" and "endorsement of inequality." The study suggests that conservatives are particularly receptive to political messaging that warns of internal and external threats, making the Southern Strategy a complete package for national distribution. The message is that a mortal threat to American traditions is posed by African Americans and immigrants, among others, who are manipulated into government dependency by liberals bent on ever-growing federal power. Moreover, an accompanying message rouses fear that this growing menace is paving the way for the complete destruction of American values by international forces working through the United Nations (see Chapter 5).[28]

Economists have also weighed in on the subject of American political culture. The economist David George has argued that the twentieth century brought about a shift from civic-oriented moralistic political culture to business-oriented individualistic political culture, reinforced by post–World War II consumerism. Even as federal government outlays have remained low compared to other nations (peaking under Reagan at 23 percent of GDP), public discourse has reflected increasing dissatisfaction with government and civic duty, as compared to business and personal liberty. A content analysis of newspapers conducted by George revealed a dramatic decline in references to "big business" and a corresponding increase in negative references to "big government." Similarly, references to "economic growth" surpassed references to intellectual, spiritual, and personal growth, and to economic equality, fairness, and justice. In Hartzian terms, George's analysis suggests that the nation strengthened its fundamental orientation to Lockean classical liberalism over the course of the century. Such a conclusion is muddied, however, by the success of the Southern Strategy with its emphasis on social conservatism. The economist Albert Hirschman conducted a similar analysis of political rhetoric, finding that "polarized debates" among political cultures have essentially left them largely intact rather than normalizing around classical liberalism. This "dialogue of the deaf," Hirschman maintains, is a continuation of the Civil War by other means, a perpetuation of the deep rift between fraternalistic and progressivistic political cultures.[29]

Elazar published his theory of political cultures in 1970, and since then cultural regions have become more diverse and political motivations more complex, as suggested by the psychological research cited above. The shift toward greater regional diversity can be explained in part by the Republican Southern Strategy, which has been reformulated as a national strategy aimed at securing suburban, exurban, and rural counties outside the South (Carville's "Alabama"). The expanded strategy seeks to implant traditional southern political priorities, such as opposition to federal authority, throughout the country, principally by arguing that the federal

Table 8. Elements of Ashley Cooper Republican Doctrine and
Their Adoption in America

Component	Ashley Cooper Republicanism	American Republicanism
Form of government	Constitutional aristocracy	Constitutional democracy
Executive authority	Through consent of nobility	Through popular election*
Balanced government	Agrarian	Nonagrarian
	Balance of powers	Separation of Powers
Elections	Regular elections to legislature	Regular elections to executive and legislature
National defense	Militia raised by Nobility**; permanent navy	Standing srmy and navy
Taxation	Limited by consent of nobility	Proposed by executive and authorized by legislature
Rights of citizens	Freedom of conscience Other rights guaranteed by the Ancient Constitution	Freedom of religion Other rights guaranteed by the Bill of Rights

* With limited legislative oversight specified in the constitution
** No standing army

government is redistributing the income of hardworking people ("makers")
to unworthy consumers of government largesse ("takers"). Nevertheless,
strong, long-standing regional patterns remain in place, as demonstrated
by the highly popular usage of the red, blue, and purple state meme.

To appreciate the genesis of traditionalistic political culture with the
Ashley Cooper Plan, one must look at Ashley Cooper's own political
milieu. Seventeenth-century Gothic republicanism, which Ashley Cooper
defined during the Restoration, became a strong influence on early
colonial leaders and eventually on the Founding Fathers. Table 8 lists the
tenets of late seventeenth-century republicanism and their translation
into southern political culture. Strains of modern libertarian and neoconservative philosophy can be traced to that source, including agrarianism, gun rights, minimal taxation, and decentralized government. On the
other hand, opposition to a standing army and foreign interventionism
run counter to modern neoconservatism, though not libertarianism.

Present-day attacks from the right on principles of sustainable development, Smart Growth, New Urbanism, environmental protection, climate science, and social equity have acquired a new intensity that is confounding to practitioners in those fields. Specific conceptual and rhetorical strategies for productively engaging with and responding to libertarian and neoconservative arguments against such initiatives can be found in the Epilogue. The following sections offer the reader a deeper look into the history and diffusion of the "Carolina way." The account will form the basis for a practical new perspective on contemporary political culture.

Expansion of Carolina Culture into Georgia

Georgia was the last of the British-American colonies. Established in 1733, it was conceived when the Enlightenment reached maturity. The plan for Georgia, the Oglethorpe Plan, reflected the full range of idealistic thought prevalent during the age. It reached back to the same philosophical roots that inspired Ashley Cooper and Locke and updated those ideals with new Enlightenment ideals of equality, humanism, and the great potential of reason and the scientific method to solve all problems. With a goal of creating a colony of yeoman farmers and a system of sustainable agrarian equality, the Oglethorpe Plan prohibited amassing of land and monopolizing of the economy by special interests. The new colony was initially welcomed and supported by South Carolina. The colony's southern flank was vulnerable to attack by Spanish, French, and Native American forces, and the Georgia settlement plan included a well-trained militia.[30]

The visionary behind the plan for Georgia, James Edward Oglethorpe, was also the leader on the front lines when it came to establishing the new colony. He led the first party of colonists to America, selected the site for the town of Savannah, and oversaw its development according to plans drawn up in London. The plan developed by Oglethorpe and his associates, a body known as the Georgia Trustees, exemplified Newtonian symmetry, logic, and rationality. It took as a given the concept of a universe governed by laws, a tenet at the heart of the Enlightenment. It also contained practical elements of frontier defense acquired by Oglethorpe from his classical studies of Roman colonization at Oxford and his military service under Prince Eugene in the Balkans.[31]

Colonists were organized into groups of ten families, with each group allocated a 10-parcel block in town, a cluster of 5-acre gardens just outside town, and a square-mile farm section containing 45-acre plots for each family. Oglethorpe believed the regimentation to be necessary to forming a militia on a hostile frontier claimed by the Spain, eyed by France, and occupied by indigenous nations. Towns would be established in a strategic pattern and settlers were organized into units of ten families, the core unit of a well-regulated militia. Once the frontier was tamed and civilized, the colony would be governed under the original principles of England's Ancient Constitution, much as Roman military camps became towns that were eventually absorbed into the republic.

Thus Oglethorpe, a military officer as well as a politician, drew his defensive design from the Roman army's colonial *castrum*, but he was also an idealist who drew from Renaissance concepts of an ideal city. Oglethorpe's formulation of the ideal city was one that allocated land fairly within and outside of the town. Families were expected to own and work their own land. Indentured servants who worked for families would receive their own grant of land once they completed their service. Slavery was prohibited, both as a corrupting influence on the system of family farming and as an inhumane practice.[32]

Oglethorpe and fellow Georgia Trustees maintained their opposition to slavery for seventeen years. Constant pressure from South Carolina slave traders and their acolytes to end the ban in Georgia was held at bay until Oglethorpe ended his involvement with the colony in 1749. Only then did the remaining Trustees relent on their opposition to slavery. Discouraged upon hearing that slaves had been secretly brought into the colony in substantial and irreversible numbers, the Trustees voted to lift the prohibition, and the chapter on the only slave-free southern colony formally closed.

When Georgia was founded in 1733, it stood in stark contrast to South Carolina. Oglethorpe, its visionary founder, conceived a model colony of yeoman farmers who worked their own family farms without underlying classes of leetmen, villeins, or enslaved laborers. Landownership was limited to 50 acres for "charity" colonists (the "worthy poor") who were initially subsidized to settle in Georgia and 500 acres for those who paid their own way. No one, regardless of class, could acquire more acreage through inheritance, purchase, lease, or any other means.

The plan for Georgia, like that of Carolina, took inspiration for its agrarian social balance and economic structure from James Harrington. The newer plan, however, combined Harrington's prescription for agrarian equality with the emerging concept of social equity. The country party of Gothic republicanism conceived by Ashley Cooper in the 1670s evolved into republicanism in the 1700s, led by men like Oglethorpe and Lord Bolingbroke (widely read in pre-Revolutionary America). Oglethorpe advanced the Lockean ideal of equality beyond where Harrington had taken it, while Bolingbroke and others retained more of Harrington's—and Ashley Cooper's—traditional class structure emphasizing reciprocity and noblesse oblige in a balanced agrarian society.

Oglethorpe was well aware of the differences between the colony he envisioned and the slave-dependent caste system that was by then entrenched in Carolina. While Oglethorpe maintained a close relationship with some of Carolina's political leaders, notably Colonel William Bull, who had helped lay out Savannah, he was increasingly at odds with the slave merchants and slaveholders, who saw Georgia as an untapped market. Oglethorpe wrote that "the people of Carolina desire to have [Georgia] entirely destroyed, and united to theirs, that they may have the benefit of the improvements here, and the liberty of oppressing both the Indians and the English poor, as they do their own." There were repeated appeals to the Georgia Trustees in London to abandon the prohibition on slavery, which Oglethorpe countered in the strongest terms: "If we allow slaves we act against the very principles by which we associated together, which was to relieve the distressed. Whereas, now we should occasion the misery of thousands in Africa, by setting men upon using arts to buy and bring into perpetual slavery the poor people who now live free there."[33]

Georgia's effort to regulate trade with Native Americans to prevent abuses and its interception and destruction of rum imports angered Carolina upcountry traders as well as Charleston merchants. They attempted to stir up animosity between the Georgia colonists and their indigenous neighbors, a move that backfired. The Carolinians blamed Georgia settlers for encroachment on their territory, when it was they who had engaged in greater encroachment. While there had been a small "indiscreet action" by the Georgians in Uchee territory, the matter was resolved. "But what vexed the Uchees more was [that] some of the Carolina people swam a great heard of cattle over Savannah and sent up Negroes and began a plantation on the Georgia side, not far from the Uchee's town." Instead of blaming the Georgians, they informed Oglethorpe that his actions affirmed the strength of their treaty, and they would not be provoked by the Carolinians. They even offered to fight with him against the Spanish in Florida if hostilities broke out. Oglethorpe concluded by writing to the Trustees, "You see how God baffles the attempts of wicked men."[34]

Oglethorpe's early success in establishing a slave-free colony and good relations with Native Americans became increasingly agitating to Carolina slaveholders, merchants, and traders. Additionally, Oglethorpe believed they had undermined settlers at Port Royal Sound (an assessment he may have acquired from his friend Colonel Bull) because it does not want competition, and that they intended to do the same to Georgia to preserve power in Charles Town. Facing the hostility, Oglethorpe wrote, "There is hardly a man in the universe that has had more lies raised of him." And "this general clamour of idles, wicked and ungrateful people must have had some root," one that could go all the way to England, where the Carolinians had allies within the commercial class in Bristol.[35]

With all the disdain cultivated in Charles Town for Oglethorpe and Georgia, visitors from South Carolina were sometimes surprised at its progress. When one group toured the Savannah area with William Stephens, the Trustees' secretary in the colony (and later its president), they were impressed with its progress, admitting that production "exceeded any thing about Charles-Town." Nevertheless, the visitors argued, slavery was essential to lower production costs. Stephens observed that whites in South Carolina had to be "perpetually" on guard against revolt as a result of their dependence on an enslaved labor force, a mortal threat that did not exist in Georgia.[36]

Soon afterward, Stephens spoke with seven others who had left Georgia to settle in Carolina and were now returning. One by the name of Williamson, a relative of a Charleston slave merchant, observed that Georgia was much better off than previously, and he spoke of the "vanity" of South Carolinians and their "inveterate ill-will" toward their neighbor. The Carolinians spoke of Georgia with "great contempt" yet were apprehensive that the new colony would overtake them in "trade and manufactures" in a matter of a few years, principally because Carolina was invested almost exclusively in rice. Stephens speculated that if St. Augustine were taken, Carolinians might be inclined to settle in Georgia and live under its "constitution." Williamson let on that the attorney general in South Carolina would assert a claim to land in Georgia, implying that Carolinians were returning in anticipation of overturning the Trustee system and claiming larger tracts on which to institute the "Carolina way."[37]

For a brief period of time, Georgia appeared as if it might succeed in spite of the efforts of Carolinians and their acolytes in Georgia, known as the Malcontents. In August 1740, Stephens wrote, "The town had the great blessing of health to a degree far beyond its neighbors across the river in Carolina, which it was to be wished might not be impaired, as the Fall came on, though the immense quantity of peaches growing every where, which our people have long eaten with greediness, alike with the swine, that have in great part been fed with them."[38]

The aggressive stance taken by Carolina toward Georgia might be characterized as that of a tyrannical regime fighting to preserve aristocratic privilege. The observation of historian Robert Weir cited earlier that described Carolina rule as one of "pervasive conservatism that retarded change in many areas of life" exposes a related form of aggression born of an instinct for self-preservation. Samuel Johnson's comment about the loudest yelps for liberty coming from those who defend slavery can be appreciated all the more in light of the relationship between Carolina and the infant Georgia Colony.

Carolina's persistence in undermining Georgia was a major factor in unraveling Oglethorpe's plan of agrarian equality. The Carolinians promoted dissent in Savannah with promises of wealth built on slavery, they attempted to undermine Georgia through allies in government in England, and they constantly worked to undermine Oglethorpe's reputation. When Oglethorpe relocated from Savannah to Frederica to prepare for conflict with the Spanish at St. Augustine, the Carolinians took advantage and did everything possible to clandestinely introduce slavery and sabotage the first principles of the new colony.[39]

In 1749, Stephens informed the Trustees that the prohibition against slavery was impractical to enforce and recommended that it be lifted but carefully regulated to be both humane and limited in scope so as to avoid the potential for revolt. The Trustees responded with indignation that such a request should be made, but Stephens held firm, maintaining that slaves had been secretly brought over from Carolina for some time and it was now impossible to stop. The Trustees, with Oglethorpe on military duty and no longer attending meetings, relented. Two years later, when the Georgia Trustees surrendered management of the colony back to the crown, plantation owner Jonathan Bryan took sixty-six slaves to the Savannah area, leading a "parade" of Carolina planters into Georgia Colony.[40]

The Trustees enacted regulations that they viewed as humanitarian for the treatment of slaves before surrendering the colony. Those regulations, however, were soon replaced by the repressive South Carolina slave code. The former had provided for treatment of enslaved blacks in a manner similar to that of white servants. The latter, initially modeled on the Barbados code and made even more severe after the Stono Rebellion of 1739, was consistent with Locke's description of slavery as a "vile and miserable" institution of mankind. As the geographer Donald Meinig wrote, "One of the most distinctive colonies in America was being rapidly transformed into a replica of its neighbor. In terms of cultural geography, Georgia had become simply the westernmost district of Greater Carolina." Georgia was the first new province to fall to the "Carolina way," but the political culture would move westward at an accelerating rate over the last half of the eighteenth century.[41]

Displacement of Native Americans

The westward advance of the "Carolina way" was initially checked by the presence of numerous indigenous nations. White American mythology once held that North America was sparsely populated and mostly unclaimed, making the continent wide open for European settlement. Rather than having a million or so inhabitants as once thought (and taught in schools), the population is now known to have been around 20 million. Four principal factors paved the way for Euro-American settlement across the South and through such a sizable population: disease, war, treaty violations, and relocation.[42]

The historian Alfred W. Crosby published a comprehensive assessment of European contact on Native Americans in *The Columbian Exchange*, published in 1972. The title has since become the term of choice used by scholars to describe the sudden and transformative interaction between the Old World and the New World. Crosby's work stimulated new research and led to the development of the field of environmental history. The initial impact on indigenous populations occurred in the Caribbean Basin and South America during the Spanish and Portuguese conquests of those regions. In the seventeenth century, the English and other northern Europeans entered the Columbian Exchange through the Caribbean and North America, with similarly momentous results.[43]

The transmission of disease was a major component of the Columbian Exchange, along with the exchange of plants, animals, culture, and technology. Europeans introduced strains of smallpox, measles, malaria, influenza, typhus, yellow fever, tuberculosis, and other diseases to Native Americans for which they had no resistance. It is estimated that up to 95 percent of the Native American population died from epidemics brought on by Europeans. The impact of disease on indigenous Americans was vastly greater than on Europeans because of the relative isolation of the Americas until 1492 and an accompanying lack of acquired immunity. Additionally, Native Americans generally did not domesticate animals, a practice that can produce crowd diseases and eventually produces immunities. The enslavement of large numbers of Native Americans in South Carolina for a half century increased exposure to disease and its rapid spread.[44]

When Carolina and Georgia were established, there was no grasp of the toll disease was already taking on Native Americans, or that wars or mass relocations would be required for European settlement. The charters for the colonies established borders to the north and south but not to the west. The British Empire was expected to grow westward, into and

across the continent. Treaties with Native American nations were anticipated, but it was also believed that England's culture, laws, and religion
would prevail—an outcome expected without the accelerants of disease,
war, or relocation. The three planned colonies—Carolina, Pennsylvania,
and Georgia—adopted explicit policies to promote goodwill and mutually beneficial relations with Native Americans. The Lords Proprietors
issued specific instructions to the first colonists to pursue good relations
with Native Americans; Pennsylvania concluded successful treaties with
the Lenape and other indigenous people; and the Georgia Trustees were
committed to a policy of "equity and beneficence" toward indigenous
people. The initial goodwill crumbled, however, as the British population
grew and sought land for expansion.[45]

At the time of the founding of Georgia in 1733, the colonies were poised
for westward expansion. When Oglethorpe arrived in America, he immediately instituted the Georgia Trustees' policy of living peacefully and
productively with the native populations. His attitude of mutual respect
led him to become a close friend of Tomochichi, chief of the Yamacraw, who
lived near Savannah, hosting him on a visit to England and even learning
to hunt buffalo with him. He traveled extensively among the indigenous
nations promoting peace and understanding and securing allies. Through
that cultural immersion, he acquired a deep respect for Native American
culture, and he insisted on mutually beneficial treaties establishing boundaries and governing relations with nearby nations—an expectation that
became a source of friction between Carolina and Georgia.[46]

With few exceptions, the posture of Carolinians toward Native Americans
after the proprietary period was one of exploitation, not cooperation.
Within a remarkably short thirty years, South Carolina laid the foundation on the frontier that would shape regional dynamics for the remainder
of the colonial period. By 1700, South Carolina was competing with the
older Virginia Colony, which had been an early model for both settlers
and backcountry influence. Soon afterward, Charles Town authorities saw
their colony as the heart of the British Empire in the Southeast. Respect
for Native American people and their nations declined, and the English
settlers dismissed them as having "nothing but the shape of Men to
distinguish them from Wolves & Tigers." They were considered by most as
savages to be subdued like everything else in the American wilderness.[47]

There were four large indigenous nations, and various smaller tribes,
still thriving in the southeastern region of North America in territory
granted to the provinces of Carolina and Georgia by their charters. The
Creek, or Muskogee, Nation encompassed much of present-day South

Carolina, Georgia, and Alabama. The Cherokee Nation was concentrated in the southern Appalachians but maintained a strong trading presence in the coastal lowlands. The Chickasaw and Choctaw populations were concentrated farther west in present-day Alabama and Mississippi but had trade relations and mutual defense pacts with Carolina and Georgia. The first European settlers in Carolina initially encountered the Yemasee people, who were primarily of Creek ethnicity. The Yamacraw people whom Oglethorpe encountered on the Savannah River were a smaller band, also associated with the Creek Nation.

Ignoring the Lords Proprietors' desire for good relations with the indigenous nations, Carolina traders became infamous for their corrupt practices, which included aggressively marketing rum and running up indebtedness to gain leverage for swindling their trade partners. These practices, together with encroachments into native lands, had precipitated the Yemasee War of 1715, which temporarily depopulated Port Royal and destabilized the southern frontier of the Carolinas. William Bull, who befriended Oglethorpe and aided in building Savannah, was among the few who advocated more progressive policies toward Native Americans. However, he and like-minded Carolinians were outnumbered and outmaneuvered by those with an appetite for quick profits.[48]

The Georgia Trustees, at Oglethorpe's recommendation, enacted a law governing trade with Native American nations. Carolina traders operating within Georgia were required to be licensed and to conduct themselves in accordance with the new law, while also respecting Trustee policies and treaties with the nations. Oglethorpe sent agents upcountry to monitor trade, and he seized and staved shipments of rum, which was banned in Georgia (unlike beer and wine). Carolina contested the law through the Board of Trade in London and fought it at home. The more powerful colony passed a law of its own requiring Georgia to compensate Carolina merchants for losses incurred by the Georgia law. Rum in particular was viewed by Charles Town merchants as essential to trade, while Oglethorpe and Native American leaders opposed it for the deleterious effect it had on native people.[49]

The Carolinians began taking Native Americans as slaves almost as soon as the colony was established and persisted with the practice for a half century, as noted earlier. Many of these slaves were prisoners of war taken captive by either enemy tribes or European settlers; others were taken by Native American raiding parties, which ranged as far south as the Florida Keys. The proprietors attempted to stop the practice but failed. The demand for indigenous slaves gradually gave way to the demand for Africans, who had no knowledge of the land and nowhere to escape, who posed no threat to trade relations, and who were resistant to many diseases. Few Native Americans were enslaved by the end of the 1720s, but slave trading had become so widespread and profitable that it altered indigenous societies and destroyed towns and agricultural practices over the remainder of the century.[50]

The Southeast was the only region in which three European powers competed and where their actions were intertwined with European geopolitics. Indigenous nations often entered into alliances with European nations to defend their interests against other combinations of native and foreign forces. Creek and English forces, for example, fought the Spanish and their allies over disputed territory between Georgia and Florida. Creeks and other nations entered into a treaty with the English to defend against the French and their allies, who posed a territorial threat in the west. Eventually, the English in South Carolina became sufficiently strong to prevail in direct confrontations with indigenous nations, beginning with the Yemasee War and culminating in a series of later hostilities and wars with the Cherokee Nation that persisted from the late 1750s to the early 1780s.[51]

A succession of treaties with the nations were contrived to facilitate European expansion and were often violated when they proved inconvenient to white settlers. Alexander McGillivray (1750–93), born Hoboi-Hili-Miko, was a Creek chief of mixed ancestry who represented multiple nations in negotiating treaties to preserve sovereignty. He attempted to prevent British expansion into Creek territory. His experience negotiating treaties with the Americans was that they were frequently violated. In 1785 he wrote, "We have received friendly talks and replies, it is true, but while they are addressing us by the flattering appellations of Friends and Brothers, they are stripping us of our natural rights by depriving us of that inheritance which belonged to our ancestors and hath descended from them to us since the beginning of time."[52]

George Washington as president, Thomas Jefferson as vice president, and Henry Knox as secretary of war, the principal representative to the Native American nations, believed that the United States should adopt a formal position that the indigenous nations were sovereign states and that a relationship should be established with them based on treaties and mutual respect. More important, as sovereign states, all relations should be conducted by the federal government. It was a policy they believed was consistent with the principles of the Revolution.[53]

Their efforts culminated in the Treaty of New York in 1790. McGillivray led a large contingent of Native Americans to the treaty conference in an impressive show of force. The treaty was designed to establish permanent borders that would ensure peaceful coexistence of whites and Native American nations. The new framework, however, was undermined in Carolina and Georgia, where state authorities and white settlers had no intention of respecting the terms of the treaty. The new federal government found that it had few enforcement resources. Whites poured across Creek borders by the thousands. Knox wrote that "a lawless set of unprincipled wretches" were violating "the most solemn treaties, without receiving the punishment they so richly deserve." Washington wrote that "scarcely anything short of a Chinese wall will restrain . . . the encroachment of settlers upon the Indian Country."[54]

Andrew Jackson, who became president in 1829, brought about the forced removal of Native Americans from their homelands through the Indian Removal Act of 1830. The act authorized the forced relocation of Native American people from the southeastern states to the present-day state of Oklahoma. The subsequent mass migration, now known as the Trail of Tears, began in 1832 and continued to 1839. Cherokee, Creek, Seminole, Chickasaw, and Choctaw nations were subject to the mass relocation. The torturous march resulted in thousands of deaths of Native Americans as well as African Americans and European Americans who endured the march with them. It was the final act in opening up southwestern territory for white settlement.

The mass depopulation, displacement, and relocation of Native Americans in the Southeast cleared the way for rapid growth of white populations in Alabama, Mississippi, Florida, Louisiana, Kentucky, Tennessee, and eventually west of the Mississippi.

Westward Expansion

By the mid-1700s, three largely independent slave societies were well established in the Southeast: Virginia, South Carolina, and Louisiana. Each, of course, was associated with a larger region. Virginia was at the center of the Tidewater region and North Carolina. South Carolina by then had succeeded in bringing Georgia under its influence. And the slave society of Louisiana encompassed the Lower Mississippi region (a province of France until the Louisiana Purchase, except from 1763 to 1800 when it was ceded to Spain). By 1742, Oglethorpe had secured the southern flank of the thirteen colonies for Britain by settling Georgia, securing treaties with indigenous tribes throughout the region, and commanding an army that repulsed an incursion by Spanish forces. A decade later, with

Oglethorpe and the Georgia Trustees out of the way, South Carolina was in control of the destiny of the Deep South.

Carolina political culture advanced westward across the southeastern region, eventually meeting and joining the established slave culture of Louisiana. At the same time, it percolated northward, blending with Virginia cultural influences in Tennessee and Kentucky. The relative influence of the two British colonies (and later as two southern states) was primarily determined by two factors: the projection of agrarian elitist influence and the volume of migration into the new territories.

On the surface, Virginia and South Carolina appear to have evolved with similar political cultures: their societies were agrarian and rigidly hierarchical, their governments were controlled by the plantation elite, and their economies were dependent on monoculture and enslaved labor. By the nineteenth century, as the historian Eugene Genovese observed, their shared "source of pride was not the Union, not the nonexistent southern nation; it was the plantation, which they raised to a political principle." Upon closer examination, however, one finds significant differences. In 1790, when Congress considered the gradual abolition of slavery, Virginia was poised to consider it. Thomas Jefferson proposed phasing out slavery by emancipating children after a certain date. He later expressed fear, shared by many, that the failure to act after the Revolution had left the state in a precarious position: "We have a wolf by the ears, and we can neither hold him nor safely let him go. Justice is in one scale, and self-preservation in the other."[55]

Such deep concern spanned generations in Virginia, culminating in a statewide debate over the future viability of slavery following Nat Turner's rebellion in 1831. During the debate, hundreds of Virginians signed petitions and attended meetings of the House of Delegates to convey their concerns. The influence of Locke was present in the statements of some: "All men are by nature free and equal"; natural rights meant that slaves could "assert and regain liberty." A small minority of Virginians, notably Quakers, who had been citing Locke since the 1770s, argued that slavery was an evil that could only be corrected through emancipation and egalitarianism. Western Virginians, who were mostly nonslaveholders, argued for emancipation and removal of freed slaves. Among those who sought a path toward emancipation was Thomas Randolph, grandson of Thomas Jefferson, who proposed that it should be put to statewide popular vote. The powerful Tidewater oligarchy, however, remained committed to preserving its slave society through tighter regulations and expulsion of free blacks. In the end, the House of Delegates passed an ambiguous resolution that favored removal of free blacks and set no definitive course toward emancipation.[56]

By contrast, South Carolina was acculturated to a slave majority and ruled by a more repressive regime, an oligarchy that perfected a language of liberty while tightening the noose of tyranny. It never considered emancipation and never wavered in its opposition to abolitionists. It had no regional section or significant minority voicing opposition to slavery. It had no leaders during the colonial or antebellum eras of the stature of Jefferson, Madison, or Monroe to articulate the new ideals of the Enlightenment, or even to question the sustainability of an ever-expanding slave society. It did not have a wide swath of Appalachian Mountains to impede westward expansion or alter established settlement patterns.

An elaborate system of slave regulations and state-supported terror was fully in place in Carolina by 1740. The Carolina model spread westward more slowly at first than the Virginia model, but ultimately it spread farther. Its harshness produced the legacy of repression associated with the Deep South. The two political cultures met west of the Appalachians and united to preserve the system of slavery upon which they both depended.[57]

The consolidation of the Southeast as a slave society began in 1767 when the Province of Georgia, by then modeled on the Carolina way, claimed most of the present states of Alabama and Mississippi. Soon after the Revolution, the area was rapidly settled through fraudulent land grants awarded by successive Georgia governors and a collusive legislature. The infamous example was the Yazoo land scandal (named after Native Americans who had once lived in the Yazoo River basin), a political contrivance that awarded vast amounts of land to cronies from among the political and plantation elite, thus perpetuating the social pyramid engrained in South Carolina.

South Carolina's influence expanded across the region by multiple means. Its influence initially spread through the colony's aggressive traders, whose reach quickly extended to the Tennessee River. Trans-Appalachian trade gained early momentum in the 1690s when the French explorer and trader Jean Couture defected to Carolina. Couture was probably the first European to follow the Tennessee River to its source in the Cherokee Nation.[58]

During the Revolution, the British settled thousands of loyalists from South Carolina and Georgia in Natchez, bringing about a "plantation revolution" along that segment of the Mississippi River. Settlers migrating from Kentucky and Tennessee to the Lower Mississippi fell under that influence, and in 1780s and 1790s a society with slaves became a slave society. With sugar plantations expanding rapidly around New Orleans in the late 1790s, an unbroken chain of plantations extended upriver for 250 miles.

Jefferson and other Virginians believed that the expansion of slavery into the west represented an opportunity to relocate slaves, thereby dispersing slavery across a larger region and reducing the threat of rebellion. Such a strategy required cutting off the importation of slaves to be effective, which the Deep South strenuously opposed.[59]

In the assessment of geographer Donald Meinig, the Lowcountry elite were the dominant southern influence for a century and a half, until interrupted by rising inland wealth and reapportionment. "South Carolina was in an excellent position to exert a very marked influence upon the newer Gulf States." Prominent Carolina planters like Wade Hampton invested heavily in Mississippi Valley plantations, and "South Carolina contributed large numbers of migrants to every state lying to the west." Their influence was especially strong in new courthouse towns, where Carolina "sociopolitical leadership" was often concentrated. South Carolina thus exerted its will across the Deep South through "the many prominent persons—governors, judges, lesser officials, and local leaders—who had received training in South Carolina." At the dawn of the Civil War, South Carolinians even outnumbered Mississippians at the Mississippi secession convention. Virginians and others from Border States wondered if it would not be preferable to be the south of the northern states rather than the north of a southern confederacy.[60]

The reticence of the Upper South to pursue a future of ever-greater dependence on slave labor may be attributable to a combination of capitalism and political culture. Narrower profit margins in the first case and moderating ideals of the Enlightenment in the second case may have produced a less virulent plantation elite. The Barbadian pragmatism of the Deep South and high profit margins on its principal crops—rice in the Lowcountry, sugar in Louisiana, and cotton across the region—created a different sort of regime. The debate over slavery between the North and the slaveholding South produced the sectionalism (political regionalism) that eventually bridged the gulf between Upper and Deep South subregions. Sectionalism then became the "dominant idiom" for debating slavery and shaped the concepts of free and slave labor, constitutionalism, and states' rights.[61]

The nature of the differences between the North and the South that led to the Civil War has been the subject of various theories. Most historians agree that the war was caused by tension between a free-labor society and a slave-labor society residing within one nation. The work of historians Eugene Genovese and James Oakes highlights differences that exist within this framework in what has become known as the Genovese-Oakes debate. In Genovese's view, "When we understand that the slave

South developed neither a strange form of capitalism nor an undefinable agrarianism but a special civilization built on the relationship of master to slave, we expose the root of its conflict with the North." To Genovese, the war was between *wage*-labor states and *slave*-labor states, the former placing labor at the disposal of capitalists, the latter placing labor, a sort of extended family, under the paternal guardianship of the plantation elite, who cared less about efficiency than a way of life. Oakes, on the other hand, views *free* labor and *wage* labor as fundamentally different from *chattel* slavery. When southern slaveholders made slaves chattel property, they created something entirely different from free labor. The supposedly paternalistic society of the South was no less capitalistic: "Modern slave societies had come into existence to serve capitalism."[62]

Building on the presumption of a cultural basis for the conflict between North and South, Genovese later asked whether we "should not be too hard on proponents of Southern slavery . . . [who are] prepared to be sanguine about capitalism's ability to avoid the commodification of every feature of life and to promote a culture in which Christian principles can flourish?" This latter view was part of a progression toward a sympathetic reading of the Southern Agrarians, particularly their embrace of natural hierarchy and rejection of "market values" (or vulture capitalism, to use a current phrase). For Oakes, however, the slaveholders' fixation on human property rights and unregulated markets to produce cash crops for the world trade made the South even more market-oriented than the North. Southern slave society was also, in some ways, more efficient than the northern wage-labor economy, as when the plantation elite readily relocated chattel labor to western territories.[63]

The Upper South had the potential to become a distinct section with features of northern and southern political culture. With its votes in Congress, the slave trade could have been ended, slavery in the territories banned, and slavery phased out in terms considered by the Virginians. An "empire of liberty" was within reach. However, incessant pressure from the Deep South, led by South Carolina, undermined any prospect of that happening. Instead, the Deep South took on the character of South Carolina as it grew dramatically after the Revolution and the Upper South fell under its sway. The influence of South Carolina across the region meant that there was no concern over the number of slaves in the population, no limit to the cruelty in maintaining the system, and no ceiling to the rhetoric defending slavery as fundamental to a great civilization. The prevailing attitude in the Deep South in this formative period was encapsulated by James H. Hammond, governor of South Carolina and senator when it seceded: "I repudiate, as ridiculously absurd, that much lauded but nowhere accredited dogma of Mr. Jefferson, 'that all men are born equal.'"[64]

In the 1850s, the phrases "King Cotton" and "Cotton Is King" were used to characterize the powerful southern economy and its influence on the world; and in 1860 a book compiling the writings of various proslavery southern intellectual leaders was published under the title *Cotton Is King*. With the rise of King Cotton in the early 1800s, the Deep South became larger and stronger. A million slaves were relocated to the Mississippi Valley, one-third as part of plantation relocations and two-thirds through the domestic slave trade. British capital, the invention of the cotton gin, the introduction of steamboats on the Mississippi, and a vast supply of slave labor reshaped the global economy and made the Deep South the richest agrarian region in the world. By the 1850s, the region was producing as much as 80 percent of the world's cotton, with most of it going to Great Britain.[65]

King Cotton monoculture dominated the Deep South from South Carolina to east Texas. A "radical simplification" of landscape accompanied the reeducation of slave labor brought in from the Upper South for the new cotton crop. The powerful regional economy acquired vulnerabilities that most of its leaders chose to ignore: reliance on a single crop, dependence on outside capital, overinvestment in land and slaves, lack of a manufacturing sector, and limited distribution networks. Local markets failed to mature as slaveholders invested all their resources in cotton, reduced their slaves to subsistence levels, and imported goods for their own needs.[66]

Over the fifty-year period from 1810 to 1850, eight new southern states were admitted to the union. Growth in the newer states and Georgia was dramatic, as shown in Table 9. Growth was particularly rapid in Alabama, Mississippi, and Louisiana, where the population increased from only 117,000 to over 2.3 million. The regional population grew from 2.9 million to 9.9 million.

The enslaved population in the United States in 1790 (the first census) stood at 40,370 in the North, 521,169 in the Upper South, and 136,358 in the Deep South. In 1860, numbers were 64, 1,530,229, and 2,423,467, respectively. As the historian Walter Johnson wrote, the population was so large and widespread that "there was a ready spot market in human beings in every southern city on every day of every week." In addition to the enslaved people of the Upper South "sold down the river" into the harsher conditions of the Deeper South, many were also marched down to Georgia and from there to plantations across the Cotton Belt. Slaveholders comprised about a quarter of the population in the South and held 93 percent of the region's agricultural wealth. Whites who were not slaveholders generally aspired to become one, and about half of those had the potential to do so. Slavery was not dying out as some have claimed; it was in a state of dynamic growth.[67]

While Virginia, Carolina, and Louisiana slave societies were blending and influencing the character of the Southeast, newer territories opened up by the Louisiana Purchase and the establishment of the Republic of Texas followed by its annexation vastly expanded the horizons of the slave states. Arkansas and Texas were the first two states fully west of the Mississippi River to be settled and admitted to the Union. Migration to Texas in particular accelerated after the overextended cotton economy formed a bubble that burst in 1837. Still the Republic of Texas at that time, it became a shelter from legal action against bankrupt planters and merchants. East Texas and the Arkansas delta joined the other states of the Deep South in adopting the South Carolina practices of unrestrained growth of slavery, harsh treatment of slaves, and the bloated antifederal, proslavery rhetoric of aristocratic destiny. Other influences in the growing region were limited to pockets, such as Germans in east Texas and Appalachian Virginians in the Ozarks.[68]

The struggle between an "empire of liberty" and an "empire of slavery" came to a head with the fight over Missouri statehood. Fear of breaking up the Union, brought on by belligerent threats from the Deep South, led instead to the Missouri Compromise. The agreement divided the lands acquired in the Louisiana Purchase into free and slave territories. In 1821, Missouri was admitted to the Union as a slave state, absorbing the militant grand vision of the future of slavery of the Deep South along with its contempt for the federal government.[69]

In the years leading up to the Missouri Compromise, the states of Ohio, Indiana, and Illinois debated and ultimately prohibited slavery, in large measure due to popular opposition. The antislavery states were left in a precarious position, however, by the 1857 *Dred Scott* Supreme Court ruling that neither Congress nor the people of a territory could ban slavery. Many historians believe the United States came very close to becoming a slaveholders' republic at this time of southern ascendancy. Instead, *Dred Scott* led the nation into the Civil War.[70]

The slaveholding plantation elite of the South had grander ambitions than annexation of western territories already under the influence of English-speaking Americans. Expansion was an essential feature of a slaveholding society. As a speaker in the Georgia legislature declared in 1856: "Whenever slavery is confined within certain specified limits, its future existence is doomed." Expansionism went beyond rhetorical claims. The proslavery advocate William Walker led several military ventures into Latin America and became president of Nicaragua after an insurrection

Table 9. Statehood and Antebellum Population in the South

| | | POPULATION | |
| | | --- | --- |
State	Statehood	1810	1860
Georgia	1788	251,407	1,057,286
South Carolina	1788	415,115	703,708
Virginia	1788	877,683	1,219,630
North Carolina	1789	556,526	992,622
Kentucky	1792	406,511	1,155,684
Tennessee	1796	261,727	1,109,801
Louisiana	1812	76,556	708,002
Mississippi	1817	31,306	791,305
Alabama	1819	9,046	964,201
Arkansas	1836	1,062	435,450
Florida	1845	n/a	140,424
Texas	1845	n/a	604,215

Source: U.S. Census of Population and Housing

in 1855. The Knights of the Golden Circle, a secret paramilitary society, supported various actions to bring about a Central American–Caribbean southern empire. The South kept an eye on the tropics to fulfill its racial imperialism, but it also kept one on the North's "hireling civilization," which it saw as advancing toward the arctic.[71]

Virginian Thomas Roderick Dew, president of William and Mary College, saw the South as a model for the world. Only slavery and obedience of lower classes could sustain republican liberties of the upper, propertied classes, while giving security to all, thereby creating a stable society. The southern model was ancient, Dew maintained, dating to Hebrew theocracy, the greatest government ever achieved. The male head of family was the appropriate model for all social organization, rather than bourgeois individualism. Aristocracy is an essential element of such a society as much as inequality. James Hammond of South Carolina wrote: "Slavery does indeed create an aristocracy—an aristocracy of talents, of virtue, of generosity and courage. In a slave country every freeman is an aristocrat." At the same time, in Hammond's view, "inequality is the fundamental law of nature, and hence alone the harmony of the universe." Another South Carolinian, William Harper, was among the many political theorists who insisted that "the institution of slavery is the principal cause of civilization." If inequality led to a "state of tyranny," according to the Confederate officer and political theorist Albert Taylor Bledsoe, it was because that was the natural abode of blacks.[72]

A strident voice for the preservation of slavery through secession was that of South Carolinian Leonidas Spratt, who spoke of two civilizations, one modeled on the white male as husband, father, and slave master and the other intent on pursuing equality as a natural right. The latter was portrayed as a "delirium of liberty" for all that would only result in a "carnival" of social disorder. The "culture wars" decried by politicians and political commentators today echo the rhetoric of the debate over slavery. A commentator in *DeBow's Review*, a popular southern business magazine, described the divide between the slave states of the South and the abolitionists of the North as between home, family, and the Bible on the one hand, with pluralism, democracy, and anarchy on the other.[73]

An urban-rural divide paralleling that of today was also evident in the nineteenth century. According to Genovese, "slave civilization" does not produce "urban centers." The South developed neither rural nor urban markets of sufficient size to develop diversified agriculture or industry. In 1860, the urban population of the Deep South was only 7 percent of the total population. There were only three cities with more than 15,000 people: New Orleans, Charleston, and Savannah. The state geologist in South Carolina warned farmers not to grow more corn than they could consume as there was no market infrastructure to sell it. Kentuckian Cassius Clay concluded: "A home market cannot exist in a slave state."[74]

Political culture and sectionalism as defining features of the United States until the Civil War did not end at Reconstruction, of course. Gradually, the regional character of the nation as defined by Elazar and others is slowly dissolving and reaggregating into finer-grained patterns at metropolitan and county levels. This new political geography carries with it beliefs and attitudes that formed during the colonial era. Like New England and New Amsterdam, the South has proven to be one of the more enduring influences, owing largely to South Carolina's unwavering adherence to traditional social hierarchy, exurban development, property rights, religion, and intense antifederalism.

Consolidation of Southern Political Culture

The southern way of life matured into a uniquely agrarian political culture during the early colonial era, a period of time in which it evolved from a society with slaves to a slave society. In the Revolutionary era and during the westward migration, the South acquired a competing national political culture dedicated to preserving the institution of slavery and adopting the tactics of states' rights and nullification to achieve that end. That formative period spanning two centuries created a culture that survives today. As W. J. Cash wrote, "The South, one might say, is a tree with many age rings, with its limbs and trunk bent and twisted by all the winds of the years, but with its tap root in the Old South."[75]

The antebellum argument that a great civilization must be built with aristocracy and slavery has faded, indeed anti-aristocratic sentiments were strong in the years immediately following the Civil War. Nevertheless, many of the attendant beliefs remained intact. Traditionally, southern honor was closely tied to the ownership of property, which included slaves. Honor, social hierarchy, and property still constitute a cluster of interrelated concerns within southern political culture. In the South of the past and the present, the chief role of government was and is the protection of property. As an organizing paradigm, it exerts a strong influence in America, often opposing collective action. The contemporary effects of this are manifested in opposition to city planning and urban design, to environmental regulation, and to new civil rights and social justice initiatives. Those issues will be taken up in Chapter 5, but first it is necessary to look a little deeper into southern political culture.[76]

As this book was being written, there were observances throughout the country of the sesquicentennial of the Civil War. The causes and effects of the war were laid out before the public by authorities ranging from historians to park rangers. Most of the lingering sentiment for a mythical antebellum South of happy slaves and caring masters driven apart by northern aggression was debunked for anyone who cared to look squarely at the record. Nevertheless, it is useful to recapitulate the arguments of the time in the interest of demonstrating the continuity of political culture.

There is an alternate claim from within popular histories about the South that slavery was not the central concern of its political culture, but the historical record thoroughly contradicts any such assertion. The words of the leaders of secession speak with clarity on this point. In a conference of the Southern Rights Associations, the Beaufort, South Carolina, contingent summed up the belief of many southern leaders that it was time "to unite in a slaveholding Confederacy, maintaining as a fundamental principle, the perpetual recognition of that institution."[77]

The seceding states made formal declarations of their reasons for leaving the union, and the overarching reason was to preserve the institution of slavery. Two specific reasons were the differences over admission of new slave states and the return of fugitive slaves. The moral justification for enslavement was the belief in white superiority, a natural condition within the Great Chain of Being within God's creation. The legal justification was the states' rights argument that federal power could be nullified by state law. A natural law argument is also found in the declarations of secession, where the rhetoric of liberty and tyranny was deployed against northern antislavery initiatives.

South Carolina declared on the eve of the Civil War that "an increasing hostility on the part of the non-slaveholding States to the institution of slavery," as well as persistent agitation against slavery as an immoral institution and election of a "President of the United States, whose opinions and purposes are hostile to slavery," made it necessary for South Carolina to declare itself "a separate and independent State." Georgia stated, "For the last ten years we have had numerous and serious causes of complaint against our non-slave-holding confederate States with reference to the subject of African slavery." This threat to "property" necessitated "new safeguards for our liberty, equality, security, and tranquility." Mississippi, however, provided the most succinct statement of motivation:

> Our position is thoroughly identified with the institution of slavery—the greatest material interest of the world. Its labor supplies the product which constitutes by far the largest and most important portions of commerce of the earth. These products are peculiar to the climate verging on the tropical regions, and by an imperious law of nature, none but the black race can bear exposure to the tropical sun. These products have become necessities of the world, and a blow at slavery is a blow at commerce and civilization. That blow has been long aimed at the institution, and was at the point of reaching its consummation. There was no choice left us but submission to the mandates of abolition, or a dissolution of the Union, whose principles had been subverted to work out our ruin.[78]

In the years immediately following the war, southern leaders reframed the conflict as one of liberty versus tyranny in which the South sought to uphold the Constitution, preserve states' rights, and protect the property rights of freemen (including "the right of property in slaves," as stated in the South Carolina declaration). The Confederacy stood for those honorable principles, they maintained, while the North acting through the federal government trampled on their fundamental liberties. Enactment of the Fourteenth Amendment, giving all citizens equal protection under the law, would be another unwanted exercise of federal authority over the states. Passage in the legislatures was required to regain representation in Congress, but it did not come easily. As one leader put it, "If I have to eat [dirt], I want to be compelled to do it, not to be hospitably invited to it as a desirable meal."[79]

The president of the Confederacy, Jefferson Davis, was particularly anxious to influence history's judgment. Davis completed *The Rise and Fall of the Confederate Government* in 1881 and went on to write *A Short History of the Confederate States of America* in 1889, near the end of his life. The books fulfilled his postwar mission to leave behind a legacy of purity in purpose. Davis succeeded in providing an alternate history of the Confederacy while also initiating a practice that can be described as "deflection of responsibility." Davis's articulation of a higher purpose in southern motives enabled those who accepted his account to avoid self-reflection in favor of blaming others of tyranny, aggression, and hypocrisy. The resulting unwillingness to break with the past after the Civil War regenerated a South without slavery but still owning the framework that supported it.

Reframing the war as one fought by the South to preserve higher principles also had the effect of freezing elements of colonial political culture within the more mature postbellum culture. Among the colonial elements frozen into the larger culture were those unique to South Carolina: Ashley Cooper's Gothic republicanism, strict constitutionalism, and legally protected social hierarchy, as well as his platform of opposition to high taxes, professionalized government, and urban power. It is worth noting that Locke's classical liberalism, modified to place emphasis on property rights and de-emphasis on labor rights, was a later element of colonial South Carolina (and Virginia) political culture frozen into southern regional culture.

Race remained at the center of white southern political culture. Whites still believed that they were a superior race. If blacks were awarded full citizenship and equal protection under the law, the natural hierarchy would be upended. Whites saw freedmen leaving the plantations and assumed it was ingratitude and laziness that drove them away. In reality, the near impossibility of forging a new relationship with former slaveholders forced freedmen to find employment elsewhere, and they were motivated as well by the desire to find family members who had been sold and relocated and to settle in more welcoming communities. Whites, failing to grasp those dynamics, became deeply fearful of black mobility, especially when blacks were seen in greater numbers near towns. Many whites believed that a race war was inevitable, an opinion with longevity, as it was heard throughout the South up to the civil rights era. Fear was a unifying influence on blacks and whites alike, a defining feature of southern culture.[80]

The South has changed political parties, but it has not changed political culture over more than three centuries. In terms of electoral history, a Solid South has been evident from the election of 1800 to the present. These election results reflect the continuity of principles and associated attitudes established in colonial times and passed down to the antebellum South, the Jim Crow South, and the New South.

Following the Civil War and the twelve-year attempt at rebuilding the South known as Reconstruction, the South rebuilt the mythology of white superiority, retrenched into its defensive positions, and developed a talent for deflecting criticism and avoiding responsibility for the ways of the past. Scholars of southern political culture consistently confirm a pattern of defensiveness. W. J. Cash called this defensiveness the "savage ideal," a deep hostility to criticism and suppression of dissent and diversity. The historian Sheldon Hackney called it a "siege mentality," a "sense of grievance . . . at the heart of the southern identity." The historian Nancy MacLean described it as "reactionary populism," antielitism coupled with racism and xenophobia. The region's defensiveness is accompanied by an inflated sense of virtue supported by ostentatious religiosity and pretensions of honor.[81]

In reframing its defensive rhetoric, the region felt justified in throwing off northern attempts to re-pattern its society and economy and resuming the old ways to the greatest extent possible. The Jim Crow South with a new system of white control replaced the Old South with its institution of slavery, retaining the same rigid social hierarchy in the process. The Jim Crow South stood opposed to the Republican Party of Lincoln, strengthening its position through a Democratic Party coalition that allowed northern progressives to make gains on behalf of labor and social reform, provided they were willing to overlook southern racial discrimination.

The coalition was ultimately unsustainable, and progressive Democrats eventually achieved sufficient power to pursue a national civil rights agenda unacceptable to most white southerners. President Truman's civil rights initiatives led to the formation of the States' Rights Democratic Party, commonly known as the Dixiecrat Party, in 1948. Its motivation was to preserve the Jim Crow system from federal intervention. It was led by the governor of South Carolina, and later senator, Strom Thurmond. The party's platform emphasized white dominance, flatly stating, "We stand for the segregation of the races. . . . We oppose the elimination of segregation." This core value was couched in the rhetoric of liberty and tyranny, stating that "the Constitution of the United States is the greatest charter of human liberty ever conceived by the mind of man" and that "the totalitarian, centralized bureaucratic government and the police nation" posed a threat to fundamental liberty.[82]

The Dixiecrat Party lasted only through the 1948 election, but Thurmond and many other southern leaders would later defect to the

Republican Party when it launched the Southern Strategy and shed its support for civil rights legislation in the early 1960s. By 2012, the Solid South had grown from the original eleven states of the Confederacy to thirteen states, with Virginia and Florida leaving the old alliance and Oklahoma, Missouri, Kentucky, and West Virginia joining it. The realignment of the Republican and Democratic parties has remade the former as the party of Jefferson Davis and the latter as the new "party of Lincoln." Emboldened by the return of southern political culture through the Republican Party, the South Carolina legislature in 2013 wrapped itself in the rhetoric of liberty and proposed new statutes to fight tyranny and nullify federal laws, with five nullification bills filed in the house and senate at the beginning of the session.[83]

W. J. Cash concluded *The Mind of the South* with a description of southern character that captures the finer details of traditional political culture:

> Proud, brave, honorable by its lights, courteous, personally generous, loyal, swift to act, often too swift, but signally effective, sometimes terrible, in its action—such was the South at its best. And such at its best it remains today, despite the great falling away in some of its virtues. Violence, intolerance, aversion and suspicion toward new ideas, an incapacity for analysis, an inclination to act from feeling rather than from thought, an exaggerated individualism and too narrow concept of social responsibility, attachment to fictions and false values, above all too great attachment to racial values and a tendency to justify cruelty and injustice in the name of those values, sentimentality and a lack of realism—these have been its characteristic vices in the past. And, despite changes for the better, they remain its characteristic vices today.[84]

In some cases, the New South has moved on. It has accepted a version of Lockean natural equality and a certain level of integration of the races. Yet the historical rhetoric of antebellum and colonial times remains embedded in the political culture. While racism and xenophobia are no longer acceptable, the rhetoric of liberty and tyranny allows southerners to feel aggrieved by any federal intervention aimed at reducing poverty, aiding public schools, protecting voting rights, or improving access to medical care. To combat such interventions, the antebellum rhetoric of constitutionalism, property rights, and states' rights is deployed anew—formerly invoked to protect the institution of slavery, now to protect white privilege from any zero-sum erosion as a result of black gains.

Diffusion of Southern Political Culture in the United States

From the late 1930s to the late 1960s, more than 6 million southerners migrated to the industrial cities of the North and to southern California. By 1970, 11 million southerners lived outside the South, 7.5 million of whom were white. By the 1960s, California had the largest share of southerners in the nation outside the South. Southern California became the southern evangelicals' city upon a hill.[85]

Southern political culture traveled with the migrants, including religious traditions that had evolved to accommodate slavery and Jim Crow. As seen in Chapter 3, the earliest ministers from England in South Carolina spoke against slavery or attempted to moderate it but were ostracized when they did so. They learned to accommodate the system of slavery to maintain their social standing. In the nineteenth and twentieth centuries, many southern ministers became advocates for their political culture and could face retribution if they failed to do so. They proclaimed its virtues and defended it from outside criticism, maintaining that southern society was modeled on Abrahamic hierarchy, that Jesus never spoke against slavery, or that the "Curse of Ham" condemned dark-skinned people to servitude.[86]

Southern churches became part of the advancing flank of southern migration, fostering segregationist and racist views along the way. Churches affiliated with the Southern Baptist Convention and the United Methodist Church and its predecessors, together with other evangelical churches, were particularly active in exporting southern traditions and drawing people of similar persuasions together in new communities outside the South. Political and religious culture moved hand in hand from the South, to some extent in reaction to the federalism and secularism of the New Deal. Southern California came to be viewed as a land of opportunity for the mass transplantation of southern political and religious culture. Southerners saw themselves as "pilgrims and patriots," part of a nationwide great awakening of conservatism and religion.[87]

The historian Darren Dochuk documented the close relationship between politics and religion in *From Bible Belt to Sun Belt* and the *Rise of Evangelical Conservatism*. Dochuk traced the evolution of southern churches in California, documenting their political influence. Many southern ministers became associates of John Birch, a Baptist missionary who had trained at the Fundamental Baptist Bible Institute in Texas. Birch became an exemplar for the Far Right John Birch Society, formed in 1958 by Robert Welch Jr., a retired manufacturer. The John Birch Society tied conservative politics to conservative southern religion. Fred Koch, the founder of Koch Industries, was an early supporter, and his sons are famously active in conservative causes today. George Pepperdine, an auto parts magnate, joined in the effort. Considering secular public education to be a threat to the nation, he founded conservative Pepperdine University. The support of grassroots conservatism by wealthy industrialists was an essential step in transplanting southern political culture throughout the nation. The model has been replicated many times, and today there are over 200 conservative advocacy and policy groups, or "think tanks," supported by conservative industrialists and benefactors that distribute guidance and financial support to local conservative groups. One of the first with a libertarian orientation was the Foundation for Economic Education, based in New York, which distributed treatises by John Locke and Adam Smith to erect a philosophical framework around southern fundamentalist conservatism.[88]

Southern evangelism coalesced into a conservative opposition force to New Deal progressivism as it became increasingly partisan and political. Its leaders viewed the policies of the New Deal as a path toward communism, anathema to those raised to believe that God ordained a class pyramid, with whites occupying the top tiers and African Americans forever at the bottom. Liberal churches seeking Christian unity in meeting the needs of the poor through New Deal programs became alarmed at the threat posed by conservative southern churches, which ironically were leading the mass exodus of poor people from a destitute region. An effort was made by southern California political leaders to slow the influx of southerners, who were fundamentally changing attitudes and making the integration struggle in Los Angeles more difficult.[89]

The spatial patterns of southern political culture and American conservatism are difficult to track in the transitional period that began during the New Deal. Southerners retained their Democratic registrations but became increasingly independent. The Civil Rights Act of 1964 was the last straw. Senator Richard B. Russell of Georgia filibustered the bill, threatening to "resist to the bitter end any measure or any movement which would have the tendency to bring about social equality." His effort to stop it failed, and Senator Strom Thurmond of South Carolina was the first Senate-level southern Democrat to change parties in reaction to the new law. Many others soon followed, endorsing Barry Goldwater, who had opposed the Civil Rights Act, for president that year. Goldwater won the Deep South, and Nixon and Reagan would follow, perfecting the Southern Strategy discussed earlier in this chapter.[90]

In view of Goldwater's defeat and Nixon's initial success as a pragmatist, Ronald Reagan cultivated a moderate image for conservatism in California by distancing the Republican Party from the John Birch Society and others on the Far Right. He offered the alternative vision for a Creative Society to replace the Great Society in an appeal to urban conservatives, and he also attempted to forge a relatively color-blind party while tactically deploying states' rights language and professing to be a born-again Christian to appeal to southern conservative audiences. The strategic refinements were sufficient to retain strong southern support while rebuilding a national political base.[91]

During the Jim Crow era, racial rhetoric had become bloated with white supremacist overconfidence, reflecting the South's success since Reconstruction in avoiding any consequences to its resumption of a racial caste system. The subtler language of the Southern Strategy proved just as effective. Moreover, Republican fiscal conservatism could be translated into traditional southern neglect of initiatives targeting social and economic advancement advocated by northern Democrats since the New Deal. However, addressing social and economic issues, particularly if they were aimed at African American advancement, would constitute a major departure from a political system based on white supremacy. No state, except Mississippi, was more extreme in its racial politics than South Carolina. As the political scientist V. O. Key wrote in 1949, the state's "preoccupation with the Negro stifles political conflict. . . . And, in the simple strategy of self-advancement, leaders possessed of an artful invective or chancing upon a timely opportunity may raise the issue and thereby place themselves in unassailable positions as skilled defenders of the highest value, almost without regard to their position on other matters." The Southern Strategy offered a way forward for southern politicians, one where fiscal conservatism and social neglect were intertwined with the older language of liberty, tyranny, constitutionalism, antifederalism, and property rights.[92]

The Southern Strategy thus proved to be a highly successful merger of the Republican Party platform and southern political culture. The presidential election map for 1996 reveals a nearly complete shift in party orientation. The South and the more rural states emerged as solidly conservative and Republican (see Table 10). At the finer-grained level of congressional districts, an urban-rural divide is seen in nearly all states, supporting James Carville's observation cited earlier that rural Pennsylvania is essentially Alabama. The rhetoric of southern political culture, an enhanced language of tyranny versus liberty, is now found in every state.[93]

Table 10. Timeline of Southern Settlement

1720	End of the 50-year proprietary period of Carolina governance
1729	Last proprietary interest bought out by the crown
1733	Georgia established in part as a buffer between South Carolina and Spanish Florida
1739	Stono Rebellion
1743	Oglethorpe returned to England the final time
1752	Georgia Trustees surrendered control of the colony back to the crown; Carolina slaveholders led a "parade" of slaves into the colony
1767	Province of Georgia claims most of the present states of Alabama and Mississippi
1790	Treaty of New York between the United States and Native American nations
1803	Louisiana Purchase
1830	Indian Removal Act
1861	Civil War begins with the Battle of Fort Sumter, South Carolina
1863	Emancipation Proclamation
1865	End of the Civil War
1877	End of Reconstruction era; resumption of southern white privilege

With its transition from overt racial rhetoric to the more sophisticated rhetoric of the Southern Strategy, southern political culture unwittingly placed colonial ideals at center stage. Ashley Cooper's Gothic republicanism and Locke's classical liberalism never completely faded from southern political rhetoric, but federal neglect of the South during the Jim Crow era left it free to ignore ideological debates and exercise only the more practical rhetoric of white supremacy described by V. O. Key. With the rise of the South as a force in national politics, the nation's three primary political cultures once again took on competing positions in a war of ideas dating to the colonial era. And once again, the South has framed the war as one among sections and classes as well as one against outside powers.

Conclusion

Theories of American political culture are in general agreement that New England and New Netherlands bequeathed several distinctive attributes to American society, including freedom of conscience, tolerance, pragmatism, and new perspectives on democracy and equality. When it comes to the South, there is less agreement about the nature and origin of its contributions. Most scholars and analysts agree that it has maintained an attachment to social hierarchy and agrarianism, which some (notably the Southern Agrarians) have argued offers a more meaningful way of life. The origin of an indisputably distinctive southern political culture, however, is a matter of debate. Many have argued that Virginia was the prototype from which the region developed. Others have argued that South Carolina was an influence of at least equal measure. Those who have taken the latter position usually trace the influence farther back to Barbados, England's first slave society in America, rather than attributing it to the Ashley Cooper Plan.

A few authorities have argued that Ashley Cooper's Grand Model was a formative influence on southern political culture, a position that is supported here. In the conclusion to Chapter 3, it was shown that five facets of the Grand Model departed from the Barbados model and survived to shape Carolina. In summarizing the findings of this chapter, one also finds five differences between South Carolina and Virginia political culture, and their ability to project it, to support the argument that the former exerted an equal or greater influence in the formation of southern regional political culture.

1. The South Carolina plantation elite, unlike that of Virginia, believed it held the authority of inerrant nobility. It consequently emerged as the stronger ideological proponent of the form of slave society that ultimately swept the South.

2. The Ashley Cooper Plan not only created a formal social hierarchy, but unlike Virginia, established a settlement plan that resulted in wealth- and culture-promoting synergies between plantation and capital city.

3. South Carolina became richer than Virginia from the success of rice monoculture, reinforcing its sense of inerrancy and privilege as well as its ability to project its vision westward.

4. The political culture of South Carolina expanded south and west into Georgia, from where it could readily advance across the Deep South, whereas the expansion of relatively moderate Virginia political culture was slowed by the Appalachians and resistance to slavery in the Midwest.

5. South Carolina's more extreme form of slave society in terms of numbers of enslaved people, terroristic methods of repression, and rhetoric used to defend the system were aggressively carried westward.

The vision of southern civilization articulated by Calhoun and so many other slaveholders in the nineteenth century was the confident vision of South Carolina and a culmination of generations of rhetorical refinements paralleling the region's dependence on slavery, monoculture, and a unique plantation way of life. It was a vision of an agrarian South, one of a highly advanced aristocracy nurturing a white underclass and providing compassionate care to a black slave class. It was also a vision of how a society uses the land, perceives the natural environment, and forms cities and their hinterlands. The next chapter examines southern political culture in contemporary context while keeping its historical roots in mind.

CHAPTER FIVE

The Grand Model and the
American City

Ashley Cooper's Grand Model was the ultimate product of English colonial policy, political philosophy, and city planning prior to the Enlightenment. The Fundamental Constitutions and "instructions," products of both Ashley Cooper and Locke, formed a body of law and policy written by two of the most astute minds of the time, tempered to be sure by the diverse opinions of the remaining seven Carolina proprietors. Within those documents, city planning (in the broad sense of the term used throughout) held an essential place in the overall design of the colony's social structure, economy, and government.

Cities of Ashley Cooper's time were necessary for government, commerce, and the cultural pursuits of aristocracy. City planning was essential to those purposes. But cities were not yet seen as great engines of prosperity and democracy, and they were not yet perceived as a medium capable of leveling class structure, providing education and upward mobility, or fostering creativity among the talented whether poor or wealthy. Urban democracy was still seen as mob rule, and it would continue to be seen that way until the Enlightenment, when the premise that all men are created equal became axiomatic.

When Carolina was founded in the predawn of the Enlightenment, an ordinary English citizen was expected to live in a village where life was well ordered and the lord of the manor or other person of authority looked after his people and represented them in London's halls of power. It was a society descended from an ancient Gothic framework, one from which Ashley Cooper and Locke saw an opportunity to perfect the English ideals of balanced government, noblesse oblige, and class reciprocity on the blank slate of American wilderness.[1]

The new cities of America envisioned by the Grand Model were planned to be healthier, more efficient, and more civilized, yet reserved for the few who had some purpose to live there. Cities were to be located on rivers at points that would be healthful and central for regional development; they were to be designed with a geometry that would provide for efficient growth; they were to have public squares and river frontage set aside for civic and commercial uses; they were to have aesthetic merit; and they were to be laid out to ensure health and public safety, benefiting from the lessons of the Great Plague and the Great Fire of 1666. Cities were designed to serve a hinterland of estates and villages where most people would find fulfillment in life within their stratum in the social hierarchy. As the colony grew, it would proceed in an orderly and efficient manner, establishing economies of scale before extending into adjacent, newly formed jurisdictions; unplanned growth would not be permitted to leapfrog into new areas until services and infrastructure were in place. In today's terminology, the model was consistent with principles of "sustainable development" and "smart growth." Yet the plan was devised by Ashley Cooper and John Locke, fathers of republicanism and classical liberalism—the foundations of modern conservatism and libertarianism, traditions that have now turned against the planning model their idols invented.

James Oglethorpe's plan for Georgia was a sequel to the Grand Model, consistent with it in many respects but updated with one great departure—the application of the premise that all men are created equal. The plan reveals how a new idea of the city emerged as the ideals of the Enlightenment supplanted those of Ashley Cooper's age. The philosophy of the city that guided Oglethorpe remained fundamentally that of Ashley Cooper: it aimed to create well-designed places to support essential regional functions, but not places that would attract the multitudes and grow indefinitely. However, the now famous Oglethorpe Plan differed from the Ashley Cooper Plan in another fundamental way: it was designed to achieve equality within the framework of a yeoman society.[2]

At the time of Georgia's founding, William Hogarth, who had earlier painted Oglethorpe's prison committee, was painting *A Harlot's Progress* and *A Rake's Progress*, each a series of scenes of country people falling prey to urban vices. In *A Harlot's Progress*, a gullible Moll Hackabout is shown being recruited into prostitution upon arrival in the city. She becomes a common prostitute, gets arrested, contracts venereal disease, and dies at age twenty-three. In *A Rake's Progress*, an unwitting Tom Rakewell inherits money, moves to London, wastes his fortune on gambling and prostitution, and winds up in prison. Both of Hogarth's subjects become caught up in the vices of the city and are forever lost to productive society.

Even a century after the implementation of the Grand Model, and thirty-seven years after the founding of Georgia, the city was still not seen as a healthy destination for the masses, as Oglethorpe's friend, Oliver Goldsmith, movingly persuaded his readers in *The Deserted Village*. The creative success of Hogarth and Goldsmith, and of so many others in their urban social circles, did not appear to strike them as ironic.

The idea that cities were the primary source of personal and societal corruption was carried from England to America where it became well established. Jefferson made his disdain for cities crystal clear: "I think our governments will remain virtuous for many centuries; as long as they are chiefly agricultural; and this will be as long as there shall be vacant lands in any part of America. When they get piled upon one another in large cities, as in Europe, they will become corrupt as in Europe."[3]

From Ashley Cooper's time to that of Jefferson four generations later, most cities were unhealthy, unsavory places. And they only got worse over succeeding generations as the Industrial Revolution further intensified earlier urban problems. It was not until the early twentieth century produced a series of reform and design movements aimed at making cities more livable that the city could be viewed in mostly positive terms. Only then were urban ills effectively addressed through city planning, including (as the term is used here) public policy, health and zoning ordinances, development standards for tenement buildings, and a whole range of new, socially ambitious urban design paradigms, beginning in the early twentieth century with the Garden Cities movement.

Although anti-urbanism lingered into the twentieth century, the rise of the modern city began with the framework for planned cities implemented with the Ashley Cooper Plan. The utility of this information rests in understanding its relationship to political heritage. The construction of anti-urban and anti–environmental regulation platforms within the Republican Party and among other conservatives, libertarians, and especially the Tea Party movement can be shown to be inconsistent with the very traditions otherwise claimed by them.

In order to restore meaningful dialogue with the new anti-urban political coalition, city planners, environmental scientists, and others oriented to inductive reasoning and the scientific method will need to understand the deductive reasoning processes of those on the right and communicate within an idiom oriented to tradition and first principles. This chapter will connect the historical traditions outlined in previous chapters with today's policy debates. The Epilogue will present specific guidance for effective dialogue between creative-progressive urban and environmental policy makers on the one hand and fraternalistic conservatives and libertarians on the other.

Political Culture and the Modern American City

The pragmatic Mid-Atlantic political culture flourished as the automobile industry took off in the 1920s and as the war industries mushroomed in the 1940s. Migrants from the South filled the inner cities, while the mobility provided by the automobile fed development in successive rings and lengthening corridors of suburbanization. Between 1910 and 1950, cities from Philadelphia to Chicago saw population increases of 50 percent or more, with Cleveland doubling and Detroit quadrupling in size. Much of the population came from the rural South, where a stagnant agrarian economy entwined with a segregated society suppressed regional economic growth and opportunity for African Americans. Urbanization represented a challenge to the southern caste system, and the opportunities the city offered were largely rejected by the South in favor of the status quo.

Southern cities were thus self-limited by their attachment to a rigid class pyramid enforced through Jim Crow laws, until liberated by the civil rights movement. The growth of Atlanta through the upheaval of civil rights progress is well documented and offers insight into the current urban-rural divide in America. The Atlanta region remained relatively small compared to northern cities until the upheaval of the 1960s, after which it quadrupled in size over the next four decades, to become one of the nation's largest urban areas. Other southern cities that accommodated integration, notably Charlotte, also entered a phase of rapid growth as civil rights were secured for African Americans and the class pyramid began crumbling.

Southern whites, however, did not become enthusiastic advocates of urbanism, despite its obvious economic benefits. They abandoned the inner cities and the poor, who were moving there with as much zeal as they had previously defended urban territory from integration. The historian Kevin M. Kruse studied the transformation that took place in Atlanta, the "city too busy to hate," as its forward-looking leaders anointed it:

Because of their confrontation with the civil rights movement, white southern conservatives were forced to abandon their traditional, populist, and often starkly racist demagoguery and instead craft a new conservatism predicated on a language of rights, freedoms, and individualism. This modern conservatism proved to be both subtler and stronger than the politics that preceded it and helped southern conservatives dominate the Republican Party and, through it, national politics as well. White flight, in the end, was more than a physical relocation. It was a political revolution.[4]

Kruse proceeded to document the widely held belief among southern whites that they were defending their liberty by supporting segregation, rather than denying liberty to others. They saw the expanding application of principles of equality as "a zero-sum game in which every advance for civil rights meant an equal loss for whites." The politics and rhetoric of the racially divided, fraternalistic South flowed almost seamlessly into that of the New Right, aided by the Republican Southern Strategy. In the congressional elections of 2014, the last white Democrat in the Deep South was defeated by a wide margin.[5]

The civic realm, which was well developed when reserved for whites, was nearly abandoned with desegregation. Public squares, parks, and recreational facilities in the cities were ceded by whites to blacks. As whites moved to the suburbs, they increasingly relied on privatized space, and since they no longer "owned" urban public spaces, they no longer wanted to maintain them with taxes. The historical republican doctrine of low taxes dating to Ashley Cooper provided a justification for the white tax revolt. Bonds for public improvements were defeated by white voters, and the white city on the hill was the suburbs beyond the city limits. When George Romney, as secretary of the Department of Housing and Urban Development, spoke of suburban integration, Nixon replaced him. Romney's policy would have run counter to the Southern Strategy. A new era of "politics of suburban secession" followed, and 54 percent of the nation's exurbs were located in the South by the year 2000.[6]

The South had a golden opportunity to reconcile itself with the broader concept of equality embraced by post-Enlightenment political cultures. Instead, it retrenched in the pre-Enlightenment tradition of republicanism, with its emphasis on class hierarchy but without Ashley Cooper's crucial ingredient of class reciprocity. The U.S. Supreme Court landmark decision on school desegregation in *Brown v. Board of Education* led to resistance instead of adaptation. A new generation of southerners might have been raised in a post–Jim Crow society, but the southern "siege mentality" and its need to blame others for all its ills rather than assume responsibility for them blocked social progress.[7]

Instead of attempting self-reconstruction, southern leaders stood defiant against change. Georgia governor Herman Talmadge declared that "Georgians . . . will not tolerate the mixing of races in the public schools or any of its tax-supported public institutions." In anticipation of the *Brown* decision, Talmadge advanced a plan to privatize schools and issue grants for white students to attend white schools in a move that presaged today's Republican endorsement of school vouchers.[8]

The "Declaration of Constitutional Principles" of 1956, also known as the Southern Manifesto, signed by politicians across the South, declared unequivocal opposition to integration. Senator Strom Thurmond of South Carolina was one of the original drafters of the document, which maintained that the Supreme Court had exceeded its constitutional authority. The Constitution, it declared, must be strictly interpreted; and since there is no mention of education, the states possess the authority to segregate schools.[9]

Southern political culture drew upon its roots, framing new challenges in familiar rhetoric. The taproot was Ashley Cooper's republican philosophy of decentralized government, leadership by the rural aristocracy, strict interpretation of the "Ancient Constitution," and low taxes. The reconstructed republicanism of the Carolina slaveholder elite, which eliminated reciprocity between the higher and lower tiers of the class pyramid, became the American version of republicanism tailored for the southern caste system of slavery and Jim Crow. The new version of republicanism emphasized opposition to federal authority, narrow interpretations of the Constitution, states' rights, and segregation of races as natural law, part of God's natural order, the Great Chain of Being.

The framing rhetoric, however, remained that of liberty versus tyranny. As southern political culture faced increasing scrutiny of its moral foundation from outside and struggled with its own deep-seated anxieties, it responded with the cultural *reaction formation* (discussed in Chapter 4), which intensified the rhetoric of liberty versus tyranny.

Three Visions of the City

The three primary political cultures have become associated with distinct visions of the American city that date to colonial times and the philosophy underlying the founding of colonies during that era. In New England, the town was the center of community and church; outlying farms were a necessary part of life, but not its essence. In the Mid-Atlantic, towns were practical places of commerce, following the Dutch model rather than Penn's vision of a pious, uncorrupted rural society. In the South, Ashley Cooper's vision of an ideal Gothic society, modified by the Barbadians to accommodate mass enslavement of a rural labor force, produced towns that served the needs of the aristocracy. Those early, sculpting forces were, of course, modified by a succession of new influences, beginning with the Industrial Revolution.

At the nation's founding, there were few large cities, and 95 percent of the population lived in rural areas. There was no formal philosophy of the city, but elements were in place for an emerging American idea of the city upon the hill. Ashley Cooper's agrarian republicanism and the influence of social critics such as Hogarth and Goldsmith, who lauded rural virtue and lamented urban ills, reinforced the neo-Gothic concept of the city. On the other hand, the Enlightenment was a paradigm of optimism about the future, and the city was beginning to be seen as having great potential for human fulfillment. America, however, had no experience with its own metropolis.[10]

In the first census of the United States, conducted in 1790, the five cities with populations of more than 10,000 were New York, Philadelphia, Boston, Charleston, and Baltimore. Eleven of twelve cities having a population of more than 5,000 were in the New England and Mid-Atlantic regions. Table 11 shows the thirteen states and their principal cities and populations. In some cases, the principal city was the commercial hub rather than the capital, as was notably the case in South Carolina, where the new capital of Columbia was a small town.

Vermont, Kentucky, and Maine were not states in 1790 but were enumerated in the census as part of the nation's total population of 3,893,635. The more urban profiles of the New England and Mid-Atlantic states, compared with the South, made them more suitable as vectors of the Industrial Revolution (see Table 11). The agrarian economy of the South was not merely a stage in its economic development— it had become a way of life. The southern economy as well as its social development centered around the plantation. The spatial organization and social hierarchy of the South resembled that of ancient Gothic England, where the lord's manor house was the center of authority. It was frozen in a pre-Enlightenment and preindustrial time, but without the noblesse oblige or class reciprocity that Ashley Cooper believed was essential to the model.[11]

Table 11. Population Profiles of the Thirteen States in 1790

State	Population	Principal City	Population	Slave Population	% Rural Population
NEW ENGLAND					
Massachusetts	378,787	Boston	18,320	0	86.6
Connecticut	237,946	New Haven	4,487	2,764	97.1
Rhode Island	68,825	Newport	6,716	948	81.4
New Hampshire	141,885	Portsmouth	4,720	158	96.6
MID-ATLANTIC					
Pennsylvania	434,373	Philadelphia	28,522	3,737	89.8
New York	340,120	New York	33,131	21,324	88.5
Maryland	319,728	Baltimore	13,503	103,036	95.7
New Jersey	184,139	Princeton	—	11,423	99.9
Delaware	59,094	Dover	—	8,887	99.8
SOUTH					
Virginia	747,610	Richmond	3,761	292,627	98.3
North Carolina	393,751	New Bern	—	100,572	99.8
South Carolina	249,073	Charleston	16,359	107,094	93.5
Georgia	82,548	Savannah	—	29,264	99.5

Source: "Historical Statistics, Colonial Times to 1970," A 195–209.
U.S. total = 3,893,635

The Southern City of Liberty

Ashley Cooper's Grand Model was the initial influence on urban form in the South, but the model was soon adapted to the confining reality of a slave society, or a land of liberty, as the enslavers emphatically called it. The resulting pattern of regional development superficially resembled that of the older English manorial system; but Carolina's large single-crop plantations were much less fine grained than the motherland's rural landscape. Locke's instructions for development emphasized siting towns on navigable rivers, first along the coast, then inland, in successive, orderly tiers. The plan he was implementing took advantage of the topography of the region, which appeared (from coastal observation) to have numerous rivers connecting inland areas to the sea. Small towns became the central places through which plantations sent their products to market. Cities, on the other hand, were not for everyone. Their role was to accommodate the aristocracy's need for business transactions and cultural expression of a higher level than suitable for the manor, or plantation, house. Southern political culture emerged from this milieu with a distinct model that enforced separation of land uses and social classes.[12]

By 1790, 98 percent of the population of the South lived in rural areas, compared to 92 percent in the North. At the same time, 94 percent of the slave population of the United States lived in the South. By 1860, just before the Civil War, 90 percent of the population in the South lived in rural areas, whereas in the North the proportion had declined dramatically to 64 percent. The difference has narrowed since 1860, but the rural character of the South remains more pronounced than in the North.[13]

Since World War II, suburbanization in the United States has profoundly changed the character of cities, creating vast suburbs and exurbs with characteristics of both city and country. The initial centrifugal force propelling city residents outward was the availability of mass-produced housing with secured financing under the Federal Housing Administration and the Veterans Administration. At the same time, the Federal Highway Administration funded new road projects to make the suburbs more accessible, and federal grants authorized by the Housing Act of 1949 funded urban renewal ("slum clearance") projects that reduced the availability of housing in city centers. The postwar trend toward physically similar environments, coupled with the advent of television, homogenized the country's white population and reduced regional differences and tensions among political cultures. For a brief period in the 1950s, the white population of the United States was relatively united.

The quest for equality endemic to American democratic ideals reignited differences among political cultures in the 1960s. Southern political culture remained committed to racial segregation, while the rest of the nation was generally willing to remove legal barriers to integration. The Republican Party, seeing an opportunity to break the Democratic Party's grip on the South, launched its Southern Strategy. Democrats outside the South, encouraged by President Johnson's landslide victory in 1964, were willing to sever their long-standing alliance with the South to build a party uncompromised in its progressivistic values. Southern politicians, having failed to form a new States' Rights Democratic Party, known as the Dixiecrat Party, accepted the Southern Strategy's invitation and began voting Republican in large numbers. The defection was led by South Carolina senator Strom Thurmond, who switched party affiliation in 1965. The merger of traditional Republican business values strongly associated with the pragmatic Mid-Atlantic culture with southern political culture resulted in less rhetorical stridency on race issues. Lee Atwater, an architect of the Southern Strategy, had this to say about shifting away from hard-edged racism:

All you have to do to keep the South is for Reagan to run in place on the issues he's campaigned on since 1964 and that's fiscal conservatism, balancing the budget, cut taxes, you know, the whole cluster. . . . You start out in 1954 by saying, "Nigger, nigger, nigger." By 1968 you can't say "nigger"—that hurts you. Backfires. So you say stuff like forced busing, states' rights and all that stuff. You're getting so abstract now [that] you're talking about cutting taxes, and all these things you're talking about are totally economic things and a byproduct of them is [that] blacks get hurt worse than whites. And subconsciously maybe that is part of it. I'm not saying that. But I'm saying that if it is getting that abstract, and that coded, that we are doing away with the racial problem one way or the other. You follow me—because obviously sitting around saying, "We want to cut this," is much more abstract than even the busing thing, and a hell of a lot more abstract than "Nigger, nigger."[14]

The Southern Strategy succeeded in uniting the rhetoric of southern political culture and the Republican Party, and in doing so attracting a blue-collar base known as the Reagan Democrats. Thus George Wallace was able to ascend the national stage speaking of the virtues of states' rights over the "welfare state" in fueling soft-core racial anxiety while returning to hard-core racist rhetoric at home, warning Alabamians of out-of-control blacks creating conditions where whites "cannot walk the streets at night . . . without fear of mugging, raping, killing, or other physical assault." The multipurpose strategy failed, however, to reverse civil rights legislation and a widening social acceptance of racial integration. Since the civil rights era, racial barriers have been reduced, enabling nonwhites increasingly to participate in suburbanization. A leading driver of suburbanization and exurbanization became the attraction to higher-quality school districts, replacing the search for racially pure neighborhoods and inexpensive tract housing.[15]

The southern political idiom of white supremacy and racial segregation ended with the Southern Strategy, but the subtext of race remained coded in political discourse. Instead of "doing away with the racial problem," as Atwater put it, race remained a deeply divisive political wedge issue. Politicians courting white voters promised to cut taxes by withdrawing support for the city as the economic, cultural, and transportation hub of metropolitan regions. The "takers" in the city could be left behind.

Kruse concluded from his study of Atlanta that suburbanites "came to see their isolation as natural and innocuous. In the end, the ultimate success of white flight was the way in which it led whites away from responsibility for the problems they had done much to create."[16]

Mobility provided by the automobile and the suburban street network became a natural barrier to preserve the suburbs from encroachments by the city's poor. Opposition to public transportation and pedestrian facilities became standardized as part of southern political rhetoric. Kruse quoted Newt Gingrich promoting suburban segregation as a "values" issue:

> People in Cobb don't object to upper-middle-class neighbors who keep their lawn cut and move to the area to avoid crime. What people worry about is the bus line gradually destroying one apartment complex after another, bringing people out for public housing who have no middle-class values and whose kids as they become teenagers often are centers of robbery and where the schools collapse because the parents that live in the apartment complexes don't care that the kids don't do well in school and the whole school collapses.[17]

The exodus from the city to the suburbs and the exurbs profoundly reshaped the American city, especially in the South. By 2000, 54 percent of the nation's exurbs were located in the South, where rural political and economic power had resided since the time of Ashley Cooper. The modern conservative political agenda of suburban secession, individualism, unrestrained free enterprise, and opposition to federal authority dated not just to the resistance of southern whites to desegregation, but, in its basic form, to the founding of Carolina.[18]

In South Carolina today, there are very few working plantations still using the name "plantation." However, in addition to historic properties that have retained the name, planned communities called plantations abound in coastal Carolina. The latter are typically semirural white enclaves served by a mostly nonwhite workforce. The historical parallel goes mostly unnoticed by residents, but not by others who have a sense of slavery's continuing effects. The Beaufort County school system in coastal South Carolina, where modern gated plantations are a popular form of development, prohibits using the word in naming its facilities.

Those who do not understand the past are destined to repeat it, as the saying goes. So it is with the southern city of liberty, where cultural reaction formation with the anxious rhetoric of liberty versus tyranny steers politics today. The fraternalistic southern city of liberty remains one of class, not restricted by race through law or even geography, but designed to benefit the affluent and isolate the poor by limiting the power and influence of cities. From within, the fraternalistic city of liberty is part of one nation, under God, with liberty and justice for those who believe they are the true Americans who possess and guard the country's first principles. There is no visible reflection on how such supreme confidence mirrors that of the antebellum South as it sought the high ground in defending slavery.

The historic citadels of South Carolina are an apt metaphor for the siege mentality central to fraternalistic political culture. The economy of the early South could only grow by enslaving more people, and it grew until freedom was the preserve of a small minority surrounded by a vast labor force up to eight times the size of the minority. A citadel was built in Charleston in 1822 for a militia and as a refuge for whites after an insurrection plot was discovered. Another was built in Beaufort, Carolina's second city, where the ratio of enslaved people to free people was highest.

Fraternalistic political cultures are often associated with a sense of siege at their core, as Sheldon Hackney and many other southern scholars have written and as psychological research cited in Chapter 4 suggests. South Carolina faced a long list of threats as a frontier colony in a region where multiple European and Native American nations competed for territory. Those threats were replaced by new threats as South Carolina became a slave society, including the ever-present possibility of slave rebellion and outside pressure from nonslaveholding societies. After the Civil War, new threats emerged, as catalogued by Hackney: "carpetbaggers, Wall Street and Pittsburgh, civil rights agitators, the federal government, feminism, socialism, trade-unionism, Darwinism, Communism, atheism, daylight-saving time, and other by-products of modernity." Add to that a fear of social disorder and taxation sold by the Republican Southern Strategy and in 2008 the fear that an African American president would redistribute the wealth and overturn the privilege of "real" Americans.[19]

The city of today's fraternalistic political culture is one that promotes a strong defense against the threats of the day, through avoidance of cultural diversity; personal independence offered by the automobile; a retreat to safety in the suburbs and exurbs made possible by the automobile; preventing of the "47 percent" from advancing toward those havens of cultural uniformity by opposing use of tax funds for pedestrian, bicycle, and transit facilities; and holding the line with a gun culture and "stand your ground" laws. Southern fraternalistic society has self-deported to remote and gated enclaves, even as its legislatures ironically pass laws to defend against a sinister United Nations scheme to concentrate people in human habitat zones (a subject to be taken up subsequently).

Southern political culture, perceiving itself under siege, articulated a self-righteous devotion to a race-based class system in the articles of independence published by Confederate states, and again and again in justifying Jim Crow laws, in the writings of the Southern Agrarians, in the Dixiecrat Party, in the Southern Manifesto, in the White Citizens Councils, in the Council of Conservative Citizens, in the realignment of the Republican Party around the southern platform, and blended into the rise of Tea Party and libertarian political philosophy—successive manifestations of white fear that black empowerment constitutes a mortal threat. Today, fraternalistic political culture, inheriting the southern siege mentality, is mounting a reinvigorated liberty-versus-tyranny defense against the twin threats of sustainable development and social equity with their embrace of urban diversity. The defense is articulated by conservative and libertarian think tanks and delivered locally by the Tea Party movement and its fundamentalist allies, self-described as "teavangelicals."[20]

America's mix of political cultures sufficiently dilutes fraternalistic angst to prevent it from creating a pervasive national obsession over race and government. The nation's pragmatic and egalitarian political cultures do not harbor a sense of siege or feel compelled to issue manifestos to define and defend a just cause. What the broader strains of American political culture accept, and often embrace, is a tolerance for new arguments for the improvement of society as a whole, allowing the arc of history to bend toward a more vigorous pursuit of justice within the context of a broad spectrum of equality.

Throughout most of America, there is no reflexive opposition to federal involvement in urban development, no concern that city planning or environmental science is driven by a United Nations goal of world domination, no revulsion over ideas that might be associated with Europe, no obsession that tyranny looms large and freedom is under imminent threat. The city of America is generally a city of practical solutions and rational progress rather than one of reaction to external threats. It is a city of continuous advancements in the tradition of colonial planners like Ashley Cooper and Locke, who saw London's Great Fire of 1666 as an opportunity to renew or reinvent the city. Washington and many other American cities, as discussed in the Preface, were designed in that tradition. And as older cities were rebuilt from within, they were continuously improved, their slums made incrementally more livable through ordinances to provide better plumbing, electricity, ventilation, sunlight, and fire exits. Civic facilities, public parks, and public education were built for all with a sense of pursuing the greater good for society.

An uncompromising ideological divide over how to plan America's cities is a relatively new phenomenon. The philosophical debate over private-versus-civic good was one that could be resolved, if need be, in the courts. Constitutional principles and settled law were the bedrock of final arbitration. Communities had the right to constrain private development through planning and zoning, as the Supreme Court made clear in the 1926 *Euclid v. Ambler* decision. At times, local and state governments have leaned too far in the direction of civic interests, and the courts set boundaries for such "regulatory takings." Since the 1920s, the Supreme Court has made numerous takings decisions, thereby establishing a basic framework from which private and civic interests are able to find their way forward. The courts have determined that if a regulation does not destroy the economic benefits of a property, it does not constitute a taking. Cities continue to balance private and civic interests based on legal precedent and objective considerations of fairness. However, the new ideological argument now thrown into the equation is one that defies rational interpretation. It is an argument that external forces (the federal government and the United Nations) and their internal accomplices (such as planners and environmental scientists) are seeking to undermine the first principles upon which the nation was founded, "shredding" the Constitution as they do so.

The conflicts across the new ideological divide arise over several matters basic to how the American city is perceived, planned, and developed. Planning-related activities, such as comprehensive planning, environmental policy, zoning, transportation planning, bicycle and pedestrian facilities planning, provisions for affordable housing, and environmental justice advocacy, create flashpoints that are really surrogate issues that disguise a larger "culture war," one with roots in race and class hierarchy.

The Essence of the Conflict

On the most basic level, the cultural divide is one of ancient (virtually innate) social norms versus new (noninstinctual) social norms that arose during the Enlightenment. On the one hand is the hierarchical society that has evolved from prehistoric chiefdoms to republicanism. On the other hand is the much newer egalitarian society of many democracies. The two, of course, overlap in the modern democratic republic, where democracy and oligarchy often coexist. It has been argued here that the highest refinement of the first type of society is displayed in Ashley Cooper's Grand

Model, while the first glimmer of the second type of society can be seen in Oglethorpe's plan for Georgia. The two plans, in one sense, were related: they descended from the idea of stable government built upon agrarian balance as set out by James Harrington in *The Commonwealth of Oceana*. Ashley Cooper placed Harrington's ideal state in an ancient English context. Oglethorpe placed it in an updated context guided by the new eighteenth-century vision of "agrarian equality."[21]

As arcane as those two distinct ideals may at first appear to the modern observer, they are nevertheless the bedrock of today's political landscape. Fraternalistic political culture, the base of American conservatism, posits *liberty* to be the highest value of society. The nation's other political cultures posit that *equality* is the highest value of society. Liberty in the context of traditional social hierarchy is always available more to those in the upper tiers of the pyramid than to those farther down. To paraphrase Samuel Johnson, the loudest yelps for liberty come from those who possess the advantages of being in the upper tiers, advantages that may be conferred by race, class, or wealth. Equality is quite different because it is self-consciously classless; it not only seeks to remove class barriers but anticipates upward mobility as the lower tiers of society dissolve and a flatter democratic society emerges. Moreover, it continuously expands the scope of its pursuit, a feature that distinguishes it dramatically from the banner of liberty held by fraternalistic political culture. The benefits of equality at the founding of the nation were unavailable to the majority of Americans—women, blacks, and those not owning property, among others. All of those groups over time acquired the benefits of equality, and more are being added (notably, at present, lesbian-gay-bisexual-transsexual communities). The ideal of liberty can be self-limiting, but the ideal of equality is fundamentally unlimited.

Fraternalistic political culture is perpetually under siege because the liberty afforded to its component classes is continually assaulted by the equality available to other classes. Such assaults are, one may argue, self-constructed, since they are based on an assumption of zero-sum benefits. That is, as those lower in the social pyramid seek to advance upwardly, they take benefits from those occupying a place in the upper tiers. An effective dialogue with fraternalistic political culture has to address the fear of losing benefits and offer the alternative idea of expanding benefits for all.

Race has historically been the deepest of concerns for fraternalistic political culture. In Ashley Cooper's Carolina, as the historian Peter Wood wrote in *Black Majority*, race and class were not rigid barriers; people of all sorts worked together to meet the challenges of the frontier. Race became all-consuming after a slaveholding class led by West Indian sugarcane planters developed a lucrative rice monoculture. The high ratio of enslaved to free people, mostly black and white, necessitated an increasingly rigid social hierarchy with a legal system to perpetuate it and eventually a theory of white supremacy to justify it. Fear of black rebellion never subsided, since the more repressive the system became, the greater the motivation by its victims to overturn it.

Following the election of 2012, the conservative thought leader and former senator from South Carolina Jim DeMint wrote, "We must take our message of freedom and opportunity for all and connect with every neighborhood in America." The idea of "opportunity" is one designed to appeal to the minority populations that defeated Republican aspirations in that year's election. However, the idea of "opportunity," which is embedded in conservative rhetoric, does not have the same force as the idea of "equality," which is embedded in American law. DeMint's example of opportunity is one of allowing an inner-city student to attend a private school, leaving behind a failing public school. Public schools, historically, have been America's great equalizers, offering true opportunity to American children of all classes. Since the earliest stirrings of the civil rights movement, southern or fraternalistic political culture has persistently attempted to diminish public education and emphasize private alternatives. The pursuit of equality, however, is not amenable to privatization; it stands above and beyond private interests, which necessitates some degree of public (government) oversight.[22]

The notion that private interests, the "miracle of free enterprise," will bring about opportunity and equality is central today in fraternalistic political culture. The city upon a hill will be achieved, it is believed, by the invisible hand of a free market made up of private individuals, associations, and corporations acting within a freedom-loving context in their own self-interest. Government actions, it is maintained, disrupt the free market and take away the freedom of individuals.

There is a body of social and economic theory attached to free markets independent of race and class that warrants serious consideration. However, the loudest demands for free markets, and freedom in general, in America have historically been uttered in the context of advances of racial and class equality or surrogate issues of the sort cited by Lee Atwater. From the eloquent supremacist rhetoric preceding the Civil War, to the formation of White Citizens Councils in opposition to civil rights legislation, to the spontaneous formation of the Tea Party movement after the election of an African American president, the loud yearning for freedom in America has race (or the appearance of it) at its core, while the soft yearning for equality has true opportunity at its core.

Most opposition to city planning, environmental science, urban public policy, and social justice advocacy can be traced to racial angst or to the constructs of southern political culture bequeathed to its derivative, fraternalistic political culture. This does not mean that conservatives are racists, but rather that there is a symbiotic association between historical racism and the inherited rhetoric of the contemporary Far Right. The struggle against racial integration mounted by southern political culture bequeathed a rhetoric to fraternalistic political culture that is now deployed in three notable areas shaping the future of American cities: public spaces, suburbanization, and transportation. Many on the right believe that these are battleground issues because of policies pursued through a United Nations program known as Agenda 21.

Agenda 21: A Contemporary Focus of Conflict

American political cultures refresh their scripts periodically with new angels and demons. Their narratives, however, change very little: they draw heavily from the historical languages of liberty versus tyranny and equality versus injustice to describe anxieties that remain constant over time. Within the southern fraternalistic political culture continuum, a new demon has arisen to pose an existential threat to liberty, a demon that epitomizes the sense of siege that has always been a source of anxiety within the culture. That new demon is Agenda 21, the body of policy for *sustainable development* facilitated through the United Nations.

Within fraternalistic political culture, Agenda 21 represents a conspiracy by foreign and domestic enemies of liberty to end national sovereignty, impose tyrannical socialistic rule, and force Americans to live in high-density containment areas in the name of the false god of environmentalism. To egalitarian political culture, Agenda 21 represents a global, broadly participatory collaboration to envision a better world, identify common problems, and promote sustainable development.

The new aversion on the right to principles of sustainable development poses a fundamental problem for practitioners such as city planners, who have placed those principles at the very core of their practice. The new script similarly disadvantages policy makers, regulators, and scientists who work in urban and environmental fields. Their inductive, scientific approach to problem solving has been placed starkly at odds with the deductive, ideological worldview of fraternalistic political culture. The problem of "gridlock in Washington" has filtered down to the state and local level, where fraternalistic influence, often through Tea Party groups, is committed to restoring an idealized version of the past rather than addressing the future.

The framework for Agenda 21 was adopted at the United Nations Conference on Environment and Development held in Rio de Janeiro in 1992. It was an action plan for implementation of protocols of sustainable development assembled from the work of scientists, public health officials, economists, and others since the 1960s. As the United Nations has no territorial jurisdiction, Agenda 21 is implemented voluntarily and tailored to fit the needs of national and local governments. Opposition to the initiative in the United States was limited to right-wing fringe groups such as the John Birch Society with long-standing conspiratorial views of the United Nations.

Agenda 21 was based on an earlier report of the World Commission on Environment and Development, better known as the Brundtland Commission, after its chair, Gro Harlem Brundtland. The commission's report, "Our Common Future," advanced a concept of sustainable development that embraced a multidisciplinary approach to addressing such global challenges as clean energy, population growth, food production, viability of ecosystems, and international economic interdependence. The report defined "sustainable development" as "development that meets the needs of the present without compromising the ability of future generations to meet their own needs."[23]

Gro Harlem Brundtland began her career as a physician and scientist with Norway's public health system, where she investigated the relationship between children's health and environmental quality. She was appointed minister of the environment in 1971, and in 1981, at the age forty-one, she became the youngest person and first woman to hold the office of prime minister. She later became director-general of the World Health Organization, and since 2007 she has served as a UN Special Envoy for Climate Change. Brundtland received the Thomas Jefferson Foundation Medal in Architecture, which recognizes outstanding achievement. The medal is one of the three highest external honors bestowed by the University of Virginia, which does not grant honorary degrees. The university's three high awards "recognize achievements of those who embrace endeavors that the author of the Declaration of Independence, third U.S. president and founder of the University of Virginia, himself, excelled in and held in high regard."[24]

The subtitle of "Our Common Future" is "From One Earth to One World." Most people interpret that phrase as a lofty vision of a rising consciousness of global interdependence coupled with the recognition that humanity's greatest challenges are not confined to national borders. However, to many adherents of fraternalistic political culture, the term "One World" triggers the twin fears of loss of sovereignty associated with southern political culture and government tyranny dating to Ashley Cooper's time. They find themselves once again under siege, believing that federal and international authorities will conspire to rob them of liberty by using the ruse of sustainable development. Of further concern, Brundtland's Norwegian origins indicate a tie to "European socialism," or social democracy, regularly maligned by the Far Right as a "welfare state" that falls but little short of totalitarian communism.

While President Obama and the federal government were the first targets of the Tea Party movement, protest activities quickly worked their way down to the local level, with support from Far Right think tanks and advocacy groups, including the revitalized John Birch Society. Such groups portray Agenda 21 as a grave threat to American liberty being secretly spread to communities across the nation by socialists, internationalists, and their dupes in local government. Local Tea Party groups have trained their sights on planning and zoning commissions, which they believe are carrying out a global conspiracy to trample American liberties and force citizens into Orwellian "human habitation zones." Protests have taken many forms, such as opposition to a bike-sharing program in Denver that would turn the city into a "United Nations Community," Tea Party outrage in Maine that a transportation project to improve U.S. Highway 1 amounted to "the centralized planning for the de-industrialization of large segments of Maine, and the relocation and isolation of the population into human habitation zones," and a Virginia Tea Party leader's call for resistance to the "global agenda to actually abolish private property and abolish the Constitution." City planners regularly encounter Tea Party activists outraged over Agenda 21 and the introduction of sustainable development practices into their communities. Local officials are often caught off guard and intimidated by the sudden onslaught of conspiratorial thinking.[25]

The Southern Poverty Law Center, founded in 1971 to promote civil rights and expose extremist groups, issued a special report in April 2014 on opposition to Agenda 21. The report found that a "paranoid parade" of Far Right opponents of Agenda 21 is making it increasingly difficult to address "the serious problems that confront our nation and our planet." A case study of Baldwin County, Alabama, reveals a climate of conspiracy-fueled fear over Agenda 21 bringing about the repeal of the fast-growing coastal county's long-range development plan—an action that led the county's nine-member planning commission to resign en masse. In the words of one commission member, "It's the age of the Tea Party, all government is bad. That's why they threw an amazing, award-winning plan into the trash."[26]

Tea Party groups are political advocacy organizations, most of which were founded during or soon after the 2008 presidential election that brought Barack Obama to the White House. These new political actors purport to be independent grassroots groups fed up with government spending. However, they are supported by a wide range of older organizations dedicated to conservative causes partly funded by petrochemical magnates and other oligarchs. In Beaufort County, South Carolina (Ashley Cooper's chosen site for Carolina's first city), local Tea Party opponents of zoning code amendments with form-based (New Urbanist) elements presented an anti–Agenda 21 slide show consistent with John Birch Society talking points. Local planners were perplexed that anyone would think the amendments, which offered more use options and greater physical access to more persons, could be construed as a taking of freedoms. In Murfreesboro, Tennessee, Tea Party opponents of a new comprehensive plan and zoning ordinance distributed anti–Agenda 21 information also supplied by the John Birch Society. The central themes presented in such local venues are virtually identical across the country.[27]

Texas-based Tea Party 911, an informational organization supporting other Tea Party groups, warns that Agenda 21 is nothing less than an existential attack on America:

> If you were to hear that in the very near future the United States will have no privately owned property, no air conditioning, no dams, no paved roads, no way to correct rivers for flood control, no golf courses, no pastureland used for grazing, would you believe it?
>
> These are all mandates of a United Nations program called Agenda 21 which was born in Rio de Janeiro in 1992. All delegates watched as four men, holding poles attached to an "Ark of Hope" which contained this Agenda 21 document! Within its pages are a substantial attack on the American Declaration of Independence and our Constitution. The primary target for the changes proposed in 1992 is the United States of America.[28]

Language such as this from ostensibly diverse organizations is remarkably similar in its assertions as well as its wording. Broadly, these documents suggest that Agenda 21 is the implementing mechanism of a socialist plot to establish a new world order in which humans will be herded into urban areas, stripped of their liberty, and subjected to a redistribution of their assets to those who have become dependent on government rather than showing personal initiative. The supposedly diverse organizations distributing this information about a plot for a new world order are heavily funded by the old world order of oligarchs who have operated behind the scenes to influence political outcomes for decades. They see a new opportunity in the reaction to the election of President Obama and the rise of the Tea Party movement to expand their influence, especially at the state and local level.

National Tea Party organizations such as Tea Party Express, Americans for Prosperity, FreedomWorks, and the National Tea Party Federation avoid the subject of Agenda 21 and other conspiracy theories, preferring to remain focused on the core issues of limited government, fiscal responsibility, and free markets. It is at the local level where fear of Agenda 21 is being stoked by the more extreme policy institutes and advocacy organizations. While local Tea Party groups draw conservative citizens together, the information brought to those venues by citizens often comes from the far right of the conservative media spectrum.

The John Birch Society is one such organization now intensely active at the local level. Marginalized for decades for its political extremism, it has come out of the political shadows on the coattails of the Tea Party movement. In an attempt to resonate with the movement, the John Birch Society joined the attack on Agenda 21 with a community-organizing effort and educational tracts purportedly exposing a worldwide plot. "This United Nations program," it claims, "lays out a comprehensive plan of sustainable development locally, nationally, and globally in every area where humans affect the environment. Basically it's the UN's plan to establish control over all human activity, including man's reputed contribution to climate change. The UN is at the hub of a global network working to submerge the independence of all nations in a world government controlled by the elites." Use of the terms "comprehensive plan" and "sustainable development," common terms of local planners, undoubtedly raises concerns among those reading John Birch Society materials, promoting the view that local governments have become puppets of conspirators at the United Nations.[29]

John Birch Society tracts pinpoint sustainable development as the mechanism by which local governments will be seduced into adopting the anti-American goals of Agenda 21. "Sustainable development," it explains, "is really just disguised Marxism, with its top-down control of economic decisions, violation of private property rights, and emphasis on

Social Justice." They move next to the fear that may be at the heart of the oligarchs who fund the John Birch Society: "We strongly reject the U.N. Agenda 21 as erosive of American sovereignty, and we oppose any form of U.N. Global Tax." The John Birch Society has long been opposed to U.S. participation in the United Nations, and arousing fear of Agenda 21 within the general population builds a political base from which to oppose all things related to the United Nations, especially as they might relate to taxes on fossil fuel industries. Fred Koch, co-founder of Koch Industries, an energy conglomerate, was a founding member of the John Birch Society. Two of his sons, Charles and David Koch, have emerged as increasingly visible supporters of conservative think tanks and the Tea Party movement.[30]

American Freedom Watch Radio is one of several Far Right media outlets with a focus on Agenda 21, which it describes as a "plan for a New World Order through global governance." It endeavors to educate its listeners and website visitors to an even more extreme interpretation of Agenda 21. A group they call the Agenders has been tasked with a mission "to educate the people, expose the lies, promote the American rule of law and return America to the Constitutional Republic that makes America unique and successful." Agenda 21, according to the website, was instigated by "10,000 people from the Council on Foreign Relations (CFR), International Monetary Fund (IMF), United Nations (UN), the Club of Rome, the Bilderbergs and the Tri-Lateral Commission." These nefarious plotters "have decided to rule the world in a One World Government." In order to do so "they must reduce the population and put controls in place to insure future civilizations of indentured servants whose sole purpose will be to work for the state."[31]

The portrayal of Agenda 21 by the Far Right (as well as by conservative state legislatures, as will be seen later) as a socialist plot for a New World Order that will deprive the "makers" and reward the "takers" presumes that seditious intentions of the UN initiative are hiding in plain sight. The process leading to Agenda 21 was remarkably open to leaders worldwide, the media, and citizens; and its subsequent implementation activities are notably transparent. The claim that there is a plot depends on a portrayal of city planners, urban designers, environmentalists, advocates for social justice such as legal aid attorneys, and many others as enemies within, socialist plotters or their unwitting dupes, who will bring about the end of personal liberty, property rights, and national sovereignty.

Public sector city planners are required to meet public participation laws of state and local government; additionally, they must follow community-oriented planning standards published by the American Institute of Certified Planners. Such requirements make planners a visible target for local groups who have become alarmed about Agenda 21 and sustainable development. Planners are accustomed to an occasional delusional individual making irrational claims at public meetings; but they are at a complete loss when required to respond to large groups claiming that planners and other local officials are agents of global conspiracy. Ultimately, they must learn the language of the Far Right (much of it loosely derived from Ashley Cooper republicanism and Lockean liberalism) to respond to the radical claims about Agenda 21. While their responses may not appease the most determined conspiracy theorists, a demonstrated knowledge of relevant history and political philosophy will provide elected officials and other decision makers with a greater level of comfort and political cover in supporting new planning proposals.

A concerted effort to halt Agenda 21 and sustainable development is well under way. On the national level, the Republican National Committee adopted a resolution in January 2012 declaring that "United Nations Agenda 21 is a comprehensive plan of extreme environmentalism, social engineering, and global political control . . . being covertly pushed into local communities throughout the United States of America through the International Council of Local Environmental Initiatives (ICLEI) through local 'sustainable development' policies such as Smart Growth, Wildlands Project, Resilient Cities, Regional Visioning Projects, and other 'Green' or 'Alternative' projects." It is a "plan of radical so-called 'sustainable development'" that "views the American way of life of private property ownership, single family homes, private car ownership and individual travel choices, and privately owned farms . . . as destructive to the environment." The resolution goes on to characterize "social justice" under Agenda 21 as a scheme for "socialist/communist redistribution of wealth." The resolution "recognizes the destructive and insidious nature of United Nations Agenda 21 and hereby exposes to the public and public policy makers the dangerous intent of the plan."[32]

This formal action by the Republican Party in concert with numerous conservative organizations and many Tea Party groups creates a serious disconnect with the American tradition of city planning as understood by the planning and design professions. City planners are by implication unwitting accomplices of forces that are out to destroy national sovereignty, impose a reign of United Nations tyranny, force the populace to live in urban areas, and redistribute the wealth of deserving Americans to government-dependent takers.

The American Planning Association launched an effort in 2012 to dispel rumors about Agenda 21 and clarify its nonbinding status, to explain the benefits of sustainable development, and to educate planners on how to respond to citizens fearful of a grand conspiracy. However, according to Tom DeWeese, a ubiquitous speaker spreading the message that Agenda 21 is a threat to America, "the latest tactics by the American Planning Association reveals the dark intent of the Sustainablists and the lengths they will go to hide their goals. Honest intent doesn't have to hide in lies and double speak. Those are the tactics of tyranny."

It has become extremely difficult for planners and others being accused of deception and scientific hoaxes to challenge such inflammatory and inaccurate messaging. Any direct confrontation carries the risk of a political chain reaction on the right that would harden opposition to sustainable development and its practitioners. The activism of the Right and wary passivity of those under attack is deepening the divide in the country between those who subscribe to a pre-Enlightenment view of America and those who subscribe to Enlightenment values. The moderating influence of pragmatic conservatives is on the wane, and the inflammatory rhetoric aimed at sustainable development, climate science, and environmental justice is likely to persist.

At the state level, several bills have been introduced in legislatures to prohibit "implementation" of Agenda 21. The State of Alabama was the first to enact legislation, which simply stated, "The State of Alabama and all political subdivisions may not adopt or implement policy recommendations that deliberately or inadvertently infringe or restrict private property rights without due process, as may be required by policy recommendations originating in, or traceable to 'Agenda 21.'"[33]

Bills directed against Agenda 21 had been introduced in the Georgia, Louisiana, and Tennessee legislatures by the end of 2012. The North Carolina Republican Party passed a resolution in June 2012 calling Agenda 21 a "comprehensive plan of extreme environmentalism, social engineering and global political control" that "is incompatible with the Declaration of Independence and the Constitution of the United States and is a danger to the American way of life." North Carolina governor Pat McCrory, elected in 2012, supports the anti–Agenda 21 position. The South Carolina "Agenda 21 Protection Act," as drafted in June 2014, would "prohibit this state and its political subdivisions from adopting and developing environmental and developmental policies that, without due process, would infringe or restrict the private property rights of the owner of the property."[34]

Such bills have not always been enacted, even by conservative legislatures. A bill in the Oklahoma senate asserting that Agenda 21 is "a comprehensive plan of extreme environmentalism, social engineering, and global political control . . . being covertly pushed into local communities throughout the United States of America through the International Council of Local Environmental Initiatives" did not pass. The bill associated "smart growth," the "wildlands project," "resilient cities," "regional visioning projects," and "green" projects with the plan for "United Nations world domination."[35]

The Tea Party–influenced U.S. House of Representatives has sought cuts in the Environmental Protection Agency, and the Office of Smart Growth is one of its targets. In particular, House Republicans would like to undercut President Obama's urban policy initiative, the Partnership for Sustainable Communities, which coordinates a multiagency approach to urban challenges. The attack would prevent the EPA from working more effectively with the Department of Housing and Urban Development and the Department of Transportation on targeted problems and in sharing knowledge about best practices for solving urban problems. An example of the coordinated Smart Growth success is Saginaw, Michigan, which was caught in a cycle of population loss, disinvestment, and decline. A Smart Growth grant is helping Saginaw to reduce vacancy rates and attract private investment.[36]

Conservative and libertarian energy magnates are active in efforts to discredit Agenda 21, Smart Growth, sustainable development, environmental regulation, and many other planning initiatives. Charles and David Koch epitomize America's Far Right oligarchy. Their combined worth of $35 billion is exceeded only by Bill Gates and Warren Buffett. Koch Industries, a conglomerate of petrochemical and other resource-based industries, ranks as the second-largest private company in the United States. Ironically, they are behind-the-scenes supporters of the Tea Party movement. In July 2010, they underwrote an event in Austin, Texas, billed as a summit to educate populist Tea Party activists about vested corporate power. Yet speaker after speaker railed against President Obama and the federal government, not corporate excesses. Although the Kochs have denied involvement with the Tea Party, their minions are more candid. A speaker representing Americans for Prosperity, a Koch-funded advocacy organization, told attendees at the Texas conference that her group's role was in providing policy education and "next-step training" for Tea Party activists. A libertarian economist from a Koch-funded think tank observed that the libertarian movement has "been all chiefs and no Indians." The emergence of the Tea Party meant that for the first time there was a base of political power, with the Kochs "trying to shape and control and channel the populist uprising into their own policies." A Republican strategist who worked for the Koch brothers credited the pair with providing "the money that founded it. It's like they put the seeds in the ground. Then the rainstorm comes, and the frogs come out of the mud—and they're our candidates!"[37]

The Kochs are ideologues of the right, true believers in the virtue of laissez-faire capitalism and the inherent destructiveness of government. They also clearly benefit financially from the lack of regulation by a minimalist government presence, which may well reinforce their Far Right political philosophy. They believe that government has only one legitimate purpose, that of the protection of individual rights, especially property rights. In order to reverse the direction of government since the New Deal, they have adopted a vertically and horizontally integrated strategy linking think tanks, endowed college programs, media, lobbying, litigation, and local advocacy groups (primarily the Tea Party).[38]

The political scientist Jeffrey A. Winters, an authority in the study of oligarchy, has found that the richest Americans have always influenced the nation's political landscape. "The complex truth," Winters writes, "is that the American political economy is both an oligarchy and a democracy," where one exercises "material power" and the other "non-material power." For decades, the former has been able to reduce its share of the national tax burden despite popular sentiment that favors the opposite, and during the Reagan and George W. Bush administrations, it has been able to reduce regulation of industry. On the other hand, American democracy has managed to expand the doctrine of equality to women and racial, ethnic, and sexual minorities. Figure 15 illustrates the notable success of the nation's oligarchy in reducing its tax burden since 1970.[39]

The American political economy is a finely balanced system not only in terms of its branches of government but also in the less transparent interplay between the interests of the ultrawealthy and the general population. While the oligarchy portrays itself as a beneficent "job creator" class that only requires lower taxes and less regulation to be the rising tide that lifts all boats, the lower tax rates shown in the chart have not been accompanied by increased incomes for the lower- and middle-income segments of the population. Oligarchs derive two great benefits from a stable nation with a balanced government: armed defense of property and legal defense of property. Oligarchs historically had to pay an enormous cost for militias, citadels, and fortified cities to protect their assets. Now they enjoy the

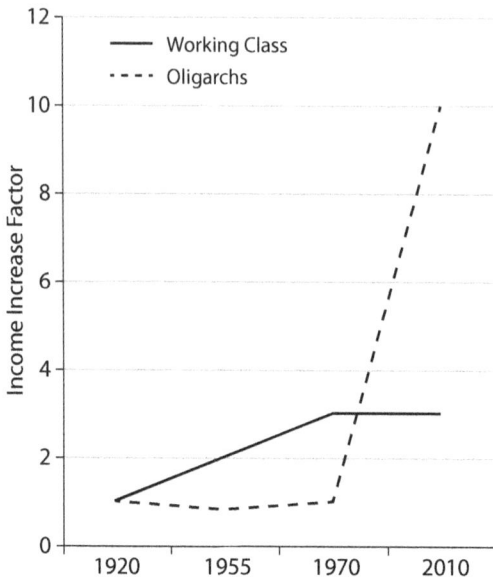

Figure 15. Working-Class and Oligarch Income Increase, 1920–2010. The rise of the working class abruptly ended in the 1970s. At the same time, the ultrarich experienced a dramatic rise in income. Source of data: Jeffrey Winters, *Oligarchy*.

benefit provided by the government of their property being protected by the nation's military and intelligence apparatuses. The nation's laws and its massive judicial system offer protection of intellectual and material property. Protection of property rights is a first principle of fraternalistic political culture derived from the emphasis in southern political culture on the right to hold slaves as chattel property. Beyond these vital functions of wealth protection, oligarchs have little use for government, a top-down view that is very different from the democratic bottom-up view of equality and social justice.[40]

Property rights are a core American principle, strongly reinforced by the existential concerns of the oligarchy and the traditional concern about land and chattel property deeply rooted in fraternalistic political culture. As Aristotle made clear, the physical and legal protection of property enables the creation of a state that combines the virtues of oligarchy and democracy, magnifying the benefits of each. An imbalance is created when oligarchs seek behind-the-scenes power that increases their wealth without increasing the wealth and maintaining the freedoms of the general population. An imbalance may also be created when the general population through the power of the majority takes more of the wealth from the oligarchy than can be justified by the benefits it receives from the wealth protections and national stability provided by the state. The acceleration of wealth accumulation by affluent Americans coupled with the stagnation of earnings by those in middle- and lower-income ranges demonstrates that the system is out of balance. The growth of political action committees, the removal of restraints on political spending by oligarchs made possible by the Supreme Court's Citizens United decision, and the vertical and horizontal integration of political strategies on the right supports the conclusion that the imbalance will persist or grow worse.

The importance of property rights in a democracy is linked to liberty, rather than to a balanced political economy, by the Far Right. The simple proposition that freedom produces an exceptional class of people to make money, thus creating a tide that lifts all boats, provides the rationalization for a continual pursuit of lower taxes and less regulation on high incomes. The political justification for this position is traced by conservative theorists to John Locke, who was an indisputable influence on the Founders. Locke's work on Ashley Cooper's plan for Carolina demonstrates a commitment to the ideal of reciprocity discussed earlier, in which an accumulation of wealth by the oligarchy is inseparable from its commitment to the well-being of the people—that is, a fundamental sharing of the benefits of a balanced political economy. Locke's venture into applied political philosophy with Ashley Cooper was tempered by the other proprietors, but his ties to it were not transitory; he maintained an interest in the colony past the Glorious Revolution, and he remained close to the Ashley Cooper family to the end of his life.[41]

Locke was clear in stating that the main purpose of government was to protect property, a tenet often interpreted outside the context of the time in which it was written. Locke and Ashley Cooper were influenced by Harrington's concept of balance of agrarian interests in which unlimited and unchecked acquisition of land and power constituted a fatal flaw in any political economy. Locke also emphasized, in the Harrington tradition, that a balanced government is one of laws. (Harrington wrote that "a commonwealth is a government of laws and not of men.") Locke added that the arrangement is rooted in a compact (he also used the word contract) between the people and their government. In other words, power rests with the majority, who reserve the right to hold leaders, including power-wielding oligarchs, accountable to the public interest. It is also important to understand that Locke's use of the word "property" was broader than typically found in current usage, even with the expansion of meaning in modern times to include intellectual property. Locke saw property as one's life and free will, as well as one's material possessions, a concern that is more consonant with progressivistic political culture.[42]

City planning has historically been rooted in a Lockean compact with respect to land rights. The compact anticipates interplay between private and civic interests, which may ultimately be arbitrated by the courts. This formal dance has generally maintained the kind of balance that Locke would expect in a government of laws. Many practicing planners in a challenging growth environment have heard accusations of communism hurled at them by special interests, but not from major institutions representing an entire political culture. Locke would not recognize today's assault on city planning from his perspective as a philosopher or a planner. The historian Peter Laslett, who reconstructed Locke's intended version of *Two Treatises* (incomplete and corrupted versions had long circulated), observed that if one assumes a definition of property as material only, Locke can be seen as arguing to make an "uncompromising defense of wealth and power." On the other hand, if one finds in Locke's work a much broader definition, as Laslett did, then property would include immaterial possessions and apply to all citizens of a commonwealth. Labor, for example, is "the unquestionable property of the laborer"—a tenet that would appeal to labor unions but not to neoconservatives or libertarians.[43]

From the perspective of fraternalistic political culture, which now dominates the Republican Party, two great enemies—the United Nations and the federal government—are threatening national sovereignty and the liberty and property rights of Americans. Proposals for public spaces, urban revitalization, public transportation facilities (even sidewalks), form-based development codes, resource protection, habitat restoration, pollution prevention, and carbon footprint reduction are seen as part of an orchestration of events leading to worldwide socialist tyranny and seizure of private lands. There is no easy response to such claims, which seem paranoid and delusional to pragmatists and progressivists. For city planners and others who want to avoid stepping off a political cliff, the best hope to avoid misperception is historical knowledge and informed rhetorical persuasion. Three conflicts arising over misunderstandings between political cultures over formerly benign planning proposals are examined in the sections that follow.

The Conflict over Public Space

The American tradition of city planning has historically placed great emphasis on the public realm. That tradition is highlighted at Monticello in an exhibit on city planning: "Jefferson advocated a comprehensive approach to city planning that considered site, transportation, and growth." His two "checkerboard" model city plans left alternating squares available for "turf and trees."[44]

The Ashley Cooper Plan for Carolina began the planning tradition with Anglo-America's first comprehensive plan for town and regional development. The plan set aside land for civic squares, wide streets, and public access to riverfronts. The importance of public space grew in large part from the intense discussions of public health, fire prevention, mobility, public facilities planning, and aesthetics that followed the Great Plague and the Great Fire. The later influence of Classical design, for which there was a strong current of interest during the Enlightenment, solidified America's planning ethic with a strong sense of the value of public space.[45]

Before the United Nations was created, a succession of popular movements that shaped American cities emphasized the value of public space. The City Beautiful movement of the late nineteenth century and early twentieth century emphasized beauty and harmony in the public realm and created many of America's most attractive urban environments. The tenets of the movement were reinforced by the Garden Cities movement imported from England during the same period. Later movements such as Modernism emphasized public space amid high-rise urban development.

America's traditional emphasis on urban public space began to diminish in the South during the 1950s in parallel with advances in civil rights. Following the Supreme Court's *Brown v. Board of Education* decision on school desegregation, Georgia governor Herman Talmadge declared, "Georgians . . . will not tolerate the mixing of races in the public schools or any of its tax-supported public institutions." Mixing of the races in any form other than one based on white superiority was almost inconceivable to white southerners in the 1950s. Talmadge told crowds while campaigning: "I was raised among niggers and I understand them, I want to see them treated fairly and I want to see them have justice in the courts. But I want to deal with the nigger this way; he must come to my back door, take off his hat, and say 'Yes, sir.'"[46]

Although Atlanta promoted an image as "the city too busy to hate," as already noted, the underlying racial caste system was unyielding. White politicians capitalized on the racial angst of their constituents by promoting a more individualistic approach to city and regional planning rather than encouraging biracial community dialogue and problem solving. Public space was increasingly ceded to blacks, leading to greater reliance on private space by whites. The loss of public space that whites had previously felt they "owned" led to a backlash in the form of a tax revolt, and bonds for public improvements were defeated by white voters.[47]

Post–World War II suburbanization brought about a similar effect in metropolitan areas across the country. Those who left the cities for the suburbs developed an affinity for the privatized space of malls and shopping centers and retained little interest in the urban treasures of the past, even the relatively recent achievements of the City Beautiful movement. Elected officials responded by forming suburban voting blocs that fragmented planning processes and generally opposed creation or maintenance of parks and other public spaces. Decades of work by urban policy makers to restore regional support for parks, public waterfront facilities, museums, highway corridor beautification, and similar efforts to improve the public realm now face a new form of resistance from conspiracy-minded groups that see such facilities as symptomatic of socialist or globalist subversion.

The Conflict of City versus Suburb

The suburbanization of American cities began with electric streetcars in the late nineteenth century. Streetcars offered extended mobility at modest cost to city residents, who until then had relied on walking and horses for transportation. Most streetcar suburbs were developed between 1890 and 1920, and they can readily be identified by the architecture of the period, including Victorian, neoclassical, and craftsman styles. New Urbanism was inspired in part by urban design patterns established at that time. A strong economy and mass production of automobiles in the 1920s stimulated a second phase of suburban development. Suburbs of the streetcar era and the early automobile era remained oriented to their historic city centers. It was not until the baby boom era that followed World War II that a third phase of suburbanization altered traditional urban fabric by creating major commercial corridors and centers outside of the historic downtown. The new postwar suburbs were made possible through federal government investment in regional highways and freeways, coupled with federally insured home loans tailored to suburban specifications.[48]

As the nation became increasingly suburbanized and auto-oriented, a fourth phase of suburban and exurban development took form. This new phase of growth began in response to several factors, including lower land costs, flight from urban ills, avoidance of urban schools, and availability of natural and planned amenities. Master planned (and sometimes gated) communities became standard in fourth-ring suburban development, although less expensive tract developments of third-ring design planted on the rural fringes also became common.

Resistance to integration during the civil rights era gave impetus to the relocation of first- and second-phase residents to third- and fourth-phase suburbs. Kevin Kruse, in his study of Atlanta, found that "much of the modern suburban conservative agenda—the secessionist stance toward the cities, the individualistic outlook, the fervent faith in free enterprise, and the hostility toward the federal government—was, in fact, first articulated and advanced in the resistance of southern whites to desegregation." Fraternalistic political culture was largely formed out of southern political culture at this time and expanded outward into national politics through the Republican Southern Strategy.[49]

Kruse describes the new, tacit system of segregation resulting from this outmigration as the "politics of suburban secession." In the phrase of former labor secretary Robert Reich, it is a "secession of the successful" in which those with means stake out a new identity, leaving the older city underfinanced and in perpetual decline. Fraternalistic political culture then seized the opportunity to drive a wedge between city and suburb, recruiting a majority of voters based on fear of the urban minority.[50]

An essential part of the Southern Strategy involved forming an alliance with white conservative Christian groups. As land-use planning, transportation planning, zoning, public facilities finance, and school facilities and financing have become political issues dividing poor and affluent, city and suburb, conservative religious leaders have sided with the social concerns of their membership in the suburbs. In Atlanta, the evangelical leader Ralph Reed, as the state's Republican Party chairman, orchestrated a successful anti-urban campaign in 2002 that swept many new Republicans into office. The party platform made these promises: "Shorter commutes. More time with family. Lower mortgages." It was effective on multiple levels, conflating the personal goals of suburban and exurban secessionists with fundamentalist values. Underlying the platform was a fundamentalist sense of exile from the city, where corruption and degeneracy had taken hold, and a rebuilding of Christian society in the suburbs and exurbs.[51]

In parallel with political and religious initiatives supportive of suburban interests, several conservative think tanks have built expertise in urban theory that favors a suburban growth model. In doing so, they deemphasize the more integrated planning model known as regionalism that attempts to balance urban, suburban, and exurban interests. They also attack the "creative class" theory that complex, mixed-use urban environments attract skilled people and spark diversified and sustainable forms of economic development. Think tanks supported by ultraconservative oligarchs that publish articles and reports on urban and regional planning include Reason Foundation, Competitive Enterprise Institute, Heartland Institute, Manhattan Institute, and the Koch-supported Cato

Institute. A small number of authors are responsible for most of the publications: Jonathan Adler, Wendell Cox, Joel Kotkin, Randall O'Toole, and Samuel Staley. Their work provides technical detail for use by Tea Party groups to oppose principles of sustainable development, regionalism, and creative cities. More conspiratorial Tea Party groups can combine this material with that supplied by other right-wing groups on purported Agenda 21 threats to national sovereignty and individual liberty.

Joel Kotkin, who is affiliated with conservative institutions such as the Koch-supported Cato Institute, is perhaps the most ubiquitous voice of advocacy for suburban growth. Kotkin argues that middle-class families are better served by the suburban model: "The battle's over. For half a century, legions of planners, urbanists, environmentalists and big city editorialists have waged war against sprawl. Now it's time to call it a day and declare a victor. . . . The winner is, yes, sprawl." The victory, he declares, is for the good of the nation because suburbs represent the American Dream—giving us "space, quality of life, safety and privacy." Since making that claim in 2005, which was tempered with an acknowledgment of some failures of the suburban model, Kotkin has increased his defense of the suburbs and his assault on urbanism.[52]

In an attack on Richard Florida, author of *The Rise of the Creative Class*, Kotkin claims that creative-class strategies "packaged and pedaled" by Florida have been a disappointment to cities that have implemented them. The "real geography of opportunity," Kotkin argues, is in cities like Houston and Oklahoma City, where growth of "family-friendly suburbs and exurbs" has been fueled by energy and manufacturing sectors, not technology and other creative industries. Richard Florida's response to Kotkin, whom he describes as "America's leading cheerleader for urban sprawl," is that solid research proves that "cities and density spur economic growth." Florida acknowledges that growth of a "creative knowledge economy" presents challenges, but he maintains that cities can meet such challenges if they embrace a new "social contract" that addresses wages and affordable housing. In fact, new research consistently shows that cities are proving more resilient than suburbs.[53]

Kotkin's credentials are burnished with scholarly titles from think tanks and from Chapman University, where he holds the title of professor. However, his website bio reveals no degrees or credentials from academic or professional institutions. Rather, he is a journalist who "attended Berkeley" and writes about urban geography and city planning. A content analysis of recent articles he has authored finds that they are sprinkled with references to academic research findings that appear to bolster his arguments, but his arguments are advanced primarily with rhetorical flourishes and denigrating phraseology designed apparently to relegate urbanists (along with advocates of sustainable development and Smart Growth) to an elitist category in a manner consistent with conservative messaging. Kotkin then proceeds to commit three types of logical errors in presenting his pro-suburbia arguments. First, he engages in a logical sleight of hand by setting up a straw-man argument against urbanist principles. He describes suburban growth as driven by its attractiveness to a majority of Americans, invoking an image of automobile-dependent third- and fourth-phase suburbs. Then, however, he proceeds to embellish the suburbs to include urbanized, mixed-use, transit-served communities such as those in the Silicon Valley corridor, falsely contrasting them with San Francisco as if urbanists propose big-city living for everyone. Kotkin is thus arguing against a construct of his own making in which his elitist adversaries oppose suburban living in favor of the city core. In truth, urbanists embrace precisely the kinds of places that Kotkin drew into his suburban domain—the vibrant towns in the transit-served, urbanized corridor between San Francisco and San Jose.[54]

Kotkin's straw-man argument against the city core is not only a false issue, but is also one that leads him to commit a mathematical error. In comparing employment generation in core areas with outlying suburbs, he fails to make adjustment for the simple fact that the larger the circumference of metropolitan geography, the greater the area. Thus, when he cites data published by Wendell Cox, another conservative critic of urbanism, showing that areas within 2 miles of metropolitan city centers have added 206,000 residents between 2000 and 2010 and then compares that with areas 10 to 20 miles from the core, he is comparing the urban core to a suburban area that is seventy-five times larger. On a square-mile-area basis, urban cores have attracted more residents than Kotkin's suburban ring, an amazing feat considering the limited amount of available residential land (due to existing development, industrial brownfields, and zoning regulations) in most city centers. A more revealing comparison of change in urban-versus-suburban residential preference would be to compare urban transit corridors from the city center to the end of the urbanized area with areas zoned for single-use residential development.[55]

The third type of logical error committed by Kotkin is that of a *category mistake*. In this Kotkin is not alone (the author has called attention to the same mistake made by planners and urban designers). In talking generally about urban and suburban growth, one needs to take great care to compare functionally equivalent geographic categories rather than overgeneralized geographic concepts. Kotkin flirts with this notion but fails to do much with it when he says that the city is a complex "protean form that is always changing." If Kotkin could bring himself to engage in a more rigorous dialogue without the name calling, he would find that his conclusions are not polar opposites to those of urbanists. In fact, the purpose of Kotkin's relentless critiques may be to reinforce a political dichotomy on behalf of his employers rather than to advance knowledge of urban dynamics.[56]

Many conservative think tanks like the Cato Institute receive much of their funding from the conservative oligarchs of extractive and energy industries, which calls into question their objectivity in stridently defending the suburban growth model to the point of glorifying urban sprawl. In recent years, the Republican Party has harmonized its messaging with the suburban bias. The detailed party platform adopted in 2012 contains scant reference to urban challenges except, for example, to prescribe school vouchers and weaker gun laws for the District of Columbia. The Republican aversion to urban populations is a relatively recent phenomenon, strengthened with the party's Southern Strategy and implemented during the period of white flight to suburbs and exurbs.[57]

The vote-getting power of anti-urban, often racially tinged, politics is only one part of the urban-suburban strategic calculation. The underlying motivation for conservative thought leaders is the libertarian sense of individuality and its close association with the automobile. This philosophy of private mobility is, of course, melded with wealth derived from petrochemical industries. Virtually unlimited mobility in a growing population consuming polluting, nonrenewable resources goes unquestioned, as long as the accumulation of wealth from petroleum-associated industries can be perpetuated. Principles of sustainable development articulated long before Agenda 21 was conceived force policy makers to evaluate the long-term consequences of petroleum-driven growth, a challenge resented by America's energy oligarchs, who believe fervently that their business and leadership acumen is essential to American civilization.

The great irony of the conservative defense of individualism and automobile mobility is that those two facets of society became interrelated as a result of federal government "central planning" and investment. The great expansion of the suburbs would not have been possible at the scale it occurred without mortgage insurance provided by the Federal Housing Administration and the Veterans Administration, without the Federal Highway Administration and the Interstate Highway System, without federal grants for water and sewage treatment facilities, and without federal planning grants to cities. Those federal planning grants, authorized under section 701 of the 1954 Housing Act, enabled hundreds of America's cities to prepare land-use plans for guiding the vast postwar baby boom expansion.

Another irony can be found in the utter rejection of the city planning principles prescribed by Anthony Ashley Cooper and John Locke, men otherwise exalted by conservatives and libertarians for their presumed roles in defining transatlantic republicanism and classical liberalism (the basis of modern libertarianism). Ashley Cooper and Locke, in beginning the American tradition of city planning, prescribed orderly and compact growth patterns that made efficient use of resources and produced essential economies of scale. They could not have been clearer in their "Instructions" of May 1671 and June 1672, where planning guidelines were laid out for sustainable development similar to those of Agenda 21 and the American planning initiative known as Smart Growth.[58]

The Conflict over Public Transportation and Personal Mobility

Nothing epitomizes the divide between political cultures more than public transportation. Egalitarian political culture, looking to the future, sees technological advancements as presenting an opportunity for bringing back intercity trains, commuter trains, and urban trolley lines. Fraternalistic political culture, drawing from its tradition of government skepticism, rejects virtually any innovations in transit that involve taxation and public sector operation. Many conservative policy institutes receive funding to counter public transportation proposals, including the Heritage Foundation, the American Enterprise Institute, and the Reason Foundation. The conservative Free Congress Foundation is an anomaly in its support from multimodal systems and "maximum choices for the traveling public." In a report released in June 2013, the Free Congress Foundation argued that America has underinvested in public transportation and that future economic growth will depend on rail and other alternatives to the automobile.[59]

Metropolitan Tampa, Florida, is a model of fraternalistic transportation planning. It is true to Tea Party fiscal conservatism in resisting taxation for public investment in transportation infrastructure, except for roads, which are funded through gas taxes (an acceptable form of "user fee"). At the same time, it has avoided downtown investment in pedestrian enhancements essential to attracting the creative class. Although the city is more progressive than the metropolitan region, it is impeded from becoming a dynamic regional hub by Tea Party–controlled county governments. A proposed tax to build a light-rail system was overwhelmingly rejected by county voters even as a majority of city voters supported it, and the city's ambitions to improve its vitality are scaled back to what it alone can afford. Forbes magazine ranked Tampa dead last among major cities for ease of commuting, while Transportation for America and Smart Growth America ranked it second among the most dangerous cities for pedestrians. A 2007 survey found it to be the only city of thirty studied with no walkable destinations. The city has been described as having "a windswept, desolate feel outside of business hours." The sprawling city that hosted the Republican National Convention in 2012 had to charter 400 buses to shuttle conventioneers between the downtown venue and distant suburban and exurban accommodations.[60]

Portland, Oregon, stands in sharp contrast to Tampa. With regional and state coordination, Portland has built one of the best multimodal transportation networks in the nation. Its transportation facilities have been planned in concert with development initiatives aimed at attracting the creative class to its vibrant urban neighborhoods. The cost feasibility of public transportation systems depends on the distribution of population in a metropolitan area. Populations that are widely dispersed, as in Tampa, are generally not well distributed for rail-based transit systems, although a high growth rate provides an opportunity to develop nodes of transit-oriented development.

The U.S. Census Bureau has published a table of "population-weighted density" for the 2010 census that measures population concentrations within metropolitan areas. The table reveals that Metropolitan Statistical Areas experienced an overall decline from 6,725 to 6,320 persons per square mile from 2000 to 2010, a 6.0 percent drop over ten years. The population-weighted density of Tampa declined from 3,444 to 3,323 during the same period, a 3.5 percent drop; that of Portland, by contrast, increased from 3,994 to 4,372, a rise of 9.5 percent.[61]

The difference between the two cities is one of political culture and associated city planning. Tampa's fraternalistic political culture is more segregated, hierarchical, and laissez-faire. The autonomy of the automobile is the highest priority for mobility. The Tampa region has successfully resisted state-level planning guidelines that until recently promoted the concepts of sustainable development and Smart Growth. The metropolitan area also defaulted to a traditional hierarchical pattern in which the conservative, fraternalistic suburbs relegated the diverse and more progressive city to a lower and isolated status. Portland's egalitarian political culture and its creative-progressive professional culture, in contrast, resonated with state-level sustainable development strategies adopted in the 1970s as well as a more communitarian sense of regionalism than that exhibited in Tampa.

Sidewalks and other pedestrian facilities are another concern of conservatives, particularly on the Far Right. Such concerns are magnified by fear of Agenda 21 and sustainable development. In Savannah, Georgia, in 2012, the Tea Party rose up against a proposal by County Commissioner Patrick Shay to install sidewalks along a stretch of highway serving six schools. The highway, which once traversed the rural outskirts of the city, is now densely developed and serves the city's eastern suburb. Commissioner Shay believed that sidewalks would offer greater safety for schoolchildren walking along the highway. He was shocked when his modest proposal met with fierce opposition over a presumed connection to Agenda 21. Pedestrians, including hundreds of schoolchildren, will continue to walk in rutted and sometimes muddy conditions at the edge of the highway.[62]

In Atlanta, pedestrians are also treated as second-class citizens, if not criminals. The city's pedestrian advocacy group, PEDS, has found that police officers in the metropolitan area tend to cite pedestrians hit by automobiles rather than drivers, sometimes even while they are hospitalized. Georgia law makes it illegal to use the roadway where sidewalks are present, and police officers are citing pedestrians and runners for crossing the street even though sidewalks are often in poor condition and "jaywalking" laws are primarily designed for application in downtown areas (Georgia law currently requires pedestrians to use a crosswalk between signalized intersections). Atlanta is one of the nation's most hazardous cities for pedestrians, and the state's political culture is unlikely to fund pedestrian facilities with the same concern it places on roadways.[63]

The disdain for nonmotorized modes of transportation found in fraternalistic political culture now extends beyond sidewalks to recreational hiking and biking trails. Planning professor Andrew Whittemore has followed the Tea Party in the Dallas area, finding that it perceives the hand of the United Nations in the North Central Texas Council of Government's economic blueprint, "Vision North Texas," and in the "Hike and Bike System Master Plan" for Arlington, Texas. The cities of Garland, Rowlett, and McKinney have also been targeted by Tea Party groups for purportedly following UN Agenda 21 directives. Planning initiatives once seen as wholesome improvements are increasingly under assault as un-American.[64]

The New Divide

Anthony Ashley Cooper and John Locke were committed to the idea that human settlements require planning in order to thrive. Ironically, their ideological descendants in today's conservative movement, dominated by fraternalistic political culture, are suspicious of planning and the paradigm of sustainable development on which it is largely based. Many of today's right-shifting conservatives believe that the built environment is best left in the hands of profit-making businesses with little regulation, and that mostly from local authorities. This view is bolstered by evangelical conservatives who believe the natural environment is a bequest from God for human consumption rather than the complex system perceived by the sustainable development paradigm. In this view, advocates of sustainable development are misguided dupes marching to orders from the federal government or, in the extreme view, from the United Nations.

Although many conservative investors and entrepreneurs privately disagree with the conspiratorial view, some nevertheless encourage it because it advances their interests—primarily property rights without government regulation. Many in the building industry have long sought legislation that would prevent local governments from enacting strict environmental and zoning laws. Known as *takings* legislation, such laws require cities and counties to compensate land developers for loss of value as a result of regulations. Until recently, such legislation has been argued on theoretical, legal, and practical grounds, and more often than not been rejected on those grounds by courts and legislatures. Now, however, advocates of takings legislation have new allies among Tea Party culture warriors determined to protect traditional American society from domestic and foreign threats to its way of life. The new dynamic resets the dialogue from one of practical and legal issues to one that is cultural and political. Planners and a large cast of others are pushed unwillingly onto a stage where multiple political dramas are unfolding—First Amendment interpretations regarding religion, Second Amendment interpretations of gun rights, immigration policy, climate science, health care reform, and a woman's control over reproductive rights.

The roots of this new political divide can be traced to the modified Grand Model, which established a rural ethic in South Carolina that spread across the South and filtered through the nation. The Solid South that emerged was built on an agrarian economy based on slavery, Jim Crow, and racial politics with an idealized self-image steeped in the rural landscape. Southern whites and their ideological heirs remained connected with that rural heritage, and they retained the familiar language of liberty and tyranny as new cultural challenges such as civil rights emerged. The contemporary planning issues of environmental quality, resource protection, sustainable development, and multimodal transportation became challenges to the revered suburban, exurban, and rural lifestyles.

The political divide is particularly evident in the debate over gun safety regulation. While guns were essential for security in a rural environment without police protection, for hunting game, for maintaining a militia (the original purpose of the Second Amendment), and for protection against slave revolts, the reverence for the gun remained after its principal purposes faded away. What was essential in early times became recreational with the end of slavery and the taming of the frontier. Yet revulsion of federal authority inherited from ancestral political culture stoked fear that guns would be taken away by a tyrannical government. The danger now faced by advocates of sustainable development is that their goals will become associated with government tyranny as much as gun safety regulation is at present.

Jim Bacon, formerly publisher and editor-in-chief of *Virginia Business* magazine, has taken on the mission of bridging the growing chasm between the Right and the Left in the area of Smart Growth, the city planner's perspective on sustainable development. He launched Bacon's Rebellion blog, which supports sustainable principles for local planning while rejecting federal involvement. As a wary conservative, Bacon predicts "an eventual collapse of federal government finances." He calls for less government, lower taxes, and strong protection of property rights; but once those basics are in place he favors local application of the principles of Smart Growth, warning conservatives not to throw out "the smart-growth baby with the liberal bathwater." He notes that leapfrog development and "scatteration" are "more expensive to serve with roads, utilities and public services than compact development." Combined with zoning that segregates land use, this kind of planning (or lack of it) "drives up the cost of local government and transportation." The American tradition of city planning contains many elements that should appeal to conservatives, as Bacon maintains; however, the tradition is also built upon progressive principles of the Enlightenment, which will continue to make it a tough sell for conservatives.[65]

The fast-growing divide between the American tradition of city planning and fraternalistic political culture will be difficult to bridge. However, in addition to improving their knowledge of history and historical rhetoric, planners have another option to improve communication. Planners might embrace a concept of ruralism that balances a trendy predilection for urbanism. An opportunity for doing so can be developed from the "design with nature" prescription made famous by the landscape architect Ian McHarg. His work has long been considered foundational to the modern concept of sustainable development. An urban-rural equation that places principles of New Urbanism and urban creativity side-by-side with beneficial ruralism (as described by the Southern Agrarians) could represent an overarching paradigm with greater appeal to conservatives.[66]

Conclusion

It is difficult to predict whether fraternalistic political culture will continue to gain strength at the national, state, and local levels and how that might affect the sustainable development paradigm and practices such as city planning that embrace it. Factors that favor the persistence of attacks on sustainable development and those who practice it—essentially an attack on Enlightenment-inspired first principles—are the concerted efforts among oligarchs funding the attack, the effectiveness of Far Right media in delivering their message, the success of the Tea Party conservatives in securing more control at the state and local levels of government, tighter control of messaging in national elections to avoid the gaffes that undermined Tea Party–endorsed candidates in 2012, the extent to which southern political norms become central to the Republican Party, and the presence of xenophobia and racism within the electorate requiring surrogate issues such as Agenda 21 to find expression. Factors favoring a decline in angst within fraternalistic political culture over sustainable development and those who practice it are a loss of motivation following the Obama presidency, demographic trends that will dilute the influence of the Tea Party movement, and increasingly effective messaging by progressivistic groups in portraying the Far Right as predominantly old, white, racist, and xenophobic and prone to believe conspiracy theories.

The conservative tide is unlikely in any case to go out as fast as it came in during and immediately after the 2008 presidential election. The Far Right has constructed an infrastructure of think tanks and media organizations that will be maintained at any cost by conservative oligarchs, encouraged by their successes in the 2014 midterm elections. The Tea Party movement is well organized and enjoys a sense of connectedness among groups coast-to-coast. It may decline slightly as some members lose hope in the effort to "take back our country" or simply resume a more mundane, less politically active life. The Tea Party will remain strong in "red states" where the influence of southern political culture and other conservative political cultures such as Mormonism keep it in the mainstream. It will also remain a force in the "purple states," where it will be heavily supported by the traditional conservative infrastructure as well as oligarchic investment. It is in the "blue states" that the Tea Party movement and Far Right activity is most likely to recede in the immediate future.

Enlightenment-inspired American traditions such as city planning, like many allied professions in the social and natural sciences, will likely remain under attack in fraternalistic areas, whether they are red and purple states or conservative exurbs and rural communities. That likely scenario cannot be ignored by those who practice the American tradition of city planning or other professions built on science and inductive reasoning. They must be prepared for a sustained counter-effort to preserve their values and practices. The effort on the Far Right to portray city planners and so many others as actors in an international scheme to undermine personal liberty, end national sovereignty, and herd people into urban containment areas will persist in American political culture into the foreseeable future, even if it wanes in the nation's larger urban areas.

There are three elements to an effective counter-effort by creative-progressive professionals supported by the findings in this book. The first is knowledge of history and the political philosophy as it shaped the nation's first principles. Anthony Ashley Cooper and John Locke are at the top of the list of people who influenced the nation—Ashley Cooper because his design of Carolina contributed to the formation of an American political culture and Locke because of his close association with Ashley Cooper, his influence on the Founders, and his continued influence today, particularly among libertarians and conservatives. While planners across the nation have found it virtually impossible to find common understanding with those who have bought into the Agenda 21 conspiracy theory, they must at least be able to interpret the historical and philosophical references sprinkled throughout conservative discourse to elected officials and other decision makers as they assure them that American values will not be violated by their planning and zoning recommendations.

A second element, more specific than that of first principles, is that of the physical planning and design of regions. Early plans, dating to the Ashley Cooper Plan, contain basic precepts that are remarkably similar to those found today in the principles of sustainable development and Smart Growth. As shown earlier, Ashley Cooper, with Locke's able assistance, created a growth model that would accommodate most people in well-planned towns, that would prevent "sprawl" and "leapfrog" development, and that would place strong emphasis on civic facilities. During the colonial period and the formative years of the republic, the principles of the Ashley Cooper Plan and later the Enlightenment guided city planning and the vision of what cities are in American civilization. Those principles were not those of laissez-faire capitalism or unrestricted property rights, but a balanced system of many interests, above all human rights. Within this context, the idea of an urban-rural equation is one that offers hope of bridging differences and strengthening support for sustainable development among conservatives.

A third element is that of language, or the historic forms of discourse appropriated by the Right to attack sustainable development. To mitigate such attacks, one must again return to Ashley Cooper and Locke. The republicanism resurrected by Ashley Cooper in the 1670s, following the mid-century failed experiment with a commonwealth, was established with a well-defined philosophy and vocabulary. Republicanism entered America through Carolina, and later Georgia, and has survived to the present. Many of its components can be found in the political platform of the modern Republican Party, and many can be found in the Democratic Party platform as well. Locke began his career as a philosopher steeped in republican philosophy, and a branch of it known today as classical (or Lockean) liberalism has developed. Understanding the language of the Right and its historical roots is essential to an effective rebuttal.

The Epilogue will take up the third element, an answer to those who characterize sustainable development, Smart Growth, New Urbanism, Agenda 21, environmentalism, environmental urbanism, landscape urbanism, resiliency planning, and social justice and those who practice within those frameworks as part of an international socialist plot to bring an end to the American way of life. Specific suggestions are laid out in the form of a metalanguage for communication across political cultures. If the principles of the Enlightenment that emphasize equality and justice are to remain strong and coexist with libertarian disengagement and neoconservative nationalism, then advocates of those principles must development a rhetoric as effective as that honed by the Right.

Epilogue

Political Culture and the Future of the City

Anthony Ashley Cooper reached a ceiling in human potential with his design of Carolina. All societies with which he was familiar through his study of history had been rigidly hierarchical, formed into social pyramids of well-defined classes, each class-tier performing a function for the maintenance, or ideally the betterment, of the whole. Carolina was intended to be the ultimate refinement of the social pyramid based on an understanding of history from Classical Greece to England's Gothic traditions. The design would secure stability through balanced government and ensure fairness to all classes through reciprocity of duties and benefits throughout society.

John Locke later broke through the ceiling that he and Ashley Cooper reached with the design of Carolina. The rupture was made possible by regime change in England—the Glorious Revolution that brought William and Mary to power. The prospect of regime change, bringing with it Dutch values of pragmatic tolerance and elective leadership, prompted Locke to think further about the nature of man and the structure of society. With publication of *Two Treatises of Government*, Locke not only laid a foundation for England's new government, as was his intention; he also laid a substantial part of the foundation for the Enlightenment. The idea that humans are equal in the state of nature, and that they relinquish some of their natural rights through a compact (or contract) in order to attain the greater benefits of society, was so new and profound as to demolish the ceiling that had previously limited human potential.

Carolina did not advance toward the Enlightenment with Locke but instead went the other direction. It rigidified the social pyramid

227

and modified Ashley Cooper's language of liberty to rationalize a slave society rivaling that of ancient Rome. The idea of *liberty* was compartmentalized in Carolina in a way that allowed its beneficiaries to complain of tyranny if their oligarchic benefits were reduced by the gains of the lower classes. The language of liberty and tyranny that evolved in southern political culture was one that served those at the top of the pyramid; and the framing properties of that language, which guide fraternalistic political culture today, remain in place. Gains by a class of people lower in the social pyramid were seen as bestowed by a tyrannical North, stealing liberty and property from those higher in the pyramid. The language of liberty and tyranny evolving from the Carolina experience coupled with a sense of siege by enemies foreign and domestic reinforced the sense of a zero-sum society through succeeding generations.

A new language of equality and democracy alien to Carolina emerged from Locke's *Two Treatises*. The framing properties of that language—a language of the Enlightenment—guide egalitarian political culture and the creative-progressive professions today. The language of equality and democracy is based on civic dialogue rather than authoritarian pronouncements. It forces one to think in terms of the larger society rather than self, class, or fraternal milieu. The language of liberty and tyranny supporting an archaic class pyramid receded with the end of slavery, the demise of Jim Crow, and the greater integration of society.

City planners, urban and environmental policy makers, design professionals, and social justice advocates, among other creative-progressive professionals, were secure in adopting the language of equality and democracy as a central tenet of their professional paradigms. There was no sense of pursuing a political agenda since it was language that came from the Declaration of Independence and was well established in American discourse. With the Southern Strategy, however, the language of liberty and tyranny reemerged. A great culture war took form over deep divisions unresolved by the Civil War and the battles over civil rights. With the election of President Obama, fraternalistic political culture instantly found a new voice in the Tea Party. Professions advocating a role for government in setting urban and environmental policy are now confounded by the rhetoric from a language they never learned. Their instinctive response has been to invite more open discussion, to say, "Let us reason together." But fundamental cultural and rhetorical differences now appear unbridgeable by openness and reason alone.

Finding a way to depoliticize current public discourse over sustainable and resilient cities, of basing public policy where possible on science, or on the value of pursuing social justice, is a new challenge for many professions. The dominant movement of a major political party views such activities as not only political but in the service of tyranny, putting creative-progressive professionals on the defensive. More public meetings with more open discussion will not resolve differences when people are not sharing the same linguistic terrain. Nor will such meetings bring consensus or compromise when underlying cultural assumptions are inherently nonrational. To paraphrase Jonathan Swift, you cannot reason someone out of something they were not reasoned into.

The only nonpolitical method of successfully countering nonrational arguments is to respond in the same language using similar rhetorical frameworks. That is, first, to argue with a knowledge of history and first principles that is so well informed and respectful of traditions that it highlights the origin and oversimplified nature of contemporary anti-urban, anti-environmental rhetoric. Then, second, to present policies and initiatives within a strategic planning format, thereby framing recommendations in the context of value systems. Strategic plans, especially those within city and county comprehensive plans, typically begin with vision statements and goals that reflect community values.

Cognitive science has shown that 98 percent of thought is unconscious. Even much of what scientifically oriented people think of as reason occurs in part at an unconscious level. Rational thought is built on language, and language in turn is built on metaphors and other constructs with physical and emotional properties. Pure logic and rigorous reasoning have an essential role within professional discourse, but when the professional is engaged in discourse with broader audiences, different forms of communication are required. The cognitive linguist George Lakoff goes so far as to say that objectivism is a myth, and that effective communication occurs within "frames" that have emotional and experiential content. Inevitably, "frames trump facts," according to Lakoff.[1]

There is no simple solution to the present challenge, but the foregoing may be the only one that might work. To implement the solution, seminars should be conducted to enable professionals to develop strategic plans with greater emphasis on vision statements and values-oriented goals. At the university level, courses should be required and retooled to enable practitioners to respond effectively to contemporary political challenges. In city planning, a course in the history and theory of planning might cover the historical roots of contemporary rhetoric.[2]

Enlightenment versus Gothic Traditions in
Contemporary America

Prehistoric human society took the form of hunter-gatherer bands. Many anthropologists believe that those primitive groups evolved with primary traits of cooperativeness and egalitarianism but secondarily were also competitive and sufficiently aggressive for males to demand parity within their community. Women too may have had generally equal status within the group because of the critical roles they played in ensuring group survival. Such societies were able to hold aggrandizers in check to maintain basic equality. The anthropologist Christopher Boehm has hypothesized that late in the Paleolithic era hunter-gathers began developing substantial cognitive ability in concert with acquiring social traits such as *coalition formation* conducive to the evolution of moral and egalitarian society. Such traits prepared the way for more complex hierarchical societies such as chiefdoms and kingdoms, but also for the rise of egalitarian civilizations.[3]

Modern human societies, by contrast, are naturally hierarchical; and over the last 5,000 years the trend has been distinctly so, often favoring despotism. Aristotle's social pyramid, a benchmark for this book, has emerged recurrently from mankind's "state of nature," in Locke's phrase, producing the monarchies, oligarchies, and commonwealths of highly stratified societies. The powerful and wise sit atop the pyramid, with a toiling or slave class supporting it from the bottom. In between are warriors, tradesmen, farmers, and others, all with defined social roles.[4]

In 1767, Anthony Ashley Cooper and John Locke set out to refine Aristotle's pyramid in a way that would reflect mankind's accumulated knowledge of systems of government from ancient Greece through Gothic England to their own time. It was in part a course correction to republicanism gone awry under Oliver Cromwell, but also a utopian vision that would play out in the American wilderness. Their new system of government, codified into the Fundamental Constitutions of Carolina and the detailed "instructions," comprised the Grand Model, a guiding instrument that was both a constitution and a comprehensive development plan. In addition to defining governmental functions, it prescribed the physical and social form of an entire society. It was a vision of the city, figuratively and physically—a new city upon a hill.

Ashley Cooper died in exile fifteen years after he and Locke began designing their ideal society. Locke, however, lived to be part of the Enlightenment. Keeping one foot planted in Ashley Cooper republicanism, he extended the other into fresh new territory. In stating that men are born equal in their natural state, that slavery is "so vile and miserable an estate of man," and that law is "to preserve and enlarge freedom," he opened the door to an entirely new vision of society, one that broke free from the bonds of the Aristotelian pyramid. The Enlightenment, for the first time in history, taught that human beings, through their capacity for reason, had virtually limitless capacity. They could create a more equitable society, put an end to slavery, enable social mobility, harness science for the betterment of human institutions, design better human habitats, and create more dynamic cities.[5]

The Enlightenment paradigm in which reason, freedom, and equality are basic principles was one that required purposefulness, careful planning, and constant vigilance. It was a better route to broad human advancement, but it was not an easy route. In Boehm's words, "Egalitarianism does not just happen." Reversing natural hierarchy and placing the rank and file in charge of a society's future requires a moral framework, intentionality, and a practical blueprint such as a constitution. Even with the principles of the Enlightenment firmly implanted in many modern political cultures, it remains far easier to continue to refine the social pyramid than to reshape society in a reverse hierarchy through reason. The contrast between the progressive stance of the Enlightenment and the traditional order of the world was new and dramatic. America was founded with ideals from both: fraternalistic culture developed from Ashley Cooper's pre-Enlightenment republicanism, and Lockean egalitarian and progressivistic culture developed from the new ideals of the Enlightenment. The former was adapted to the disposition of post–hunter-gatherer humans to form hierarchical societies. The latter, by contrast, was a revolutionary departure from the constraints of the traditional social pyramid and the Great Chain of Being.[6]

Figure 16 illustrates the divergence of political cultures in America. Transatlantic republicanism, introduced by Ashley Cooper, became a pillar of American political culture. However, the new ideas of the Enlightenment concerning equality, freedom, and ultimately democracy split the founding principles into two branches, with Gothic republicanism growing separately. Table 12 contrasts the new doctrine of the Enlightenment with that of traditional Gothic republicanism.

American fraternalistic and egalitarian traditions have converged and diverged from colonial times to the present, strengthening and weakening the nation as they have vacillated. The two traditions came together to create a brilliant framework for liberty and equality between 1776 and 1789. They joined in designing a model city for the capital and in planning the

Table 12. American Fraternalistic and Egalitarian Traditions

	CULTURAL TRADITION	
Characteristics	*Fraternalistic*	*Egalitarian*
Cultural Origin	Gothic England	the Enlightenment
Political and Philosophical Origin	Agrarian republicanism	Egalitarian republicanism, pragmatism, utopianism
Regional Origin	South	New England, Mid-Atlantic
Epistemological Foundation	Tradition, a priori reasoning, National mythology	Reason, a posteriori reasoning, Scientific method
Social Organization	Traditional pyramid, paternalistic authority, social uniformity, individualism	Enlightenment diamond, empathic authority, social diversity, civic responsibility
First Principles	Freedom of conscience (Judeo-Christian), small government, low taxes, property rights, laissez-faire economy, public/private education mix	Freedom of conscience (broadly construed), activist government, progressive taxes, human rights, social justice, public education
Political Motivation	Action poses danger; actions produce zero-sum or negative consequences	Inaction poses danger; actions can produce new benefits to improve society
Geographic Base	Southern, rural, ex-urban	Northeast, West Coast, urban
Thought Leaders	Oligarchic class	Progressive-creative classes
Rhetorical Model	Liberty-tyranny	Equality-injustice
Modus Operandi	Maintenance of traditions	Continual refinement and advancement

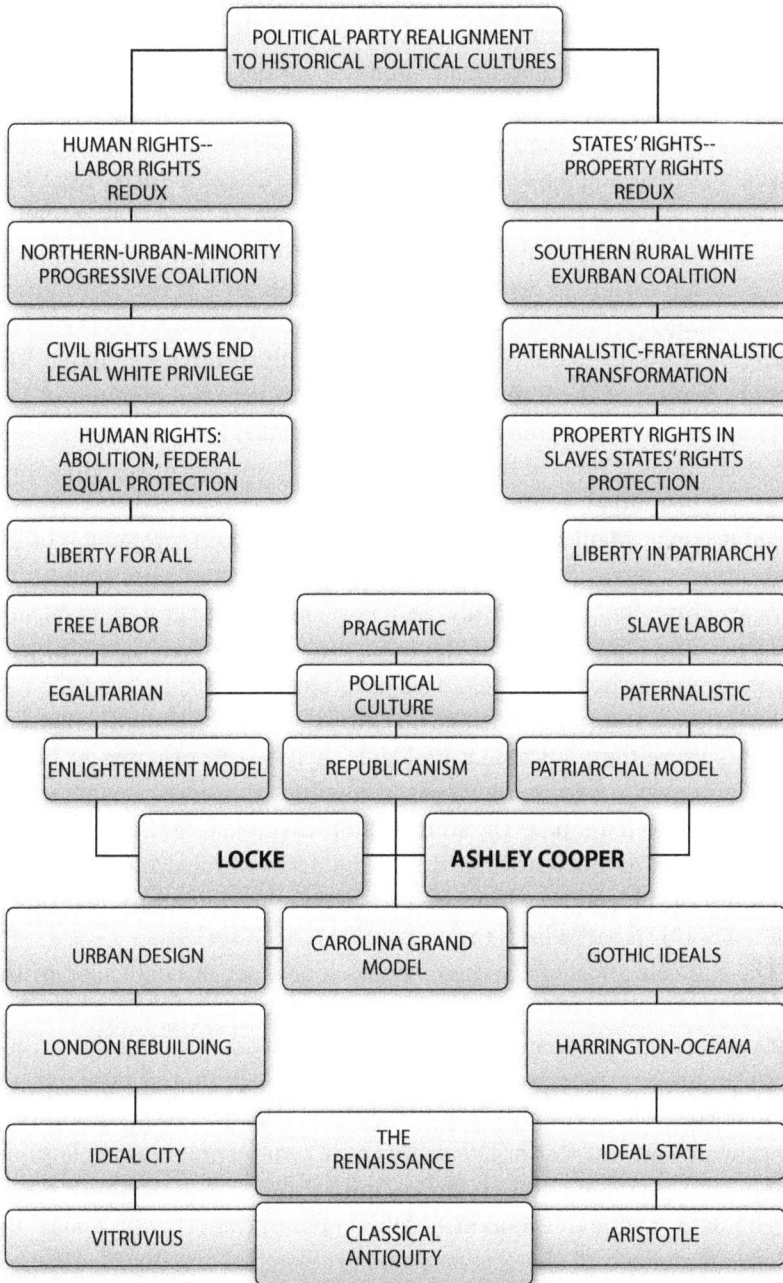

Figure 16. Origin and Evolution of American Political Culture. Progressive
and conservative traditions can be traced to Ashley Cooper and Locke. Ashley
Cooper reinvented republicanism after the fall of the Commonwealth to become
the dominant political model of modern civilization. Locke shifted emphasis from
paternalistic hierarchy to the idea that the people engage their leadership
through a compact. Paternalistic political culture became increasingly
fraternalistic after the Civil War. Illustration by Teri Norris.

settlement of western lands. They set aside differences to fight two world wars, to develop a modern nation, and to become the leader in space exploration. They also failed time and again to attain common ground, allowing slavery to persist until it resulted in civil war, allowing Jim Crow to persist until the social upheaval of the 1960s overturned it, allowing the ideal of public education to fade and the social safety net to falter in the face of partisanship.

The tension between fraternalistic and egalitarian ideals has entered a new phase in the era of the Tea Party where consensus and compromise are often impossible to achieve and the outlook for a progressive future is increasingly grim. Fraternalistic culture sees opportunity in the crisis, taking radical stances the way progressivistic culture did in the 1960s. The thought leaders of the Right are determined to seize the moment in history to turn the tide against Enlightenment challenges to orthodoxy and the institutions it erected during the New Deal and the civil rights era— government-funded employment initiatives, unemployment insurance, Social Security, Medicare, Medicaid, affirmative action, protection of the environment, scientific research. The Right has created a political action infrastructure that is vertically and horizontally integrated to ensure efficiency and effectiveness at the local, state, and federal levels in promoting leaders who will attack those programs.

Egalitarian and progressivistic culture is in the position of defending its gains more than advancing its ideals. It has seen progress in health care, immigration reform, rights of sexual minorities, and other areas; but the gains are as tenuous as the shifting political balance in Congress. Such national issues are increasingly being conflated with local and state issues as more radical leaders within fraternalistic political culture form well-defined political battle lines throughout American society.

The radicalization of the Right poses a new set of challenges to the creative-progressive professions. Until recently, such professions have cultivated a nonpartisan approach to their work. A majority within those professions may well be Democrats, but substantial numbers are Republicans. And certainly among local elected officials, Republicans (historically, at least) as often as Democrats have favored progressive planning, design, and environmental protection initiatives for their communities.

The late political economist Albert Hirschman wrote about the debilitating effects of rhetoric on social problem solving. In *The Rhetoric of Reaction*, he identified three forms of recurring argument against progressive action. The first is what Hirschman calls the *perversity* thesis, or arguments that reforms will have unintended consequences that will only worsen existing conditions. The second is the *futility* thesis, arguments that reform is hopeless. And the third is the *jeopardy* thesis, arguments that reforms represent a threat to historic balance. Under the first, a raise in the minimum wage, for example, would worsen conditions for most workers. Under the second, reforms are perceived as a waste of money. And under the third, expanded voter rights will only lead to abuse and fraud thereby undermining legitimate government. Hirschman concludes that "democracy-friendly" dialogue is repeatedly stifled by these self-limiting rhetorical mechanisms.[7]

City planners and others unwittingly caught up in today's political rhetoric do not want to politicize their practices and further alienate their critics by responding in kind. Their preferred response is one of respectful, apolitical, reasoned dialogue. In some cases, this, as in the past, will be sufficient to inform and persuade skeptics, to reach compromises with them, or to learn from them and change direction accordingly. In today's political climate, however, more is often required, including an understanding of both the historical and the rhetorical dimensions of ultra-conservative arguments. Lakoff argues that progressive politicians must realize that framing issues is essential to winning minds. Creative and progressive professionals, having been put under a political spotlight by conservatives, will need to absorb the same lesson.

The remaining sections look at the nature of new challenges to Enlightenment ideas, egalitarian political culture, and the creative-progressive professions. A strategy is then laid out for a more assertive response to current challenges in the form of a dialogue based on American history, the nation's first principles, and its long tradition of progressive city planning. The new challenge comes from two ostensibly different political traditions, libertarianism and neoconservatism, bolstered by allies among fundamentalist Christians. But the two are united in the belief that their primary constituents are social conservatives aligned with their political traditions. In the words of Dr. Richard D. Land, recent past president of the Ethics and Religious Liberty Commission of the Southern Baptist Convention, social conservatives are "hardwired to be pro-family, religious and entrepreneurial. . . . Let the Democrats be the party of dependency and ever lower expectations. The Republicans will be the party of aspiration and opportunity." Across the spectrum of conservatism, the egalitarian and pragmatic (progressivistic) traditions are deemed illegitimate and degenerate. This unceasing rhetoric of the Right is met with only feeble responses from egalitarian political culture, which (outside of pure politics) prefers to focus on deeds that it believes will promote equality, reasoned solutions, and social justice.[8]

The Language of Libertarians

The language of libertarians infuses the Tea Party movement and is prominent in today's political discourse. It invokes the authority of history: the struggle to preserve liberty against tyranny; the doctrine of free markets; the virtue of individualism; and the danger of Big Government. It is a language that descends from the seventeenth-century republicanism of Ashley Cooper and Locke and the eighteenth-century philosophy of Adam Smith and the American Founders, without the emphasis on equality and cooperation.

Compared to other conservative factions, the libertarians and their disdain for an expensive military-industrial complex and foreign interventions are truer to Gothic tradition and Ashley Cooper's republicanism, which decried the standing army of the king as tipping the balance of power from Parliament to court (legislative to executive), thus inviting tyranny. Libertarians prefer to put guns in the hands of the people, who can raise militias in perilous times, as was done in Gothic England for centuries. They resent taxation and regulation as government-forced stifling of individual initiative while favoring its constituent groups, much as Ashley Cooper advocated agrarian power over the rise of centralized power in London.

The authority of historical doctrines has a mystical quality to libertarians. Their policy institutes and informational outlets churn out phrases and memes loaded with authoritative historical references: quotes from John Locke, Adam Smith, and Thomas Jefferson; assertions about traditional values; references to first principles and the U.S. Constitution. The John Locke Foundation, based in North Carolina, articulates the broad concerns of libertarians: "government corruption and wasteful spending," "crushing tax burdens," "destructive welfare state," "oppressive rules and regulations on business," and the "decline of individual freedom and self-reliance." It connects these core issues with the everyday concerns of Americans: "basic education to every child," " safe, civil communities," "traffic congestion," and "economic opportunities."[9]

The rhetorical structure or framing of libertarian messaging thus has three levels: American first principles, codified in the Constitution; political catchphrases such as "oppressive regulations"; and the issues and anxieties of concern to everyone on a daily basis, such as traffic and schools. The middle level is the operational level, which enables a special interest group to oppose regulations of Big Government and to enlist community support in doing so, because the oppressive hand of government is implicated in the problems of daily life. Moreover, it is implied, government regulations too often run counter to the first level—counter to the highest ideals of the American nation.

Recognizing that personal freedom has a strong appeal to young voters, conservative think tanks have shifted their messaging toward libertarianism. In doing so, they avoid an association with their wealthy antiregulatory benefactors seeking to conflate their agendas with broader personal freedoms. To the extent that this strategy is successful, it will turn more and more people against government-led action on urban and environmental problems.

The Language of Neoconservatives

Aristotle posed the question, "Are good laws primarily good for the higher classes, or are they good in an immediate and direct way for the many?" Today's republicans, who generally conform to the politics of the modern American Republican Party, believe laws favoring the higher classes are "good" laws. Laws that maintain order but exact little from the nation's "job creators" provide social stability and a growing economy that ultimately will advance an entire society.[10]

Conservatives introduced a resolution in the 2001–2 session of Congress affirming that the United States is a republic. Ostensibly, the resolution affirmed the election of George W. Bush by the Electoral College over the majority vote received by Albert V. Gore. Among the fourteen "whereas" clauses, the resolution stated that "the constitutionally prescribed system in the 2000 election for choosing electors for President and Vice President continues to function as originally designed, protecting minority and States' rights from the exercise of majority power."[11]

The resolution, however, serves an implicit and controversial purpose in asserting a distinction between republican government and pure democracy. Under the former, a class of wise leaders represents the masses. Under the latter, there is a reign of chaotic mob rule creating "spectacles of turbulence and contention [that] have ever been found incompatible with personal security or the rights of property." The distinction opens the door to bring a modern version of the Great Chain of Being and the traditional class pyramid back into America's social fabric. In so doing, evangelical conservatives may claim that leaders are chosen by God to rule over the masses; and it sets the stage for conservative oligarchs to, covertly and under the cover of religion, claim their rightful authority to lead or influence events beyond their number.[12]

The latter claim is associated with neoconservatism, the faction of conservatism that gained prominence in advocating the invasion of Iraq in 2003. Self-identified neoconservatives are not large in numbers, nor are they organized to advertise their existence. On the contrary, they prefer to remain behind the scenes, allowing libertarians, religious conservatives, and Tea Partiers to step to the fore. Their stance is consistent with their belief in a structured social pyramid and in the decline of Western Civilization resulting from erosion of the pyramid resulting from humanism and relativism.

Neoconservatism has emerged as an influential strand of American republicanism, binding its intellectuals with its warriors. The neoconservative movement can be traced to the political philosophy of Leo Strauss (1899–1973). Strauss emigrated from Germany to England in 1935, where he taught briefly at Cambridge University. In 1937, he immigrated to the United States, where he taught at a number of colleges and universities, including twenty years at the University of Chicago, the institution with which he is most often identified.

Strauss is a controversial figure who taught an intentionally arcane philosophy. He espoused a belief that humans are intrinsically political and that philosophy must therefore engage on some level with the "city," by which he means the intellectual and political domain of a civilization. The political nature of humans is such that even empirical science is lodged within its larger framework. Strauss was particularly critical of social science, which he deemed to wear a deceptive cloak of empiricism in advancing Enlightenment relativism.[13]

Strauss's social pyramid consisted of great thinkers and scholars in its upper tiers, the "philosophers" conceiving bold and creative answers to the greatest challenges of the time. Strauss believed with Nietzsche that realities are relative and that successful societies must create their own reality, or mythology. While such relativism seems, on the surface, to be antithetical to the strident advocacy of "values" and "principles" found in American conservatism, such stridency is perfectly consistent with the commitment to mythology and illusion he believed necessary to the survival of a superior society.

Since society's great thinkers and scholars communicate downward through the social pyramid, they require separate languages for lower and upper tiers, one "exoteric" (directed to outsiders, or the masses) and another "esoteric" (directed to insiders). The former means of communication creates the illusion of exactitude and certainty necessary to reinforce the sense of "values" and "principles" craved by the vast population residing within the lower tiers of the social pyramid. The latter means of communication allows for a more challenging and relativistic dialogue among thinkers in the upper tiers of the pyramid, a dialogue infused with contradictions and illusions so as to make it incomprehensible to the masses. Moreover, such communication is delivered much as a song, according to the political philosopher Shadia Drury, with dual components of words and tune.[14]

Strauss maintained that esoteric communication has been common throughout history, even throughout most of the Enlightenment. Difficult questions and unsettling truths were not believed to be suitable subjects to place before an unwise populace. To do so would be irresponsible and would undermine the plans of wise men and subvert their political calculus. As the Bible admonished, one who digs a pit must cover it or be responsible for the fools who fall in.[15]

Exoteric communication by "philosophers," the wisest of men, is accomplished through the use of many techniques, including contradictions, intentional blunders, statements of false principles, confusing repetition, pseudonyms, arcane terminology, ambiguity, and stylistic oddities, all of which are used quite deliberately to communicate to the few who are capable of grasping a complex, subtle, and hidden message. Exoteric communication for mass consumption may also contain strategically placed messages, sometimes buried in the middle of a text rather than in plain sight at the beginning or the end, to allow the wise reader (or listener) to find the pearls in the muck. The esoteric message of the philosopher is embedded within exoteric communication that contains sufficient truth to lead the less able person to believe he or she is learning while keeping confined to a necessary world of myth and illusion. But such messages are hidden in long-winded sermons containing much that has nothing to do with the real message.[16]

It is important to differentiate between Strauss and his followers. Straussians, as they are known, have acquired a more defined political framework to the right of the political spectrum than their master. Notable Straussians include Dick Cheney, Jeane Kirkpatrick, William Kristol, Paul Wolfowitz, and David Frum. As Shadia Drury has observed, creative-progressive professions are considered detrimental to Western Civilization: "Kristol blames most of the ills of our society on the liberal intellectuals . . . the 'new class,' which is to say, a new ruling class that includes journalists, educators, city planners, government bureaucrats, as well as scientists, doctors, and lawyers who work in the public sector."[17] The concern is that Enlightenment values propagated by such professions open the door to moral relativism, which should be reserved for the wisest of society's "philosophers." This view is consistent with that of Ashley Cooper and Locke as they designed Carolina. Unlike traditional conservatives and libertarians, neoconservatives recognize that Locke subsequently opened the door to the Enlightenment, which they believe changed the course of history for the worse.

The Language of Fundamentalist Christians

Christian sectarianism in colonial America mirrored the zeal of dissenting denominations in Britain but evolved with new idioms and rhetorical devices. The political life of eighteenth-century America was intimately tied to religious sectarianism and shared its language, and many earnest believers pursued spiritual and secular goals as if they were one. Others used religion for political purposes as well as personal agendas. The Anglican missionary Gideon Johnston, serving in South Carolina, wrote, "Among all those that have the church continually in their mouths, few of them have any concern either for it or religion. More than as it serves for a cloak to carry on their worldly designs."[18]

The Founders conceived government as a neutral arbiter capable of maintaining national stability amid religious and regional tensions. The conception of liberty in New England was strikingly different from that in the South. New Englanders conceived of liberty as consisting of soul, individual, group, and political components. In the assessment of historian David Hackett Fischer, the attainment of soul liberty—the free pursuit of true faith—was entirely "consistent with the persecution of Quakers, Catholics, Baptists, Presbyterians, Anglicans and indeed virtually everyone except those within a very narrow spectrum of Calvinist orthodoxy."[19]

This religious and political understanding of liberty stood in sharp contrast to the hierarchical conception of liberty in the South. Addressing Parliament, Edmund Burke described the southern "spirit of liberty as still more high and haughty" than in the North. In Virginia and Carolina, with their "vast multitude of slaves," he said, "those who are free are by far the most proud and jealous of their freedom. . . . In such a people, the haughtiness of domination combines with the spirit of freedom, fortifies it, and renders it invincible." Such differences made it essential for the Founders to establish a neutral form of government that would not capsize on the rough waves of religious and regional rhetoric.[20]

In addition to avoiding interdenominational conflict, the Founders were motivated to avoid the entanglement of religion and state that had plagued Europe with centuries of war brought on by tyrannical rulers who invoked "divine right" in building their empires. The political chaos that consumed England in the seventeenth century and spilled over into the colonies (disastrously so in Maryland), brought on in part by the disjunction of religion and government, was a specific instance of history that lighted the path of the Founding Fathers as they sought a "wall of separation." They recognized that an intertwining of religion and state produces a form of Big Government that is virtually impossible to challenge, an irresistible alliance for many ambitious politicians. Thus George Washington, like other Founders, insisted that "the bosom of America" was "open to receive . . . the oppressed and the persecuted of all Nations and Religions; whom we shall welcome to a participation of all our rights and privileges."[21]

Since religion has the weight of final authority for its adherents, it has a special appeal in the slaveholding states, where an edifice of divine justification was essential to reconciling the dual obsession with liberty and enslavement. The survival of mass enslavement in the face of Enlightenment humanism required a new language infused with religion and historicism. The eighteenth century began with democratic ideas, such as Locke's contention that government subsists as a contract between the leaders and the governed; it then ended with the American and French revolutions, which decisively crushed rule by divine right and the inevitability of a rigid social pyramid.

Christianity has always been torn between those who would join with political leaders to construct a powerful class pyramid, as the Catholic Church did in Rome, and those who would seek the humble life that Jesus lived, which they established in monasteries and agrarian communities throughout Christendom.

Multiple American belief systems have grown from the seeds planted in the colonies by Anglicans and dissenting believers such as Puritans, Quakers, and Catholics, as well as utopians and secularists. The seed planted in Carolina that created such a rigid pyramidal class structure meshed ever more tightly with religion as it spread across the South. It produced a classic form of political hegemony in which the power of the state and the power of organized religion were interwoven into the strongest possible fabric of power. That political structure maintained the institution of slavery for two and a half centuries and replaced it with a repressive system of white dominance for another century.

The Southern Strategy instituted by the Republican Party in the 1970s enabled it to recover from the stinging defeat of Barry Goldwater in 1964 and form a new alliance that would create a path for the party from moderation to extreme conservatism. The 350-year history of repression in the South had only been curbed by civil rights legislation for a mere decade, and white resentment and fear of social disorder was a latent force available for harnessing to the Republican leadership.

It did so, first with Goldwater, then with Nixon, more with Reagan, then again with the Bush administrations, all artfully deploying code that evoked and justified the past glory of white domination. They invoked the twin injustices of "welfare queens" siphoning hard-earned income from working people and criminals left at large by liberals to prey on an overtaxed middle class. The anger over such injustices could mask the deep resentment over enforced equality, and any government action that prescribed equality could be cleanly opposed under the banner of states' rights, just as it had been before the Civil War. As Richard Viguerie, a Republican fund-raiser, admitted, people "are more strongly motivated by negative issues than positive ones."[22]

At the same time, the Southern Strategy would be deployed to unite conservative religious traditions with evangelicals across the country. The politicization of abortion became a particularly effective tool of the strategy. But there were deeper resentments to tap into that were shared by southerners and blue-collar Americans elsewhere. The Great Migration of African Americans to the industrial cities of the North and the Midwest had deposited large communities in the older core of those cities, a new group in a succession of immigrants to be resented. But the resentment grew more intense as the nation deindustrialized and those communities deteriorated. To the uninquiring mind, those were simply bad places full of bad people who needed to be harshly repressed, not coddled with government assistance.

The Southern Strategy reached its final stage with the nearly complete realignment of white southerners with the Republican Party. Southerners were accompanied by many in other regions who felt a kinship with their attitudes. The transformation included the politicization of conservative churches, which integrated themselves at the leadership level with the Republican Party.

As a political-religious leadership class took form, it created a self-serving body of philosophy to justify its increased participation in politics. In *The Family* and *C Street: The Fundamentalist Threat to American Democracy*, author Jeff Sharlet shed light on the extent to which religion had insinuated itself into politics at the highest levels. Sharlet's work also revealed the emergence of a new class pyramid very much resembling the rule of divine right claimed by rulers throughout history. Some of these Christian politicians believe themselves to be among the "chosen," which means their destiny is to "reconstruct early Christian society" and welcome Jesus upon his return. They assert that "the powers that be are ordained by God," and those who acquire power are therefore God's chosen leaders (much like the Fifth Monarchist "saints" whom Ashley Cooper served with in Parliament). Moreover, as in a class unto themselves, they are above the rules that govern the masses. What appears to be scandalously outrageous behavior to ordinary people is simply the action of "elite fundamentalist" leaders pursuing their uniquely qualified course of life. Thus former South Carolina governor Mark Sanford's abandonment of government duties for an illicit affair in Argentina and former Nevada senator John Ensign's purchase of rights to another man's wife are actions by C Streeters that cannot be brought down to a level where they can be compared with the standards of ordinary human behavior.[23]

With the emergence of a combined religious and political agenda, there has been an increase in secrecy. The C Street "Family" was initially open, but it has adopted a policy of not keeping written records and decentralizing to avoid public scrutiny. The level of secrecy parallels that of the neoconservatives, and to some extent there is an overlap in membership that creates an overlap in ideology and organizational policy. Christian leaders of the movement emphasize their ties to Judaism, with some success in drawing neoconservatives, many of whom are Jewish, into the fold. For the neoconservatives, however, it is likely to be an alliance of convenience, not one of the heart, as many are disinclined to embrace and endorse American fundamentalism.[24]

Religion has played an increasing role in city planning, most recent in its opposition to what is viewed as UN interventions in traditional American lifestyles through such initiatives as Agenda 21. Many fundamentalists believe cities are inherently dangerous for spirituality. Influences such as homosexuality lurk everywhere. Sharlet discovered that even Christian conservatives in Colorado Springs, one of the most godly of cities, would warn him "away from downtown's neat little grid of cafés and ethnic joints." Stay with the suburban chains, they urged. Such sentiments can be found in the Bible if one wants to find them, but the fusing of politics into religion is the primary source of anti-urbanism. Conservative fundamentalists have won elections in recent years by making gains in the suburbs and exurbs of cities. They have done so on political platforms that appeal to those populations rather than by espousing religious doctrine. In Georgia, fundamentalist Ralph Reed made political gains (described in Chapter 5) as the state's Republican Party chairman by advocating such attractive platforms as more jobs in the suburbs and shorter commute times.[25]

The Rhetoric of Fraternalistic Political Culture

Religion plays a central role in elevating fraternalistic political culture to a position of legitimacy before an ultimate arbiter. From that elevated position, adherents may authoritatively condemn progressivistic values. Religion is an essential paradigm for fraternalistic political culture, not only in attaining a sense of being on the moral high ground, but also in providing it with a framework for reasoning. That framework is one in which principles and values are drawn upon to interpret reality. As a system of reasoning, it is a priori, or deductive in its methodology, that is, it reasons from the general to the specific.

Bruce Bartlett, an official in the Reagan and first Bush administrations, predicted a major struggle within the Republican Party with the rise of fraternalistic political culture under the second Bush, a battle in part of reason versus religion. Bartlett worried about George W. Bush's a priori certainty: "Absolute faith like that overwhelms a need for analysis. The whole thing about faith is to believe things for which there is no empirical evidence." In counterpoint to that, a Bush administration official went so far as to complain about hindrance from the "reality-based community" made up of those who "believe that solutions emerge from . . . judicious study of discernible reality." He added: "That's not the way the world really works anymore. We're an empire now, and when we act, we create our own reality."[26]

Unreality pays dividends in politics, as Thomas Frank demonstrated in *What's the Matter with Kansas*, an examination of a state with progressivistic (egalitarian *and* pragmatic) founding principles that has absorbed fraternalistic political culture. In Kansas, Frank writes, "the gravity of discontent pulls to the right," and going farther and farther in that direction, the Right's less-effective approaches of the past will be corrected. To oppose the liberal elites thought to be destroying America, Kansans, like many others, are willing to enter into a complete disconnect in embracing the Right. Frank points to the Kansas Republican policy platform in 1998, which bemoaned "degenerating society," homosexuality, and gun control, then proposed a flat tax, abolition of capital gains taxes and estate taxes, deregulation, and privatization of Social Security, among other measures that had no bearing on the social problems it bemoaned.[27]

If John Locke's place at the head of the table of conservative political philosophers may be challenged, his place in the study of knowledge, known as epistemology, is clearly at odds with fraternalistic political culture. Locke is the founder of the school of thought known today as British Empiricism (George Berkeley and David Hume were later luminaries of the school). Empiricism finds that knowledge is based on observation, experimentation, accumulation of factual data, and the gradual development of theories based on inductive, a posteriori, reasoning. In *An Essay Concerning Human Understanding*, published in 1689, Locke expressed the view that all human knowledge in fact is based upon experience, a view that became a central tenet of the Enlightenment.[28]

Anyone today who seeks to build a bridge of communication between fraternalistic and progressivistic cultures needs to understand the two worlds on either side—one built on faith and deductive reasoning, the other a "reality-based community" that applies inductive reasoning. The two cultures not only reason differently, but their languages contain shibboleths—words or expressions of one culture that are unfamiliar to the other. Detection of a shibboleth can quickly limit communication by introducing prejudice. City planners holding public meetings for the purpose of hearing out all sides of an issue (as planners frequently do) are not building bridges, they are exchanging shibboleths. As discussed further in the next section, there are only two ways a creative-progressive professional can build a bridge to a fraternalistic audience: by demonstrating a thorough knowledge of the facts surrounding the "values" and first principles, and by communicating not only to the audience but also to an interpreter. An interpreter is, in the best of circumstances, an appointed or elected official who can speak to each group without shibboleths. The interpreter is also someone who can act upon reasoned argument and then explain the proposed action in terms of values and first principles. The progressive presenter is thereby giving the interpreter reasoned arguments that offer political cover. Although there is ultimate legitimacy derived from the conviction of being a people of God, fraternalistic believers must justify themselves in relation to the messier context of the social pyramid within which their daily lives are conducted.

The Creative-Progressive Response

City planners and others in the *creative-progressive fields*, defined in the Preface, find themselves unintentionally at odds with Tea Party–swayed contemporary conservatism. Such occupations are progressive in the sense that they are oriented to the Enlightenment ideals of equality, democracy, social justice, and human advancement, through reason, controlled experimentation, and the scientific method. Practitioners within those fields may be somewhat more politically progressive in number than the general population, but many are politically conservative or simply apolitical. Nevertheless, the city planner or urban designer or environmentalist who advocates sustainable development, resilience theory, Smart Growth, or especially Agenda 21 is increasingly sucked into a vortex of antiprogressive rhetoric, as is the scientist who finds compelling evidence for climate change, advances the theory of evolution, or estimates the age of the earth to be a number of years with more than four digits.

The great dilemma facing practitioners in such creative-progressive fields is how to remain politically neutral in the face of a national political realignment in which the right side of the political spectrum is increasingly hostile to them. There is a possibility of self-correction as the Right comes to terms with its alienation of so many subsets of the population—in addition to the mentioned occupations, women, African Americans, Latinos, immigrants, and sexual minorities have experienced and come to resent conservative intolerance. The numbers were sufficient to cause major setbacks in the 2012 election. The momentum, however, is with the Far Right, as shown in the 2014 midterm elections, not the moderates who would broaden the base of the conservative movement. The intensity of right-wing rhetoric will therefore most likely increase in coming years. Creative-progressive professionals should be prepared to counter the rhetoric rather than ignoring it on the assumption that it is so extreme and unsupportable by facts that it will fade away.

As yet, creative-progressive professionals have not responded effectively to the claims made by the Tea Party and the many organizations created and funded to support it. One of the core claims asserted by the Right is that its members constitute a political culture of values while the Left is the political culture of dependency. The target of the dependency argument asserted by the Right has widened to include city planners and others concerned with sustainable development. While the Right has long made the claim about dependency, its spokespersons sharpened their case during the 2008 presidential campaign following an encounter between Barack Obama and Joe Wurzelbacher (who subsequently became known as "Joe the Plumber"). The two men had a lengthy exchange about small businesses and taxes in which Wurzelbacher expressed concern about higher taxes proposed by the Democrat and Obama responded with an account of the increasing disparity of income in the country and the need to restore the income-earning potential of average Americans.

You would get a 50% tax credit so you'd get a tax cut for your healthcare costs. . . . If your revenue is above 250 [$250,000]—then from

250 down, your taxes are going to stay the same. It is true that from 250 up—from 250—300 or so, so for that additional amount, you'd go from 36 to 39%, which is what it was under Bill Clinton. And the reason why we're doing that is because 95% of small businesses make less than 250. So what I want to do is give them a tax cut. I want to give all these folks who are bus drivers, teachers, auto workers who make less, I want to give them a tax cut. And so what we're doing is, we are saying that folks who make more than 250 that that marginal amount above 250—they're gonna be taxed at a 39 instead of a 36% rate.[29]

Obama was arguing for an increase of three percentage points in the tax rates of higher-income Americans in order to lower taxes on middle- and lower-income Americans. He concluded his explanation with a choice of words that fed the conservative claim that liberals wanted to perpetuate dependency on government: "My attitude is that if the economy's good for folks from the bottom up, it's gonna be good for everybody. If you've got a plumbing business, you're gonna be better off if you've got a whole bunch of customers who can afford to hire you, and right now everybody's so pinched that business is bad for everybody and I think when you spread the wealth around, it's good for everybody."[30]

To Obama, the phrase "spread the wealth" meant lowering taxes for most Americans so that once again incomes would rise for everyone, not only the wealthy. To conservatives, the phrase "spread the wealth" has had a long history of meaning something quite different: taking money from hardworking people and giving it to undeserving "takers" through the bureaucratic machinery of the "nanny state."

Conservatives seized the opportunity to cast Obama as a socialist or Marxist. Fox News executive Bill Sammon repeatedly linked the "spread the wealth around" phrase to socialism and Marxism in various on-air appearances and urged others to do the same, even though he privately admitted the allegation was "rather far-fetched." Nevertheless, Obama's use of the phrase was too good to pass up, Sammon admitted, since it "is red meat when you're talking to conservatives and you start talking about 'spread the wealth around.' That is tantamount to socialism."[31]

This example is relevant to creative-progressive professionals because they now fall squarely within the reach of conservative wrath over perceived loss of individual liberty and national sovereignty, existential threats being effected, as they see it, by Agenda 21 and sustainable development. Even those on the right who do not subscribe to the more extreme views of Tea Party activists, such as the New World Order conspiracy theory, are quick to question the premises of sustainable development, the science of climate change, or the theory of evolution. And they are quicker to do so since southern fraternalistic political norms have moved to the center of the Republican Party.

The natural creative-progressive response is to listen and reason with intellectual opponents. Many of these adversaries on the right, however, are not intellectual opponents; they are aggrieved people who feel that their way of life, their individual liberty, and their nation are under attack by evil and malicious forces. The natural response to listen and reason does not need to be abandoned, since there are still some on the right who will respond in kind. But this listening needs to be augmented with an understanding of the rhetorical devices used by the Right, a mastery of facts of history related to those devices, and a new and effective use of language with emotional as well as factual content. While many will not be swayed by any form of argument or any presentation of facts, the leaders and policy makers can be influenced and brought back from the brink of extreme decisions driven by conspiracy hysteria. Five strategies for rational as well as intuitive communication are available to city planners and other creative-progressive professionals when confronted with counterfactual claims:

Demonstrate knowledge of values and principles. A creative-progressive professional can build credibility by demonstrating an in-depth knowledge of the values and principles that lead to objections to an initiative, such as a proposal to expand regional transit or adopt sustainable development practices that address climate change. In many cases, those objecting to such initiatives will have obtained their talking points from conservative media or educational outlets. Those talking points will be framed in terms of American values, and the initiative will be associated with un-American intentions, whether misguided or downright evil. As the cognitive linguist George Lakoff has pointed out, reasoned arguments from an Enlightenment tradition of discourse make little headway in the realm of politics. By demonstrating knowledge of the moral principles contained in conservative talking points, the professional will open the door for communication. If the objector enters the door, then healthy debate may ensue; in the more likely event the open door is not entered, the professional knowledge is also presented to an appointed or elected official (or other influential person) who can act as an interpreter, explaining that the rational arguments being presented are built on a moral foundation.[32]

Communicate through an "interpreter." People who are capable of "interpreting" or "translating" the language of political cultures can be difficult to find. City planners will often rely upon elected or appointed officials to fulfill that role. Such officials often give planners the task of holding public meetings and hearing everyone out and absorbing criticism, enabling an official to thereby stay clear of politically damaging situations (whether in attendance or not). The planner must therefore create a meeting environment that would highlight the official's prominence and promise political benefits. If an "interpreter" is available, then this person will be able to speak in both languages and gauge for himself or herself who is presenting the stronger argument. However, if an "interpreter" declines to attend, he or she can still be useful. A report on the meeting will bring him or her up to speed, and well-crafted highlights will supply him or her with rhetoric that can be used to support a progressive position. This interpreter will need to translate the position to the other language, with offending shibboleths, but a translator can readily do so.

Communicate nonverbally. City planners are accustomed to frequent public meetings, which are integral to the democratic ethic of the profession. The practice must continue, even when language barriers are virtually insurmountable. Language barriers can often be circumvented through visual communication. Urban designers employ the charrette, or public design workshop, as a means of getting an audience to think visually. Charrettes are typically conducted over several days, beginning with a presentation on the history of the subject matter followed by an open microphone for public comment, then progressing through one or two days of hands-on visualization, and concluding with professional illustrations of public-generated concepts. While city planners and others confronted with a hostile audience often do not have the time, expertise, or resources to conduct a true charrette, there is much they can draw from the technique—such as group reminiscences and visualizations—to modify and enhance the civility of conventional public meetings.

Present compelling evidence. Effective city planning produces tangible results that constitute proof of the value of planning. Public sector planners, particularly those in the regulatory realm, can draw from the experiences in other communities with similar values. In presenting such case studies, they should emphasize balance in public and private benefits. City planners often make the mistake of drawing their examples from progressivistic communities such as *egalitarian* Portland, Oregon, or *individualistic* Cary, North Carolina, even when their own community may have more fraternalistic values. Finding success stories from communities with similar political cultures is essential.

Assert community values. City planners have often been guilty of avoiding explanations of local public policy, and the values underlying them, preferring instead to assert that they are merely following state law. It has been easy for city planners to point to the state as driving local planning; and the state, in fact, is the authority that authorizes local government planning through enabling legislation. Comprehensive planning, zoning, historic preservation, and resource protection laws enacted by states enable cities and counties to adopt planning ordinances and policy resolutions tailored (ideally) to local situations. In many states, such laws have sufficient detail to ensure consistent statewide implementation of public policy. However, local plans and implementing ordinances should be made attractive to the public on the basis of local policies and the values associated with them. To point the finger at the state is to fall into the trap of affirming the fear that Big Government is behind planning. All city planning should be local planning based on local values, and city planners should emphasize those shared values in their public presentations. Where local values appear to conflict with professional protocols and best practices, then it is the task of the planner to sort out the apparent conflicts with the help of policy makers rather than pointing a finger of blame at a higher authority.

The language of fraternalistic culture is natural, complex, and evolving. Specific idioms and rhetorical devices within the broader culture are constructed by politically astute thought leaders and policy analysts. The horizontal and vertical integration of conservative policy institutes, media outlets, coordinating agencies, and grassroots organizations (primarily local Tea Party groups) ensures that those devices are distributed uniformly throughout the culture. A content analysis of websites of conservative policy institutes and planning-related tracts distributed nationally by Far Right advocacy groups is summarized below.

LITERATURE CONTENT ANALYSIS OF
CONSERVATIVE POLICY INSTITUTES AND ANTI–SUSTAINABLE
DEVELOPMENT ADVOCACY GROUPS

Frequently occurring terms used by policy institutes:[33]

- Liberty; individual liberty; universal principles of liberty (versus tyranny and Big Government)

- Constitution; constitutional government; limited constitutional government; rule of law (versus unelected agencies, czars)
- Founding principles; America's principles; first principles; foundational principles (versus relativism)
- Representative government; commonwealth (versus mob rule democracy)
- Limited government (versus government intrusion, modern liberalism, and the rise of unlimited government)
- Economic freedom; free enterprise; free markets; economic freedom (versus European-style socialism)
- Individual responsibility and family (versus social justice)

Frequently occurring terms used by advocacy groups:

- Liberty; individual liberty; limited government (versus tyranny and Big Government)
- Constitution; constitutional government; legitimate government (versus unelected agencies, czars)
- National sovereignty (versus globalism, One World Government)
- Property rights and free enterprise (versus socialism, communitarianism, use of eminent domain)
- Limited government (versus bureaucracy)
- Individual responsibility and family (versus social justice)

The content analysis for advocacy groups reveals the following themes, composed as black-and-white dichotomies, which are listed with a progressive response.

Theme 1: Liberty versus Tyranny

The first principles on which the United States was founded guarantee liberty; they are stated in the Declaration of Independence and written into law in the Constitution and Bill of Rights. City planners, environmentalists, social justice advocates, and climate scientists, among others, want to dictate where people can live, force them to use public transportation, and even restrict the number of children they can have. Agenda 21, sustainable development, Smart Growth, climate change, and social justice are the justifications used by socialists and radical environmentalists to attack individual liberty.

Analysis and response: The literature driving these claims uses extreme terms in setting up a black-and-white, liberty-versus-tyranny dichotomy:

"the tyranny of Sustainable Development," "force," "manipulate," "dictate," "control," "forbid," and "seize." The *exoteric* message is that tyrannical forces now swooping down on your community are on the verge of crushing your liberty. The *esoteric* message is consistently one of "property rights," which is the core concern of those sitting atop the social pyramid and funding the message. The response is that indeed liberty is a precious shared value guaranteed by the Bill of Rights. Nothing being proposed is substantively different from the American city planning tradition that dates to George Washington and Thomas Jefferson, and to John Locke, whose words are found in the Declaration of Independence. An effective response to the *exoteric* message is equally important to address the concerns of those who sit atop the social pyramid of the local community. They are often the people who fund the distribution of materials and bring in speakers. The message will have to be tuned to the audience; however, a principle that may be discussed is "average reciprocity of advantage," a term offered by Justice Oliver Wendell Holmes to describe how a regulation can benefit a property owner even as it places limits on use. Planners may wish to use a more intuitive term, such as "reciprocal benefits of community planning," a concept at the heart of Locke's compact-based political philosophy. The central idea that benefits flow from limitations are obvious in historic districts, research parks, scenic corridors, and many other easily identified examples.[34]

Theme 2: National Sovereignty versus Globalism

Sustainable development is the means of implementing Agenda 21, the UN plan for global government (sometime called the New World Order). The forces behind it—socialists, radical environmentalists, and power seekers—will control every aspect of your life. The New World Order they are implementing through Agenda 21 will replace the United States and dictate how you live.

Analysis and response: The *exoteric* message is that city planners are among those in the creative and creative-progressive professions who are betraying America and conspiring with globalists to end national sovereignty; as enemies of the state, constructive dialogue is futile. The *esoteric* message to those at the top of the social pyramid is that the United Nations is an enemy of the oligarchy. City planners, environmentalists, human rights advocates, scientists, and others attain a larger forum and a louder voice through the United Nations, thereby challenging the established (itself global) network of financial institutions, extractive industries, and the military-industrial complex. The response to such a patently absurd claim is handicapped since it will not have credibility. This particular area in most cases is best left to policy makers or community leaders, who need to assure audiences that they have faith in their staff and consultants and know them to be honorable Americans. Subsequent staff presentations may include references to American values. John Locke, as a progenitor of American political philosophy, is someone who can be cited often to build trust among those who doubt one's loyalty to American values.

Theme 3: Property Rights versus Communitarianism

Sustainable development is part of a communitarian ideology spread by globalists who want to seize private property.

Analysis and response: Communitarianism sounds like communism, which gives it a certain appeal as a target. It resonates with the thesis of redistribution of wealth wherein Big Government taxes hardworking people and gives their money away to unproductive people. Ironically, actual usage of the term outside the sphere of Far Right rhetoric contains aspects that are conservative, libertarian, and liberal. Reliance on community-based organizations, such as churches, rather than government, is a central idea of communitarianism. Communitarian values were observed to be a defining component of American culture by Tocqueville in his travels through the young nation in the 1830s, originating with the Puritans. In attacking communitarianism as a form of communism, the Far Right sets up an *exoteric* false dichotomy of a nation based on individual initiative versus one of government-orchestrated wealth-sharing in which private property can be readily seized for public benefit. The *esoteric* message is that communitarianism strengthens Enlightenment democracy ("mob rule") at the expense of Gothic republican government. The best response is one that invokes a sense of balance, as expressed in the famous quote, "Your right to swing your arms ends just where the other man's nose begins." Allowing anyone to swing a fist anywhere is anarchy, not liberty. One person's negative environmental impact sometimes must be prevented before it can reach another person's nose. Government has a legitimate role in setting standards for the benefit of everyone, while also respecting the rights of private property owners.[35]

Theme 4: The American People versus Bureaucracy

Big Government threatens individual freedom through strangling regulations, taxation, and even seizure of private property through eminent

domain. Government planners are using words like sustainable development, open space, and Smart Growth "to threaten your property rights
and our American way of life" and herd people into containment zones of
"high density living."

Analysis and response: The rhetorical device in this *exoteric* message
is one of people versus government, a device with roots that go back to
seventeenth-century England, strongly reinforced in southern political
culture during slavery and Jim Crow. Many people are thus instinctively
receptive to antigovernment rhetoric. The *esoteric* message is that suburban voters have been easier to recruit to Gothic-based politics than urban
voters, and thus revitalizing and growing urban areas will increase the
strength of Enlightenment-based communities. An effective response to
the exoteric message is to emphasize that Americans will always have freedom of choice about where they live; the goal of planners is to expand
choice, not limit choice. Many areas reached a point where the only housing option was in the suburbs, and suburbs were being built farther and
farther out, necessitating long commutes. Planners are encouraging alternatives to that pattern, not replacing it.[36]

Theme 5: Legitimate Government versus Unelected Agencies

Agenda 21, sustainable development, and Smart Growth are being implemented by circumventing the will of the people, as expressed through
legitimate government by boards, commissions, nongovernmental organizations, and executive action.

Analysis and response: This concern is found in most literature from
the Far Right opposing sustainable development, paralleling the national
concern that the Obama administration is running the nation through
illegally empowered "czars." The *exoteric* message is that government has
been corrupted, seized by the same illegitimate forces that are committing
voter fraud to win elections—reinforcing the idea that it is time to "take
back our government." The *esoteric* message is that the accountability of
elected representatives to traditional authority (for example, oligarchs) is
diluted through unelected, government-enlarging agencies. The response
is that local governments appoint boards to get more, not fewer, citizens
and "stakeholders" involved in formulating recommendations. To the extent they endorse principles of sustainable development, it is because they
find those principles locally beneficial. Moreover, state statutes, such as
zoning-enabling acts, prevent unelected agencies from passing laws (that
is, ordinances).

Theme 6: Individual Freedom and Family Autonomy
versus Social Justice

The goal of sustainable development is to force everyone into high-density containment areas and take away their private vehicles. The suburbs and private automobiles provide freedom and mobility to individuals and families.

Analysis and response: Pitting the suburbs against the city is a calculated strategy adopted by the Right, as shown in Chapter 5. The *exoteric* message is that the concept of "social justice" is another facet of the attempt to take resources from middle-class suburbanites and redistribute them to undeserving lower classes. The *esoteric* message is that social justice initiatives empower people to vote against the agenda of the upper tier of the social pyramid. The response can focus on the fact that planning is not a zero-sum process, but one that aims to improve conditions for everyone. Audiences should be reassured that sustainable development entails offering new options, not taking away options. The complexities of the concepts of social justice make it a difficult topic to take up at public meetings; however, those concepts can be illustrated through concrete examples of success stories in similar communities. Professional associations such as the American Planning Association should compile a catalogue of success stories for use in a wide range of localities.

THE LAST DICHOTOMY pits the personal mobility offered by the automobile against public transportation and nonmotorized modes of transportation. Sidewalks, trails, bicycle plans, and pedestrian facilities are all ideas linked to Agenda 21 and are therefore perceived as being threats to suburban and exurban mobility. Seemingly innocuous plans for sidewalks and bike lanes can trigger a strong reaction from local Tea Party groups that have been advised to be on the lookout for these kinds of initiatives. The *exoteric* message is that people who walk or ride bicycles are either part of the elite that conspires to implement sustainable development, or they are expensive facilities paid for by hardworking people to benefit government-dependent people. The *esoteric* message is that nonmotorized modes of transportation represent a challenge to established energy and manufacturing industries. The response to this concern should once again focus on increasing mobility options in contrast to restricting mobility.

Agenda 21, sustainable development, Smart Growth, conservation design, resource preservation, social justice, public transportation, and even sidewalks are terms that radical Right organizations are warning their audiences signify that national sovereignty and individual liberty are being challenged by globalists. Such claims are now in the mainstream, supported by state legislation and Republican Party resolutions. While most conservative and libertarian policy institutes avoid overtly radical claims, they selectively feed such claims with articles attacking multimodal transportation plans, mixed-use development, pedestrian facilities, the creative class, New Urbanism, biodiversity protection plans, and climate science. The vertical and horizontal integration of right-wing funding and messaging is such that it is difficult to construct any scenario in which rational dialogue resumes.

The responses suggested above are framed in rational language; however, the creative-progressive professional responding to fraternalistic rhetoric will need to weave in interpreter responses and nonverbal materials, as suggested earlier. The current state of creative-progressive professions such as city planning and environmental science is such that elaborate dance steps may be required to avoid political pitfalls. This state of affairs is not likely to end soon; the heavy investment by the Right will continue to pay dividends, as evidenced by state laws prohibiting implementation of Agenda 21—laws that could be interpreted by judges as prohibiting a wide range of planning practices.

The Progressive City upon a Hill

Progressivistic ideals are a difficult pursuit against strong headwinds. The ideals of equality, democracy, and the power of reason to solve human problems were inconceivable until the Enlightenment. While those values have taken hold in America and many other parts of the world, and whereas they appear to have permanence, they remain challenging to implement, maintain, and refine.

The course of a sailing ship is an apt metaphor for comparing Enlightenment progressivism with fraternalistic culture. Until the eighteenth century, sailing was understood as a means of traveling with prevailing winds and currents. Ships sailing from Europe to America typically sailed south to the coast of Africa, then west to the Caribbean, north to British America, and then northeast back to Europe. The round-trip journey lasted about four months.

During the eighteenth century, advancements in sailing technology greatly improved the performance of sailing vessels in using the wind's energy to sail *against* the wind. The aft deflection of the wind against a sail makes forward, upwind motion possible by virtue of Newton's Third

Law of Motion (the physics of sailing was later modeled in terms of the property of lift, like the effect of air on an airplane wing). Sailboats are now designed to sail toward the direction of the wind by as much as 35 degrees, allowing a more direct route to one's destination.

The challenge of conceiving the science of forward motion against prevailing winds illustrates how the bonds of tradition can be shed through progressive breakthroughs. The difficulty of sailing upwind, which requires tacking with considerable skill and diligence, provides another level to the metaphor. In stormy conditions, the captain can release the helm and a sailboat will right itself as it naturally comes into the wind. No forward progress is made and the ship may go backward, but it is a safe strategy. Fraternalistic political culture would prefer that the ship of state sail with the wind, and to release the helm in stormy conditions.

Progressivism, whether in politics or professions like city planning, pushes forward against the wind with new ideas and new science. It challenges tradition and perpetually seeks to advance the understanding of the world and improve the human condition. In doing so, it runs up against those who fear change or have a vested interest in maintaining the status quo. But despite powerful forces often aligned against it, progressivism is the inevitable victor in the struggle. The arc of history is long, as Dr. King said, but it bends toward justice—toward Enlightenment values.

The progressivistic city is one that strives for democracy and equality, that values tolerance and diversity, that takes a civic-oriented approach to visioning and problem solving, that shares the benefits of economic growth, that harnesses reason and the scientific method as engines of advancement, that above all invests in public education to ensure that its citizens are capable of directing the arc of history toward Enlightenment values and the fulfillment of human potential. The progressivistic city is not one of dependence, as its fraternalistic detractors assert, but one that strives to push every person toward his or her full potential.

Anthony Ashley Cooper and John Locke were progressivistic thinkers who set out to reinvent a better society in the wilderness of America. They drew from the Ancient Constitution of England, from Renaissance idealism, and from Classical Greece and Rome in constructing their new society. Then they added their own original thinking: there would be permanent reciprocity of duties and benefits or advantages among classes. There would be justice for all guaranteed by a model constitution. There would be better cities designed for resilience and sustainable development. After Ashley Cooper's death, Locke leaped past the Carolina experiment to define the new paradigm of the Enlightenment.

Ashley Cooper and Locke sailed against the wind in search of a better world. They helped to establish an American tradition of continual betterment, the progressivistic tradition. The nation's fraternalistic tradition will perpetually exist as a counterpoint, seeking a better future by returning to a past time. The essential tension between the two worldviews, moderated by the nation's pragmatic third worldview, will gradually discover new human potential—if they learn to speak each other's languages.

Appendix

Anthony Ashley Cooper, 1st Earl of Shaftesbury (1621–83). Ashley Cooper was born in Dorset on the southwest coast of England on July 22, 1621, to Sir John Cooper and Anne Ashley, both of prominent landowning families. His mother died in 1628 and his father in 1631, leaving their large estate to be managed by incompetent trustees until settled by the court. Once affairs were put in order, he inherited the remainder of the estate, after which he attended Exeter College, Oxford, and then Lincoln's Inn, one of England's four historic law schools. He married Margaret Coventry, daughter of Lord Coventry, in February 1639, and the young couple lived with her family in London.

Cooper was elected to Parliament in March 1640 while still a minor, with help from his father-in-law. He represented the borough of Tewkesbury, Gloucestershire, in the west of England. The English Civil War broke out two years later, and Ashley Cooper initially remained loyal to Charles I. For his service in raising forces to defend the king, he was rewarded with the positions of high sheriff and president of the war council in Dorset. In 1644, however, he resigned those positions and joined forces of Parliament opposed to the king, who he had come to believe was under Roman Catholic influence. Parliamentary forces led by Oliver Cromwell defeated the royal army in 1648, and Charles I was executed in January 1649. Cromwell established the Commonwealth of England in 1649, later organizing the government into a more authoritarian Protectorate. Ashley Cooper served on Cromwell's Council of State, which had replaced the king's Privy Council; but as the vision of a utopian commonwealth faded, he became increasingly disaffected with the government.

Ashley Cooper's wife, Margaret, died childless in 1649, soon after creation of the Commonwealth. He then married seventeen-year-old Lady Frances Cecil (1633–52) the following year. The bride was the daughter of David Cecil, 3rd Earl of Exeter. She bore two children before dying, one of whom was named Anthony Ashley Cooper after his father. The other son, Frances, died in childhood. Ashley Cooper married a third time, in 1655, to Margaret Spencer (1627–93), daughter of William Spencer, 2nd Baron Spencer of Wormleighton.

John Berkeley, 1st Baron Berkeley of Stratton (1602–78). Berkeley was a soldier and royalist close to James, Duke of York, who succeeded his brother, Charles II, to the throne as James II. Berkeley went into exile in Paris during the Commonwealth years. Following the Restoration, he was assigned to the admiralty. In 1663, he was made a member of the

Privy Council. Charles granted him an interest in both Carolina Colony and New Jersey, where he became a joint proprietor with Sir George Carteret in 1664. With Colleton, he was an active proprietor in the early years. In 1665, he participated in drafting a proclamation for New Jersey that provided freedom of religion in the province.

Sir William Berkeley (1605-77). The younger brother of John Berkeley was favored in the household of Charles I, and he became an accomplished playwright in the court literary circle known as "The Wits." He served as governor of the Virginia Colony from 1641 to 1652 and from 1660 to 1677. He experimented in growing silkworms and supported diversification of the tobacco-based economy. He sought equitable treatment of Native Americans, which led to a revolt by planters in 1676. Afterward, he was recalled to England by Charles II. Although he was a progressive governor with respect to Native American relations and economic diversification, he opposed public education and tolerance of religious diversity. He was not an active proprietor and did not contribute financially to the colonial venture.

Vice Admiral Sir George Carteret, 1st Baronet (1610-80). During the English Civil War, Carteret initially left the navy and retired to Jersey, but he later joined the royalists. During the Commonwealth period, he protected the Prince of Wales in Jersey, where he was bailiff until Jersey was taken by Cromwell's forces. He then went into exile in France, and later in Venice. At the Restoration, he was named to the Privy Council and appointed treasurer of the navy. He and Berkeley were named proprietors of both New Jersey and the Carolina Colony, where they issued a proclamation on freedom of religion. Carteret County, North Carolina, and the town of Carteret, New Jersey, are named for him, and the city of Elizabeth, New Jersey, is named after his wife. He has been documented to have been an active proprietor from the beginning of the venture and one of the three most active at the time Charles Town was founded.

Sir John Colleton, 1st Baronet (1608-66). Colleton was loyal to Charles I during the Civil War and rose through the ranks of the king's army. As a result, his properties were seized by parliamentary forces. Following the Restoration, he was made baronet. He was an experienced planter in Barbados. His son, Peter, succeeded him as an active proprietor, arranging for settlers from Barbados and their slaves to begin rice cultivation in Carolina. Colleton County, South Carolina, is named after him. His family maintained plantations in the Carolina Lowcountry after his death.

William Craven, 1st Earl of Craven (1608-97). Craven was a nobleman and soldier who remained in the service of the monarchy throughout his career. After the Restoration, he was rewarded for loyalty and financial support by being made earl and receiving court appointments. During the Great Plague of 1666, he remained in London, unlike most noblemen, and helped to maintain order. He was not one of the more active proprietors. Craven County, North Carolina, is named after him.

Edward Hyde, 1st Earl of Clarendon (1609-74). When the charter was granted, Clarendon was lord high chancellor, the highest office in Charles II's government. His eldest daughter was married to James, Duke of York, who succeeded his brother, Charles II, as king. He was the grandfather of both Queen Mary II and Queen Anne. He was impeached by the House of Commons and fled to France in 1667. He spent the remainder of his life in exile, during which time he completed work on *History of the Rebellion and Civil Wars in England.* Clarendon had virtually no involvement in planning, financing, or administering the Carolina Colony.

George Monck, 1st Duke of Albemarle (1608-70). Monck was an active proprietor and the Carolina Colony's first palatine, or titular head. He was an English soldier and politician who fought for Cromwell in the Civil War, but later he was instrumental in the restoration of Charles II. After Cromwell's death, he led forces to London, and he appears to have negotiated with both royalist and parliamentary leaders and is credited with ending the republican era without bloodshed. He was elected to Parliament in 1660. Charles II rewarded him with several honors and positions following the Restoration. In 1666, he maintained order in the city of London during the Great Fire. Albemarle Sound in North Carolina is named after him.

Sources: *Dictionary of National Biography*; Ramsay, *History of South Carolina*; Lesser, *South Carolina Begins*; and Edgar, *South Carolina: A History.*

Notes

PREFACE

1. The term "creative class" as used herein is a subset of the definition of the term as defined by Richard Florida, and thus is written in lowercase. Florida's definition includes two main categories, the Super-Creative Core (for example, scientists, engineers, educators, computer programmers, research analysts) and Creative Professionals, a more traditional category of professionals in such areas as business, health care, and law. See Florida, *Rise of the Creative Class*, 68–69, for full definitions.

PROLOGUE

1. The term "compact" was used several times (see Chapter 2 for specific instances). The terms "consistency" and "concurrence" are drawn from State of Florida growth management policies adopted in the 1970s and 1980s. Through the leadership of Dr. John M. DeGrove, these three principles influenced the emergence of Smart Growth policies of the 1990s.

2. See Pocock, *Politics, Language, and Time*, 94, and Pocock, *The Machiavellian Moment*, 388, for the use of the term "Gothic balance." Although Ashley Cooper does not appear to have anticipated dependence on an enslaved labor force, one of the eight Lords Proprietors, John Colleton, held an interest in a Barbados sugar plantation and facilitated the expansion of that activity into Carolina.

3. See Fries, *Urban Idea in Colonial America*, for an assessment and comparison of the utopian visions behind the three colonies. See Wilson, *The Oglethorpe Plan*, for more detail on the Georgia plan.

4. See Dochuk, *From Bible Belt to Sun Belt*, for a detailed description of the religious and political dimensions of the southern diaspora.

5. Armitage, "John Locke, Carolina, and the *Two Treatises*," 603–4.

6. Fischer, *Albion's Seed*, 47. The phrase was not Winthrop's invention but was in use among theologians in England.

7. Winthrop, "A Modell of Christian Charity."

8. Hall, *A Reforming People*, xi–xii.

9. Glaab and Brown, *History of Urban America*, 5; Reps, *The Making of Urban America*, 117–40. The term "communitarian" is frequently used by scholars to describe New England political culture and its descendants; see, for example, Elazar, *American Federalism*, 96–99, 102.

10. Historians have long neglected Dutch cultural influence, in part for lack of primary source material. See Shorto, *Island at the Center of the World*, for an account of that influence based on recently translated documents.

11. Clark, *Language of Liberty*, 39–43.

12. Reps, *The Making of Urban America*, 94–95; Maryland Historical Trust website.

13. Political scientist Daniel Elazar has identified the three dominant political cultures: *traditionalistic* (southern), *moralistic* (Mid-Atlantic), and *individualistic* (New England); see Elazar, *American Federalism*, 93.

14. Historian Lawrence Stone (*The Crisis of the Aristocracy*, 746, attributing T. H. Marshall as the source) offered the following "classic definition" for traditional class society containing the ideal of reciprocity: "The essence of social class is the way a man is treated by his fellows (and, reciprocally, the way he treats them), not the qualities or the possessions which cause that treatment."

15. Reps, *The Making of Urban America*, 165; Glaab and Brown, *History of Urban America*, 6; Fries, *Urban Idea in Colonial America*, 84–85; Voltaire quoted in Rothbard, *Conceived in Liberty*, 394.

16. Fries, *Urban Idea in Colonial America*, 96–99.

17. Wilson, *The Oglethorpe Plan*, chap. 1.

18. Reps, *The Making of Urban America*, 88–103.

19. Ibid., 103–6.

20. Home, *Of Planting and Planning*, 8–9.

21. Reps, *The Making of Urban America*, 95–99; Home, *Of Planting and Planning*, 8–9.

22. Edgar, *South Carolina: A History*, 52–53.

23. Reps, "Thomas Jefferson's Checkerboard Towns," 108; National Park Service, "The L'Enfant and McMillan Plans."

24. See Kruse, *White Flight*, for a case study of the genesis of the urban-exurban divide in Atlanta.

25. Southern mythology maintains that a philosophy of "states' rights" drove secession and opposition to civil rights legislation. However, historians have thoroughly documented secession statements claiming that slavery was foundational in the South, and that in the civil rights era a belief in "segregation now, segregation tomorrow, segregation forever" (George Wallace, 1963) drove the region's political agenda. The principle of "states' rights" was merely legal doctrine that supported slavery and later segregation, not a sacred principle that by itself had to be protected to the death.

26. See Bogucki, *The Origins of Human Society*, for a chronology of human society; for Uruk, see ibid., 339–40, 355.

27. Pocock, *Politics, Language, and Time*, 116–17.

28. The concept of a social contract is found in the second treatise of Locke's *Two Treatises of Government*. Jean-Jacques Rousseau also advanced the concept during the Enlightenment. See Strauss, *The City and Man*, 6; and Drury, *Leo Strauss and the American Right*, 154–55.

29. American Institute of City Planners, Code of Ethics, www.planning.org/ethics/.

30. Mitt Romney fund-raiser address; Mitt Romney speech.

31. Cited in Lepore, *The Whites of Their Eyes*, 44.

32. John Locke Foundation website, "About the Foundation."

33. Ludwig von Mises Institute website, "About the Mises Institute."

34. Rothbard, *Conceived in Liberty*, 397–401.

35. Ibid., 605–18; Wilson, *The Oglethorpe Plan*, 128–33, 201–6.

36. Rothbard, *Conceived in Liberty*, 112.

37. Samuel Johnson, "Taxation No Tyranny."

CHAPTER 1

1. Stelter, "Military Consideration and Colonial Town Planning," 222; Kubler, "Cities of Latin America," 17.

2. See Alexander, *New Jim Crow*.

3. Marshall, "Mechanic Tyrannie," 27, 37. See Spurr, *Anthony Ashley Cooper, First Earl of Shaftesbury, 1621–1683*, for an assessment by modern historians.

4. Glassey, "Shaftesbury and the Exclusion Crisis," 211–12.

5. Ibid.; Philip Milton, "Shaftesbury and the Rye House Plot," 245; J. R. Milton, "The Unscholastic Statesman," 174n95.

6. J. R. Milton, "The Unscholastic Statesman," 174.

7. Glassey, "Shaftesbury and the Exclusion Crisis," 220, 223.

8. Marshall, "Mechanic Tyrannie," 38; Harris, "England's 'Little Sisters without Breasts,'" 186.

9. Marshall, "Mechanic Tyrannie," 32.

10. Rich, "First Earl of Shaftesbury's Colonial Policy," 47; Home, *Of Planting and Planning*, 2–8.

11. Spurr, "Shaftesbury and the Seventeenth Century," 15–17.

12. Spurr, "Shaftesbury and the Politics of Religion," 143; Spurr, "Shaftesbury and the Seventeenth Century," 17.

13. Spurr, "Shaftesbury and the Seventeenth Century," 18; J. R. Milton, "The Unscholastic Statesman," 161, 166; Pocock, *Politics, Language, and Time*, 116.

14. Goldie, "Annual Parliaments and Aristocratic Whiggism," 82–83; Harris, "Cooper, Anthony Ashley." See Goldie, "Annual Parliaments and Aristocratic Whiggism," 100, for the following quote on frequent parliaments by Jonathan Swift: "I adore the wisdom of that Gothic constitution, which made them annual; and I was confident our liberty could never be placed upon a firm foundation until that ancient law was restored."

15. Spurr, "Shaftesbury and the Seventeenth Century," 20–23.

16. Leng, "Shaftesbury's Aristocratic Empire," 103–14. For more on the transition of Barbados to a slave society, see Dunn, *Sugar and Slaves*, especially the statistics on pp. 87, 312; and Stuart, *Sugar in the Blood*, 73.

17. Compare Carolina Proprietors, "Articles of Agreement," 41–45; with Ashley Cooper et al., "Instructions to Governor and Council," 119–23; and Ashley Cooper et al., "Agrarian Laws," 355–59. The death of Barbados slaveholder John Colleton in 1666 and the retention of John Locke the following year may have contributed to the change of emphasis. For Ashley Cooper's expectation of slavery in Carolina see, Ashley Cooper, "Lord Ashley to Capt. Halstead," December 16, 1671.

18. Shaftesbury Estate website, Burnett excerpt (accessed June 20, 2012).

19. Ibid.

20. Personal communications with Ashley Cooper, 12th Earl of Shaftesbury.

21. J. R. Milton, "The Unscholastic Statesman," 154–60.

22. *American Treasures of the Library of Congress*, Thomas Jefferson to John Trumbull, February 15, 1789.

23. J. R. Milton, "The Unscholastic Statesman," 180.

24. Locke, *Two Treatises of Government, First Treatise*, § 1.

25. Glausser, "Three Approaches to Locke," 199; Bourne, *Life of John Locke*, 195–96. See the discussion of Ashley Cooper and slavery in the previous section for cites of documents written by Locke in which references to slavery were removed.

26. Armitage, "John Locke, Carolina, and the *Two Treatises*," 609.

27. Brewer, "Friday Interview: John Locke and Slavery"; Sidney quote from http://politicalquotes.org/node/60823.

28. Brewer, "Friday Interview: John Locke and Slavery."

29. See Edgar, *South Carolina: A History*, 44–45, in which a system of "intra-class 'fairness'" is described (without using the term "reciprocity").

30. Harrington, *Commonwealth of Oceana*, ix.

31. Ibid., ix–x.

32. Pocock, *Politics, Language, and Time*, 116–17.

33. Ibid.; Marshall, "Mechanic Tyrannie," 37.

34. Pocock, *Politics, Language, and Time*, 116, 197, 97.

35. "Rule, Britannia!" was composed by Thomas Arne in 1740, based on the poem of the same title written by James Thomson. Additional republican philosophy was later added to the song by Henry St. John Lord Bolingbroke, a leader of Ashley Cooper's republican tradition, who contributed several stanzas.

36. Harrington, *Commonwealth of Oceana*, 80, 24, 22.

37. Ibid., 12, 231.

38. Ibid., 12, 232.

39. Leng, "Shaftesbury's Aristocratic Empire," 105–6, 116.

40. Goldsmith, *Deserted Village*, 4; see also *The Oglethorpe Plan*, 198. Johnson and Oglethorpe maintained overlapping social circles, and they frequently dined together debating the issues of the time. Oglethorpe, who was famously stoic, took the rural-virtue position, while Johnson argued the benefits of urbanity. Discussing food, Oglethorpe argued that "if we can be as well satisfied with plain things, we are in the wrong to accustom our palates to what is high-seasoned and expensive." Johnson took the contrasting position: "To be merely satisfied is not enough. It is in refinement and elegance that the civilized man differs from the savage."

41. Goldsmith, *Deserted Village*.

42. Quoted in Krall, "Thomas Jefferson's Agrarian Vision," 134.

43. Edgar, *South Carolina: A History*, 42.

44. Home, *Of Planting and Planning*, 8.

45. Edgar, *South Carolina: A History*, 42–43.

46. Ibid., 43–46.

47. Ibid., 46.

48. Stone, *The Crisis of the Aristocracy*, 748–49; Campbell, *The English Yeoman*, 67–73.

49. Derived from Campbell, *The English Yeoman*, chaps. 1 and 2. See ibid., 67–73, for an examination of the forces behind the rise of the yeomanry since the reign of Henry VIII.

50. Ibid., 36, 41–42, 50, 67–73.

51. Ibid., 315.

52. Plato, *The Republic*, 6.488d.

53. Aristotle, *Politics*, bk. 3, chaps. 6, 7, 15 .

54. Ibid., 324–25.

55. Ibid., 294, 305, 335.

56. MacCulloch, *Christianity*, 114 (citing Romans 13:1), 591–92.

57. For the history of the concept, see Lovejoy, *Great Chain of Being*; Bynum, "The Great Chain of Being after Forty Years," 8–14; and Wilson, *The Oglethorpe Plan*, 202–6.

58. Publication of Newton's *Philosophiæ Naturalis Principia Mathematica* (Mathematical Principles of Natural Philosophy) in 1687 and Locke's *Two Treatises of Government* in 1689, immediately followed by the Glorious Revolution, are considered the events that launched the British Enlightenment.

59. See Wilson, *The Oglethorpe Plan*, especially the epilogue.

60. Philip D. Morgan, *Slave Counterpoint*, 1–2, 58–61, 96–99.

CHAPTER 2

1. Pocock, *Politics, Language, and Time*, 124–25; Christie, *A Life of Anthony Ashley Cooper*, appendix V, p. vi.

2. Bancroft, *History of the United States*, 417.

3. Word totals are standardized counts using Microsoft Word.

4. Subjects taken up by the Fundamental Constitutions are organized as follows: class property and civil divisions, articles 1–27; governance, articles 28–60; the justice system, articles 61–70, and 111 (on juries); parliament, articles 71–80; local administration, articles 81–94; religion, articles 95–106; slavery, articles 107–10; property and taxation, articles 112–15; military duty, article 116; enactment and authority of the constitutions, articles 117–20.

5. For a list of those who claimed Carolina nobility, see http://www.carolana.com/Carolina/Nobility/home.html.

6. Leng, "Shaftesbury's Aristocratic Empire," 106–7.

7. See Oakes, *Slavery and Freedom*, xii, for a discussion of the distinction between a slave society and a society with slaves.

8. The provision of a trial by a jury of peers is found later in the constitutions in article 111.

9. Spurr, "Shaftesbury and the Politics of Religion," 131–35.

10. Ibid., 141.

11. Ibid., 151.

12. Fox Bourne, *Life of John Locke*, 1:237.

13. Ashley Cooper et al., "Instructions to Governor and Council," 119–23.

14. Ashley Cooper et al., "Instructions," May 1, 1671, *Shaftesbury Papers*, 322–23.

15. Ashley Cooper et al., "Temporary Laws," May, 1671? [*sic*], *Shaftesbury Papers*, 325.

16. Wood, *Black Majority*, 27.

17. Dunn, *Sugar and Slaves*, 4–5, 20, 26.

18. Ibid., 112.

19. Stuart, *Sugar in the Blood*, 31, 102.

20. Dunn, *Sugar and Slaves*, 70–72, 312.

21. Stuart, *Sugar in the Blood*, 85–86.

22. Ibid., 91, 180–81.

23. Dunn, *Sugar and Slaves*, 65; Walter Johnson, *River of Dark Dreams*, 159, 176, 208, 283.

24. Wood, *Black Majority*, 8, 14; Dunn, *Sugar and Slaves*, 114.

25. Lords Proprietors, "Instructions," November 8, 1691, in Rivers, *A Sketch*, Appendix, 60–67.

26. Ibid., 60–67.

27. Salley, *Commissions and Instructions*, 51–60.

28. Randolph, "E. Randolph to the Lords of Trade," 443.

29. Ibid., 445.

30. Francis Bacon's *New Atlantis* offered an earlier vision for an alternatively structured society, although scientists may have been at the top of a tacit pyramid in which wise academics communicated with esoteric and exoteric languages (see the discussion of Leo Strauss in the Epilogue).

31. Sirmans, *Colonial South Carolina*, 88.

32. Salley, *Narratives of Early Carolina*, 232. This volume contains Daniel Defoe, "Party-Tyranny, or an Occasional Bill in Miniature; as Now Practiced in Carolina," from 1705.

33. Ibid., 235.

34. Sirmans, *Colonial South Carolina*, 51, 77–78, 81.

35. Rogers and Taylor, *South Carolina Chronology*, 8; the authors provide population figures for decadal years throughout the *Chronology*.

36. Sirmans, *Colonial South Carolina*, 41–42.

37. Rogers and Taylor, *South Carolina Chronology*, 16–20.

38. Ibid., 20–22, 28.

39. Sirmans, *Colonial South Carolina*, 105–6.

40. Rogers and Taylor, *South Carolina Chronology*, 28.

CHAPTER 3

1. Locke may have been involved with Carolina after 1680, but by 1682 correspondence from the proprietors is written in a markedly different style.

2. Reps, *The Making of Urban America*.

3. The Greco-Roman city planner Vitruvius was rediscovered during the Italian Renaissance, but that knowledge and the ideas it stimulated among Italian designers would not fully reach England until the early eighteenth century. Perhaps future research can find a link between Locke and Renaissance designers such as Leon Battista

Alberti (1404–72), Georgio Vasari il Giovane (1511–74), Vincenzo Scamozzi (1548–1616), Pietro di Giacomo Cataneo (c. 1510–74), and Bernardo Morando (1540–1600). For Aristotle on planning, see *Politics*, bk. 2, chap. 8.

4. Aristotle, *Politics*, bk. 2, chap. 7.

5. Ashley Cooper et al., "Agrarian Laws."

6. Harrington, *Commonwealth of Oceana*, 44.

7. Wilson, *The Oglethorpe Plan*, prologue.

8. Ashley Cooper et al., "Agrarian Laws," 356.

9. Ibid.

10. Ibid.

11. Ibid., 356–57.

12. Ibid., 357–58.

13. Ibid.

14. Ibid., 358.

15. Ibid.

16. Ibid.

17. Ibid., 359; Smith, *Historical Writings*, 1:3.

18. Smith, *Historical Writings*, 1:10.

19. Lord Ashley Site.

20. Smith, *Historical Writings*, 1:xi, 2, 20.

21. Ibid., 1:3, 19.

22. Ibid., 1:12–17, 19–20, 24.

23. Ibid., 1:29–30.

24. Ibid., 1:29, 37–39. Information on the history and current status of plantations is maintained at www.south-carolina-plantations.com.

25. Edgar, *South Carolina: A History*, 49. Historians generally portray the Barbadians as unprincipled and suggest that they would be considered "ruthless rogues" from a modern perspective. Locke quoted in Wood, *Black Majority*, 24.

26. Quoted in Smith, *Historical Writings*, 1:77–78.

27. Ashley Cooper et al., "Agrarian Laws," 358, 365–67.

28. Ibid., 365.

29. Ibid., 359.

30. Ashley Cooper et al., "Instructions," May 1, 1671, in *Shaftesbury Papers*, 322–23; Ashley Cooper et al., "Instructions," May 1, 1671, in Rivers, *A Sketch*, 366. Rivers includes detail left out of the Shaftesbury volume.

31. Ashley Cooper et al., "Instructions," May 1, 1671, in *Shaftesbury Papers*, 323–34. The model for towns in Carolina referenced in the Proprietors' instructions of May 1, 1671, probably written by Locke, has not been located. The Locke scholar David Armitage of Harvard University discovered a document among Locke's papers in the Bodleian Library, Oxford University, which appears to have been related to the instructions and the attached model. It contains the following additional development standards: "200 acre a square plot for a towne / 100 acres at ye upper end of ye towne for a fort / 700 acres cow common whereof soe much to border on ye towne as well set the inclosures / 1/4 mile of an oblong square / 100 enclosures on ye common of 6 acres apeice ye front 2/3 of ye depth."

32. Ashley Cooper et al., "Instructions," May 1, 1671, in Rivers, *A Sketch*, 367.

33. Ibid.

34. Ibid.

35. Ibid., 365.

36. Ashley Cooper et al., "Instructions," May 23, 1674, in Rivers, *A Sketch*, 387.

37. Ashley Cooper et al., "Lords Proprietors to Governor and Council," 393.

38. Ibid., 393–94.

39. Lords Proprietors, "Instructions for Granting Land," November 21, 1682, in Rivers, *A Sketch*, 401.

40. Ibid., 402.

41. Lords Proprietors, "Instructions," November 8, 1692, in Rivers, *A Chapter*, appendix IX, 63–64.

42. Salley, *Commissions and Instructions*, 9–17.

43. Ibid., 168–70.

44. Smith, *Historical Writings*, 2:42. For a thorough accounting of the early maps of Charles Town, see Bates and Leland, *Abstracts of the Records of Surveyor General*.

45. Smith, *Historical Writings*, 2:42–43.

46. Sirmans, *Colonial South Carolina*, 104, 110–11.

47. Rogers and Taylor, *South Carolina Chronology*, 8.

48. Smith, *Historical Writings*, 2:55–59.

49. Ramsay, *The History of South Carolina*, 2:569.

50. Smith, *Historical Writings* 2:151–53 istorical WritingsH; Weir, *Colonial South Carolina: A History*, 153.

51. Bull, *The Oligarchs*, 232.

52. John Carteret, Baron Carteret (1690–1763), governor of the kingdom of Ireland, refused to sell his interest, thus retaining proprietorship of part of North Carolina.

53. Wood, *Black Majority*, 218.

54. According to Bull, in *The Oligarchs* (xi), there were six families that dominated Carolina politics through much of the 1700s, three from England and three from Barbados; see Wood, *Black Majority*, 34, 40–41, 46.

55. Wood, *Black Majority*, 51–60; Rogers and Taylor, *South Carolina Chronology*, 58.

56. Rogers and Taylor, *South Carolina Chronology*, 8; Philip D. Morgan, *Slave Counterpoint*, 96–97 (map 2).

57. Wood, *Black Majority*, 279.

58. Ibid., 79.

59. Ibid., 282–84.

60. Ibid., 135–37.

61. Ibid., 284–87; Isaac Gibbs to the Georgia Trustees, October 3, 1738, in Lane, *General Oglethorpe's Georgia, Colonial Letters*, 2:350.

62. Wood, *Black Majority*, 289–98, 308.

63. Ibid., 316–20.

64. Ibid., 323–24.

65. Jordan, *White over Black*, 26, 43. See Wood, *Black Majority*, for the Carolina experience.

66. See Stuart, *Sugar in the Blood*, 156–58, on class hierarchy from a descendant of enslaved Africans.

67. Philip D. Morgan, *Slave Counterpoint*, 96–97; Bull, *The Oligarchs*, 16.

68. Jordan, *White over Black*, 80.

69. Bull, *The Oligarchs*, 224.

70. Calhoun, "Slavery a Positive Good."

71. Conkin, *Southern Agrarians*, 81, 100; Twelve Southerners, *I'll Take My Stand*, 77.

72. Twelve Southerners, *I'll Take My Stand*, xxix; see Conkin, *Southern Agrarians*, 71, on objections to the book's title raised by Allen Tate and Robert Penn Warren, over the distraction it might cause rather than its racism. (Warren, it should be noted, evolved into an antisegregationist.)

73. Carter, *Politics of Rage*, 237. To compare the two times, see ibid.; and Carter, *When the War Was Over*, 147.

74. Wilson, *The Oglethorpe Plan*, 202–6.

75. Shillington, *History of Africa*, 99–100.

76. Ibid., 104–5.

77. Park, *Travels in the Interior Districts of Africa*, 82.

78. Ibid., 196.

79. Bogucki, *Origins of Human Society*, 367–70; Shillington, *History of Africa*, 45–49.

80. Sirmans, *Colonial South Carolina*, 10.

81. Weir, *Colonial South Carolina: A History*, 72; Rogers and Taylor, *South Carolina Chronology*, 7. South Carolina historian Walter Edgar has also stated that the Fundamental Constitutions were "responsible for the rapid and successful development of South Carolina" (Edgar, *South Carolina: A History*, 42), and that, although never formally adopted, they "nevertheless helped shape public policy and politics" in the colony (ibid., 83).

CHAPTER 4

1. Two generations descended brother to brother, hence ten generations.

2. Cash, *The Mind of the South*, 59–60, 67, 126.

3. Wyatt-Brown, *Southern Honor*, xiii, 3–4. Cash's book contains an introduction written by Wyatt-Brown titled "The Mind of W. J. Cash," in which he wrote that Cash lacked knowledge of some areas of southern cultural history but made an important contribution to the understanding of "southern cultural and class patterns" (xxii–xxiii).

4. Lane, *General Oglethorpe's Georgia, Colonial Letters*, 1:302.

5. Oxford English Dictionary, U.S. online edition; Cash, *The Mind of the South*, xii, 60–61.

6. Weir, *Colonial South Carolina: A History*, 341–42, 130, 137, 142.

7. For an early use of the term "Carolina way," see Elisha Dobree to the Georgia Trustees, February 1737, in Lane, *General Oglethorpe's Georgia, Colonial Letters*, 1:302.

8. Aistrup, *Southern Strategy Revisited*, 5–6, 151; Black and Black, *Rise of Southern Republicanism*, 203–19.

9. Some have argued that the increasing social and economic diversity in the South will moderate the effect of the white shift to the Republican Party; see Aistrup, *Southern Strategy Revisited*, 243–48; and Black and Black, *Rise of Southern Republicanism*, 3–5. Recent elections suggest this may be a long time coming.

10. Elazar, *American Federalism*, 93–102.

11. The concept of "brotherhood" as applied here suggests a parallel with South Africa's Broederbond, the extensive, informal network that gradually restored Afrikaner political power and implemented apartheid.

12. J. David Woodard, *New Southern Politics*, 6–19.

13. Key, *Southern Politics*, 16.

14. Meinig, *The Shaping of America*, 1:269, 2:292.

15. Colin Woodard, *American Nations*, 5–10, 83–91; see also the map preceding the introduction and 14 for acknowledgment of Phillips and Garreau.

16. Fischer, *Albion's Seed*; for overviews of the thesis, see 3–11, 787 (chart), 805–7, 816–18.

17. Ibid., 605–6, 609, 613–18, 626, 633–39, 642–46.

18. Ibid., 650–51, 754, 758, 778, 780, 782.

19. Wyatt-Brown, *Southern Honor*, 38; Cash, *The Mind of the South*, 72.

20. Hartz, *Liberal Tradition in America*, 6, 153, 59, 165, 146–48, 175.

21. Lakoff, *The Political Mind*, 7–8, 44, 169, 196, 203, 267–68; Boehm, *Hierarchy in the Forest*, 4, 11–12.

22. Richard Ellis, *American Political Cultures*, 1–3, 28–29, 42–44, 169.

23. Chinni and Gimpel, *Our Patchwork Nation*; a summary of categories can be found on pp. 9–10.

24. Bishop, *The Big Sort*, 5–6, 9, 46, 53–56, 143, 302–3.

25. Wikimedia Foundation, James Carville quote.

26. Rentfrow et al., "Divided We Stand," 996–1009.

27. Harrington and Gelfand, "Tightness-Looseness," 1–2, 6.

28. Jost et al., "Political Conservatism as Motivated Social Cognition," 369.

29. George, *Rhetoric of the Right*, 71, 6, 25, 122, 125–26; Hirschman, *Rhetoric of Reaction*, 167–70.

30. Spalding, "South Carolina and Georgia: The Early Days," 83–84; Wilson, *The Oglethorpe Plan*, 47–55.

31. Wilson, *The Oglethorpe Plan*; see the Prologue for more on Oglethorpe's formative years. The full name of the Georgia Trustees was The Trustees for the Establishment of the Colony of Georgia in America.

32. Wilson, *The Oglethorpe Plan*; see Chapter 1 for a description of the comprehensive design and Chapter 3 for a discussion of slavery.

33. *Colonial Records of Georgia* 21, no. 184 (October 26, 1749); Lane, *General Oglethorpe's Georgia, Colonial Letters*, 2:389 (January 17, 1739).

34. James Oglethorpe to the Trustees, May 18, 1736, in Lane, *General Oglethorpe's Georgia, Colonial Letters*, 1:265–67.

35. James Oglethorpe to James Vernon, Frederica, January 26, 1741, in ibid., 540–42.

36. Stephens, *Journal*, February 12, 1739, 2:403–4.

37. Ibid., June 24, 1740, 2:416–17.

38. Ibid., August 18, 1740, 2:481–82.

39. Wilson, *The Oglethorpe Plan*, 128–31.

40. Ibid., 116; Rowland, Moore, and Rogers, *History of Beaufort County*, 178.

41. Coleman, *Colonial Georgia*, 228–29; Locke, *Two Treatises, First Treatise*, § 1; Meinig, *The Shaping of America*, 1:182.

42. Diamond, *Guns, Germs, and Steel*, 211.

43. See Crosby, *Columbian Exchange*; and Gambino, "Alfred W. Crosby on the Columbian Exchange."

44. Diamond, *Guns, Germs, and Steel*, 211–13; Philip D. Morgan, *Slave Counterpoint*, 6–7n9; Wood, *Black Majority*, 144. Nearly a quarter of the enslaved population in South Carolina enumerated in the census of 1708 were Native Americans.

45. Ashley Cooper et al., "Instructions to Governor and Council, 120; Burton, "Duty and Reward."

46. Wilson, *The Oglethorpe Plan*, chap. 3. For a note on buffalo hunting, see *Colonial Records of Georgia* 21 (March 16, 1736): 103–5 (letter from Oglethorpe at Frederica to the Trustees).

47. Oatis, *A Colonial Complex*, 41, 74–76, 105, 143.

48. Sirmans, *Colonial South Carolina*, 30, 77–78, 81; Rowland, Moore, and Rogers, *History of Beaufort County*, 80; Philip D. Morgan, *Slave Counterpoint*, 481.

49. Weir, *Colonial South Carolina: A History*, 116; Sirmans, *Colonial South Carolina*, 187–91.

50. Oatis, *A Colonial Complex*, 60, 64; Sirmans, *Colonial South Carolina*, 33–34; Wood, *Black Majority*, 38–39, 77n50.

51. Oatis, *A Colonial Complex*, 1, 41–44.

52. Quoted in Joseph Ellis, *American Creation*, 145.

53. Ibid., 162–63.

54. Ibid., 158–59.

55. Genovese, *Political Economy of Slavery*, 31; John Craig Hammond, *Slavery, Freedom, and Expansion*, 1–3, 74; Oakes, *The Ruling Race*, 236–37; Kolchin, *American Slavery*, 86, 89.

56. Wolf, *Race and Liberty*, 8, 207–11.

57. For a comparison of South Carolina and Virginia, see Philip D. Morgan, *Slave Counterpoint*.

58. Crane, "The Tennessee River as the Road to Carolina," 5–7.

59. John Craig Hammond, *Slavery, Freedom, and Expansion*, 17–18, 34–36.

60. Meinig, *The Shaping of America*, 2:291–92, 476, 494. See also Wyatt-Brown, *Southern Honor*, 262; and Oakes, *The Ruling Race*, 236–37.

61. Walter Johnson, *River of Dark Dreams*, 372, 399. For an early use of the term "section," see Turner, *Significance of the Section in American History*, 37: "We have become a nation comparable to all Europe in area, with settled geographic provinces which equal great European nations. We are in this sense an empire, a federation of sections, a union of potential nations."

62. Genovese, *Political Economy of Slavery*, 35; Oakes, "Genovese, Slavery, Capitalism"; Oakes, *Slavery and Freedom*, 52, 56. See Philip D. Morgan, *Slave Counterpoint*, for a comparison of Tidewater and Lowcountry as a response to contrasting economic conditions.

63. Genovese, *A Consuming Fire*, 119; Oakes, "Genovese, Slavery, Capitalism."

64. John Craig Hammond, *Slavery, Freedom, and Expansion*, 1–3; Kolchin, *American Slavery*, 188; population statistics from ibid., appendix, table 3.

65. Walter Johnson, *River of Dark Dreams*, 40–41, 73–78, 86–87, 170–76, 408.

66. Ibid., 159, 176–81, 283.

67. Kolchin, *American Slavery*, 178–81; Walter Johnson, *River of Dark Dreams*, 5, 41, 72.

68. Walter Johnson, *River of Dark Dreams*, 282; Lind, *Made in Texas*, 24, 45, 162.

69. John Craig Hammond, *Slavery, Freedom, and Expansion*, 8, 66–70, 76–80.

70. Ibid., 96–97, 122–23, 150–55, 170–72.

71. Quote from Genovese, *Political Economy of Slavery*, 266–67; Walter Johnson, *River of Dark Dreams*, 366–71, 418; Genovese, *A Consuming Fire*, 89.

72. Kolchin, *American Slavery*, 195; Genovese, *Slaveholders' Dilemma*, 18, 47, 89; Walter Johnson, *River of Dark Dreams*, 203, 414–15; Oakes, *Slavery and Freedom*, 73.

73. Walter Johnson, *River of Dark Dreams*, 414–15.

74. Genovese, *Political Economy of Slavery*, 34, 171–73.

75. Cash, *The Mind of the South*, 1.

76. Carter, *When the War Was Over*, 29, 42–43; Wyatt-Brown, *Southern Honor*, 72–73.

77. Rowland, Moore, and Rogers, *History of Beaufort County*, 430–31.

78. American Civil War Homepage, "Declaration of Causes of Seceding States."

79. Carter, *When the War Was Over*, 266–67.

80. Ibid., 158–59, 210–11, 216.

81. Cash, *The Mind of the South*, 90–91; Hackney, "Southern Violence," 924; MacLean, "Leo Frank Case Reconsidered," 185.

82. American Presidency Project, "Platform of the States Rights Democratic Party, August 14, 1948."

83. "Can State Lawmakers Nullify Federal Laws?"

84. Cash, *The Mind of the South*, 428–29.

85. Dochuk, *From Bible Belt to Sun Belt*, xv–xvi, 137.

86. Genovese, *A Consuming Fire*, 3–5, 113–14. The "Curse of Ham" is an interpretation of Genesis 9:20–27, which describes Noah cursing Ham for seeing him naked and drunk by condemning his son Canaan to be a "servant of servants." Skin color is not mentioned in the passage but was an embellishment added centuries later. The lack of any mention of skin color placed this among the least invoked justifications for slavery.

87. Dochuk, *From Bible Belt to Sun Belt*, xxiv, 13–17, 29.

88. Ibid., 47–49, 52, 117. See "List of Think Tanks in the United States," in Wikipedia, for links to conservative policy groups.

89. Dochuk, *From Bible Belt to Sun Belt*, 75–82, 106–7, 166.

90. Gilliland, "Calculus of Realignment," 413–14.

91. Dochuk, *From Bible Belt to Sun Belt*, 260–65, 274.

92. Key, *Southern Politics*, 131.

93. Dochuk, *From Bible Belt to Sun Belt*, 134.

CHAPTER 5

1. Campbell, *The English Yeoman*, 315, 32. Mobility in the countryside was limited.

2. Wilson, *The Oglethorpe Plan*, 69, 98–100, 168–69.

3. Jefferson's Monticello, Thomas Jefferson to James Madison, December 20, 1787.

4. Kruse, *White Flight*, 6.

5. Ibid., 9–10, 105–6, 276–77. Democrat John Barrow was defeated in Georgia's 12th Congressional District.

6. Ibid., 106, 125–26, 129, 135, 255, 264.

7. Ibid., 131–32; Hackney, "Southern Violence," 924–25.

8. Kruse, *White Flight*, 131–32. The unanimous 1954 decision on desegregation overturned the *Plessy v. Ferguson* decision of 1896, which allowed states to segregate the races.

9. Ibid., 131.

10. U.S. Bureau of the Census, "Historical Statistics, 1789–1945," B16–17.

11. See Lind, *Made in Texas*, 172–83, for more on the urban vision versus a decentralist utopia.

12. Many waterways that appeared to be rivers were tidal channels through the Lowcountry's estuaries.

13. U.S. Bureau of the Census, "Historical Statistics, Colonial Times to 1970," A178–79; U.S. Bureau of the Census, "Historical Statistics, 1789 to 1945," B48–71.

14. Perlstein, "Exclusive: Lee Atwater's Infamous 1981 Interview."

15. Carter, *The Politics of Rage*, 160–61, 464–66.

16. Kruse, *White Flight*, 257–58.

17. Ibid., 261.

18. Ibid., 264, 266. Kruse traces the modern conservative politics to desegregation. The author finds that elements are traceable to Ashley Cooper's time.

19. Hackney, "Southern Violence," 924–25.

20. See Brody, *Teavangelicals*.

21. See Winters, "Oligarchy and Democracy," for an assessment of how the two systems coexist in America.

22. DeMint, "DeMint: Rebuilding a Land of Opportunity."

23. United Nations, World Commission on Environment and Development, "Our Common Future: From One Earth to One World," I-3.

24. Jane Ford, "International Leader in Environmental Issues."

25. Mencimer, "We Don't Need None."

26. Southern Poverty Law Center, "Agenda 21: The UN, Sustainability, and Right-Wing Conspiracy Theory," 12, 20.

27. Personal communications with Teri Norris, Beaufort County Planning Department; personal communication with Elizabeth Emslie, former assistant director, Rutherford County Planning Department (both in July 2013).

28. Tea Party 911 website, "What Is Agenda 21?"

29. John Birch Society website, "Stop Agenda 21."

30. Ibid.

31. Freedom Watch Radio website.

32. Republican National Committee Counsel's Office, "Resolution Exposing United Nations Agenda 21."

33. Altman, "United Nations Agenda 21 Bill Passes Legislature."

34. Sturgis, "Pat McCrory Dons Tinfoil Hat."

35. Green, "Oklahoma Senator's Bill."

36. Adler, "Urban Nation."

37. Mayer, "Covert Operations," 1–2; Center for American Progress, "The Koch Brothers: What You Need to Know," 2–3, 8–10.

38. Mayer, "Covert Operations," 4–5, 9–11; Center for American Progress, "The Koch Brothers: What You Need to Know," 19–24.

39. Winters, "Oligarchy and Democracy."

40. Winters, *Oligarchy*, 24; Winters, "Oligarchy and Democracy."

41. Armitage, "That Excellent Forme of Government," 1.

42. Locke, *Two Treatises*, "Introduction," 120–26; Harrington, *Commonwealth of Oceana*, 24.

43. As a scholar, Locke would have taken into account the Latin derivation of "property" from "proprietas." See http://en.wiktionary.org/wiki/proprietas: "1. quality, property, peculiarity; 2. character; 3. ownership." On labor, see Locke, *Two Treatises, Second Treatise*, § 27.

44. Jefferson and City Planning (an exhibit); see also Reps, "Thomas Jefferson's Checkerboard Towns."

45. Home, *Of Planting and Planning*, 8, 32. Home found that the Grand Model influenced the design of Philadelphia and Savannah as well as other cities throughout the empire, including Adelaide, which in turn became a model for the Garden Cities movement.

46. Kruse, *White Flight*, 131, 21–22.

47. Ibid., 104–6, 125–29.

48. Bicycles also offered additional mobility at that time, becoming popular in their "golden age" of the 1890s. For a history of the suburbs from the planning perspective, see Nelson, "Leadership in a New Era."

49. Kruse, *White Flight*, 266.

50. Ibid., 235, 246.

51. Sharlet, *The Family*, 310–11.

52. Kotkin, "Biography"; Kotkin, "Rule, Suburbia," B-1; Kotkin, "Richard Florida Concedes."

53. Kotkin, "Richard Florida Concedes"; Florida, *Rise of the Creative Class*; Florida, "Did I Abandon My Creative Class Theory." See Gallagher, *The End of the Suburbs: Where the American Dream Is Moving*, for a recent assessment that contradicts Kotkin's claims.

54. Kotkin, "Richard Florida Concedes"; Kotkin, "Triumph of Suburbia." In these two articles alone, Kotkin applies the following terms to urbanists: chattering classes and chatterers, planning class, retro-urbanist, hate affair with suburbs, urban gentry and intelligentsia, bitter, anti-suburbanites, perverse, elitism animating the urban theorists, pernicious, overhyped, worships at the altar of diversity. Kotkin's phraseology also repeatedly attempts to paint urbanists as anti-family as when he says that their

plans create a "kiddie wilderness" or when he claims that they believe single family houses as "vastly preferred by families" are "fundamentally passé."

55. Kotkin, "Richard Florida Concedes."

56. Wilson, *The Oglethorpe Plan*, 170–72; Kotkin, "Triumph of Suburbia."

57. Baker, "How the G.O.P. Became the Anti-Urban Party."

58. Ashley Cooper et al., "Instructions," *Shaftesbury Papers*, May 1, 1671; Ashley Cooper et al., "Agrarian Laws."

59. Free Congress Foundation, http://www.freecongress.org/project/center-for-transportation/ (accessed August 12, 2013). James Gilmore, former governor of Virginia, is head of FCF's research arm; support for public transportation may reflect the transportation congestion crisis in the state's Washington suburbs.

60. Doig, "Tampa: America's Hottest Mess"; Goodyear, "The Most Dangerous U.S. Cities for Pedestrians."

61. U.S. Bureau of the Census, 2010 Census and 2000 Census. Population-weighted density is calculated from the average densities of census tracts in a metropolitan area.

62. Personal communication with Patrick O. Shay.

63. Schmitt, "Greater Atlanta Continues to Treat Walking Like a Crime."

64. Whittemore, "Finding Sustainability in Conservative Contexts," 2460–62.

65. See James A. Bacon, "Smart Growth for Conservatives," an essay adapted from a speech delivered at the 2012 Congress for the New Urbanism. See also http://www.baconsrebellion.com/about for Bacon's biography (accessed December 6, 2012).

66. See McHarg, *Design with Nature*.

EPILOGUE

1. Lakoff, *The Political Mind*, 3, 7–8, 22, 196–97; Lakoff and Johnson, *Metaphors We Live By*, 4, 6, 118, 186; Lakoff, *Whose Freedom*, 13, 250–51, 258–59.

2. Ballou, *Treasury of Thought*, 433. (The quote is attributed to Swift: "It is useless to attempt to reason a man out of a thing he was never reasoned into.")

3. Bogucki, *Origins of Human Society*, 207–9; Boehm, *Hierarchy in the Forest*, 2–10, 12, 182. Boehm notes that other anthropologists see primitive bands as merely attenuated hierarchies.

4. Boehm, *Hierarchy in the Forest*, 4.

5. Locke, *Two Treatises*, "Introduction," 125–26; *First Treatise*, § 1, *Second Treatise*, § 4 .

6. Boehm, *Hierarchy in the Forest*, 11–12.

7. Hirschman, *Rhetoric of Reaction*, 7, 151–53, 170.

8. Worthen, "Love Thy Stranger as Thyself," 1.

9. John Locke Foundation, "Founding Principles."

10. Aristotle, *Politics*, bk. 3, chap. 13 .

11. Library of Congress, http://thomas.loc.gov/cgi-bin/query/z?c107:H.CON.RES.48 (accessed June 2, 2014).

12. Ibid., citing the *Federalist Papers*.

13. Drury, *Political Ideas*, 11; Strauss, *The City and Man*, 6–7.

14. Drury, "Reply to My Critics," 1.

15. Ibid., 4.

16. Drury, *Political Ideas*, 6–10, 25.

17. Ibid., 154–55.

18. Clark, *Language of Liberty*, 35, 41–44.

19. Fischer, *Albion's Seed*, 201–5.

20. Ibid., 412, 414.

21. Spellberg, "Our Founding Fathers Included Islam."

22. Carter, *Politics of Rage*, 456.

23. Sharlet, *The Family*, 44, 220, 364.

24. Ibid., 223–24.

25. Ibid., 309–10.

26. Suskind, "Faith, Certainty."

27. Frank, *What's the Matter with Kansas*, 75, 157–58.

28. Empiricism dates to Aristotle, and in England Francis Bacon is considered the founder of the modern scientific method. Locke, however, is associated with the larger adoption of empiricism during the Enlightenment.

29. Gewargis, "Spread the Wealth."

30. Ibid.

31. Hananoki, "Cruise Ship Confession."

32. Lakoff, *Moral Politics*, 3–8.

33. "Conservative Institute Mission Statements," compiled by the author.

34. Freedom Advocates website; Coletta, "Reciprocity of Advantage," 300–303.

35. See Raapana and Friedrich, "The Anti Communitarian Manifesto," for an example of the Far Right's attack on "communitarianism." The quote by Zechariah Chafee is often misattributed to Justice Oliver Wendell Holmes.

36. Conservative Society for Action, "How 'Sustainable Development' Affects Your Property Rights."

Bibliography

Adler, Ben. "Urban Nation: Don't Kill the Office of Smart Growth." *Next City* (online publication), July 7, 2012. http://nextcity.org/daily/entry/urban-nation-dont-kill-the-office-of-smart-growth (accessed March 31, 2012).

Aistrup, Joseph A. *The Southern Strategy Revisited: Republican Top-Down Advancement in the South.* Lexington: University of Kentucky Press, 1996.

Alexander, Michelle. *The New Jim Crow: Mass Incarceration in the Age of Colorblindness.* New York: New Press, 2010.

Alter, Lloyd. "Exposing the Influence behind the Anti–Agenda 21 Anti-Sustainability Agenda." Treehugger.com, Business/Environmental Policy, June 29, 2012. http://www.treehugger.com/environmental-policy/who-behind-agenda-21-paranoia-how-can-we-fight-back.html (accessed March 1, 2013).

Altman, George. "United Nations Agenda 21 Bill Passes Legislature." *Montgomery Bureau Press-Register*, May 16, 2012. http://blog.al.com/live/2012/05/united_nations_agenda_21_bill.html (accessed April 2, 2013).

American Civil War Homepage. Public Documents. "Declarations of Causes of Seceding States." http://edweb.sdsu.edu (accessed October 2, 2012).

American Freedom Watch Radio. http://americanfreedomwatchradio.com/ (accessed April 5, 2013).

American Presidency Project. "Platform of the States Rights Democratic Party, August 14, 1948." Political Party Platforms, Parties Receiving Electoral Votes: 1840–2004. http://www.presidency.ucsb.edu/ws/index .php?pid=25851#axzz1iGn93BZz (accessed February 15, 2013).

American Treasures of the Library of Congress. http://www.loc.gov/exhibits/ treasures/trm033.html (accessed May 5, 2011).

Archer, John. "Puritan Town Planning in New Haven." *Journal of the Society of Architectural Historians* 34, no. 2 (May 1975): 140–49.

Aristotle. *Politics.* In the volume *On Man and the Universe: Metaphysics, Parts of Animals, Ethics, Politics, Poetics.* Edited with an introduction by Louise Ropes Loomis. Roslyn, N.Y.: Walter J. Black, 1943.

Armitage, David. "John Locke, Carolina, and the *Two Treatises of Government.*" *Political Theory* 32 , no. 5 (October 2004): 602–27.

———. "John Locke, Theorist of Empire?" In *Empire and Modern Political Thought*, edited by Sankar Muthu. New York: Cambridge University Press, 2012.

———. Personal communications. May 20–21, 2015. Text provided for a document by John Locke found in 2001 slipped in the 1648 edition of the Bible in Harrison and Laslett's Library of John Locke, item 309 (Bodleian Locke 16.25).

———. "That Excellent Forme of Government: New Light on Locke and Carolina." http://scholar.harvard.edu/armitage/publications/%E2%80%98-excellent-forme-government%E2%80%99-new-light-locke-and-carolina (accessed February 12, 2015).

Ashley Cooper, Anthony. "Lord Ashley to Captain Halstead," December 16, 1671. In *The Shaftesbury Papers*, 364–65. Charleston: South Carolina Historical Society, 2000.

———. et al. "Agrarian Laws," June 21, 1672. In *A Sketch of the History of South Carolina*, by William J. Rivers, 355–59. Charleston: McCarter and Co., 1856.

———. "Instructions," May 1, 1671. In *The Shaftesbury Papers*, 322–24. Charleston: South Carolina Historical Society, 2000.

———. "Instructions," May 1, 1671. In *A Sketch of the History of South Carolina*, by William J. Rivers, 366–69. Charleston: McCarter and Co., 1856. This transcription contains more detail than the version in *The Shaftesbury Papers*.

———. "Instructions to Governor and Council," July 27, 1669. In *The Shaftesbury Papers*, 119–22. Charleston: South Carolina Historical Society, 2000.

———. "Instructions," May 23, 1674. In *A Sketch of the History of South Carolina*, by William J. Rivers, 387. Charleston: McCarter and Co., 1856.

———. "Lords Proprietors to Governor and Council," May 17, 1680. In *A Sketch of the History of South Carolina*, by William J. Rivers, 393–94. Charleston: McCarter and Co., 1856.

———. "Temporary Laws, Carolina," May, 1671? [*sic*]. In *The Shaftesbury Papers*, 324–25. Charleston: South Carolina Historical Society, 2000.

Ashley Cooper, Anthony, 1st Earl of Shaftesbury. *The Shaftesbury Papers*. Charleston: South Carolina Historical Society, 2000.

Ashley Cooper, Anthony, 3rd Earl of Shaftesbury. *Characticks of Men, Manners, Opinions, Times*. 1711. Indianapolis: Liberty Fund, 2001. This is a reprinting of the 1732 edition. Introduction by Douglas J. Den Uyl, 2000.

Ashley Cooper, Nicholas Anthony, 12th Earl of Shaftesbury. Personal communications, October 30, 2013, and November 14, 2014.

Bacon, Edmund N. *Design of Cities*. New York: Penguin Books, 1974.

Bacon, Francis. *The New Atlantis*. Oxford: Clarendon Press, 1915.

Bacon, James A. "Smart Growth for Conservatives." http://www.baconsrebellion.com/articles/2012/05/smart_growth_conservatives.html#jump (accessed May 31, 2012).

Baker, Kevin. "How the G.O.P. Became the Anti-Urban Party." *New York Times*, October 6, 2012. http://www.nytimes.com/2012/10/07/opinion/sunday/republicans-to-cities-drop-dead.html?_r=0&adxnnl=1&adxnnlx=1349978553-dKZC2ckOFk1/4/lcXSMqkg&pagewanted=print(accessed October 6, 2012).

Ballou, Maturin M. *Treasury of Thought Forming an Encyclopedia of Quotations from Ancient and Modern Authors*. 15th ed. Boston: Houghton Mifflin, 1894.

Bancroft, George. *History of the United States*. Vol. 1. New York: Appleton, 1924.

Barry, John M. *Roger Williams and the Creation of the American Soul: Church, State, and the Birth of Liberty*. New York: Viking, 2012.

Bartels, Larry M. *Unequal Democracy: The Political Economy of the New Gilded Age*. New York: Russell Sage Foundation, 2008.

Bates, Susan B., and Harriot C. Leland. *Abstracts of the Records of Surveyor General of the Province, Charles Towne, 1678–1698*. Vol. 3 of *Proprietary Records of South Carolina*. Charleston, S.C.: History Press, 2007.

Bennett, Ralph, ed. *Settlements in the Americas: Cross-Cultural Perspectives*. Newark: University of Delaware Press, 1993.

Bishop, Bill. *The Big Sort: Why the Clustering of Like-Minded America Is Tearing Us Apart*. Boston: Houghton Mifflin, 2008.

Black, Earl, and Merle Black. *The Rise of Southern Republicans*. Cambridge: Belknap Press of Harvard University Press, 2002.

Boehm, Christopher. *Hierarchy in the Forest: The Evolution of Egalitarian Behavior*. Cambridge: Harvard University Press, 1999.

Bogucki, Peter. *The Origins of Human Society*. Malden, Mass.: Blackwell, 1999.

Brewer, Holly. Address to the John Locke Foundation, Shaftesbury Society Luncheon, March 17, 2008. http://www.lockefan.org/affiliates/biography.html?id=8 (accessed September 2, 2011).

———. "Friday Interview: John Locke and Slavery." *Carolina Journal Online*, July 24, 2009. http://www.carolinajournal.com/exclusives/display_exclusive .html?id=5532 (accessed August 19, 2013).

Brody, David. *The Teavangelicals: The Inside Story of How the Evangelicals and the Tea Party Are Taking Back America*. Grand Rapids, Mich.: Zondervan, 2012.

Bronzini, Michael S. "Transportation and the Economic Health and Attractiveness of Metropolitan Regions." Free Congress Foundation, June 2013. http://www .freecongress.org/project/center-for-transportation/ (accessed August 12, 2013).

Bull, Kinloch, Jr. *The Oligarchs in Colonial and Revolutionary Charleston: Lieutenant Governor William Bull II and His Family*. Columbia: University of South Carolina Press, 1991.

Burton, John. "The Duty and Reward of Propagating Principles of Religion and Virtue Exemplified in the History of Abraham: A Sermon Preach'd before the Trustees for Establishing the Colony of Georgia in America." Sermon delivered at the First Anniversary Meeting of the Trustees. March 15, 1732. Gale Digital Collections: Eighteenth Century Collections Online, accessed through Hargrett Rare Manuscripts Library, University of Georgia. Originally published, London: Mount and Page, 1733.

Bynum, William F. "The Great Chain of Being after Forty Years: An Appraisal." *History of Science* 13 (1975): 1–28.

Calhoun, John C. "Slavery a Positive Good." Speech on the Senate Floor, February 6, 1837. http://en.wikisource.org/wiki/Slavery_a_Positive_Good (accessed February 22, 2013).

Campbell, Mildred. *The English Yeoman under Elizabeth and the Early Stuarts*. 1942. London: Merlin Press, 1983.

"Can State Lawmakers Nullify Federal Laws?" *Columbia State*, February 18, 2013, 1A, 9A. Originally published in *Beaufort Gazette*.

Candler, Allen D., et al., eds. *The Colonial Records of the State of Georgia*. 25 vols. Atlanta: Franklin, 1904–1916.

Carolina Proprietors. "Articles of Agreement." In *A Sketch of the History of South Carolina*, by William J. Rivers, 41–45. Charleston: McCarter and Co., 1856.

Carter, Dan T. *The Politics of Rage: George Wallace, the Origins of the New Conservatism, and the Transformation of American Politics*. New York: Simon & Schuster, 1995.

——. *When the War Was Over: The Failure of Self-Reconstruction in the South, 1865–66*. Baton Rouge: Louisiana State University Press, 1985.

Cash, W. J. *The Mind of the South*. Introduction by Bertram Wyatt-Brown. 1941. New York: Vintage Books, 1991.

Center for American Progress. "The Koch Brothers: What You Need to Know about the Financiers of the Radical Right." http://www.americanprogressaction.org/wp-content/uploads/issues/2011/04/pdf/koch_brothers.pdf (accessed April 11, 2013).

Chinni, Dante, and James Gimpel. *Our Patchwork Nation: The Surprising Truth about the "Real" America*. New York: Gotham Books, 2010.

Christie, William Dougal. *A Life of Anthony Ashley Cooper, First Earl of Shaftesbury: 1621–1683*. Vol. 1. London, 1871.

——. "Memoirs, Letters, and Speeches of Anthony Ashley Cooper, First Earl of Shaftesbury, Lord Chancellor, with Other Papers Illustrating His Life from His Birth to the Restoration." 1859. *North American Review* 91, no. 189 (October 1860): 385–420.

Clark, J. C. D. *The Language of Liberty, 1660–1832: Political Discourse and Social Dynamics in the Anglo-American World*. Cambridge: Cambridge University Press, 1994.

Coleman, Kenneth. *Colonial Georgia: A History*. New York: Charles Scribner's, 1976.

Coletta, Raymond R. "Reciprocity of Advantage and Regulatory Takings: Toward a New Theory of Takings Jurisprudence." *American University Law Review* 40, no. 1 (Fall 1990): 297–366. http://www.wcl.american.edu/journal/lawrev/40/coletta.pdf (accessed May 29, 2013).

Conkin, Paul K. *The Southern Agrarians*. Nashville: Vanderbilt University Press, 2001.

Conservative Society for Action. "How 'Sustainable Development' Affects Your Property Rights." http://www.csa-1776.org/sustaindev.php (accessed May 21, 2013).

Coulter, E. Merton, ed. *The Journal of William Stephens. 1741–1743*. Athens: University of Georgia Press, 1958.

——. *The Journal of William Stephens. 1743–1745*. Athens: University of Georgia Press, 1959.

Courtenay, William A. *The Genesis of South Carolina, 1562–1670*. Privately printed, Columbia: State Company, 1907.

Cox, Wendell, Ronald D. Utt, and Brett D. Schaefer. "Focus on Agenda 21 Should Not Divert Attention from Homegrown Anti-Growth Policies." Heritage Foundation. Backgrounder series no. 2628, December 1, 2011.

Crane, Verner W. "The Tennessee River as the Road to Carolina: The Beginnings of Exploration and Trade." *Mississippi Valley Historical Review* 3, no. 1 (June 1916). 3–18.

Cranston, Maurice. "Locke and Liberty." *Wilson Quarterly* 10, no. 5 (Winter 1986): 82–93.

Craven, William, 1st Earl of Craven, et al. "Instructions for Granting Land in Carolina," November 21, 1682. In *A Sketch of the History of South Carolina*, by William J. Rivers, 399–408. Charleston: McCarter and Co., 1856.

Crosby, Alfred W. *The Columbian Exchange: Biological and Cultural Consequences of 1492*. 30th anniversary ed. Westport, Conn.: Praeger, 2003.

Cutler, Harry Gardner. *History of South Carolina*. Vol. 1. Chicago: Lewis Publishing Co., 1920.

Dailey, Jane, Glenda Elizabeth Gilmore, and Bryant Simon. *Jumpin' Jim Crow: Southern Politics from Civil War to Civil Rights*. Princeton: Princeton University Press, 2000.

DeMint, Jim. "DeMint: Rebuilding a Land of Opportunity before Winning America, Conservatives Must Win the GOP." *Washington Times*, March 22, 2013. http:// www.washingtontimes.com/news/2013/mar/22/rebuilding-a-land-of-opportunity /?page=2#ixzz2OJbNeIrX (accessed March 22, 2013).

Desaguliers, John. "The Newtonian System of the World, the Best Model of Government: An Allegorical Poem." 1728. Online publication of Google Books.

Diamond, Jared. *Guns, Germs, and Steel: The Fates of Human Societies*. New York: W. W. Norton, 1999.

Dochuk, Darren. *From Bible Belt to Sun Belt: Plain-Folk Religion, Grassroots Politics, and the Rise of Evangelical Conservatism*. New York: W. W. Norton, 2011.

Doig, Will. "Tampa: America's Hottest Mess." *Salon*, August 18, 2012. http://www .salon.com/2012/08/18/tampa_americas_hottest_mess/ (accessed August 19, 2012).

Doyle, John A. *The Colonies under the House of Hanover*. Vol. 5 of *The English in America*. 1907. New York: AMS Press, 1969.

Drury, Shadia B. *Leo Strauss and the American Right*. New York: St. Martin's Press, 1997.

———. *The Political Ideas of Leo Strauss*. New York: St. Martin's Press, 1988.

———. "Reply to My Critics." http://phil.uregina.ca/CRC/vitalnexus.html. Originally published, *Vital Nexus* 1, no. 1 (May 1990).

———. "Review: Thomas L. Pangle, The Spirit of Modern Republicanism: The Moral Vision of the American Founders and the Philosophy of Locke." *Canadian Journal of Political Science* 22, no. 2 (June 1989): 442–44.

Dunn, Richard S. "The English Sugar Islands and the Founding of South Carolina." In *Shaping Southern Society: The Colonial Experience*, edited by T. H. Breen, 48–58. New York: Oxford University Press, 1976.

———. *Sugar and Slaves: The Rise of the English Planter Class in the English West Indies, 1624–1713*. Chapel Hill: University of North Carolina Press, 1972.

Duvall, Tim. "The New Feudalism: Globalization, the Market, and the Great Chain of Consumption." *New Political Science* 25, issue 1 (November 2003): 81–97.

Edgar, Walter. *South Carolina: A History*. Columbia: University of South Carolina Press, 1998.

Elazar, Daniel J. *American Federalism: A View from the States*. 2nd ed. New York: Thomas Y. Crowell, 1972.

————. *The American Mosaic: The Impact of Space, Time, and Culture on American Politics*. Boulder: Westview, 1994.

Elliott, E. N., ed. *Cotton Is King and the Pro-Slavery Arguments: Comprising the Writings of Hammond, Harper, Christy, Stringfellow, Hodge, Bledsoe, and Cartrwright on This Important Subject*. Augusta, Ga: Pritchard, Abbott & Loomis, 1860. Retrieved through Project Gutenberg.

Ellis, Joseph. *American Creation: Triumph and Tragedies at the Founding of the Republic*. New York: Alfred A. Knopf, 2007. Augusta, Ga.: Pritchard, Abbott & Loomis, 1860.

Ellis, Richard J. *American Political Cultures*. New York: Oxford University Press, 1993.

Farr, James. Professor, Northwestern University. Personal communications. May 18–21, 2015.Fischer, David Hackett. *Albion's Seed: Four British Folkways in America*. New York: Oxford University Press, 1989.

Florida, Richard. "Did I Abandon My Creative Class Theory? Not So Fast, Joel Kotkin." The Daily Beast, March 21, 2013. http://www.thedailybeast.com/ articles/2013/03/21/did-i-abandon-my-creative-class-theory-not-so-fast-joel-kotkin.html (accessed March 21, 2013).

————. *The Rise of the Creative Class*. New York: Basic Books, 2002.

Ford, Jane. "International Leader in Environmental Issues to Receive U.Va.'s 43rd Thomas Jefferson Foundation Medal in Architecture," February 14, 2008. *UVa Today*. http://news.virginia.edu/node/4182?id=4182 (accessed March 29, 2013).

Ford, Worthington Chauncey. "Early Maps of Carolina." *Geographical Review* 16, no. 2 (April 1926): 264–73.

Fox Bourne, Henry Richard. *The Life of John Locke*. 2 vols. London: Henry S. King, 1876.

Frank, Thomas. *What's the Matter with Kansas? How Conservatives Won the Heart of America*. New York: Metropolitan Books, 2004.

Free Congress Foundation. http://www.freecongress.org/.

Freedom Advocates. http://www.freedomadvocates.org/images/pdf/Michael%20 Shaw%20bio%202009.pdf (accessed May 15, 2013).

Freedom Watch Radio. http://americanfreedomwatchradio.com/?page_id=1173 (accessed April 2, 2013).

Fries, Sylvia Doughty. *The Urban Idea in Colonial America*. Philadelphia: Temple University Press, 1977.

"Fundamental Constitutions of Carolina." Ashley Cooper, Anthony, 1st Earl of Shaftesbury. In *The Shaftesbury Papers*. Charleston: South Carolina Historical Society, 2000.

Gambino, Megan. "Alfred W. Crosby on the Columbian Exchange." Smithsonian.com, http://www.smithsonianmag.com/history/alfred-w-crosby-on-the-columbian-exchange-98116477/?no-ist (accessed June 25, 2014).

Garreau, Joel. *The Nine Nations of North America*. Boston: Houghton Mifflin, 1981.

Genovese, Eugene D. *A Consuming Fire: The Fall of the Confederacy in the Mind of the White Christian South*. Athens: University of Georgia Press, 1998.

————. *The Political Economy of Slavery: Studies in the Economy and Society of the Slave South*. Toronto: Vintage Books, 1967.

──. *The Slaveholders' Dilemma: Freedom and Progress in Southern Conservative Thought, 1820–1860*. Columbia: University of South Carolina Press, 1992.

George, David. *The Rhetoric of the Right: Language Change and the Spread of the Market*. New York: Routledge, 2013.

Gewargis, Natalie. "Spread the Wealth?" October 14, 2008. http://abcnews.go.com/blogs/politics/2008/10/spread-the-weal/ (accessed May 13, 2013).

Gilliland, Jason W. "The Calculus of Realignment: The Rise of Republicanism in Georgia, 1964–1992." *Georgia Historical Quarterly* 96, no. 4 (Winter 2012). 413–52

Glaab, Charles N., and A. Theodore Brown. *A History of Urban America*. 2nd ed. New York: Macmillan, 1976.

Glassey, Lionel K. J. "Shaftesbury and the Exclusion Crisis." In *Anthony Ashley Cooper, First Earl of Shaftesbury 1621–1683*, 207–31. Surrey, England: Ashgate, 2011.

Glausser, Wayne. "Three Approaches to Locke and the Slave Trade." *Journal of the History of Ideas* 51, no. 2 (June 1, 1990): 199–216.

Goldie, Mark. "Annual Parliaments and Aristocratic Whiggism." In *Anthony Ashley Cooper, First Earl of Shaftesbury 1621–1683*, 77–100. Surrey, England: Ashgate, 2011.

Goldsmith, Oliver. *The Deserted Village: A Poem*. London: W. Griffin, 1770.

Goodyear, Sarah. "The Most Dangerous U.S. Cities for Pedestrians." *Atlantic*. http://www.citylab.com/commute/2014/05/the-most-dangerous-us-cities-for-pedestrians/371253/ (accessed July 19, 2014).

Gouldner, Alvin W. "The Norm of Reciprocity: A Preliminary Statement." *American Sociological Review* 25, no. 2 (April 1960): 161–78.

Green, Wayne. "Oklahoma Senator's Bill Targets Controversial U.N. Agenda 21 Plan." *Tulsa World*, December 24, 2012. http://www.tulsaworld.com/article.aspx/Oklahoma_senators_bill_targets_controversial_UN_Agenda/20121224_16_a1_cutlin218146 (accessed April 6, 2013).

Hackney, Sheldon. "Southern Violence." *American Historical Review* 74, no. 3 (February 1969): 906–25.

Haley, K. H. D. *The First Earl of Shaftesbury*. Oxford: Oxford University Press, 1968.

Hall, David D. *A Reforming People: Puritanism and the Transformation of Public Life in New England*. New York: Alfred A. Knopf, 2011.

Hamburger, Philip. *Separation of Church and State*. Cambridge: Harvard University Press, 2002.

Hammond, James Henry. *Secret and Sacred: The Diaries of James Henry Hammond*. Edited by Carol Bleser. New York: Oxford University Press, 1988.

Hammond, John Craig. *Slavery, Freedom, and Expansion in the Early American West*. Charlottesville: University of Virginia Press, 2007.

Hananoki, Eric. "Cruise Ship Confession: Top Fox News Executive Admits Lying On-Air about Obama." March 29, 2011. http://mediamatters.org/blog/2011/03/29/cruise-ship-confession-top-fox-news-executive-a/178013 (accessed May 13, 2013).

Harrington, James. *The Commonwealth of Oceana*. 1656. Tutis Digital Publishing, 2008.

Harrington, Jesse R., and Michelle J. Gelfand. "Tightness-Looseness across the 50 United States." *Proceedings of the National Academy of the Sciences*. Approved for publication April 2014. http://www.pnas.org/content/early/2014/05/15/1317937111.full.pdf.

Harris, Tim. "Cooper, Anthony Ashley." *Oxford Dictionary of National Biography*. Oxford: Oxford University Press, 2004–7.

———. "England's 'Little Sisters without Breasts': Shaftesbury and Scotland and Ireland." In *Anthony Ashley Cooper, First Earl of Shaftesbury 1621–1683*, 183–205. Surrey, England: Ashgate, 2011.

Hartz, Louis. *The Liberal Tradition in America: An Interpretation of American Political Thought since the Revolution*. Orlando: Harcourt, 1955.

Hirschman, Albert O. *The Rhetoric of Reaction: Perversity, Futility, Jeopardy*. Cambridge: Belknap Press of Harvard University Press, 1991.

Home, Robert. *Of Planting and Planning: The Making of British Colonial Cities*. London: Chapman & Hall, 1997.

Huffmon, Scott H. "Selected Quotations from 1830–1865." http://faculty.winthrop .edu/huffmons/SlaveryQuotations.htm (accessed February 22, 2013).

Hutson, James. "'A Wall of Separation': FBI Helps Restore Jefferson's Obliterated Draft." Library of Congress, LC Information Bulletin, May 1998. http://www.loc .gov/loc/lcib/9806/danbury.html.

Hyndman, Charles S., and Donald S. Lutz, eds. *Colonial Origins of the American Constitution: A Documentary History*. Indianapolis: Liberty Fund, 1998.

ICLEI USA (International Council for Local Environmental Initiatives). "About ICLEI: Local Governments for Sustainability." http://www.icleiusa.org/about-iclei/faqs/faq-about-iclei-local-governments-for-sustainability (accessed March 29, 2013).

Jacob, Margaret C. *The Radical Enlightenment: Pantheists, Freemasons, and Republicans*. London: George Allen & Unwin, 1981.

Jefferson and City Planning (an exhibit). Monticello.org (accessed November 5, 2012).

Jefferson's Monticello. http://www.monticello.org/site/research-and-collections/ chain-email-10-jefferson-quotations#footnote1_215rsgd (accessed March 1, 2013).

John Birch Society. "Stop Agenda 21." http://www.jbs.org/issues-pages/stop-agenda-21 (accessed April 5, 2013).

John Locke Foundation. "Founding Principles." http://www.johnlocke.org/about/ founding_principles.html (accessed December 14, 2012, and May 16, 2013).

Johnson, Samuel. "Taxation No Tyranny." http://www.samueljohnson.com/tnt.html (accessed October 16, 2012).

Johnson, Walter. *River of Dark Dreams: Slavery and Imperialism in the Mississippi Valley*. Cambridge: Harvard University Press, 2013.

Jones, Katherine M. *Port Royal under Six Flags*. New York: Bobbs-Merrill, 1960.

Jordan, Winthrop D. *White over Black: American Attitudes toward the Negro, 1550–1812*. Chapel Hill: University of North Carolina Press, 1968. 2nd ed. published for the Omohundro Institute, 2012.

Joseph, J. W. "White Columns and Black Hands: Class and Classification in the Plantation Ideology of the Georgia and South Carolina Lowcountry." *Historical Archaeology* 27, no. 3 (1993): 57–73.

Jost, John T., et al. "Political Conservatism as Motivated Social Cognition." *Psychological Bulletin* 129, no. 3 (2003): 339–75.

Kennedy, John F. Address of President-Elect John F. Kennedy Delivered to a Joint Convention of the General Court of the Commonwealth of Massachusetts, January 9, 1961; John F. Kennedy Presidential Library.

Key, V. O., Jr. *Southern Politics*. New York: Vintage Books, 1949.

Kolchin, Peter. *American Slavery, 1619–1877*. New York: Hill and Wang, 1993.

Kostof, Spiro. *The City Shaped: Urban Patterns and Meanings through History*. New York: Little, Brown, 1999.

Kotkin, Joel. "Biography." http://www.joelkotkin.com/content/004-biography (accessed April 16, 2013).

———. "Richard Florida Concedes the Limits of the Creative Class." The Daily Beast, March 20, 2013. http://www.thedailybeast.com/articles/2013/03/20/richard-florida-concedes-the-limits-of-the-creative-class.html (accessed March 21, 2013).

———. "Rule, Suburbia: The Verdict's In. We Love It There." *Washington Post*, February 6, 2005, B-1.

———. "The Triumph of Suburbia: Despite Downtown Hype, Americans Choose Sprawl." The Daily Beast, April 29, 2013. http://www.thedailybeast.com/articles/2013/04/29/the-triumph-of-suburbia-despite-downtown-hype-americans-choose-sprawl.html (accessed October 19, 2013).

Krall, Lisi. "Thomas Jefferson's Agrarian Vision and the Changing Nature of Property." *Journal of Economic Issues* 36, no. 1 (March 2002): 135–66.

Kramnick, Isaac. *Bolingbroke and His Circle: The Politics of Nostalgia in the Age of Walpole*. Cambridge: Harvard University Press, 1968.

Kruse, Kevin M. *White Flight: Atlanta and the Making of Modern Conservatism*. Princeton: Princeton University Press, 2005.

Kubler, George. "Cities of Latin America since Discovery." In *Settlements in the Americas: Cross-Cultural Perspectives*, edited by Ralph Bennett, 17–27. Newark: University of Delaware Press, 1993.

Lakoff, George. *The Political Mind: Why You Can't Understand 21st-Century American Politics with an 18th-Century Mind*. New York: Viking, 2008.

———. *Whose Freedom? The Battle over America's Most Important Idea*. New York: Picador, 2006.

———. *Moral Politics: How Liberals and Conservatives Think*. Chicago: University of Chicago Press, 2002.

Lakoff, George, and Mark Johnson. *Metaphors We Live By*. Chicago: University of Chicago Press, 1980. New afterword, 2003.

Lane, Mills, ed. *General Oglethorpe's Georgia, Colonial Letters, 1733–1743*. 2 vols. Savannah: Beehive Press, 1990.

Lawler, Peter Augustine. "Praising the Puritans." *First Principles*. ISI Web Journal. Wilmington, Del.: Intercollegiate Studies Institute, December 2, 2010. http://www.firstprinciplesjournal.com/articles.aspx?article=1467 (accessed June 27, 2012).

Leng, Thomas. "Shaftesbury's Aristocratic Empire." In *Anthony Ashley Cooper, First Earl of Shaftesbury, 1621–1683*, 101–25. Surrey, England: Ashgate, 2011.

Lepore, Jill. *The Whites of Their Eyes: The Tea Party's Revolution and the Battle over American History*. Princeton: Princeton University Press, 2010.

Lesser, Charles H. *South Carolina Begins: The Records of a Proprietary Colony,*
    1663–1721. Columbia: South Carolina Department of Archives and History, 1995.
Library of Congress. http://thomas.loc.gov/cgi-bin/query/z?c107:H.CON.RES.48.
Lichtblau, Eric. "Cato Institute Is Caught in a Rift over Its Direction." *New York*
    Times, March 6, 2012.
Lind, Michael. *Made in Texas: George W. Bush and the Southern Takeover of*
    American Politics. New York: Basic Books, 2004.
Locke, John. *Two Treatises of Government.* Edited with an Introduction by Peter
    Laslett. New York: New American Library, 1960.
Lord Ashley Site (a blog maintained by the archaeological team). http://
    lordashleysite.wordpress.com/about/ (accessed September 30, 2013).
Lords Proprietors. "Instructions for Granting Land," November 21, 1682. In *A Sketch*
    of the History of South Carolina, by William J. Rivers, 401. Charleston: McCarter
    and Co., 1856.
Lovejoy, A. O. *The Great Chain of Being: A Study of the History of an Idea.*
    Cambridge: Harvard University Press, 1936.
Ludwig von Mises Institute. "About the Mises Institute." http://mises.org/page/1448/
    About-The-Mises-Institute (accessed June 18, 2012).
MacCulloch, Diarmaid. *Christianity: The First Three Thousand Years.* New York:
    Viking, 2009.
MacLean, Nancy. "The Leo Frank Case Reconsidered: Gender and Sexual Politics in
    the Making of Reactionary Populism." In *Jumpin' Jim Crow: Southern Politics*
    from Civil War to Civil Rights. Edited by Jane Dailey et al., 183–218. Princeton:
    Princeton University Press, 2000.
Marshall, Alan. "'Mechanic Tyrannie': Anthony Ashley Cooper and the English
    Republic." In *Anthony Ashley Cooper, First Earl of Shaftesbury, 1621–1683,* 27–50.
    Surrey, England: Ashgate, 2011.
Martyn, Benjamin. *The Life of the First Earl of Shaftesbury.* Edited by G. Wingrove
    Cooke. 2 vols. London: Richard Bentley, 1836.
Maryland Historical Trust. http://www.mht.maryland.gov/nr/NRDetail
    .aspx?HDID=30&COUNTY=Saint%20Marys&FROM=NRCountyList
    .aspx?COUNTY=Saint%20Marys (accessed June 16, 2012).
Mayer, Jane. "Covert Operations, The Billionaire Brothers Who Are Waging a War
    against Obama." *New Yorker,* August 30, 2010.
McCrady, Edward. *The History of South Carolina under the Proprietary Government,*
    1670–1719. New York: Russell & Russell, 1897.
McHarg, Ian. *Design with Nature.* Wiley Series in Sustainable Design. Hoboken:
    Wiley, 1995.
Meinig, D. W. *The Shaping of America: A Geographical Perspective on 500 Years of*
    History. 2 vols. New Haven: Yale University Press, 1993.
Mencimer, Stephanie. "We Don't Need None of That Smart-Growth Communism."
    Mother Jones, March/April, 2011. http://www.motherjones.com/politics/2010/11/
    tea-party-agenda-21-un-sustainable-development (accessed March 29, 2013).
Meroney, Geraldine M. *Inseparable Loyalty: A Biography of William Bull.* Norcross,
    Ga.: Harrison Co., 1991.

Milton, J. R. "Benjamin Martyn, the Shaftesbury Family, and the Reputation of the First Earl of Shaftesbury." *Historical Journal* 51, no. 2 (June 2008): 315–35.

——"The Unscholastic Statesman: Locke and the Earl of Shaftesbury." In *Anthony Ashley Cooper, First Earl of Shaftesbury, 1621–1683*, 153–81. Surrey, England: Ashgate, 2011.

Milton, Philip. "Shaftesbury and the Rye House Plot." In *Anthony Ashley Cooper, First Earl of Shaftesbury, 1621–1683*, 233–68. Surrey, England: Ashgate, 2011.

Minnesota Population Center. National Historical Geographic Information System: Version 2.0. Minneapolis: University of Minnesota, 2011.

Mitt Romney fund-raiser address. YouTube, posted September 17, 2012. http://www.youtube.com/watch?v=MU9V6eOFO38.

Mitt Romney speech, Peoria, Illinois. Real Clear Politics, posted March 20, 2012. http://www.realclearpolitics.com/video/2012/03/20/romney_to_contraception_heckler_if_you_want_free_stuff_vote_for_obama.html.

Morgan, Edmund S. *American Slavery, American Freedom: The Ordeal of Colonial Virginia.* New York: W. W. Norton, 1975.

Morgan, Philip D. *Slave Counterpoint: Black Culture in the Eighteenth-Century Chesapeake and Lowcountry.* Chapel Hill: University of North Carolina Press, 1998.

National Park Service. "The L'Enfant and McMillan Plans." http://www.nps.gov/history/nr/travel/wash/lenfant.htm (accessed May 23, 2012).

Nelson, Arthur C. "Leadership in a New Era." *Journal of the American Planning Association* 72, no. 4 (Autumn 2006): 393–407.

Oakes, James. "Genovese, Slavery, Capitalism." *Politics/Letters* (September 7, 2014). http://politicsslashletters.com/genovese-slavery-capitalism/ (accessed December 20, 2014).

——. *The Ruling Race: A History of American Slaveholders.* New York: Alfred A. Knopf, 1982.

——. *Slavery and Freedom: An Interpretation of the Old South.* New York: Alfred A. Knopf, 1990.

Oatis, Steven J. *A Colonial Complex: South Carolina's Frontiers in the Era of the Yamasee War, 1680–1730.* Lincoln: University of Nebraska Press, 2004.

Oglethorpe, James Edward. *The Library of Oglethorpe.* Hargrett Rare Documents Library, University of Georgia, Athens, Rodney M. Baine Papers, ms 3029, box 7, folder 7.

——. *The Publications of James Edward Oglethorpe.* Edited by Rodney M. Baine. Athens: University of Georgia Press, 1994.

——. *Some Account of the Design of the Trustees for Establishing Colonys in America.* Edited by Rodney M. Baine and Phinizy Spalding. Athens: University of Georgia Press, 1990.

Ogot, B. A., ed. *General History of Africa*, vol. 5. Berkeley: University of California Press, 1992.

Oxford English Dictionary. Oxford University Press. http://www.oxforddictionaries.com/us/definition/american_english/reaction-formation (accessed June 28, 2014).

Pangle, Thomas L. *The Spirit of Modern Republicanism: The Moral Vision of the American Founders and the Philosophy of Locke*. Chicago: University of Chicago Press, 1988.

Park, Mungo. *Travels in the Interior Districts of Africa*. 1799. New York: Arno Press, 1971.

Perlstein, Rick. "Exclusive: Lee Atwater's Infamous 1981 Interview on the Southern Strategy," November 13, 2012. http://www.thenation.com/article/170841/exclusive-lee-atwaters-infamous-1981-interview-southern-strategy (accessed March 7, 2013).

Phillips, Kevin. *The Emerging Republican Majority*. New York: Arlington House, 1969.

Plato. *The Republic*. New York: Modern Library, 1941.

Pocock, J. G. A. *Politics, Language, and Time: Essays on Political Thought and History*, New York: Atheneum, 1971.

———. *The Machiavellian Moment: Florentine Political Thought and the Atlantic Republican Tradition*. Princeton: Princeton University Press, 1975.

Raapana, Niki F., and Nordica M. Friedrich. "The Anti Communitarian Manifesto (Part 2): The Historical Evolution of Communitarian Thinking," December 19, 2003. http://www.csa-1776.org/docs/HistoryCommunitarian.pdf.

Ramsay, David. *The History of South Carolina, from Its First Settlement in 1670, to the Year 1808*. Vol. 1. Charleston: David Longworth, 1809.

Randolph, E. "E. Randolph to the Lords of Trade," March 16, 1698–99. In *A Chapter in the Early History of South Carolina*, 443–46, by William J. Rivers. Charleston: Walker, Evans, and Cogswell, Printers, 1874.

Reagan, Ronald W. "Farewell Address to the Nation from the Oval Office," January 11, 1989.

Rentfrow, Peter J., et al. "Divided We Stand: Three Psychological Regions of the United States and Their Political, Economic, Social, and Health Correlates." *Journal of Personality and Social Psychology* (October 14, 2013): 996–1012. Advance online publication: http://www.apa.org/pubs/journals/releases/psp-a0034434.pdf (accessed October 23, 2013).

Reps, John W. *The Making of Urban America: A History of City Planning in the United States*. Princeton: Princeton University Press, 1965.

———. "Thomas Jefferson's Checkerboard Towns." *Journal of the Society of Architectural Historians* 20, no. 3 (October 1961): 108–14.

Republican National Committee Counsel's Office. "Resolution Exposing United Nations Agenda 21." http://www.gop.com/wp-content/uploads/2012/06/2012_wintermeeting_resolutions.pdf (accessed April 10, 2013).

Rich, E. E. "The First Earl of Shaftesbury's Colonial Policy." *Transactions of the Royal Historical Society*, 5th series, 7 (1957): 47–70.

Rivers, William J. *A Chapter in the Early History of South Carolina*. Charleston: Walker, Evans, and Cogswell, Printers, 1874.

———. *A Sketch of the History of South Carolina*. Charleston: McCarter and Co., 1856.

Rodgers, Daniel T. "Republicanism: The Career of a Concept." *Journal of American History* 79, no. 1 (June 1992): 11–38.

Rogers, George C., and C. James Taylor. *A South Carolina Chronology, 1497–1992*. Columbia: University of South Carolina Press, 1994.

Roper, Louis H. *Conceiving Carolina: Proprietors, Planters, and Plots, 1662–1729.* New York: Palgrave Macmillan, 2004.

Rothbard, Murray N. *Conceived in Liberty.* Auburn, Ala.: Ludwig von Mises Institute, 1999.

Rowland, Lawrence S., Alexander Moore, and George C. Rogers Jr. *The History of Beaufort County, South Carolina, Volume I, 1514–1861.* Columbia: University of South Carolina Press, 1996.

Salley, A. S., ed. *Commissions and Instructions from the Lords Proprietors of Carolina to Public Officials of South Carolina, 1685–1715.* Columbia: Historical Commission of South Carolina, 1916.

———, ed. *Narratives of Early Carolina, 1650–1708.* New York: C. Scribner's Sons, 1911.

Schmitt, Angie. "Greater Atlanta Continues to Treat Walking Like a Crime," October 2, 2012. http://dc.streetsblog.org/2012/10/02/greater-atlanta-continues-to-treat-walking-like-a-crime/ (accessed October 30, 2012).

SCIWAY (South Carolina Information Highway). Internet directory of South Carolina information. http://www.sciway.net/hist/governors/apickens.html (accessed June 14, 2014)

Seaward, Paul. "Shaftesbury and the Royal Supremacy." In *Anthony Ashley Cooper, First Earl of Shaftesbury, 1621–1683,* 51–76. Surrey, England: Ashgate, 2011.

Shaftesbury Estates. www.Shaftesburyestates.com.

Sharlet, Jeff. *C Street: The Fundamentalist Threat to American Democracy.* New York: Little, Brown, 2010.

———. *The Family: The Secret Fundamentalism at the Heart of American Power.* New York: HarperCollins, 2008.

Shay, Patrick O., AIA. Personal communication, February 12, 2013.

Shepherd, William R. *Historical Atlas.* New York: Henry Holt, 1911.

Shillington, Kevin. *History of Africa.* New York: St. Martin's, 1995.

Shorto, Russell. *The Island at the Center of the World: The Epic Story of Dutch Manhattan and the Forgotten Colony That Shaped America.* New York: Vintage Books, 2005.

Sirmans, M. Eugene. *Colonial South Carolina: A Political History, 1663–1763.* Chapel Hill: University of North Carolina Press, 1966.

Skocpol, Theda, and Vanessa Williamson. *The Tea Party and the Remaking of Republican Conservatism.* New York: Oxford University Press, 2012.

Smart Growth Network. "Principles of Smart Growth." http://www.smartgrowth.org/why.php.

Smith, Henry A. M. "The Ashley River: Its Sets and Settlements." *South Carolina Historical and Genealogical Magazine* 20, nos. 1, 2 (January 1919 and April 1919): 3–51, 75–122.

———. "The Baronies of South Carolina." *South Carolina Historical and Genealogical Magazine* 11, nos. 2, 4; 12, no. 2 (April 1910, October 1910, April 1911): 75–91, 193–202, 43–52.

———. "Charleston and Charleston Neck: The Original Grantees and the Settlements along the Ashley and Cooper Rivers." *South Carolina Historical and Genealogical Magazine* 19, no. 1 (January 1918): 3–76.

———. *Historical Writings of Henry A. M. Smith, Cities and Towns of Early South Carolina*. 3 vols. Spartanburg: Reprint Company (in association with the South Carolina Historical Society), 1988.

Southern Poverty Law Center. "Agenda 21: The UN, Sustainability, and Right-Wing Conspiracy Theory." April 2014.

Spalding, Phinizy. "South Carolina and Georgia: The Early Days." *South Carolina Historical Magazine* 69, no. 2 (April 1968): 83–96.

Spellberg, Denise. "Our Founding Fathers Included Islam," October 5, 2013. http://www.salon.com/2013/10/05/our_founding_fathers_included_islam/ (accessed October 7, 2013).

Spurr, John. "Shaftesbury and the Politics of Religion." In *Anthony Ashley Cooper, First Earl of Shaftesbury, 1621–1683*, edited by John Spurr, 127–51. Surrey, England: Ashgate, 2011.

———. "Shaftesbury and the Seventeenth Century." In *Anthony Ashley Cooper, First Earl of Shaftesbury 1621–1683*, edited by John Spurr, 1–25. Surrey, England: Ashgate, 2011.

———, ed. *Anthony Ashley Cooper, First Earl of Shaftesbury, 1621–1683*. Surrey, England: Ashgate, 2011.

Stahl, Jason. "Historicizing the Conservative Think Tank." Blog of the Society for U.S. Intellectual History. http://us-intellectual-history.blogspot.com/2012/03/historicizing-conservative-think-tank.html (accessed March 13, 2012).

Stelter, Gilbert A. "Military Consideration and Colonial Town Planning: France and New France in the Seventeenth Century." In *Settlements in the Americas: Cross-Cultural Perspectives*, edited by Ralph Bennett, 210–37. Newark: University of Delaware Press, 1993.

Stephens, William. *A Journal of the Proceedings of Georgia*. 1742. 2 vols. Reprinted by the Readex Microprint Corporation, 1966.

Stone, Lawrence. *The Crisis of the Aristocracy, 1558–1641*. Oxford: Clarendon Press, 1965.

Stoney, Samuel Gaillard. *Plantations of the Carolina Low Country*. Charleston: Carolina Art Association, 1938.

Strauss, Leo. *The City and Man*. Chicago: Rand McNally, 1964.

Stuart, Andrea. *Sugar in the Blood: A Family's Story of Slavery and Empire*. New York: Alfred A. Knopf, 2013.

Sturgis, Sue. "Pat McCrory Dons Tinfoil Hat in Bid for NC Governor," June 12, 2012. http://www.southernstudies.org/2012/06/pat-mccrory-dons-tinfoil-hat-in-bid-for-nc-governor.html (accessed April 10, 2013).

Suskind, Ron. "Faith, Certainty, and the Presidency of George W. Bush," October 17, 2004. http://www.nytimes.com/2004/10/17/magazine/17BUSH.html?ex=1255665600&en=890a96189e162076&ei=5090&partner=rssuserland&_r=0 (accessed May 20, 2013).

Tea Party 911. "What Is Agenda 21?" http://www.teaparty911.com/issues/what_is_agenda_21.htm (accessed March 29, 2013).

Turner, Frederick Jackson. *The Significance of the Section in American History*. New York: Henry Holt, 1932.

Twelve Southerners (the Southern Agrarians). *I'll Take My Stand: The South and the Agrarian Tradition*. Gloucester, Mass.: Peter Smith, 1976.

United Nations. World Commission on Environment and Development. "Our Common Future: From One Earth to One World." http://www.un-documents.net/wced-ocf.htm (accessed April 3, 2013).

U.S. Bureau of the Census. 2010 Census of Population and Housing, and 2000 Census of Population and Housing.

U.S. Bureau of the Census. "Historical Statistics of the United States, 1789–1945." A Supplement to the Statistical Abstract of the United States, 1949.

———. "Historical Statistics of the United States, Colonial Times to 1970." Bicentennial ed. Part 1, 1976.

Vazquez, Leonardo. "Thomas Jefferson: The Founding Father of Sprawl?" February 20, 2006. http://www.planetizen.com/node/18841 (accessed June 22, 2012).

Weir, Robert M. *Colonial South Carolina: A History*. Columbia: University of South Carolina Press, 1997.

Whittemore, Andrew H. "Finding Sustainability in Conservative Contexts: Topics for Conversation between American Conservative Élites, Planners, and the Conservative Base." *Urban Studies* 50, no. 12 (March 5, 2013): 2460–77.

———. "Why Planners Need to Take Agenda 21 Criticism More Seriously," February 7, 2012. http://www.theatlanticcities.com/neighborhoods/2012/02/why-planners-need-take-agenda-21-criticism-more-seriously/1159/ (accessed March 25, 2013).

Wikimedia Foundation. http://en.wikiquote.org/wiki/James_Carville (accessed March 20, 2012).

Wilson, Thomas D. "Conservative Institute Mission Statements." Unpublished study, May 4, 2012.

———. *The Oglethorpe Plan: Enlightenment Design in Savannah and Beyond*. Charlottesville: University of Virginia Press, 2012.

Winters, Jeffrey A. *Oligarchy*. New York: Cambridge University Press, 2011.

———. "Oligarchy and Democracy," November/December 2011. http://www.the-american-interest.com/article.cfm?piece=1048 (accessed April 12, 2013).

Winthrop, John. "A Modell of Christian Charity." Collections of the Massachusetts Historical Society, 3rd series, 7:31–48. Boston: Massachusetts Historical Society. http://history.hanover.edu/texts/winthmod.html.

Wolf, Eva Sheppard. *Race and Liberty in the New Nation: Emancipation in Virginia from the Revolution to Nat Turner's Rebellion*. Baton Rouge: Louisiana State University Press, 2006.

Wood, Peter H. *Black Majority: Negroes in Colonial South Carolina from 1670 through the Stono Rebellion*. New York: W. W. Norton, 1974.

Woodard, Colin. *American Nations: A History of the Eleven Rival Regional Cultures of North America*. New York: Viking, 2011.

Woodard, J. David. *The New Southern Politics*. Boulder: Lynne Rienner, 2006.

Woodward, C. Vann. *Origins of the New South, 1877–1913*. Baton Rouge: Louisiana State University Press, 1951.

Worthen, Molly. "Love Thy Stranger as Thyself." *New York Times*, Sunday Review, May 12, 2013, 1, 12.

Wright, Gavin. *Old South, New South: Revolutions in the Southern Economy since the Civil War.* Baton Rouge: Louisiana State University Press, 1986.

Wyatt-Brown, Bertram. *Southern Honor: Ethics and Behavior in the Old South.* New York: Oxford University Press, 1982.

Zucker, Paul. *Town and Square: From the Agora to the Village Green.* New York: Columbia University Press, 1959.

Index

Adams, John, 26

Adlar, Jonathan, 216

Africa. *See* West Africa

African Americans: migration out of South, 187; first African American president, 199–200; Great Migration, 242; among targets of fraternalistic political culture, 246. *See also* Civil rights

Africanus, Leo, 130

Age of Discovery, 33, 67

Age of Enlightenment, x–xii, 2–3, 9–11, 13–14, 17–22, 24–26, 29–32, 35–57 passim, 62–64, 69–104 passim, 137–40, 147–213 passim, 223–26, 227–28, 230–35, 236–41, 245, 248, 256–57; British Enlightenment, 11, 102; Scottish Enlightenment, 14, 24, 63; French Enlightenment, 24

Agrarian balance, 9, 51, 68, 71, 74, 100, 103–4, 198

Albany, N.Y., 12

Albemarle Sound, 84

Alexandria, Va., 13

American Revolution, xi, 6, 63, 104–5, 241

Annapolis, Md., 11–12

Aristocracy, 32, 52. *See also* Oligarchy; Social hierarchy

Aristotle, 17–18, 29, 49, 51–52, 61, 62, 69, 102, 110, 210, 230–31, 237

Armitage, David, 269 (n. 31)

Ashley, Maurice, 94, 122

Ashley Cooper, Anthony (1st Earl of Shaftesbury and Carolina Proprietor), ix–xii; Carolina his "darling," ix, 1–34 passim; political biography, 35–43; family, 43–44; and John

Locke, 44–48; political milieu, 48–54; conceives Carolina plan, 54–57; vision of Gothic society, 57–64; effect of plan, 64–66; and Fundamental Constitutions of Carolina, 67–83; broader vision of the Grand Model, 83–89; begins implementation, with disruptions, 99–100; influenced by the Great Fire of 1666, 100–103, 103–35 passim; bequeathed an American political culture, 136–38, 138–55 passim, 175, 184–85, 191, 221, 225–28; political legacy, 230–33, 257–58; short biography, 259

Ashley Cooper, Anthony, 2nd Earl of Shaftesbury, 115

Ashley Cooper, Anthony, 3rd Earl of Shaftesbury, xii, 14, 24, 43, 93, 95, 102, 107, 115

Ashley Cooper, Anthony, 4th Earl of Shaftesbury, xii, 37, 43

Ashley Cooper, Anthony, 7th Earl of Shaftesbury, xii, 43

Ashley Cooper, Nicholas Edmund Anthony, 12th Earl of Shaftesbury, xiii, 43, 136

Ashley Cooper Plan, ix, xi–xii; principles of consistency, concurrence, compactness, 1, 2–30 passim; the first English planned colony, 31–35, 38–57 passim; implementation of the plan, 54–57; Gothic foundation, 57–60; effect of the plan, 64–66; Fundamental Constitutions and other components, 66–88, 91–230 passim; compared with American republicanism, 154; as first comprehensive plan, 213, 219;

has features of modern Smart Growth and sustainable development, 225; as a directive for the city upon a hill, 230
Ashley River, 88, 103, 107–8, 114, 117
Atlanta, Ga., 187–88, 214–15, 221
Atlantic Triangle Trade, 54, 65, 80, 89, 122, 132
Atwater, Lee, 193, 199

Bacon, Francis, 5, 44, 268 (n. 30)
Bacon, Jim, 223
Bahamas, 85
Balanced government, 1, 5, 36, 41, 51, 100, 185, 211
Baltimore, Lord, 6
Baltimore, Md., 190
Barbados, 42, 54, 85–86, 88–92, 95, 108–9, 123, 127, 129, 133–36, 144–45, 159, 167, 182, 189
Barebone, Praise-God, 38, 67
Barebone's Parliament, 38
Barony, 73, 88, 105, 109
Bartlett, Bruce, 244
Beaufort, Carolina Colony town of, 87, 118–120, 173
Beaufort County, S.C., 203
Berkeley, George, 245
Berkeley, John (1st Baron Berkeley of Stratton, Carolina Proprietor): short biography, 259
Berkeley, Sir William (Carolina Proprietor), 56; short biography, 260
Bishop, Bill, 148–49
Blackbeard (Edward Thatch or Teach), 96
Bledsoe, Albert Taylor, 177
Boehm, Christopher, 230–31
Bolingbrook, Henry St. John, Lord, 24, 156–57; idea of the patriot king, 24
Boston, Mass., 190
Brewer, Holly, 47
Britain. See England
Brundtland, Gro Harlem, 201
Bryan, Jonathan, 159
Buffett, Warren, 208

Bull, William, 95, 117, 121, 157, 162
Burke, Edmund, 240
Bush, George H. W., 242
Bush, George W., 209, 237, 242, 244

Cabal Ministry, 39
Cacique, 71–73, 75–76, 83, 106, 111, 116, 118
Calhoun, John C., 146; "Positive Good Speech," 128, 147, 183
California, 178–80
Cape Fear settlement, 84–85
Caribbean slavery, 12, 65, 81, 86, 88–89, 127; Dutch traders, 89. See also Barbados
Carolina, Province of (Carolina Colony), ix; Carolina as Ashley Cooper's "darling," ix; Lords Proprietors, 38 (see also by individual name); Fundamental Constitutions of Carolina, 67–83; structure of proprietary government, 74–77; towns, 116–21; Lowcountry, high percentage enslaved, 124; timeline of settlement, 134; "Carolina way" (slave society), 139, 158–59, 166; undermining Georgia prohibition on slavery, 155–59; Georgia brought under "Carolina way," 158–59; Native Americans and the "Carolina way," 160; exploitation of Native Americans by merchants; 161–62; primacy of the plantation, 164; westward expansion of influence, 164–72; unquestioning commitment to slavery, 166; rice monoculture, 199. See also appendix for short biographies of Lords Proprietors
Carter, Dan T., 129
Carteret, Sir George (Carolina Proprietor), 88; short biography, 260
Carville, James, 151, 153
Cary, N.C., 249–50
Cash, W. J., 137, 139, 146, 172, 177; southern persecution complex, 139;

southern taproot in slavery of Old South, 173; savage ideal, 176

Caste system. *See* Social hierarchy

Castle Doctrine, 25

Charles I (king), 36, 40, 47–48, 54, 67

Charles II (king), 32, 36, 40, 44, 47–48, 54, 67, 87, 100

Charlesfort (French colony), 84

Charles Town (Cape Fear settlement), 85

Charles Town, Carolina Colony (later Charleston, South Carolina), ix, 12, 64, 87, 89, 91–93, 107, 113–14, 116–18, 172; renamed Charleston, 91; similarity to Bridgetown, Barbados, 135; at odds with Georgia, 158

Charlestown, Md., 12

Charlotte, N.C., 187

Cheney, Dick, 239

Chicago, Ill., 187

Childsbury, S.C., 120–121

Chinni, Dante, 148, 151

Christie, William Dougal, 37

City planning, x–xi, 2, 4–23, 25, 34–35, 67, 103, 184, 228, 235; New Urbanism, xii, 155, 214, 224, 226, 256; code of ethics, 21; Garden Cities movement, 53, 213; influence of the Great Fire, 100–103; planning principles for Carolina, 103–5; regional development plan for Carolina, 105–10; urban design in Carolina, 110–15; table of Grand Model planning specifications, 112; opposition within southern and fraternalistic political culture, 173; sustainable development, 155, 185, 200, 205, 216–18, 223, 229, 246, 251–52; Smart Growth, 155, 185, 206, 217, 219, 223, 225, 246, 251; pre-and post-Enlightenment comparison, 185; antiurbanism and urban vices, 185–86, 215, 218, 229, 243; zoning, 186, 215, 222–23, 225, 254; segregated land uses, 191; post-WWII

urbanization, 192; opposition to from Far Right, 200, 205–12; American Institute of Certified Planners, 206; American Planning Association, 207; Jefferson and comprehensive planning, 212; rooted in Lockean compact, 212; conflict over public space, 212–14; Modernism, 213; City Beautiful movement, 213–14; street-car suburbs, 214; suburbanization, 214; post-WWII suburbanization, 214–19; takings legislation, 222; American tradition of, 223; planners blamed for social ills, 239; use of values language, 245–56; value of visual and nonverbal communication, 249; takings and "average reciprocity of advantage," 252

City upon a hill, xii, 3, 19, 24, 29, 199

Civil rights, 140, 144, 179, 187–88, 199, 228, 234, 242. *See also* Racism: Jim Crow

Civil War, American. *See* Political culture; Slavery

Coke, Sir Edward, 25

Class pyramid. *See* Social hierarchy

Class reciprocity. *See* Reciprocity (among classes)

Cleveland, Ohio, 187

Climate science, xii, 155, 222, 246, 248

Clinton, Bill, 247

Colleton, James (landgrave) 91, 108–9, 123

Colleton, Sir John (Carolina Proprietor), 46, 91, 108; short biography, 260, 263 (n. 2)

Colleton, Sir Peter (Carolina Proprietor), 46, 56, 91, 108–9

Colleton, Thomas (landgrave), 91, 108–9

Columbia, S.C., 190

Commonwealth of England, 11, 35, 38

Communitarianism, x, 5, 253, 263 (n. 9), 278 (n. 35)

Conroy, Pat, 119

Frederica (fort and town), Ga., 159
Freemasonry, 13–14
French James Town, S.C., 120
Freud, Sigmund, 138–39
Frum, David, 239
Fundamental Constitutions of Carolina, 32–69 passim; articles of, 72–82, 92–99 passim; planning principles, 103–7, 111–84 passim, 230. *See also* Ashley Cooper Plan

Garden, Alexander, 125
Garreau, Joel, 145
Gates, Bill, 208
Gelfand, Michelle, 152
Genovese, Eugene, 165, 167–68, 172
George, David, 153
George I (king) 122
Georgetown, 118–120
Georgia, 2, 8, 10, 15, 52, 124, 126, 129, 135, 155–55, 185, 187–89, 198, 243; Trustees as administrators, 37, 139, 155; influence of James Harrington on design, 156–57; resists "Carolina way" (slave society), 156–59; better relations with Indians than Carolina, 157; "Malcontents" under Carolina influence, 158; falls under Carolina influence, 158–59; relations with Native Americans, 161–63
Gimpel, James, 148
Gingrich, Newt, 194
Glorious Revolution, 24, 41, 44, 99, 211, 227
Goldsmith, Oliver, 52–53, 186, 190
Goldwater, Barry, 140–41, 179–80, 241–42
Goose Creek men, 96, 109, 123, 133
Gore, Albert V., 237
Gothic society and social structure, x, xii, 32, 36, 38, 40, 42, 48, 51–52, 54, 57–59, 68–70, 80, 92, 98, 104–5, 133, 135–37, 227, 230–31, 253. *See also* Reciprocity, class; Social structure

Grand Model. *See* Ashley Cooper Plan
Great Chain of Being, 19, 62–63, 72, 94, 124–25, 128, 173, 189, 231, 237
Great Fire of London (1666), 11, 35, 39, 67, 100, 103, 121, 186, 196, 213
Greece, Classical, 17–19, 49, 62, 227, 257
Green, Nathanael, 109
Gulf Stream, 65
Gullah people, 119

Hackney, Sheldon, 176, 195
Hale Commission, 38, 75
Haley, K. H. D., 37
Hall, David, 3
Hamilton, John, 14
Hammond, James H., 168–69, 171
Hampton, Wade, 167
Hancock, John, 13
Harper, William, 171
Harrington, James, 5, 8, 24, 26, 38, 48–49, 52–53, 57–58, 70, 100, 102, 104, 156–57, 198, 211
Harrington, Jesse, 151
Hartz, Louis, 146–48, 153
Helper, Hinton R., 137
Hilton Head Island, 119
Hippodamus, 102
Hirschman, Albert, 153, 234–35
Hogarth, William, 185–86, 190
Holme, Thomas, 9
Holmes, Oliver Wendell, 252
Hooke, Robert, 11, 100
Hume, David, 24, 245
Hutchinson, Francis, 24
Hyde, Edward (1st Earl of Clarendon and Carolina Proprietor), 38–39; short biography, 261

Ibn Battuta, 130
Indentured servants, 81; Irish, 123
Indians. *See* Native Americans
Industrial Revolution, 33, 104, 122, 186, 190
Instrument of Government, 38

International Council of Local
Environmental Initiatives, 206, 208
Ireland, 113

Jackson, Andrew, 20, 146, 164
James I (king), 47
James II (king, previously James, Duke
of York), 40–41, 44, 47
Jamestown, Va., 1, 31, 67
Jefferson, Thomas, 14, 20, 29, 43, 53,
163, 165–67, 186, 236, 252
John Birch Society, 22, 178–80, 201–5
Johnson, Gideon, 240
Johnson, Lyndon, 192
Johnson, Nathanial, 96, 116
Johnson, Robert, 13, 119–20
Johnson, Samuel, 28, 159, 198, 266
(n. 40)
Johnson, Walter, 91
Jones, Inigo, 43
Jordan, Winthrop, 128

Kansas, 244
Kennedy, John F., 3
Key, V. O., 144, 180–81
Kirkpatrick, Jeane, 239
Knox, Henry, 163–64
Koch, Charles, 205, 209, 215–16
Koch, David, 205, 209, 215–16
Koch, Fred, 205
Kotkin, Joel, 216–17
Kristol, William, 239
Kruse, Kevin, 187–88, 193–94, 214–15

Lakoff, George, 147, 229, 235, 248
Land, Dr. Richard D., 235
Landgrave, 71–73, 75–76, 83, 88, 91, 106,
110, 113, 116, 118
Landscape architecture, xii
Laslett, Peter, 212
Leetmen, 72–73
L'Enfant, Pierre, 14
Leng, Thomas, 71
Liberalism, classical (or Lockean
liberalism), 18, 26, 146, 206

Libertarianism, 19–20, 22, 27–30, 146,
154, 179, 185–86, 196, 208, 212, 218,
225–26, 235; language of, 236–37
Locke, John, xi, 3, 8, 14, 16–18, 20–21,
24–27, 29, 32–33, 36–37, 40,
43–48, 52, 54, 56–57, 60–61, 63,
68–70, 77–78, 80, 83, 86–87, 91–92,
99–106, 109, 113–15, 117, 122, 138,
146–48, 155, 159, 165, 175, 177, 181,
185, 211–12, 219, 225–26, 227–28,
230–36, 240–41, 244–45, 252–53,
257–58; biographical sketch, 44–48;
slavery and, 80; instructions to colonists on town planning, 86–87; on
Barbadians, 109
London, England, 11
Lords Proprietors of the Province of
Carolina, 46, 259–61
Louisiana, 135
Louisiana Purchase, 170
Louis XVI (king), 34
Lowcountry. *See* Carolina

Machiavelli, 9, 24, 36, 51
MacLean, Nancy, 176
Magna Carta, 51
Martyn, Benjamin, 37
Maryland, 6–7, 11, 13–15, 241
McCrory, Pat, 207
McGillivray, Alexander (Hoboi-Hili-
Miko), 163
McHarg, Ian, 223
Meinig, Donald, 144, 150, 159, 167
Mid-Atlantic region, x, 5, 7, 29, 67, 125,
141–43, 149, 187, 190, 192
Milton, J. R., 44
Missouri Compromise, 170
Monck, George (1st Duke of Albemarle
and Carolina Proprietor), 38, 84;
short biography, 261
Monmouth, Duke of, 41
Monoculture (in American slave socie-
ties), 91, 127, 183, 199
Montesquieu, Baron, 24
Moore, James, 96

More, Hannah, 63
More, Thomas, 5
Mulberry Plantation, 108-9
Murfreesboro, Tenn., 203

Native Americans, 8, 13-14, 54, 71,
79, 93, 95, 106-8, 116, 119-20,
124, 138-40, 142, 155-58, 160-64,
166, 195; nations in the Carolina
region, 84; Tuscarora, 96; wars with
Carolina, 96; Trail of Tears, 140, 164;
good relations with Georgia, 157-58;
devastation of Columbian Exchange,
160; enslavement by Carolinians,
160; population decline from disease
and other factors, 160; Muskogee
Nation, 161; Yamacraw people, 161;
good relations with Georgia, 161-62;
Creek Nation, 161-63; aggressively
sold rum by Carolina merchants, 162;
Chickasaw Nation, 162-63; Choctaw
nation, 162-63; Cherokee Nation,
162-64, 166; caught in European geopolitics, 163; Treaty of New York, 163;
encroachments and treaty violations,
163-64; Indian Removal Act, 164;
Seminole Nation, 164; Yazoo land
scandal, 166
Nat Turner's rebellion, 165
Navigation Act, 39
Neoconservatism, 18-19, 22, 154, 212,
235; language of, 237-40
Netherlands, 33
Newcourt, Richard, 11, 101-2; Plan of
London, 102
New Deal, 179, 209, 234
New England, x, 3, 6-7, 11, 29, 68, 94,
125, 141-43, 146, 149, 189-90
New Haven, Conn., town plans of 1638
and 1748, 4-5, 11, 13
New Jersey, 6
New Netherlands, 6
New Orleans, 34, 172
Newton, Isaac, xi, 14, 44, 60, 63
New Urbanism. *See* City planning

New York, 12-13, 94, 190
Nicholson, Francis, 11-12
Nietzsche, Friedrich, 238
Nixon, Richard M., 20, 140, 179-80, 242
Noblesse oblige. *See* Reciprocity (among
classes)
North Carolina, ix, 56, 84-85, 115-16

Oakes, James, 167-68
Obama, Barack, 203-4, 208, 224, 228,
246-47, 254
Oglethorpe, James Edward, ix, 2, 9,
27-29, 52-53, 63, 84, 104, 117, 121,
129, 135, 139, 155-59; early abolitionist, 157, 185-86, 198; resisting
Carolina slavery, 157-59; describes
Carolina elite as "wicked men," 157;
relocates to Frederica, 159; good relations with Native Americans, 161-62,
266 (n. 40)
Oglethorpe Plan (the settlement plan
for Georgia), 15, 52-53, 155; agrarian
equality, 159; 186, 198
Oligarchy, 16, 71, 209-12, 215, 218, 224,
230, 238, 245, 252, 255. *See also*
Aristocracy; Social hierarchy
Orwell, George, *1984*, 83
O'Toole, Randall, 216
Owsley, Frank, 128-29

Palatine, 70, 75, 81, 92, 116
Park, Mungo, 130
Parris Island, 119
Penn, William, ix, 2, 8-9, 27, 29
Pennsylvania, 2, 8-9, 15, 27
Percivall, Andrew, 113
Philadelphia, 12, 102, 187, 190
Philips, Kevin, 140, 145
Plato, 62
Pocock, J. G. A., 49-51
Policy institutes ("think tanks"), 179,
209, 215, 218, 237, 250-56; John
Locke Foundation, 27, 236; Ludwig
von Mises Institute, 27; Americans
for Prosperity, 208; Competitive

Institute, 215; Heartland Institute, 215; Manhattan Institute, 215; Reason Foundation, 215, 219; Cato Institute, 215–16, 218; American Enterprise Institute, 219; Free Congress Foundation, 219; Heritage Foundation, 219; Transportation for America, 220

Political culture, ix–xi, 2–3, 7–8, 16, 19, 28, 30, 32, 196; fraternalistic, egalitarian, and pragmatic nomenclature, x, 142–43; progressivism, 18, 22; political parties, 20; influence on city planning, 141; traditionalistic, moralistic, and individualistic nomenclature, 142–43; theories of, 142–55; cognitive research on, 147; map of primary political cultures in U.S., 151; and the modern city, 187–90; liberty versus equality, 198; shown in table and diagram, 232–33; shibboleths in political discourse, 245, 249; progressive "city upon a hill," 256–58

Political culture, southern, x; fraternalistic nomenclature, x; Solid South, 20, 175, 177, 222; Carolina origins, 121–26, 135; siege mentality, 127, 176, 188–89, 195, 198; culture of resistance, 138; "Carolina way" (slave society), 139, 158–59; Carolina influence spreading westward, 140, 150, 159; traditionalistic nomenclature, 142–43; racial orientation, 144; white privilege, 144; continuing Civil War, 153; southern migration, 178; national diffusion of southern political culture, 178–81; Abrahamic hierarchy; southern language of liberty and tyranny, 180; plantation way of life, 183, 190; concept of liberty, 191–96, 198; opposition to public space initiatives, 212–14; opposition to public transportation, 219; language of liberty, 222, 227; language of fraternalistic political culture, 244–45

Popish Plot, 41

Portland, Ore., 220, 249–50

Port Royal Sound, 84–87, 96, 118–20, 157

Portuguese slave merchants and slaveholders, 89; in the Columbian Exchange, 160

Pragmatic political culture. *See* Political culture

Property rights, 16, 18, 20, 210–11, 222–23, 226

Purrysburg, S.C., 121

Pyramid, class or social. *See* Social hierarchy

Racism, 189; New Jim Crow, 29; Jim Crow, 29, 34, 128–29, 138, 144, 176, 187, 228, 234, 254, 180–81, 222; origins in Carolina, 123–26; racial mythology, 126–33; southern, 140, 187–89; race at center of southern politics, 175; myth of white supremacy, 176, 193; Curse of Ham, 178, 274 (n. 83); post-WWII, 192–95; white racial anxiety, 193; modern plantation communities, 194; White Citizens Councils, 196, 213; white flight, 218; and xenophobia, 224

Radnor, S.C., 121

Raleigh, Sir Walter, 49, 67

Rand, Ayn, 27

Randolph, Thomas, 165

Reagan, Ronald W., 3, 20, 140–41, 153, 179–80, 193, 209, 242

Reciprocity (among classes), 7–8, 16–17, 28–29, 54, 56, 66, 105, 116, 126, 133, 137, 157

Reconstruction Era, 139, 172, 176; Fourteenth Amendment, 174

Reed, Ralph, 215, 243

Reich, Robert, 215

Religion, liberty of conscience and tolerance, 1, 31, 69; in the colonies, 6; priestcraft, 13; separation from state, 24–25; Islamophobia, 25; in Fundamental Constitutions, 77–80;

Viguerie, Richard, 242
Virginia, 7, 11, 13, 54–55, 65, 67–68, 71, 84, 89, 94, 135, 138, 161, 166–70, 182, 240; debate on the future of slavery and gradual abolition, 165
Vitruvius, 10, 102, 268 (n. 3)
Voltaire, 8, 24

Wadboo Barony (or plantation), 109, 123
Walker, William, 170
Wallace, George, 193, 264 (n. 25)
Washington, D.C., 14, 196; L'Enfant plan of, 14
Washington, George, 13–14, 163, 252
Weir, Robert, 139, 158
Wesley, Charles, 124
Wesley, John, 124
West, Joseph, 86
West Africa, 124, 130–32, 132 (map); early and prehistoric civilizations, 130–32
Western Civilization (path of), 136, 238–39
West Indies. *See* Barbados; Caribbean

Whig party, 37, 40, 50
White Citizens Councils, 199
Whittemore, Andrew, 221
Wilberforce, William, 130
William and Mary (joint monarchs), 41, 44, 47, 93, 99, 227
Williams, Roger, ix, 24–25
Williamsburg, Va., 11–12
William the Conqueror, 58, 70
Winters, Jeffrey A., 209
Winthrop, John, 3, 24, 29
Wolfowitz, Paul, 239
Wood, Peter, 198
Woodard, Colin, 145
Woodard, J. David, 143–44
Wren, Christopher, 11, 101
Wurzelbacher, Joe ("Joe the Plumber"), 246
Wyatt-Brown, Bertram, 137, 146
Wyche, Benjamin, 36

Yeamans, Sir John, 85–86, 88–89
Yemassee War, 96, 162

www.ingramcontent.com/pod-product-compliance
Lightning Source LLC
Chambersburg PA
CBHW030641270326
41929CB00007B/162